Ichigo Takano presents

Dreamin'
Sun

3

volume
three

Dreamin'
Sun

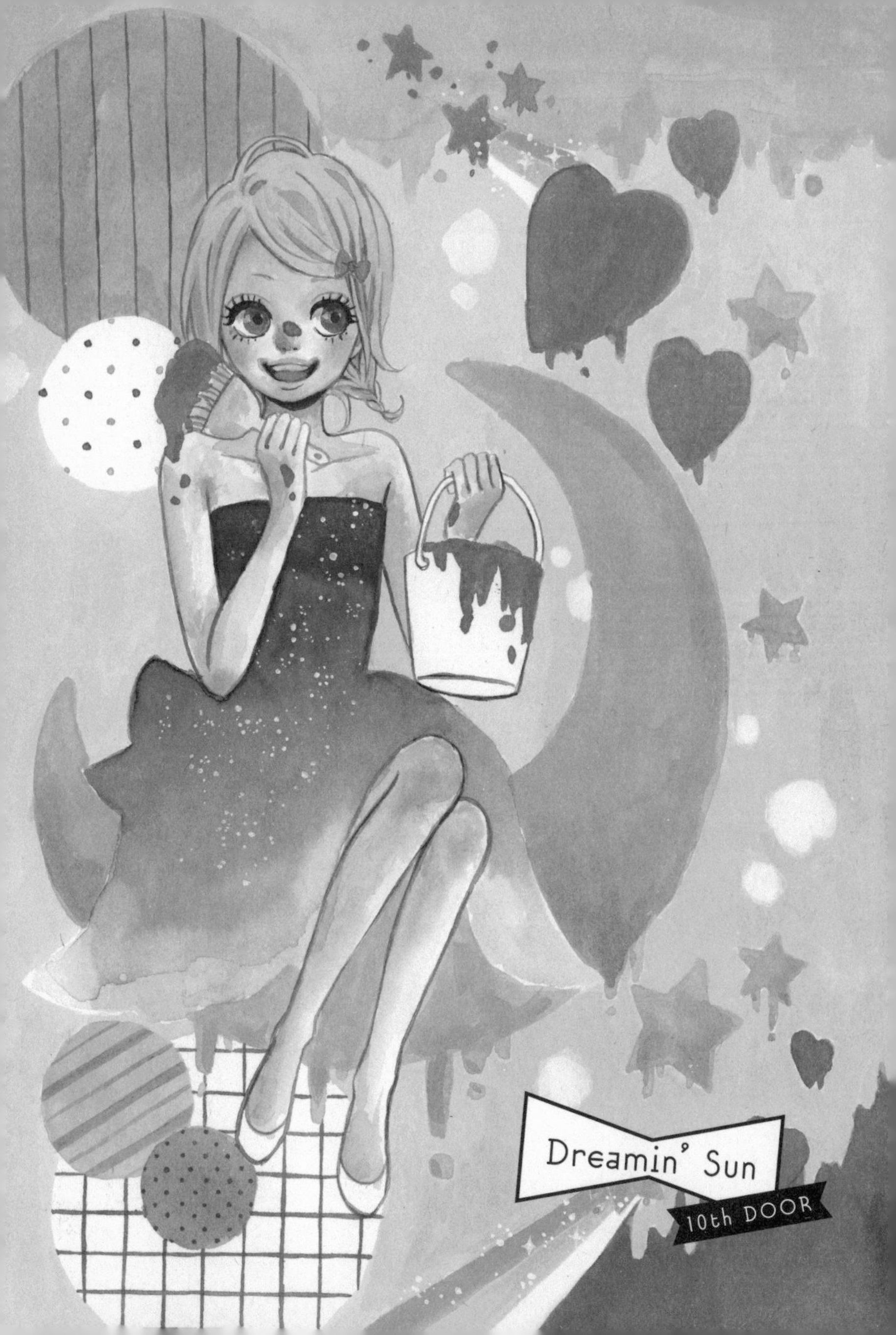
Dreamin' Sun
10th DOOR

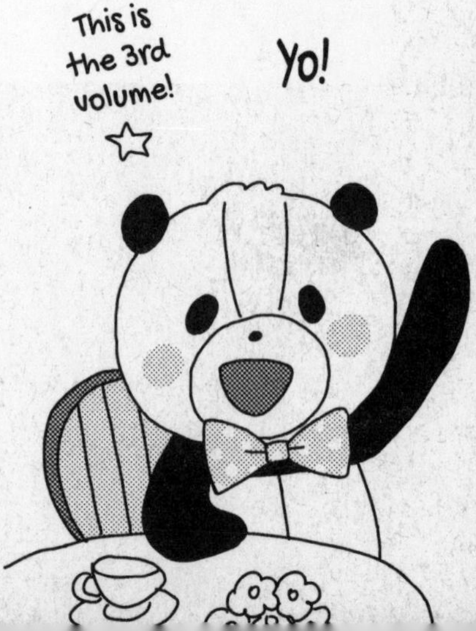
This is the 3rd volume! ☆
Yo!

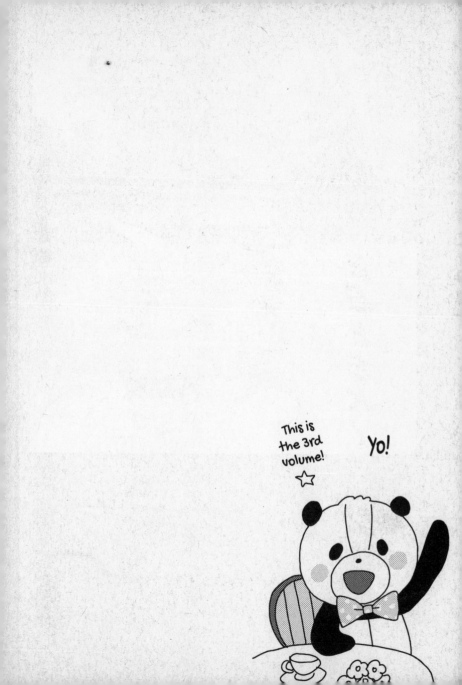

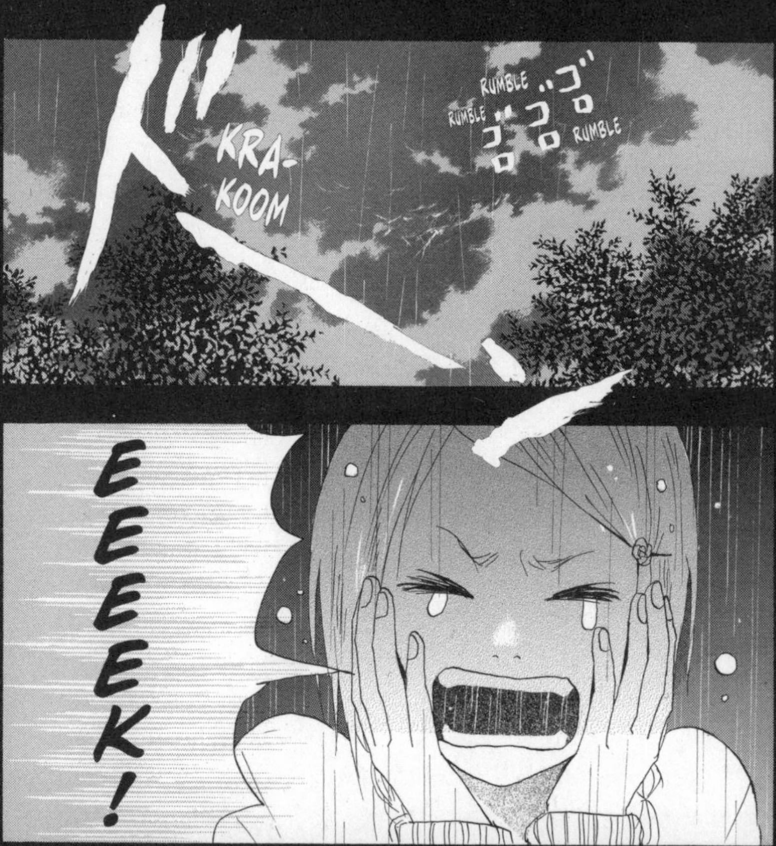
KRA-KOOM
RUMBLE
ゴロ
RUMBLE
ゴロ
RUMBLE
EEEEK!

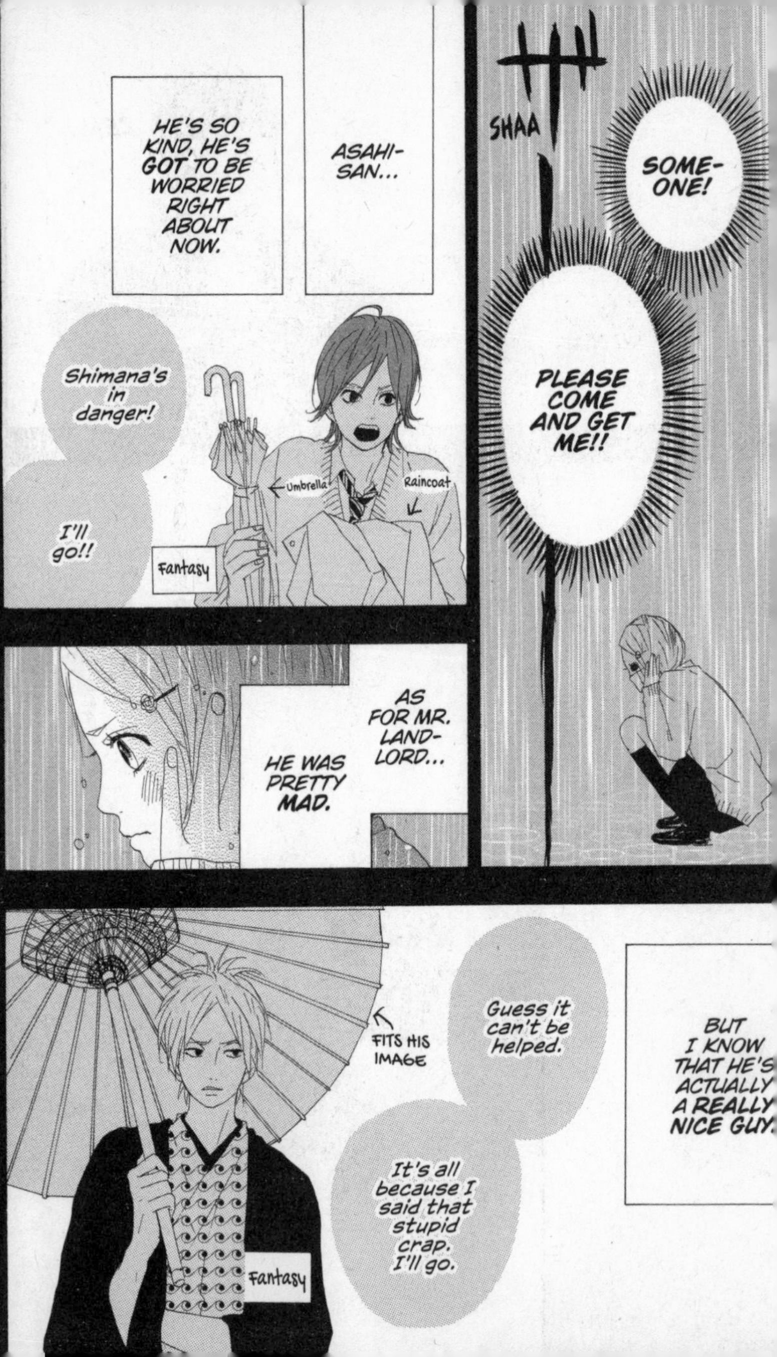
SHAA
SOME-ONE!
PLEASE COME AND GET ME!!
ASAHI-SAN...
HE'S SO KIND, HE'S GOT TO BE WORRIED RIGHT ABOUT NOW.
Raincoat
Umbrella
Shimana's in danger!
I'll go!!
Fantasy
AS FOR MR. LANDLORD...
HE WAS PRETTY MAD.
BUT I KNOW THAT HE'S ACTUALLY A REALLY NICE GUY.
Guess it can't be helped.
It's all because I said that stupid crap. I'll go.
FITS HIS IMAGE
Fantasy

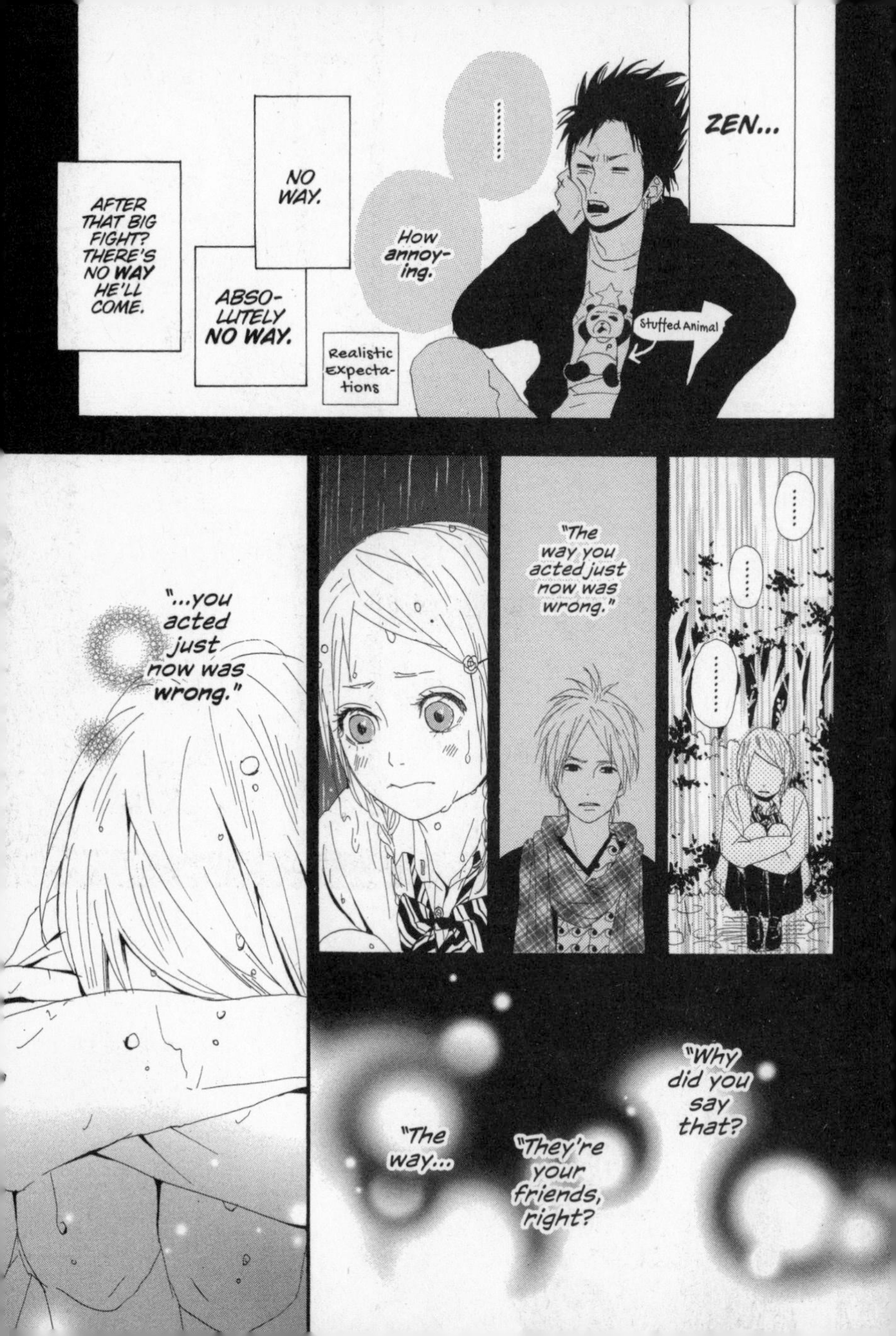
ZEN...
Stuffed Animal
......
How annoying.
NO WAY.
Realistic Expectations
ABSOLUTELY NO WAY.
AFTER THAT BIG FIGHT? THERE'S NO WAY HE'LL COME.
......
......
......
"The way you acted just now was wrong."
"Why did you say that?
"They're your friends, right?
"The way...
"...you acted just now was wrong."

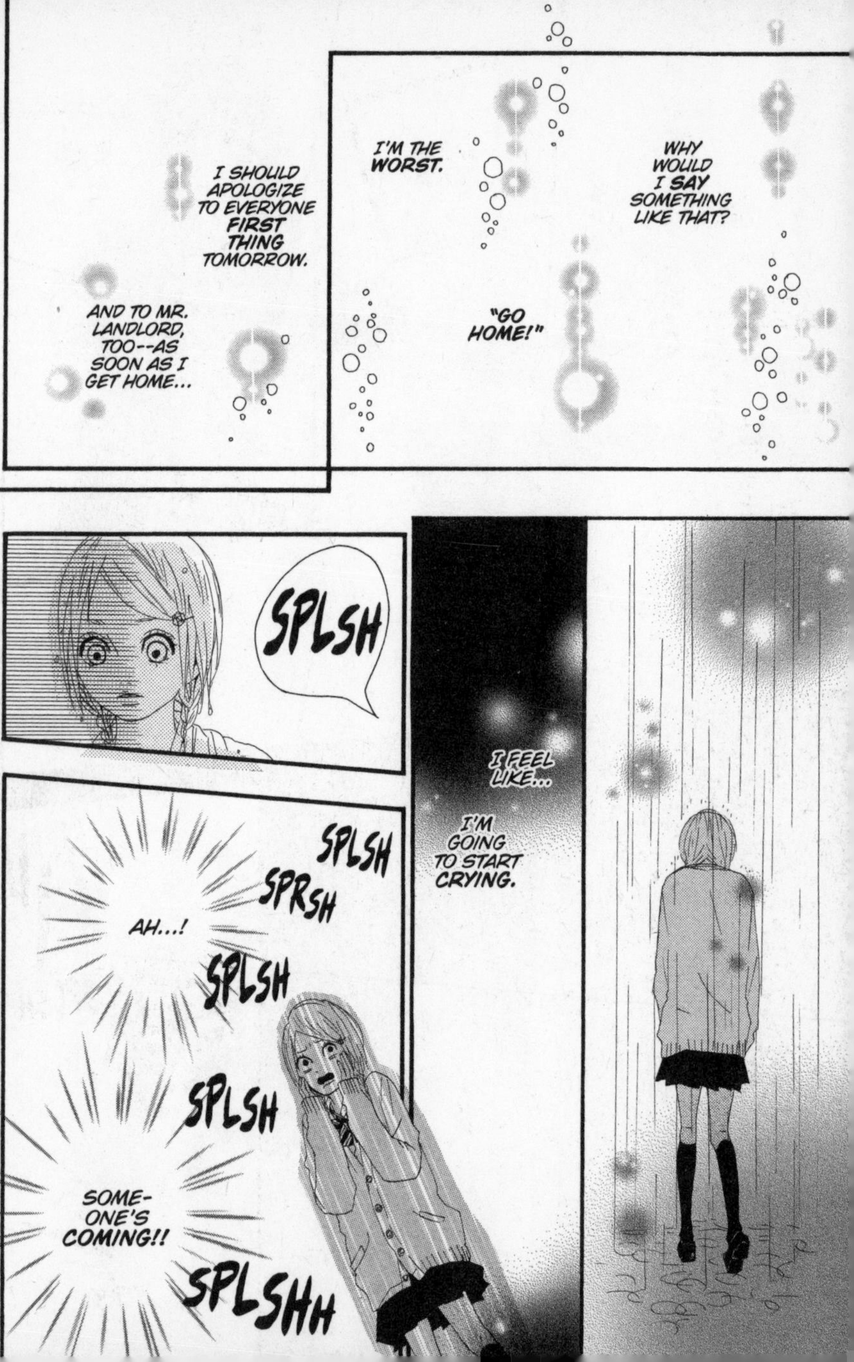
WHY WOULD I SAY SOMETHING LIKE THAT?
"GO HOME!"
I'M THE WORST.
I SHOULD APOLOGIZE TO EVERYONE FIRST THING TOMORROW.
AND TO MR. LANDLORD, TOO--AS SOON AS I GET HOME...
I FEEL LIKE...
I'M GOING TO START CRYING.
SPLSH
SPLSH
SPRSH
AH...!
SPLSH
SPLSH
SOME-ONE'S COMING!!
SPLSHH

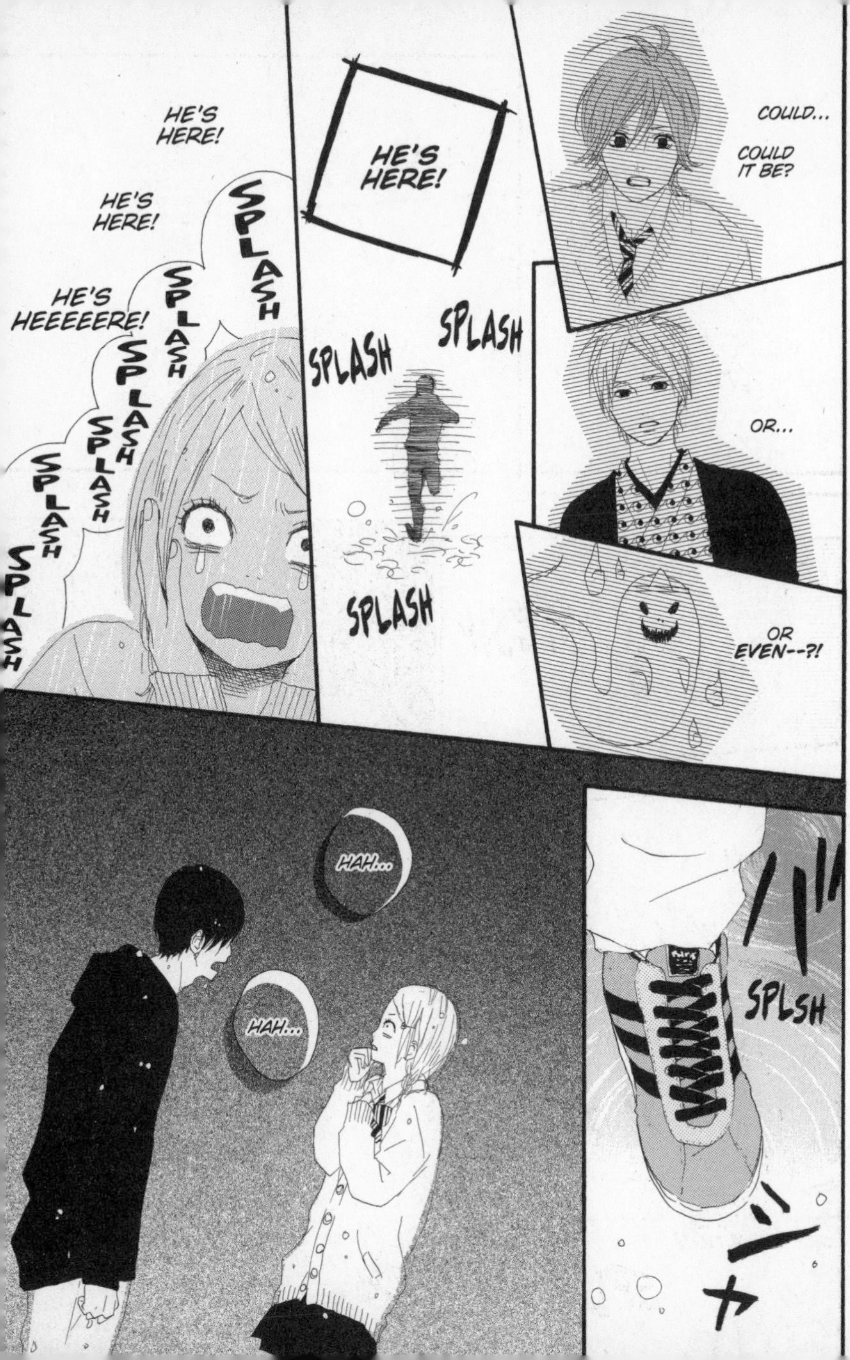

COULD...
COULD IT BE?
OR...
OR EVEN--?!
HE'S HERE!
SPLASH
SPLASH
SPLASH
HE'S HERE!
HE'S HERE!
HE'S HEEEEEERE!
SPLASH
SPLASH
SPLASH
SPLASH
SPLASH
SPLASH
SPLSH
HAH...
HAH...

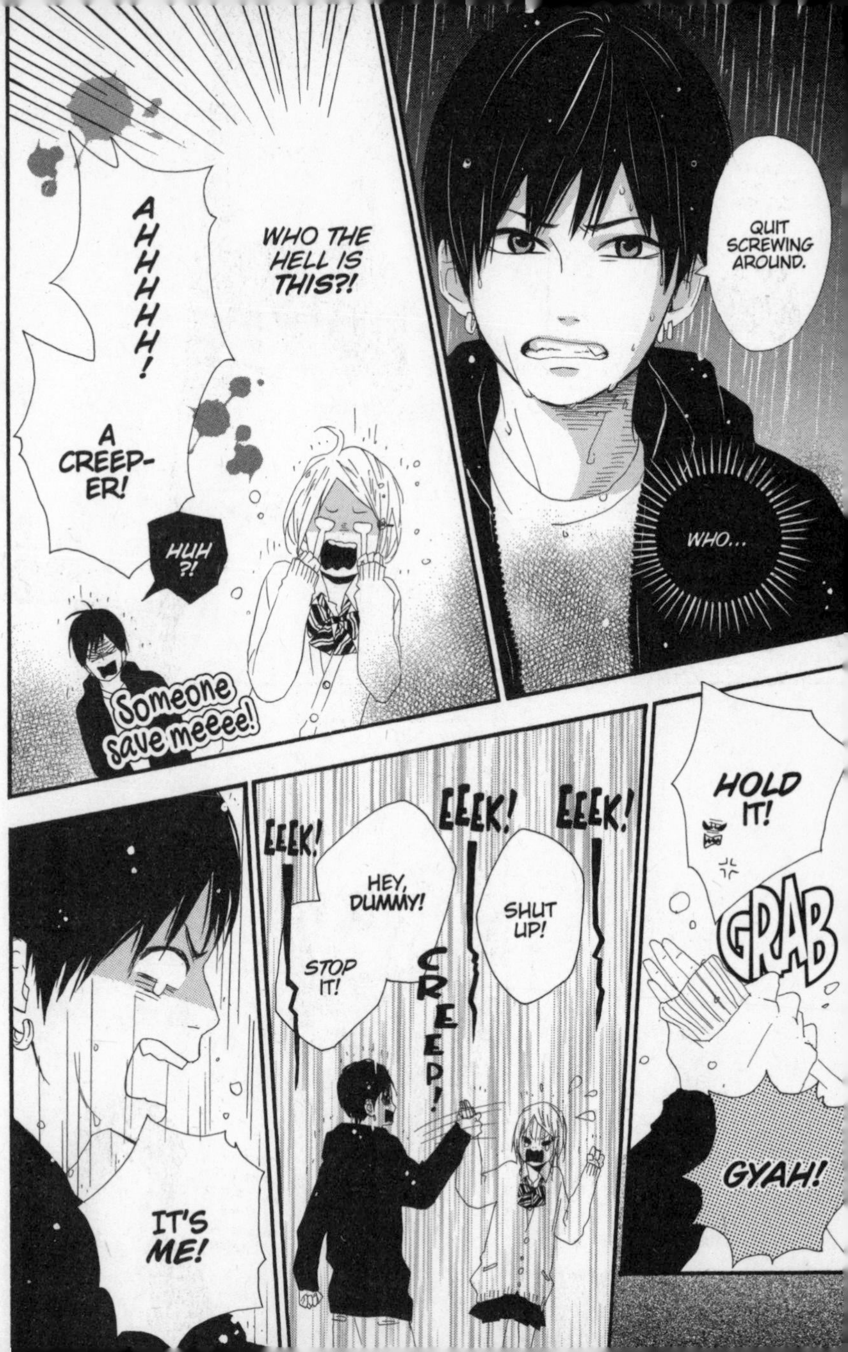
QUIT SCREWING AROUND.
WHO...
WHO THE HELL IS THIS?!
AHHHHHH!
A CREEPER!
HUH?!
Someone save meeee!
HOLD IT!
GRAB
GYAH!
EEEK!
EEEK!
SHUT UP!
CREEP!
EEEK!
HEY, DUMMY!
STOP IT!
IT'S ME!

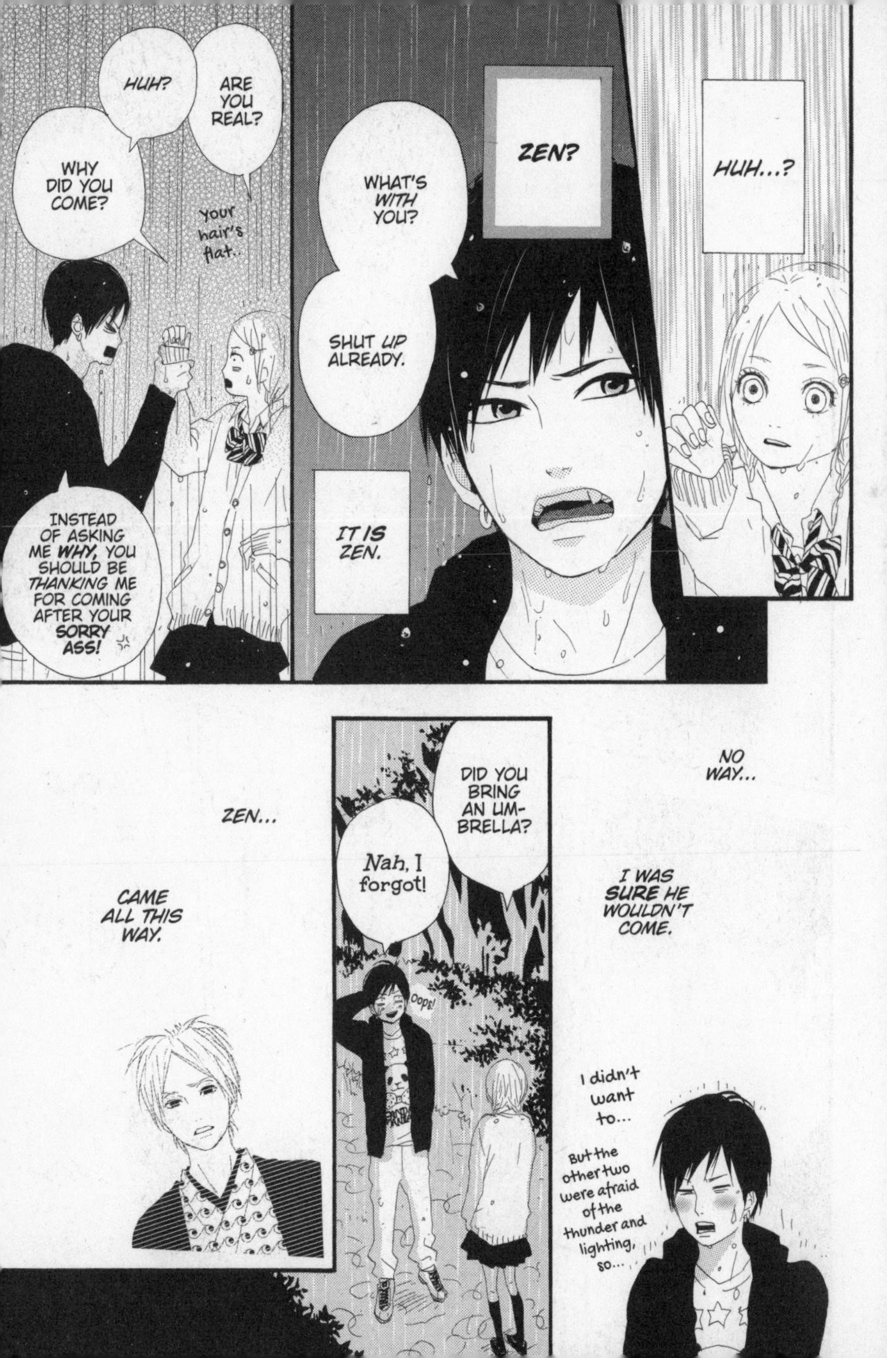
HUH...?
ZEN?
WHAT'S WITH YOU?
SHUT UP ALREADY.
IT IS ZEN.
ARE YOU REAL?
HUH?
WHY DID YOU COME?
Your hair's flat..
INSTEAD OF ASKING ME WHY, YOU SHOULD BE THANKING ME FOR COMING AFTER YOUR SORRY ASS!
NO WAY...
I WAS SURE HE WOULDN'T COME.
I didn't want to...
But the other two were afraid of the thunder and lighting, so...
DID YOU BRING AN UM-BRELLA?
Nah, I forgot!
Oops!
ZEN...
CAME ALL THIS WAY.

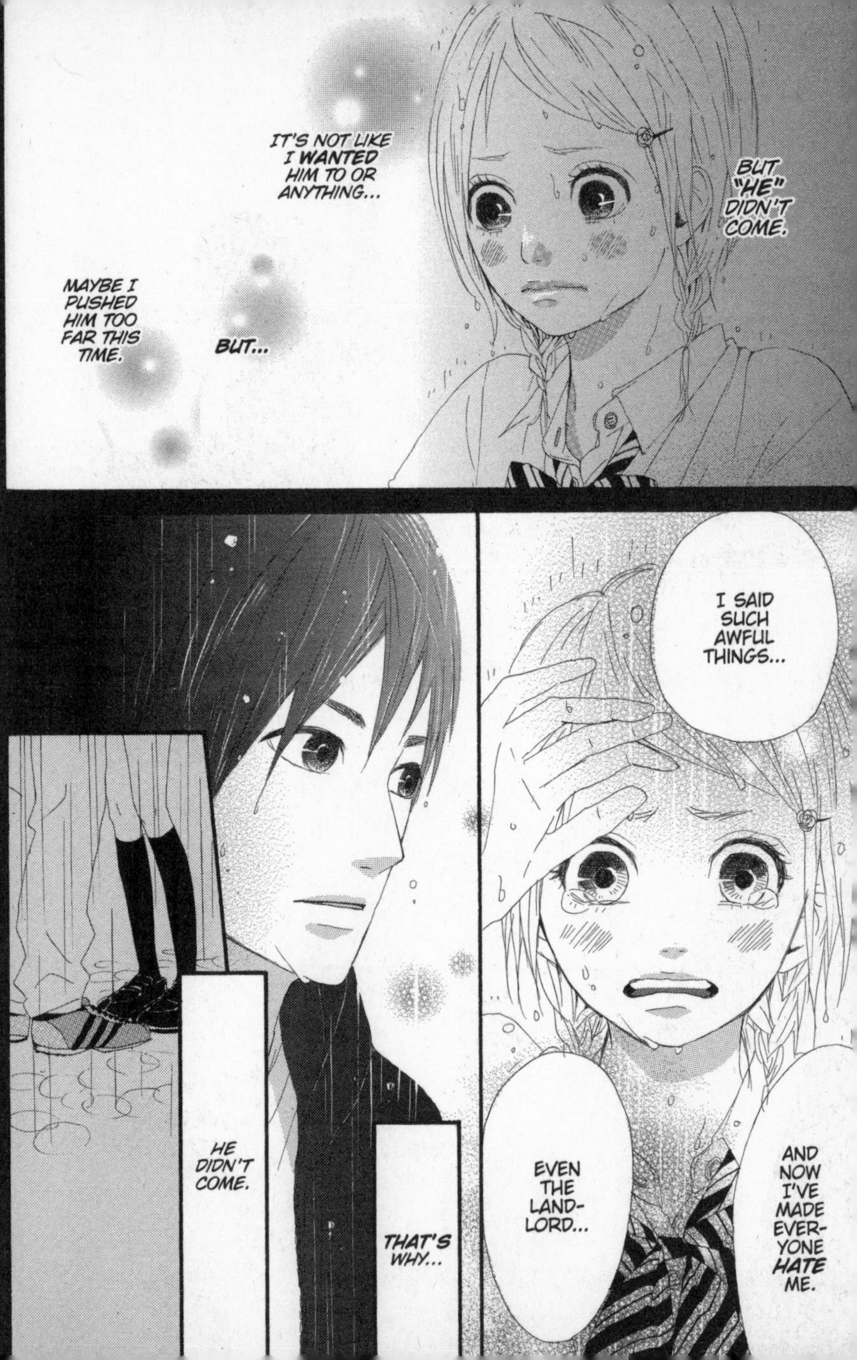
BUT "HE" DIDN'T COME.
IT'S NOT LIKE I WANTED HIM TO OR ANYTHING...
BUT...
MAYBE I PUSHED HIM TOO FAR THIS TIME.
I SAID SUCH AWFUL THINGS...
AND NOW I'VE MADE EVERY-ONE HATE ME.
EVEN THE LAND-LORD...
THAT'S WHY...
HE DIDN'T COME.

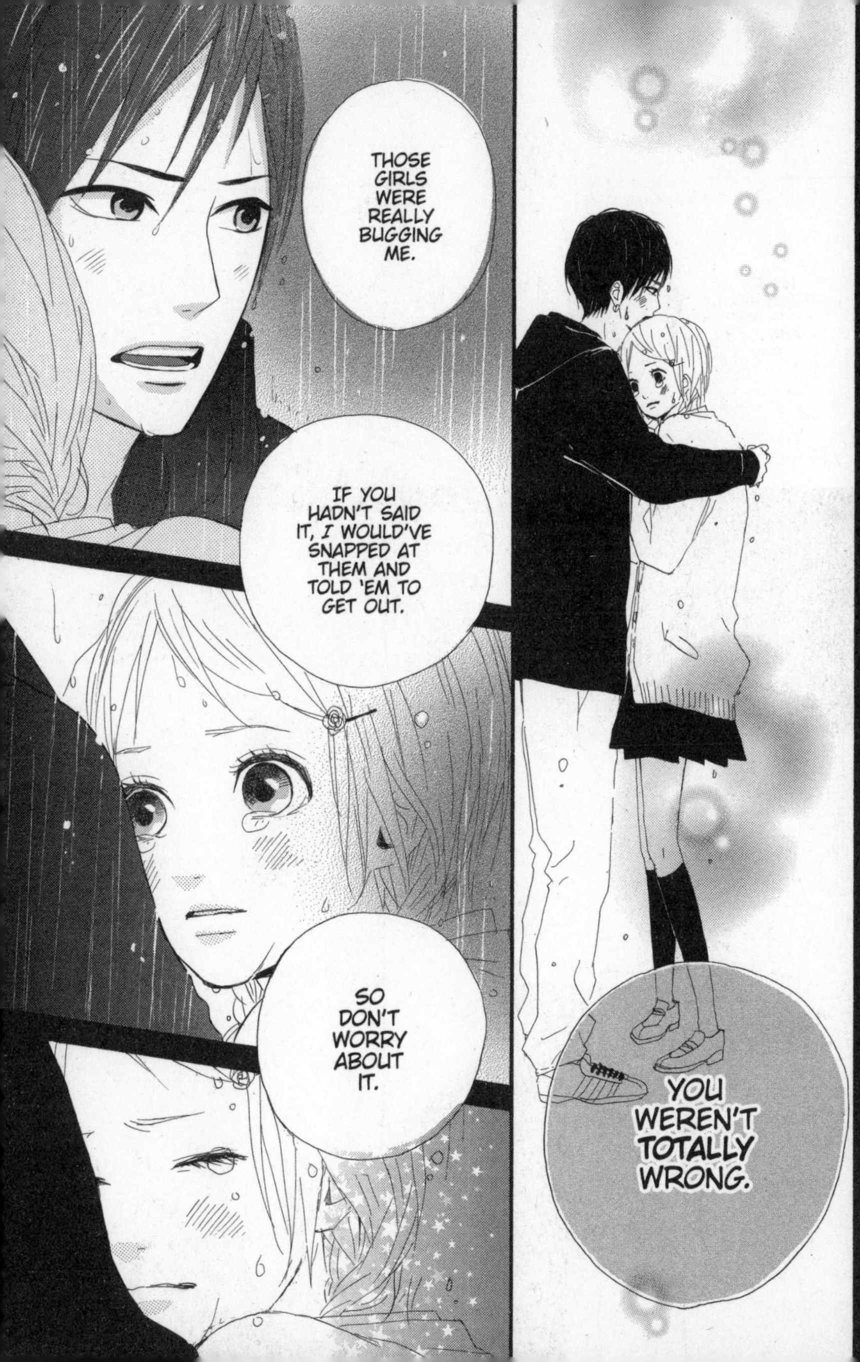
YOU WEREN'T TOTALLY WRONG.
THOSE GIRLS WERE REALLY BUGGING ME.
IF YOU HADN'T SAID IT, *I* WOULD'VE SNAPPED AT THEM AND TOLD 'EM TO GET OUT.
SO DON'T WORRY ABOUT IT.

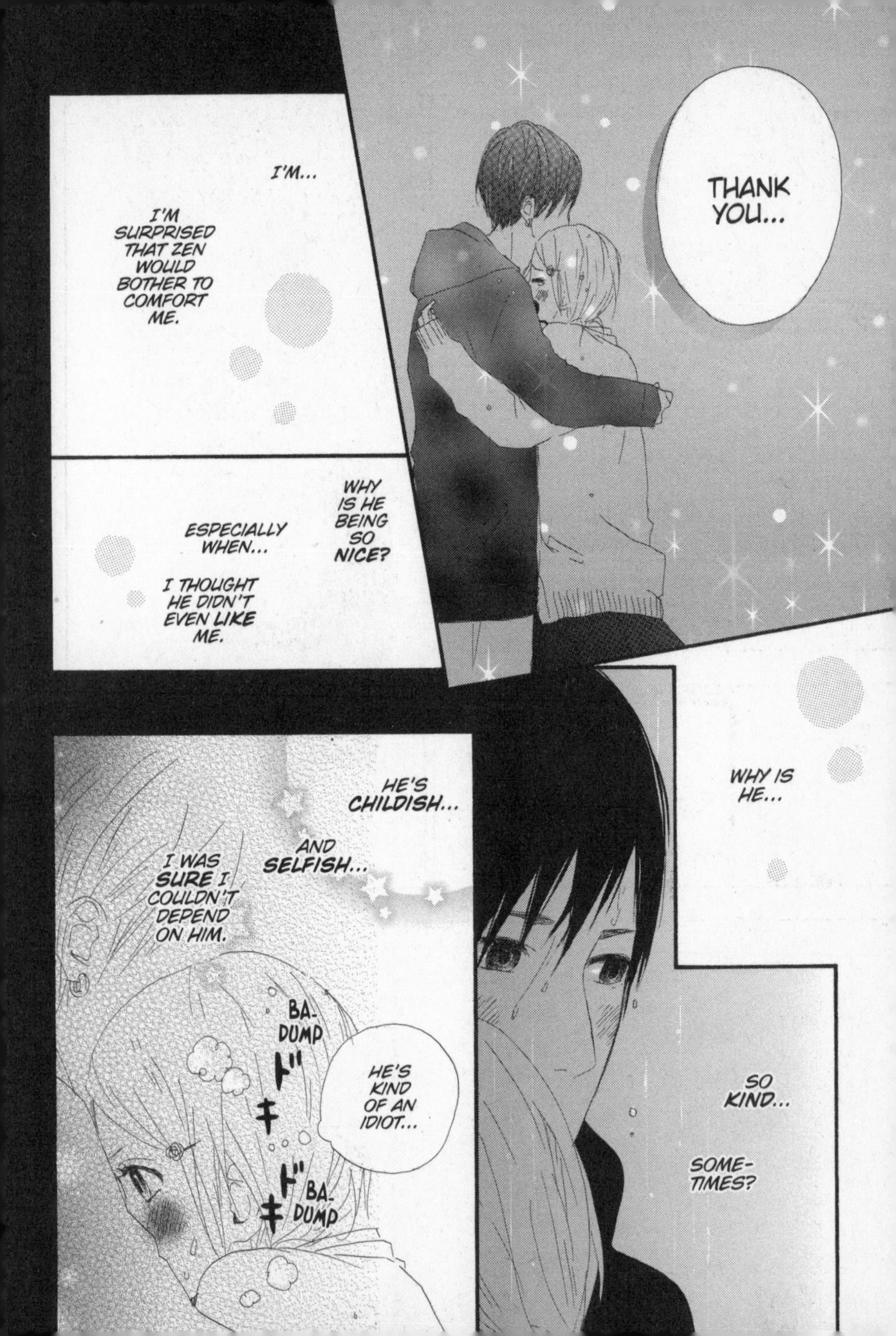
THANK YOU...
I'M...
I'M SURPRISED THAT ZEN WOULD BOTHER TO COMFORT ME.
WHY IS HE BEING SO NICE?
ESPECIALLY WHEN...
I THOUGHT HE DIDN'T EVEN LIKE ME.
WHY IS HE...
SO KIND...
SOMETIMES?
HE'S CHILDISH...
AND SELFISH...
I WAS SURE I COULDN'T DEPEND ON HIM.
BA-DUMP
ドキ
HE'S KIND OF AN IDIOT...
ドキ
BA-DUMP

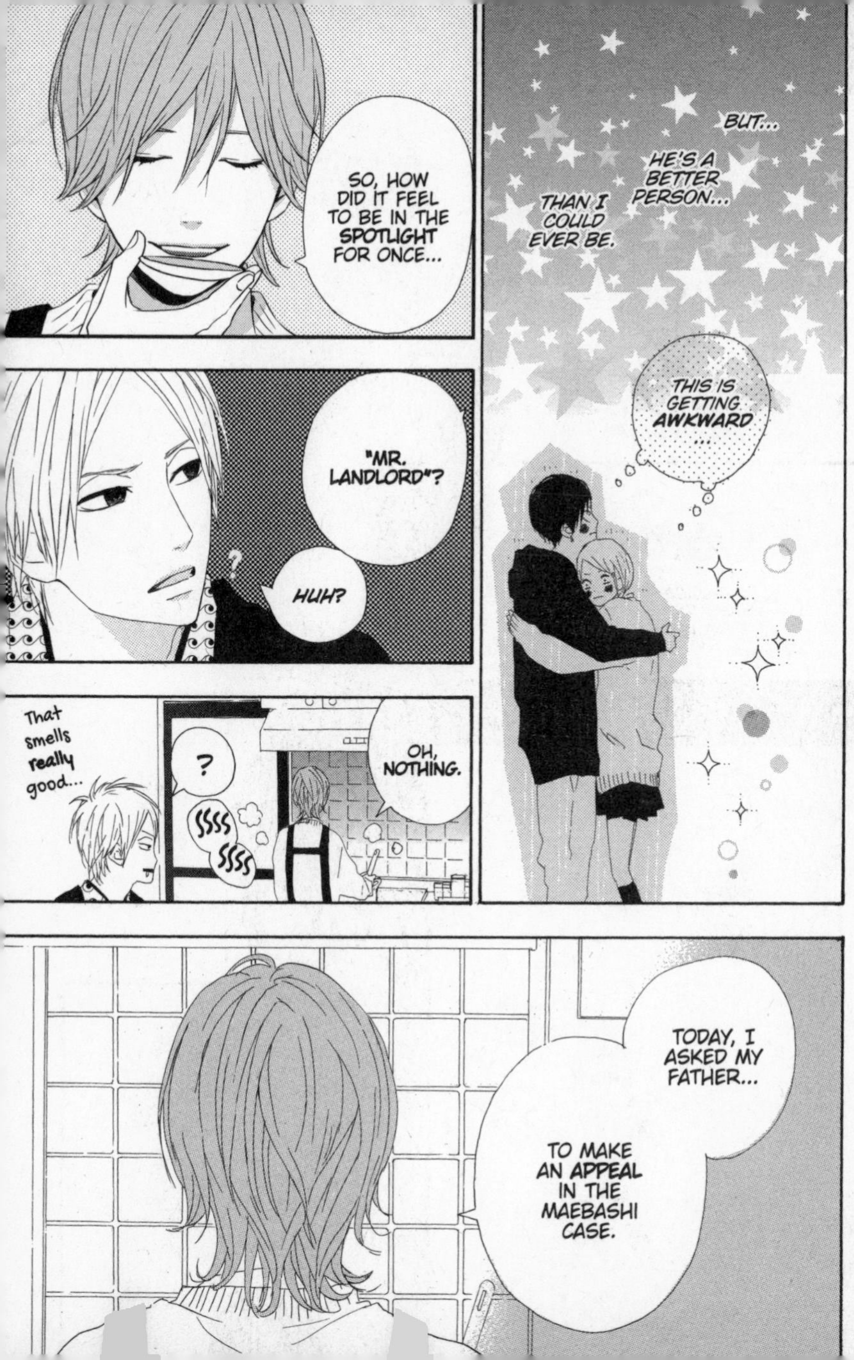
BUT...
HE'S A BETTER PERSON...
THAN I COULD EVER BE.
THIS IS GETTING AWKWARD...
SO, HOW DID IT FEEL TO BE IN THE SPOTLIGHT FOR ONCE...
"MR. LANDLORD"?
HUH?
OH, NOTHING.
?
SSSS
SSSS
That smells really good...
TODAY, I ASKED MY FATHER...
TO MAKE AN APPEAL IN THE MAEBASHI CASE.

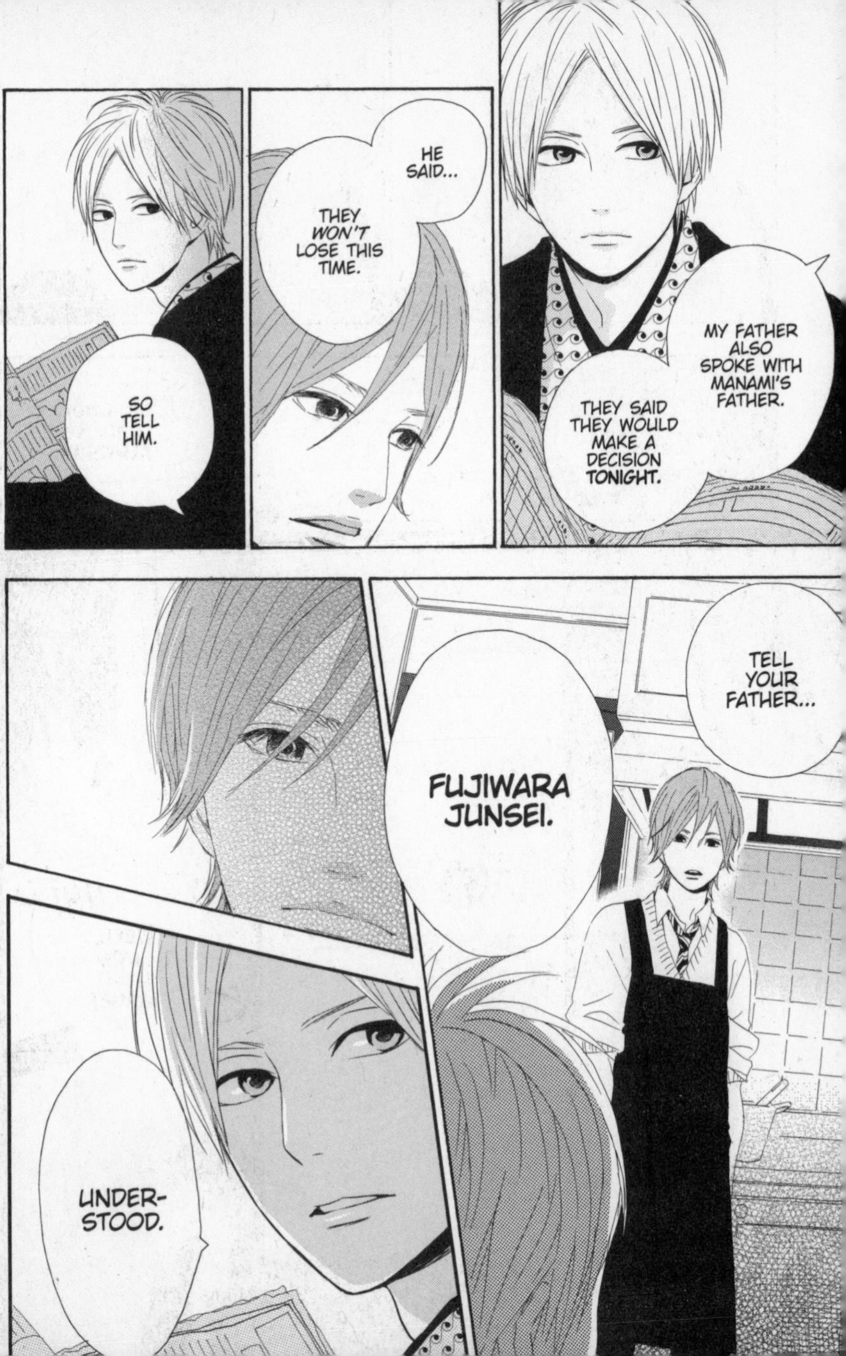
MY FATHER ALSO SPOKE WITH MANAMI'S FATHER.
THEY SAID THEY WOULD MAKE A DECISION TONIGHT.
HE SAID...
THEY *WON'T* LOSE THIS TIME.
SO TELL HIM.
TELL YOUR FATHER...
FUJIWARA JUNSEI.
UNDER-STOOD.

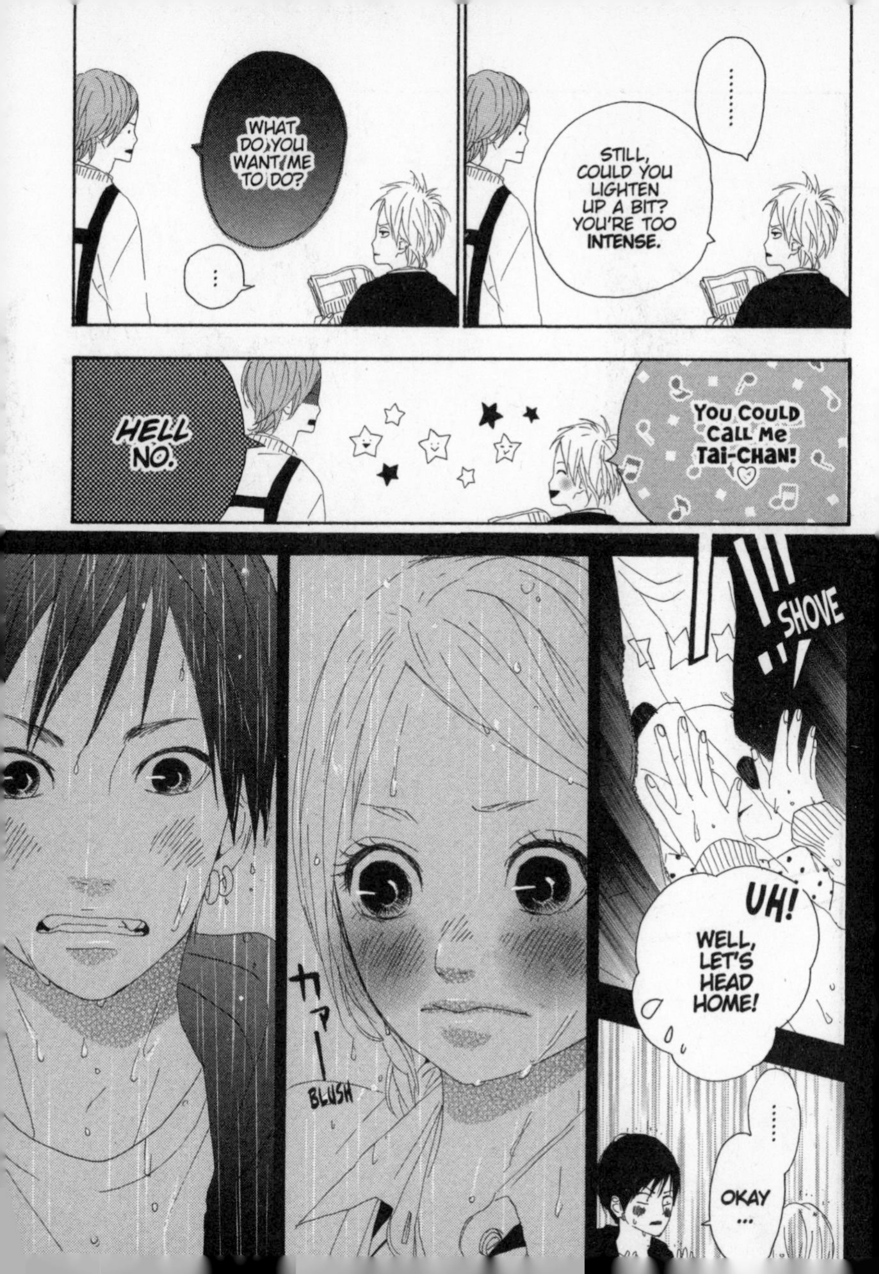
......
STILL, COULD YOU LIGHTEN UP A BIT? YOU'RE TOO INTENSE.
WHAT DO YOU WANT ME TO DO?
...
You Could Call Me Tai-CHAN!
HELL NO.
SHOVE
UH!
WELL, LET'S HEAD HOME!
......
OKAY ...
カァー
BLUSH

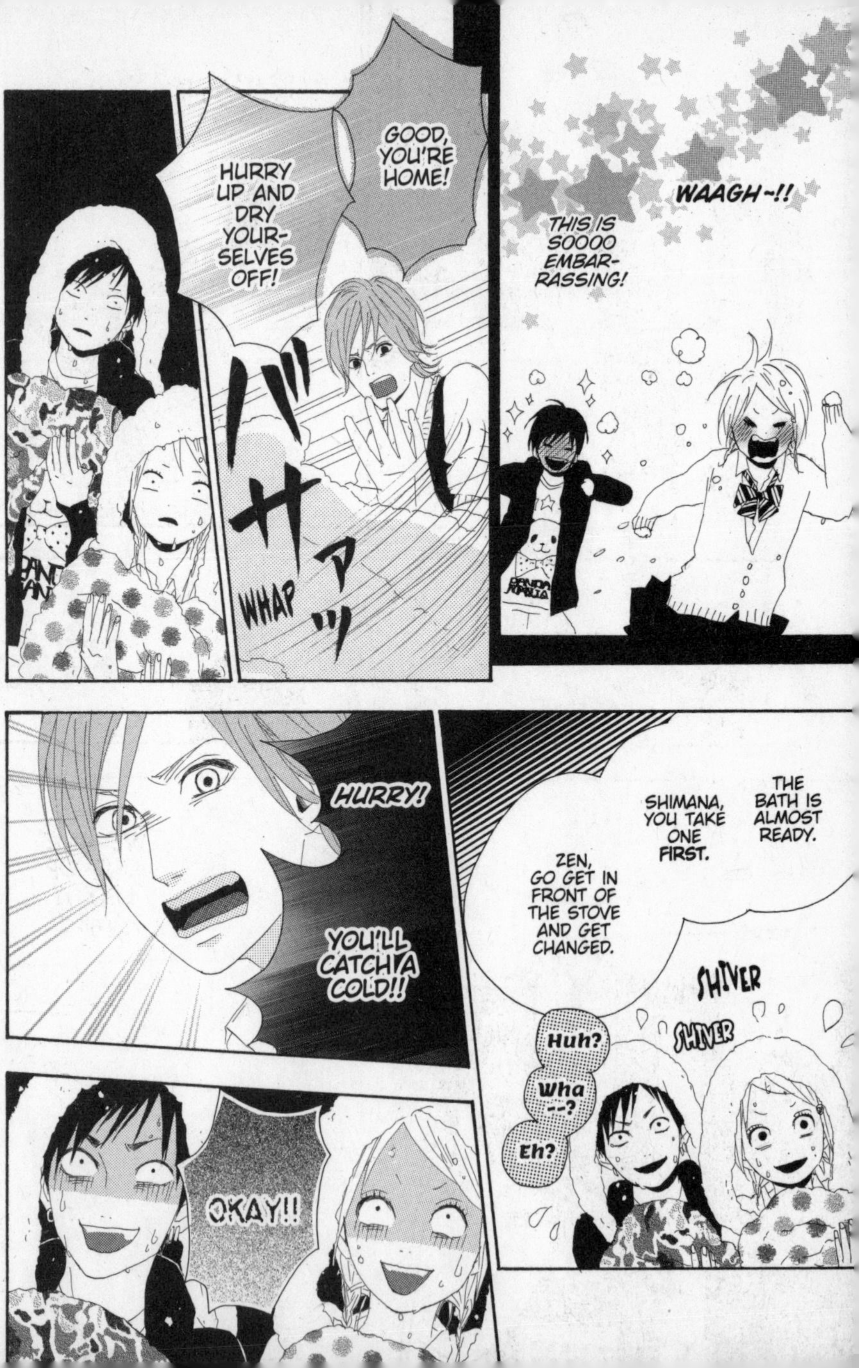
WAAGH~!!
THIS IS SOOOO EMBARRASSING!
GOOD, YOU'RE HOME!
HURRY UP AND DRY YOURSELVES OFF!
バサァッ
WHAP
THE BATH IS ALMOST READY.
SHIMANA, YOU TAKE ONE FIRST.
ZEN, GO GET IN FRONT OF THE STOVE AND GET CHANGED.
SHIVER
SHIVER
Huh?
Wha--?
Eh?
HURRY!
YOU'LL CATCH A COLD!!
OKAY!!

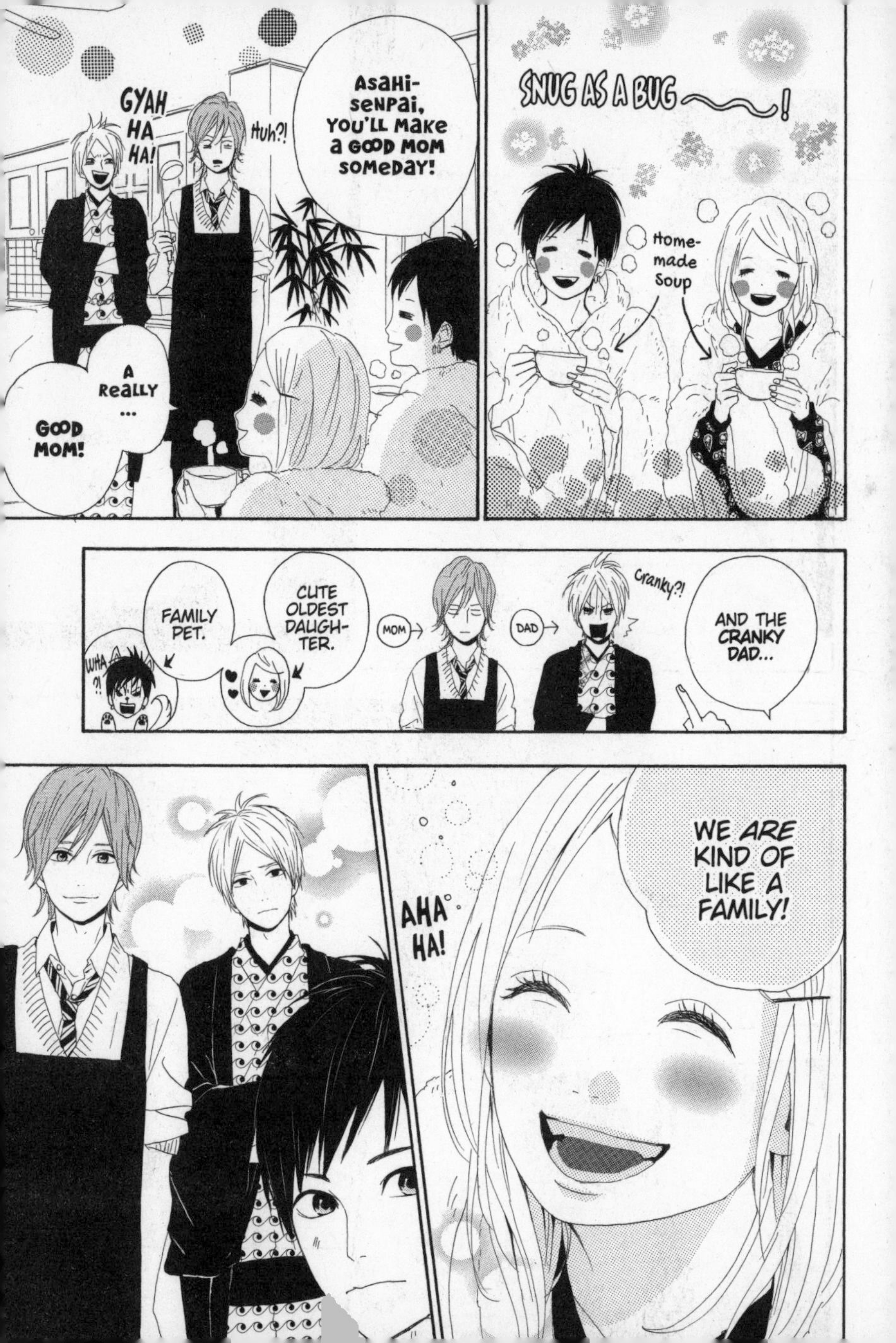

SNUG AS A BUG ~~~!
Home-made Soup
Asahi-senpai, you'll make a good mom someday!
Huh?!
GYAH HA HA!
A really...
GOOD MOM!
AND THE CRANKY DAD...
Cranky?!
DAD
MOM
CUTE OLDEST DAUGH-TER.
FAMILY PET.
WHA ?!
WE ARE KIND OF LIKE A FAMILY!
AHA HA!

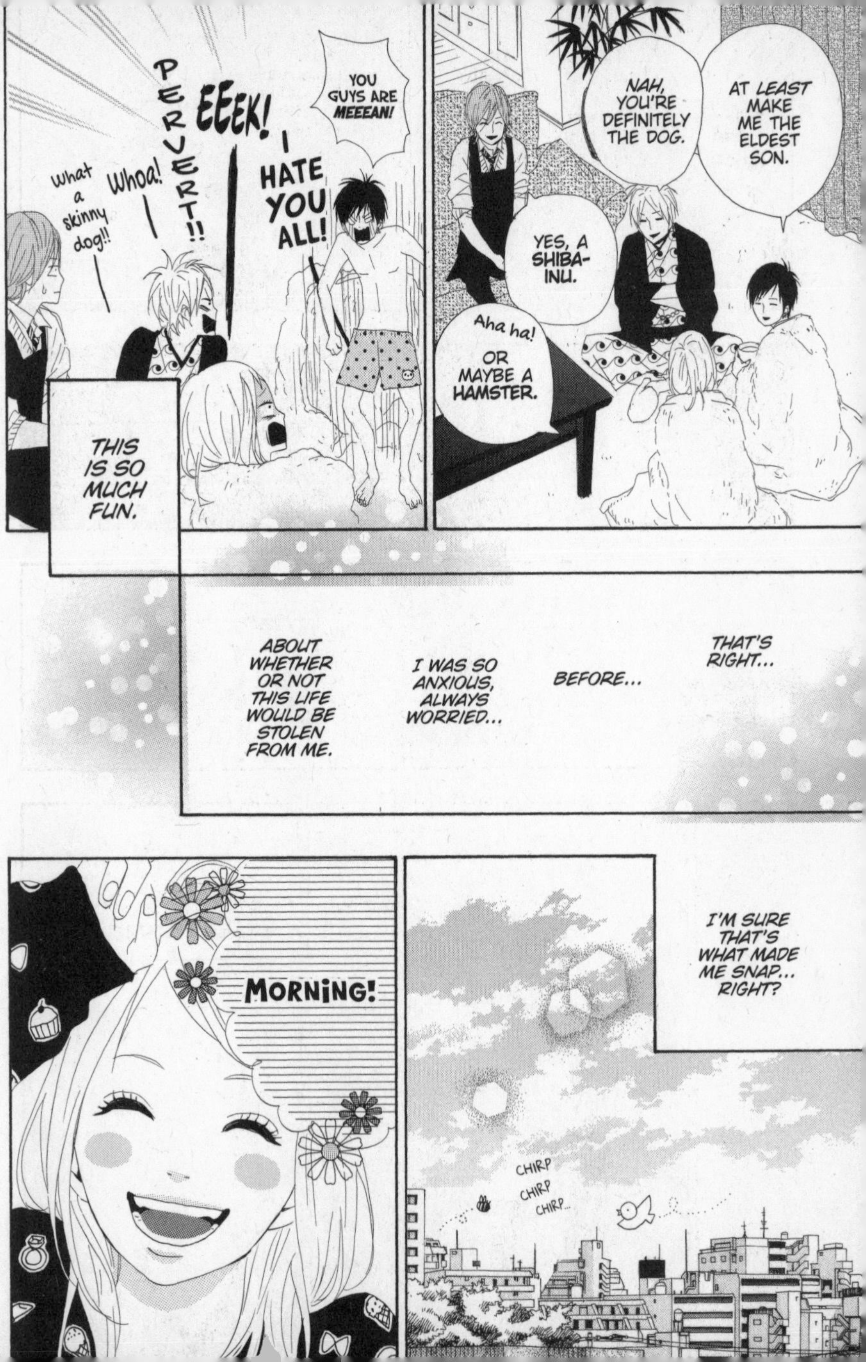
AT LEAST MAKE ME THE ELDEST SON.
NAH, YOU'RE DEFINITELY THE DOG.
YES, A SHIBA-INU.
Aha ha! OR MAYBE A HAMSTER.
YOU GUYS ARE MEEEAN!
I HATE YOU ALL!
EEEK!
PERVERT!!
Whoa!
What a skinny dog!!
THIS IS SO MUCH FUN.
THAT'S RIGHT...
BEFORE...
I WAS SO ANXIOUS, ALWAYS WORRIED...
ABOUT WHETHER OR NOT THIS LIFE WOULD BE STOLEN FROM ME.
I'M SURE THAT'S WHAT MADE ME SNAP... RIGHT?
CHIRP
CHIRP
CHIRP...
MORNING!

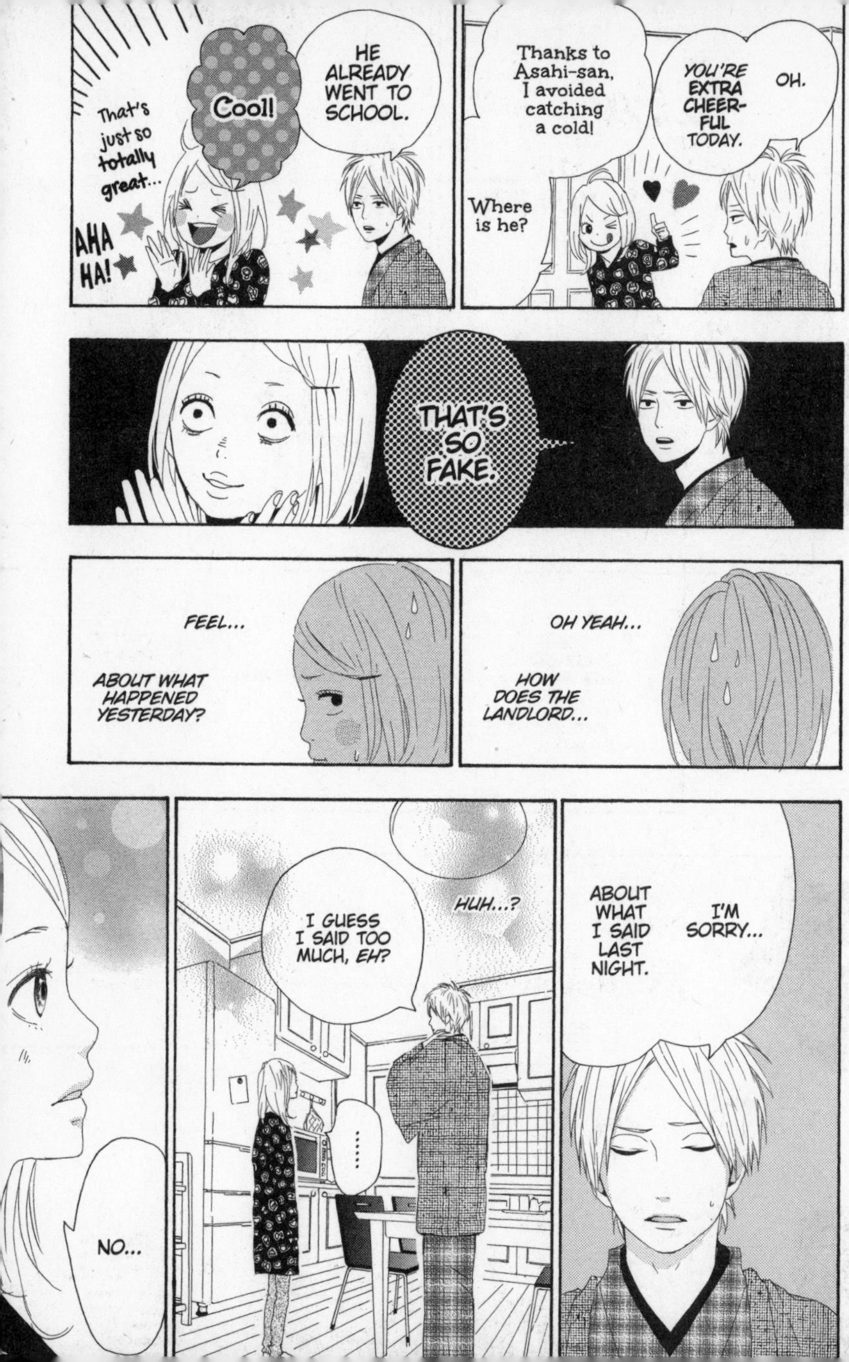
OH.
YOU'RE EXTRA CHEERFUL TODAY.
Thanks to Asahi-san, I avoided catching a cold!
Where is he?
HE ALREADY WENT TO SCHOOL.
Cool!
That's just so totally great...
AHA HA!
THAT'S SO FAKE.
OH YEAH...
HOW DOES THE LANDLORD...
FEEL...
ABOUT WHAT HAPPENED YESTERDAY?
I'M SORRY...
ABOUT WHAT I SAID LAST NIGHT.
HUH...?
I GUESS I SAID TOO MUCH, EH?
......
NO...

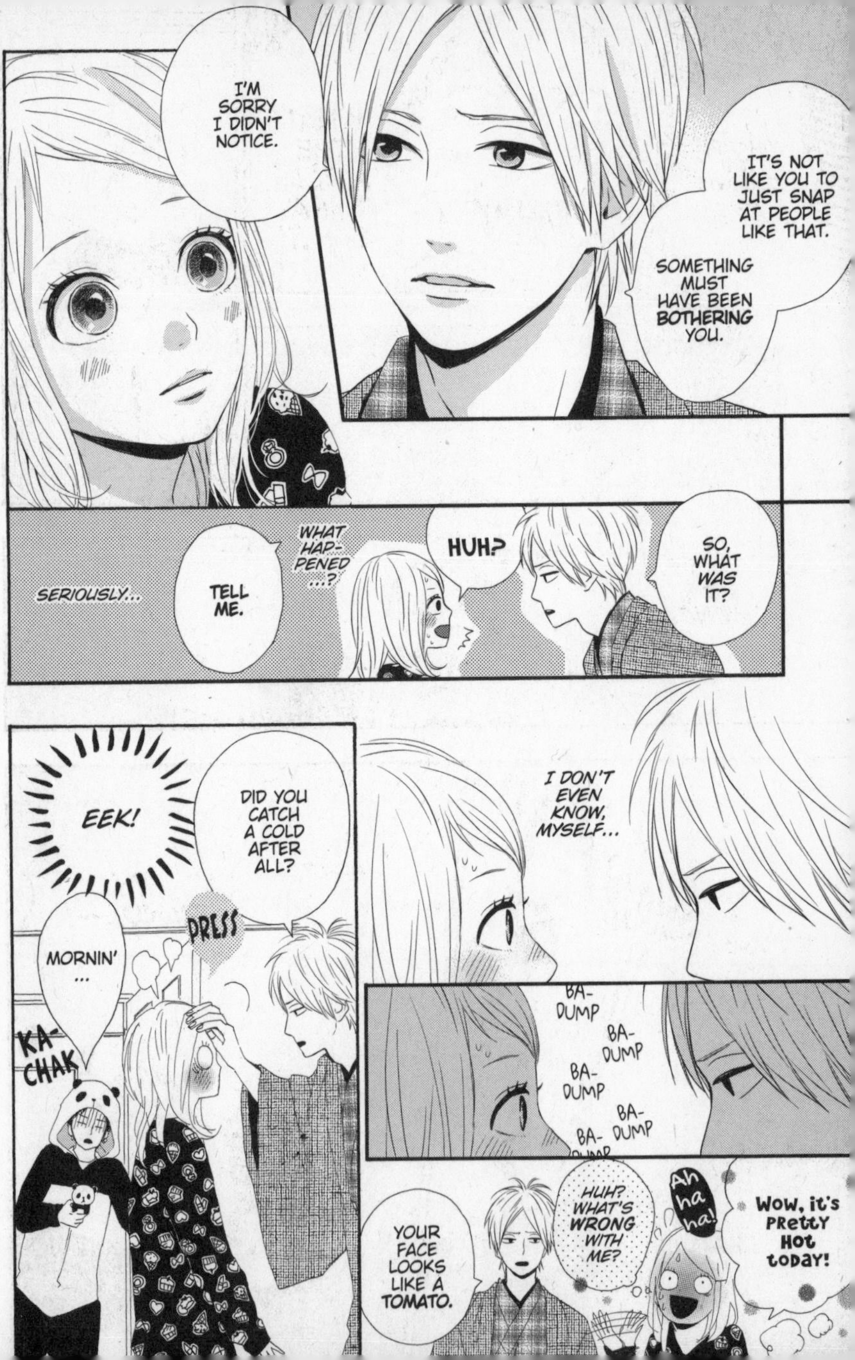
IT'S NOT LIKE YOU TO JUST SNAP AT PEOPLE LIKE THAT.
SOMETHING MUST HAVE BEEN BOTHERING YOU.
I'M SORRY I DIDN'T NOTICE.
SO, WHAT WAS IT?
HUH?
WHAT HAP-PENED ...?
TELL ME.
SERIOUSLY...
I DON'T EVEN KNOW, MYSELF...
BA-DUMP
BA-DUMP
BA-DUMP
BA-DUMP
BA-
Wow, it's pretty hot today!
Ah ha ha!
HUH? WHAT'S WRONG WITH ME?
YOUR FACE LOOKS LIKE A TOMATO.
DID YOU CATCH A COLD AFTER ALL?
EEK!
PRESS
MORNIN' ...
KA-CHAK

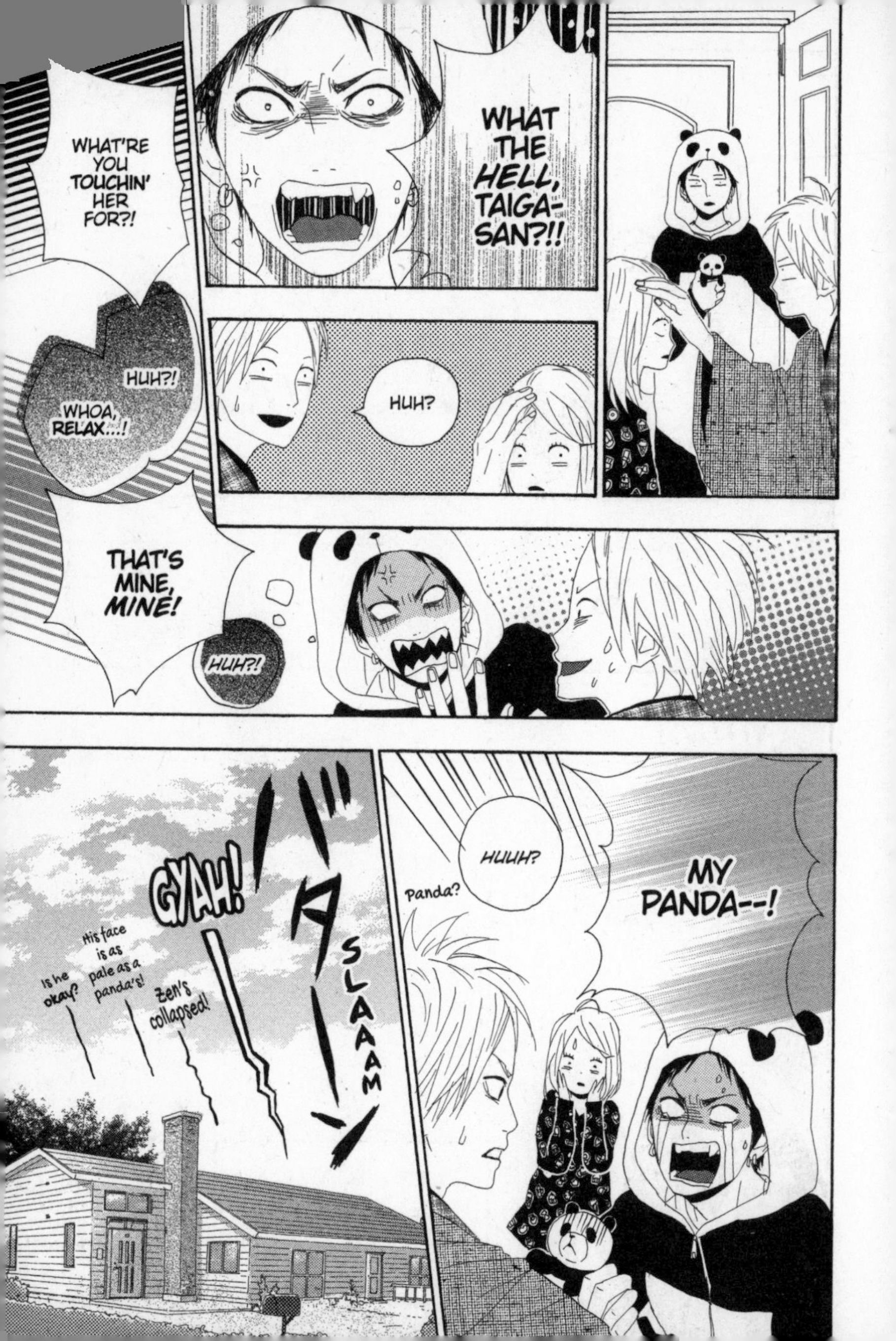
WHAT THE HELL, TAIGA-SAN?!!
WHAT'RE YOU TOUCHIN' HER FOR?!
HUH?
HUH?!
WHOA, RELAX...!
THAT'S MINE, MINE!
HUH?!
MY PANDA--!
HUUH?
Panda?
SLAAAM
GYAH!
Zen's collapsed!
His face is as pale as a panda's!
Is he okay?

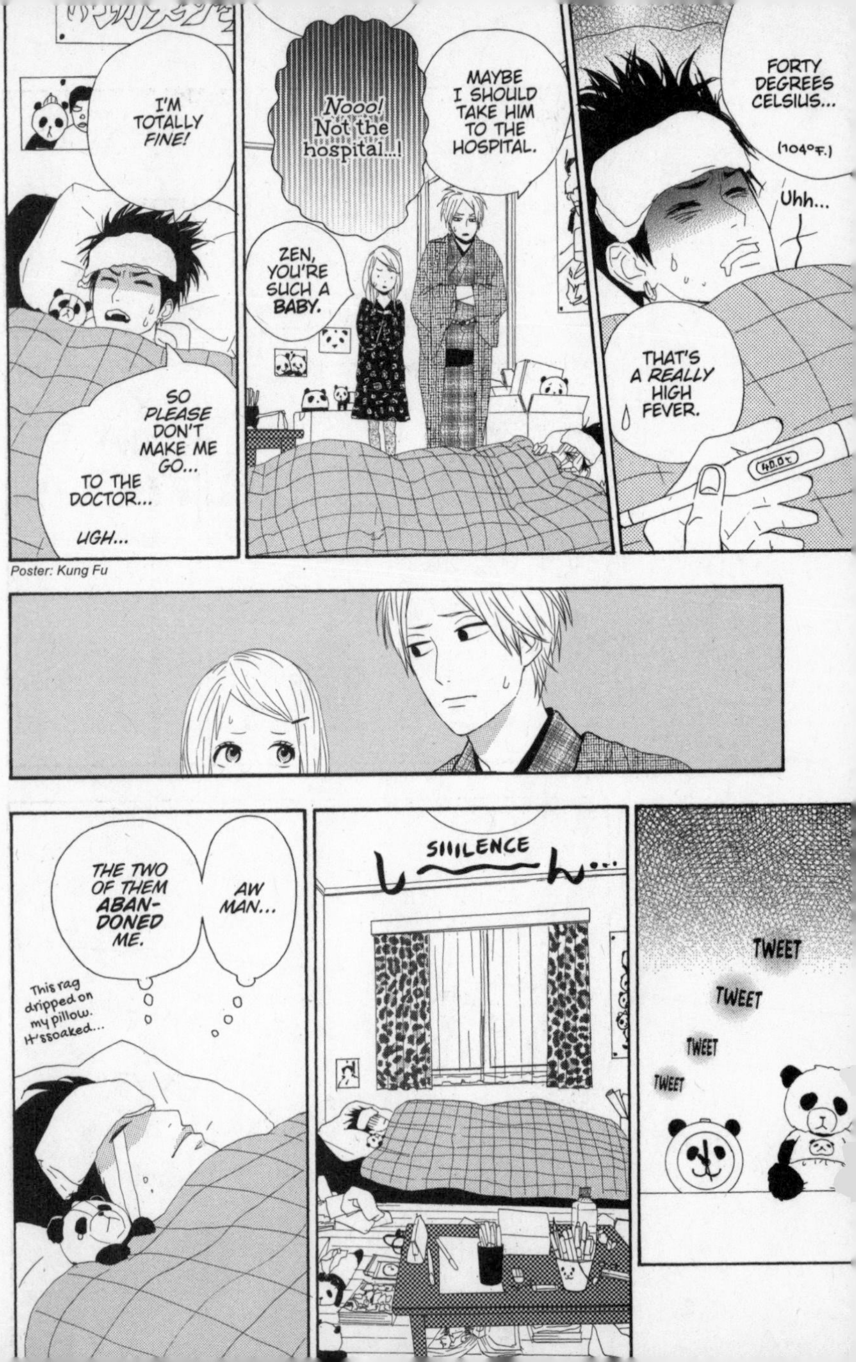
FORTY DEGREES CELSIUS...
(104°F.)
Uhh...
THAT'S A REALLY HIGH FEVER.
MAYBE I SHOULD TAKE HIM TO THE HOSPITAL.
Nooo! Not the hospital...!
ZEN, YOU'RE SUCH A BABY.
I'M TOTALLY FINE!
SO PLEASE DON'T MAKE ME GO...
TO THE DOCTOR...
UGH...
TWEET
TWEET
TWEET
TWEET
SIIILENCE
AW MAN...
THE TWO OF THEM ABANDONED ME.
This rag dripped on my pillow. It'ssoaked...

Poster: Kung Fu

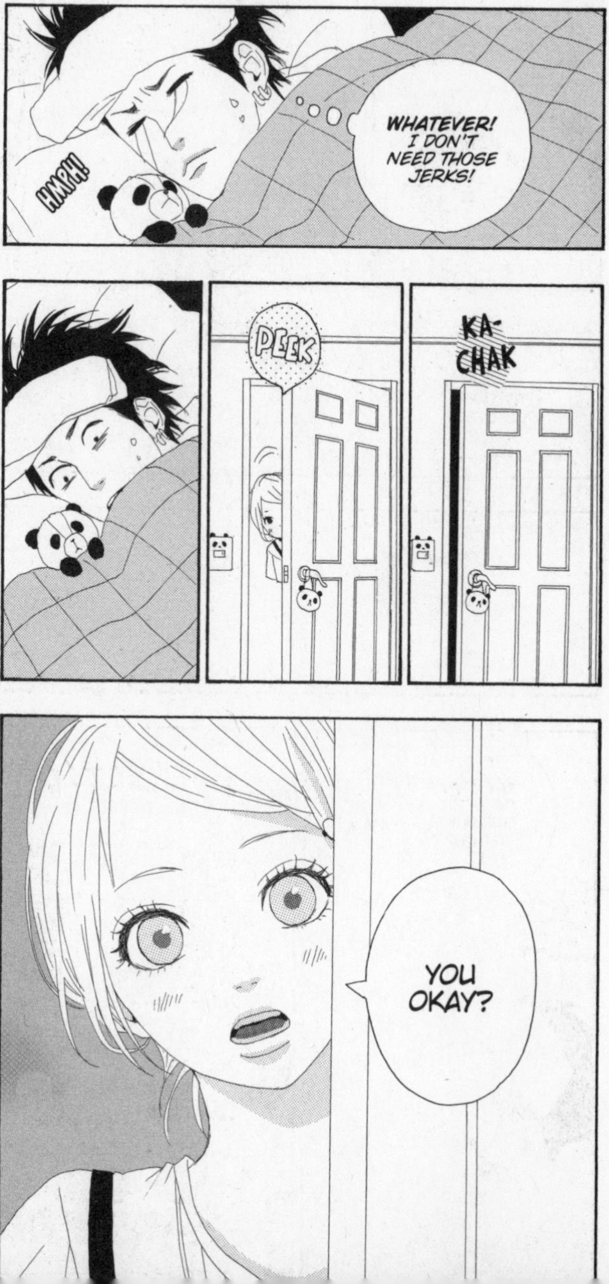
WHATEVER! I DON'T NEED THOSE JERKS!
HMPH!
KA-CHAK
PEEK
YOU OKAY?

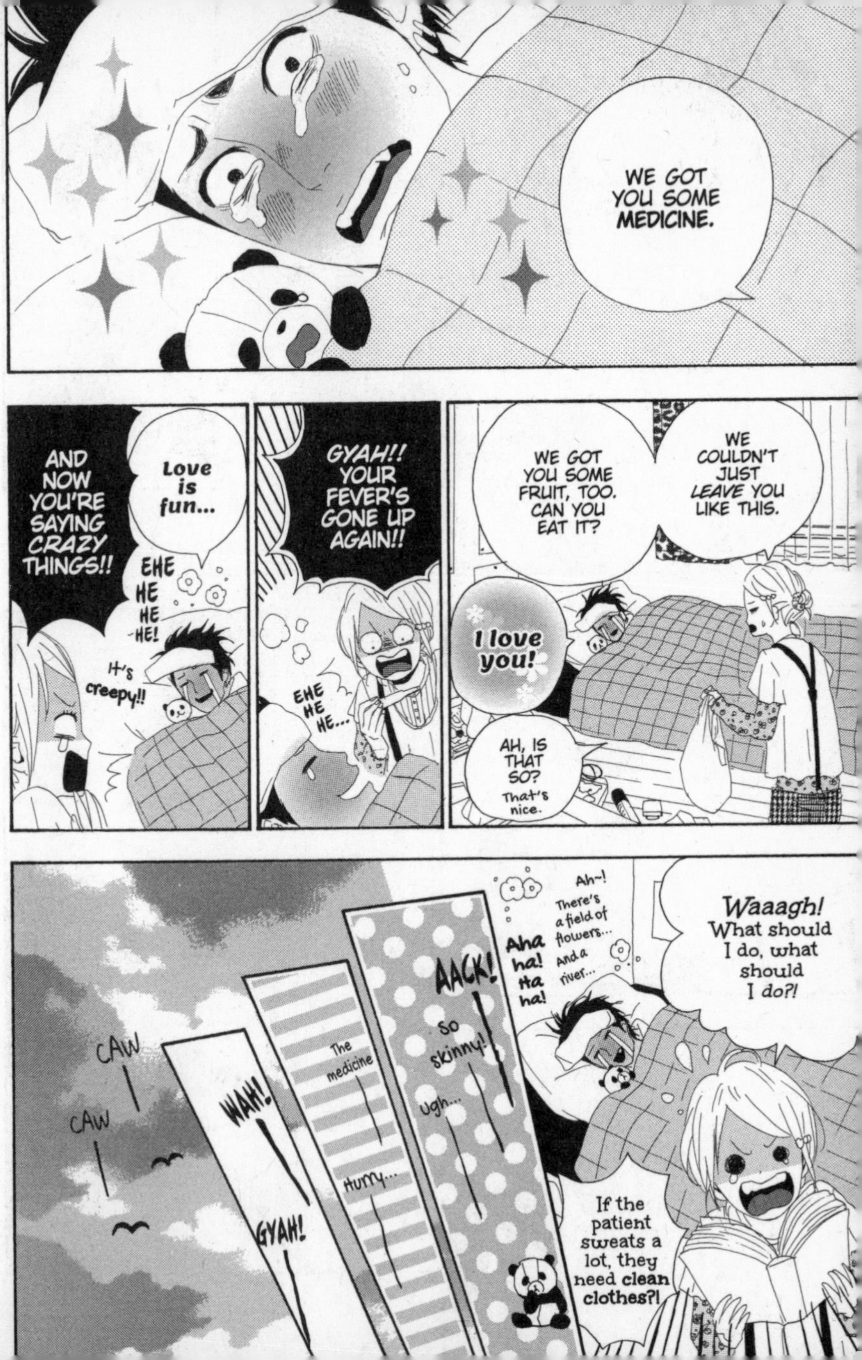
WE GOT YOU SOME MEDICINE.
WE COULDN'T JUST *LEAVE* YOU LIKE THIS.
WE GOT YOU SOME FRUIT, TOO. CAN YOU EAT IT?
I love you!
AH, IS THAT SO? That's nice.
GYAH!! YOUR FEVER'S GONE UP AGAIN!!
EHE HE HE...
Love is fun...
EHE HE HE -HE!
AND NOW YOU'RE SAYING *CRAZY* THINGS!!
It's creepy!!
Waaagh! What should I do, what should I do?!
Ah~! There's a field of flowers... And a river...
Aha ha! Ha ha!
If the patient sweats a lot, they need **clean clothes**?!
AACK!
So skinny!
Ugh...
The medicine
Hurry...
WAH!
GYAH!
CAW
CAW

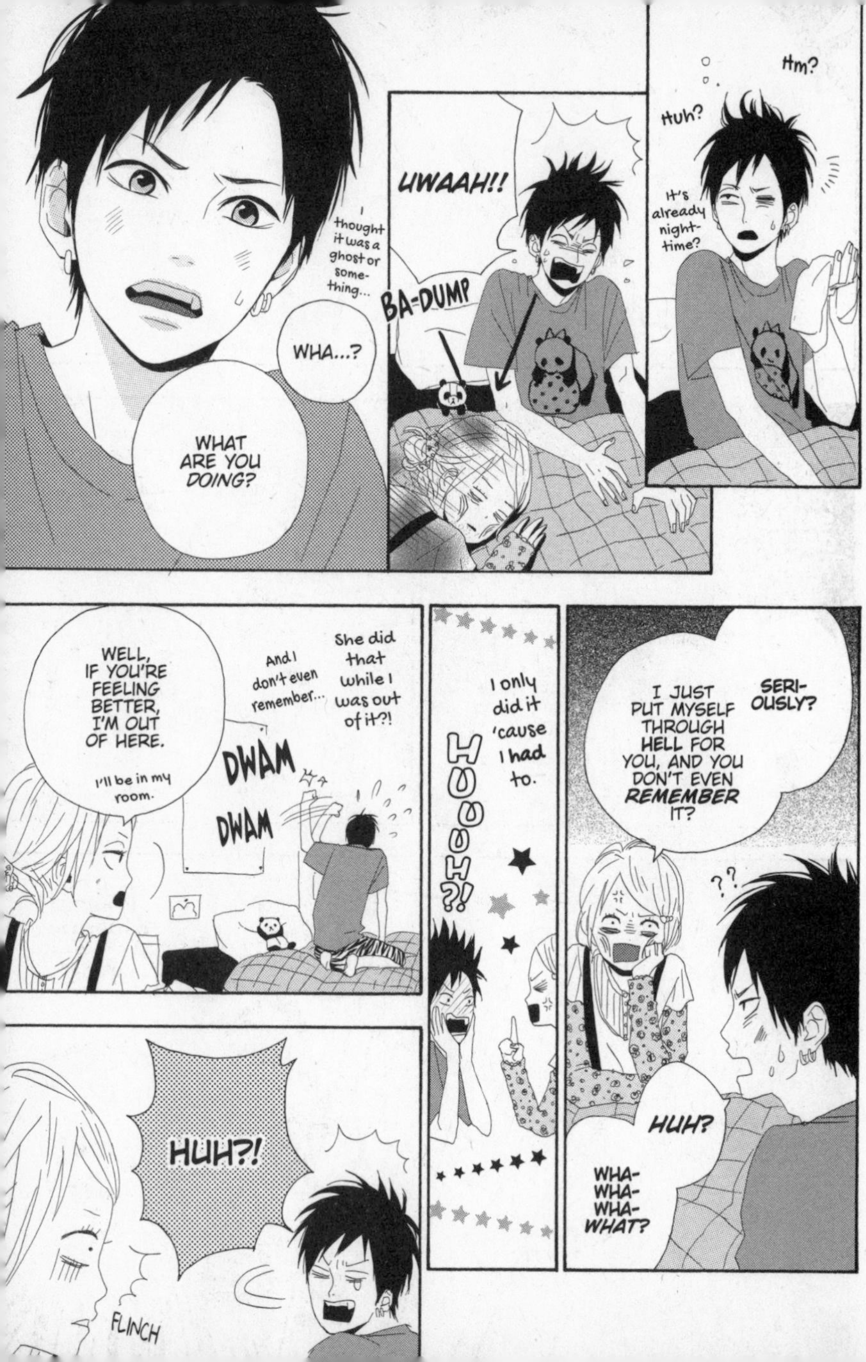
Hm?
Huh?
It's already night-time?
UWAAH!!
I thought it was a ghost or some-thing...
BA-DUMP
WHA...?
WHAT ARE YOU DOING?
SERI-OUSLY?
I JUST PUT MYSELF THROUGH HELL FOR YOU, AND YOU DON'T EVEN REMEMBER IT?
??
HUH?
WHA-WHA-WHA-WHAT?
I only did it 'cause I had to.
HUUUH?!
She did that while I was out of it?!
And I don't even remember...
DWAM
DWAM
WELL, IF YOU'RE FEELING BETTER, I'M OUT OF HERE.
I'll be in my room.
HUH?!
FLINCH

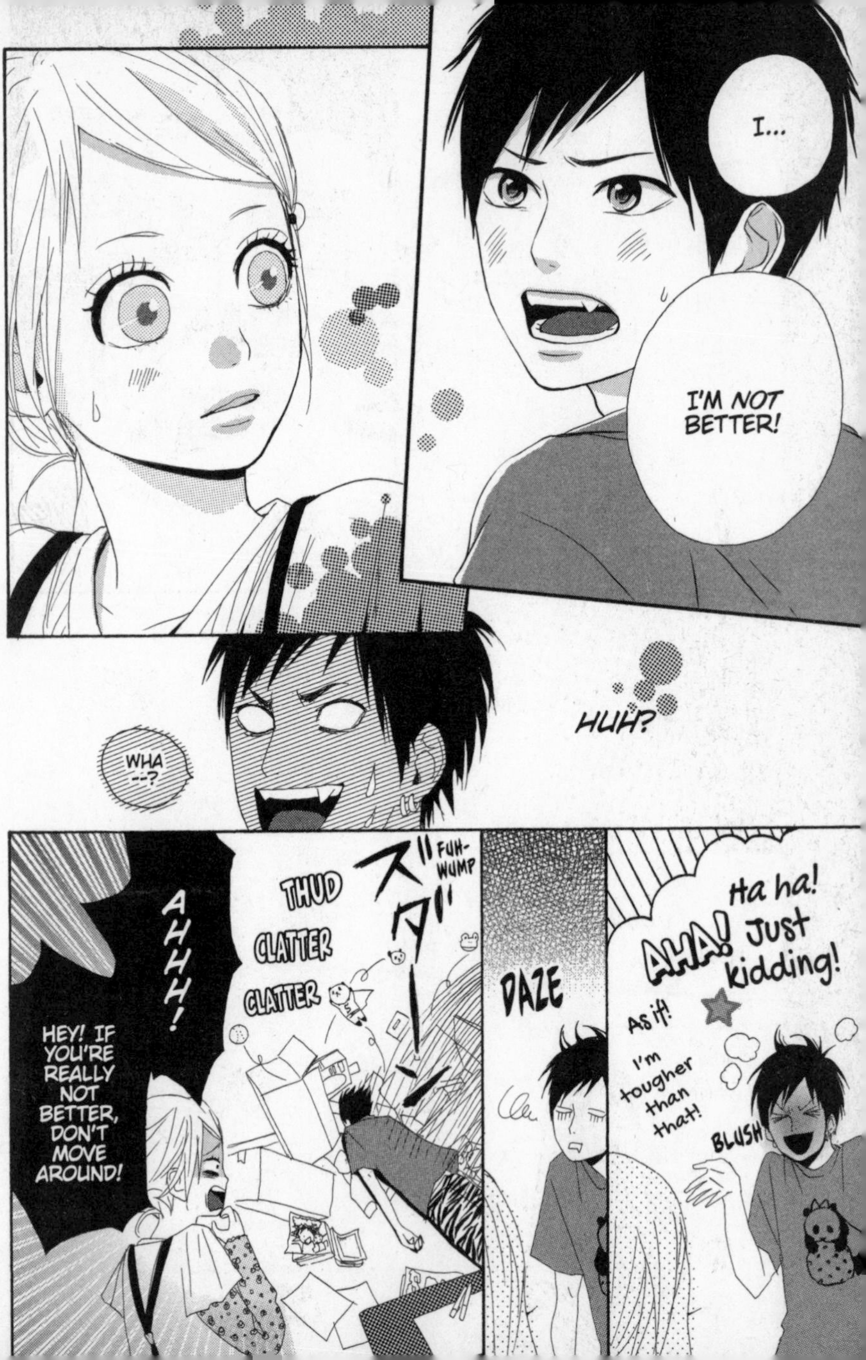
I...
I'M NOT BETTER!
HUH?
WHA --?
Ha ha! Just kidding!
AHA!
As if! I'm tougher than that!
BLUSH
DAZE
FUH-WUMP
ズダーン
THUD
CLATTER
CLATTER
AHHHH!
HEY! IF YOU'RE REALLY NOT BETTER, DON'T MOVE AROUND!

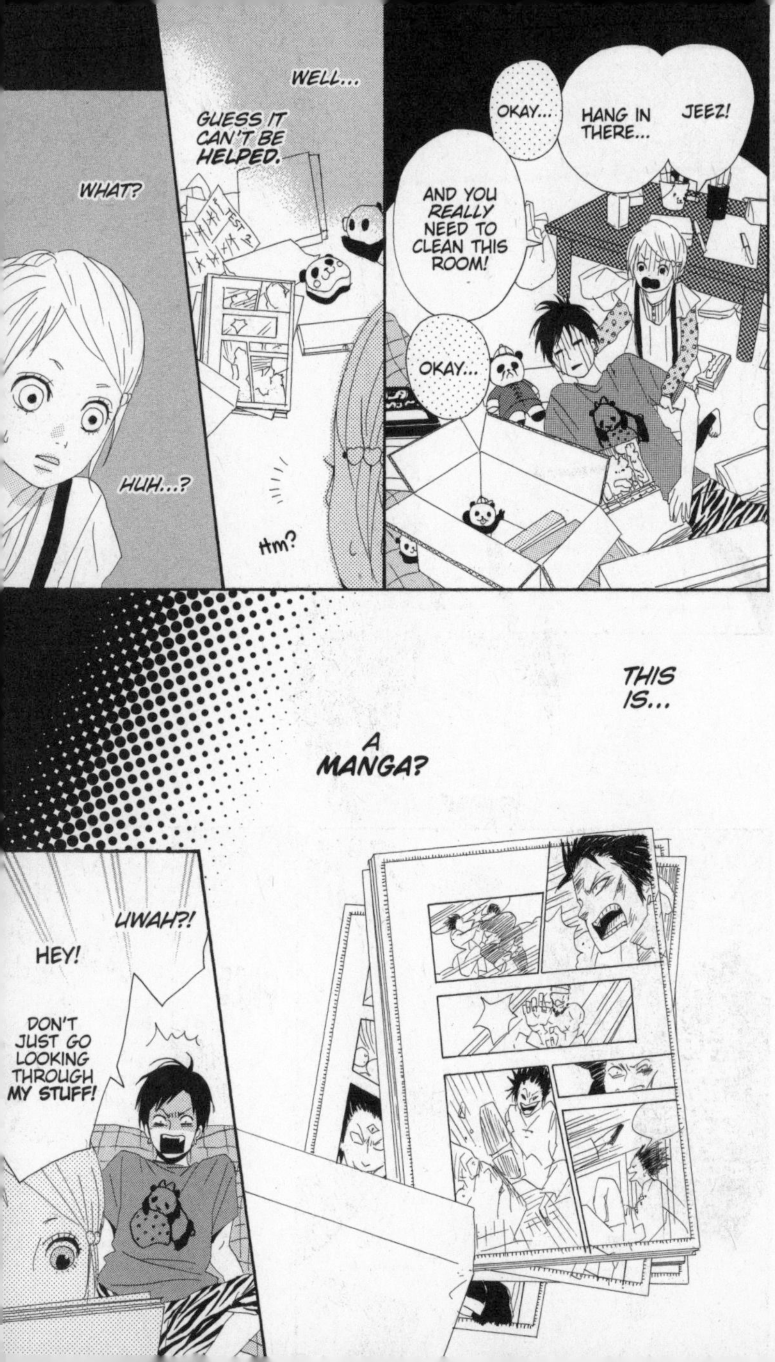
JEEZ!
HANG IN THERE...
OKAY...
AND YOU REALLY NEED TO CLEAN THIS ROOM!
OKAY...
WELL...
GUESS IT CAN'T BE HELPED.
Hm?
WHAT?
HUH...?
THIS IS...
A MANGA?
UWAH?!
HEY!
DON'T JUST GO LOOKING THROUGH MY STUFF!

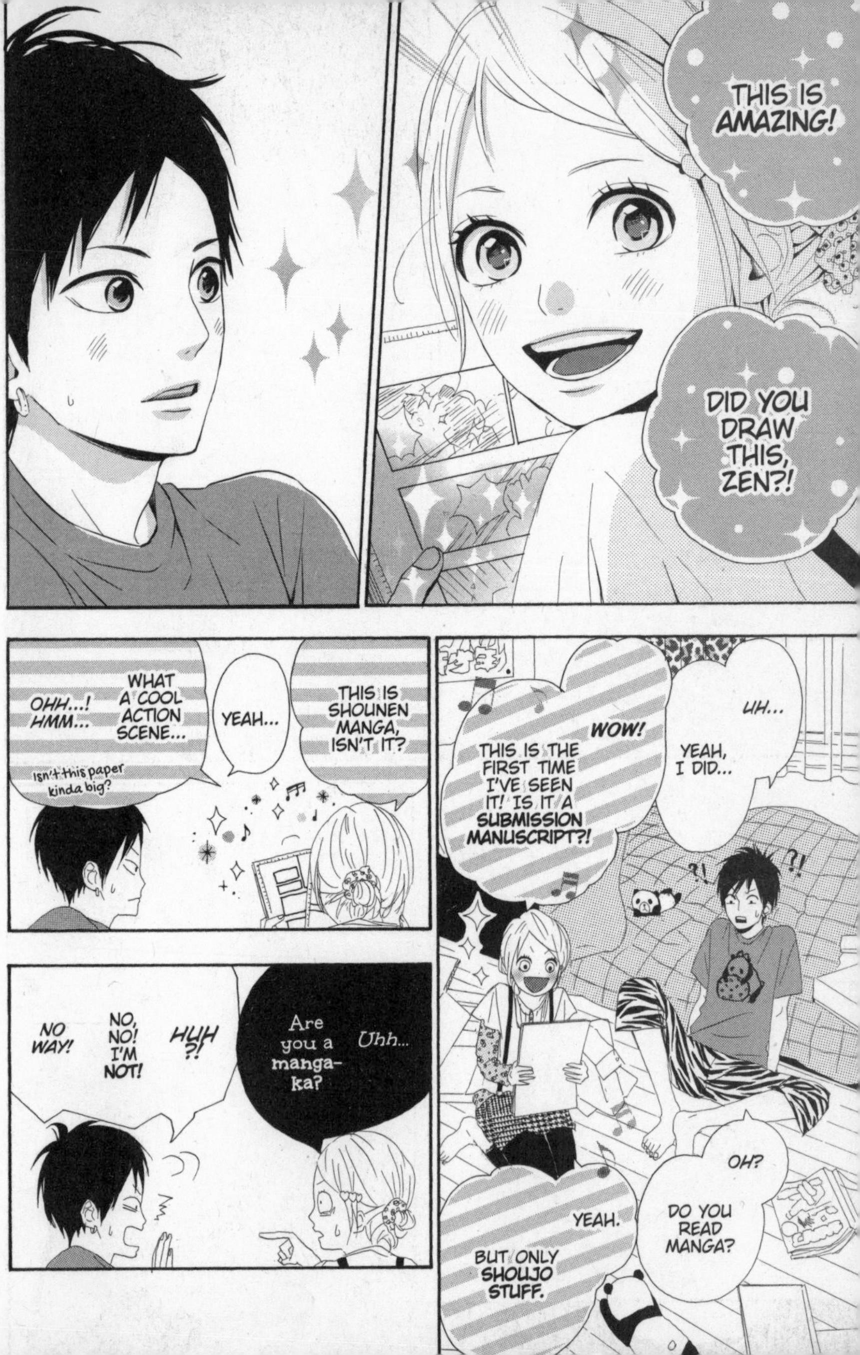

THIS IS AMAZING!
DID YOU DRAW THIS, ZEN?!
UH...
YEAH, I DID...
WOW!
THIS IS THE FIRST TIME I'VE SEEN IT! IS IT A SUBMISSION MANUSCRIPT?!
?!
?!
OH?
DO YOU READ MANGA?
YEAH.
BUT ONLY SHOUJO STUFF.
THIS IS SHOUNEN MANGA, ISN'T IT?
YEAH...
WHAT A COOL ACTION SCENE...
OHH...! HMM...
Isn't this paper kinda big?
Uhh...
Are you a manga-ka?
HUH ?!
NO, NO! I'M NOT!
NO WAY!

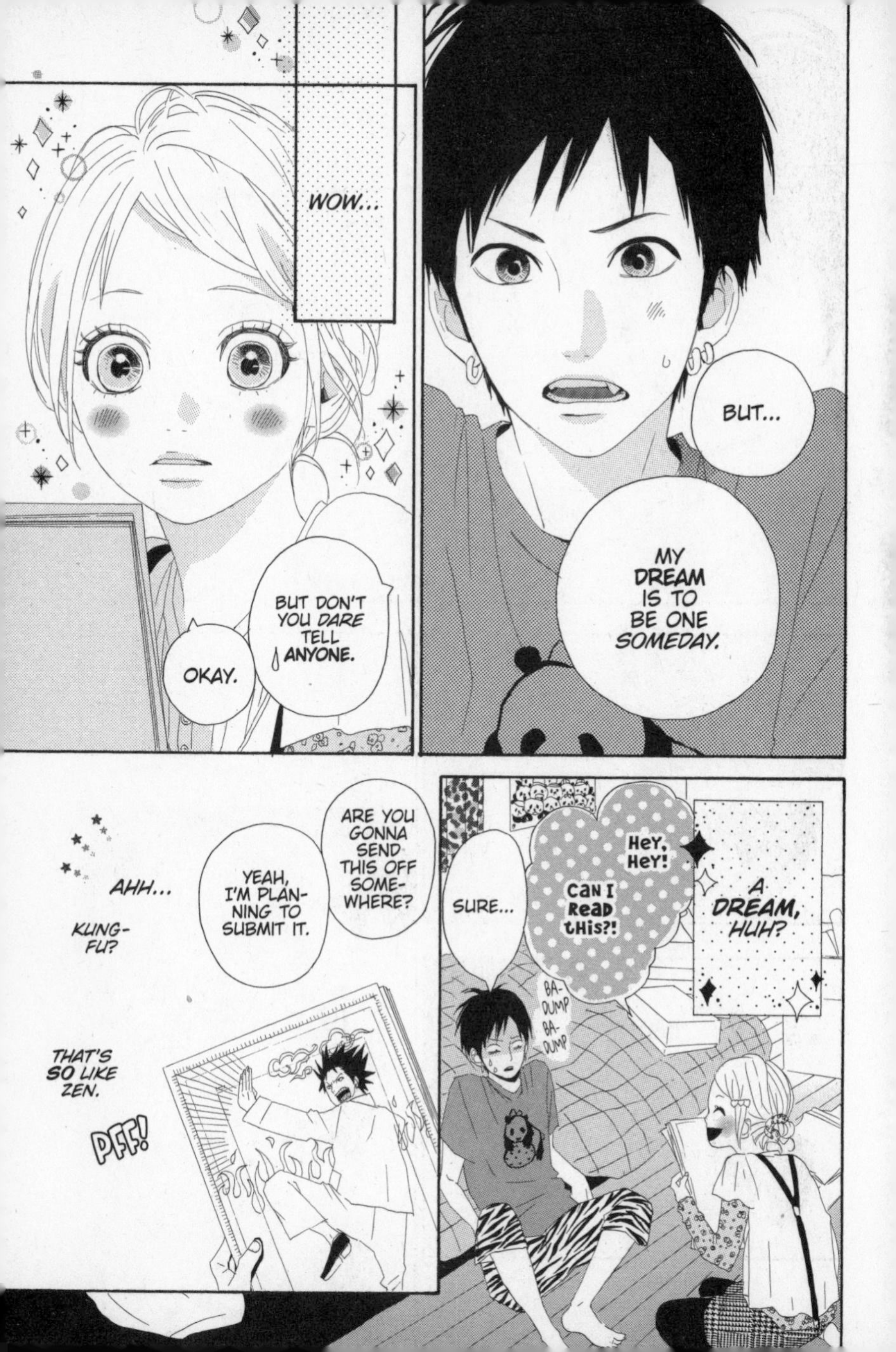
BUT...
MY DREAM IS TO BE ONE SOMEDAY.
WOW...
BUT DON'T YOU DARE TELL ANYONE.
OKAY.
A DREAM, HUH?
HEY, HEY!
CAN I READ THIS?!
BA-DUMP BA-DUMP
SURE...
ARE YOU GONNA SEND THIS OFF SOME-WHERE?
YEAH, I'M PLAN-NING TO SUBMIT IT.
AHH...
KUNG-FU?
THAT'S SO LIKE ZEN.
PFF!

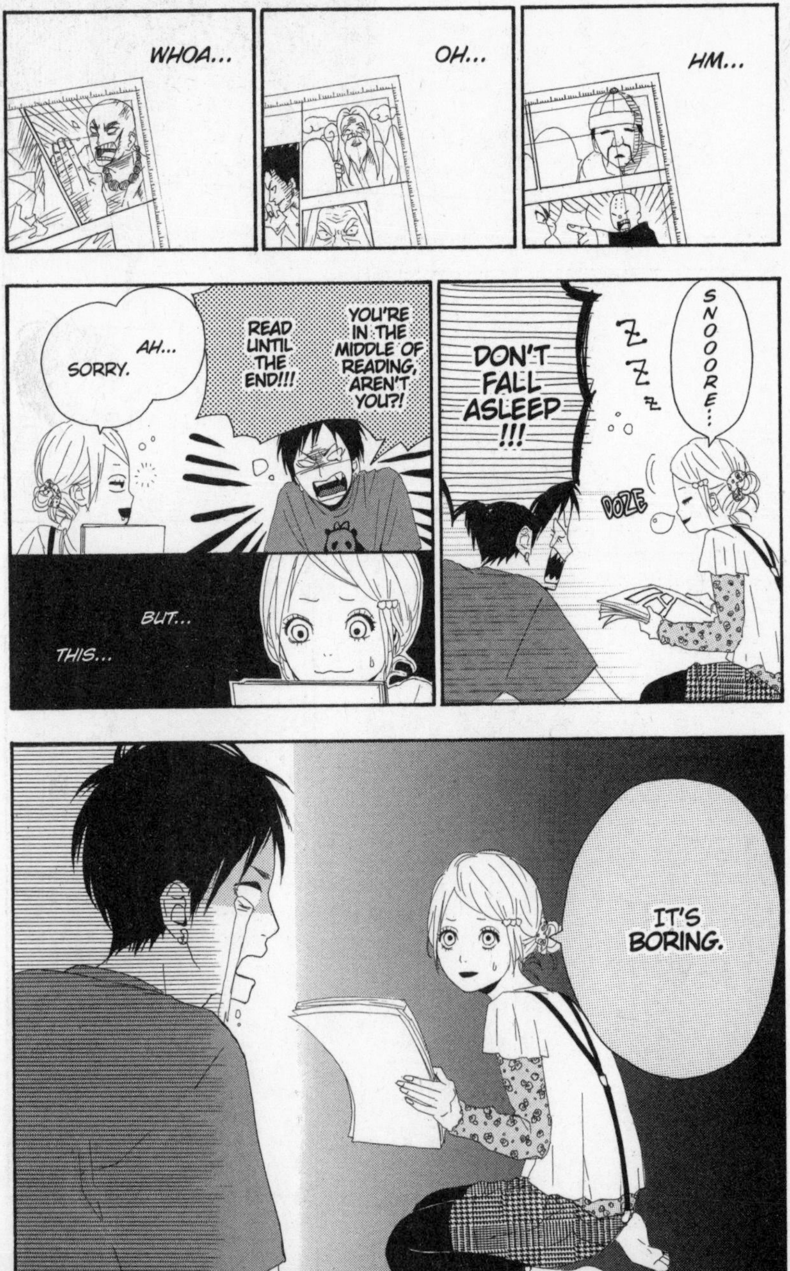
HM...
OH...
WHOA...
SNOOORE...
Z Z z
DON'T FALL ASLEEP!!!
DOZE
YOU'RE IN THE MIDDLE OF READING, AREN'T YOU?!
READ UNTIL THE END!!!
AH... SORRY.
BUT...
THIS...
IT'S BORING.

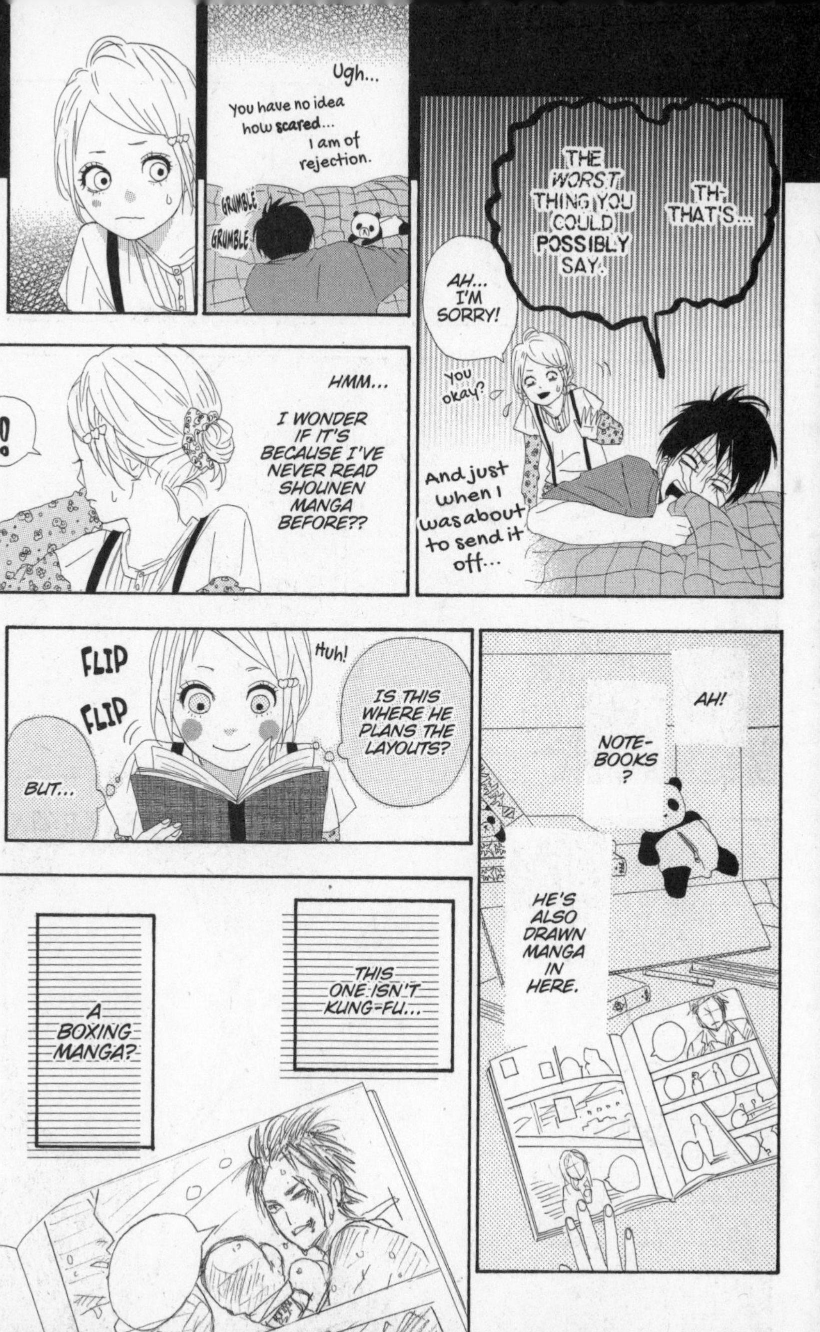
TH-THAT'S...
THE WORST THING YOU COULD POSSIBLY SAY.
AH... I'M SORRY!
You okay?
And just when I was about to send it off...
Ugh...
You have no idea how scared... I am of rejection.
GRUMBLE
GRUMBLE
HMM...
I WONDER IF IT'S BECAUSE I'VE NEVER READ SHOUNEN MANGA BEFORE??
!
AH!
NOTE-BOOKS?
HE'S ALSO DRAWN MANGA IN HERE.
Huh!
IS THIS WHERE HE PLANS THE LAYOUTS?
FLIP
FLIP
BUT...
THIS ONE ISN'T KUNG-FU...
A BOXING MANGA?

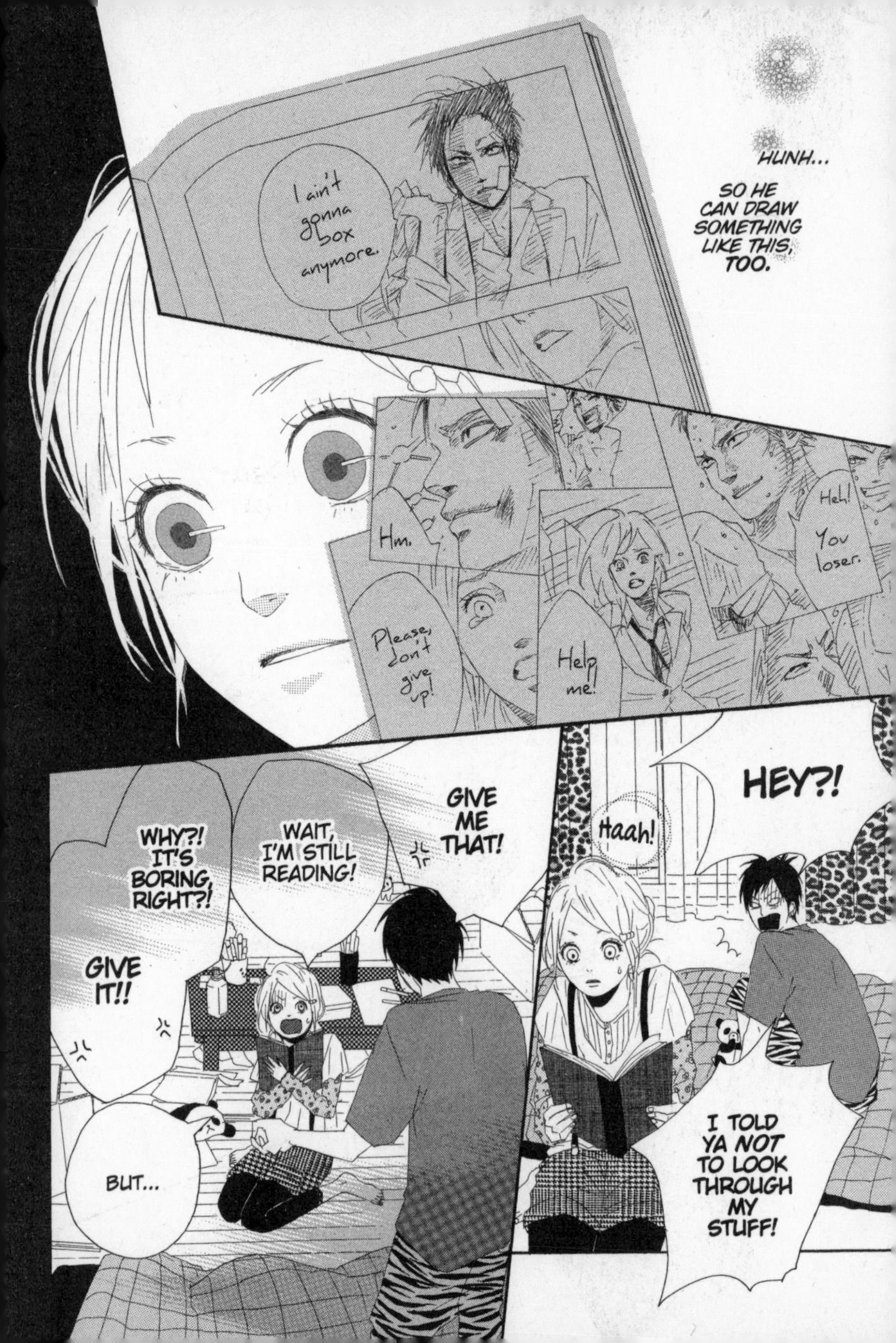
HUNH...
SO HE CAN DRAW SOMETHING LIKE THIS, TOO.
I ain't gonna box anymore.
Heh! You loser.
Help me!
Hm.
Please, don't give up!
HEY?!
Haah!
I TOLD YA NOT TO LOOK THROUGH MY STUFF!
GIVE ME THAT!
WAIT, I'M STILL READING!
WHY?! IT'S BORING, RIGHT?!
GIVE IT!!
BUT...

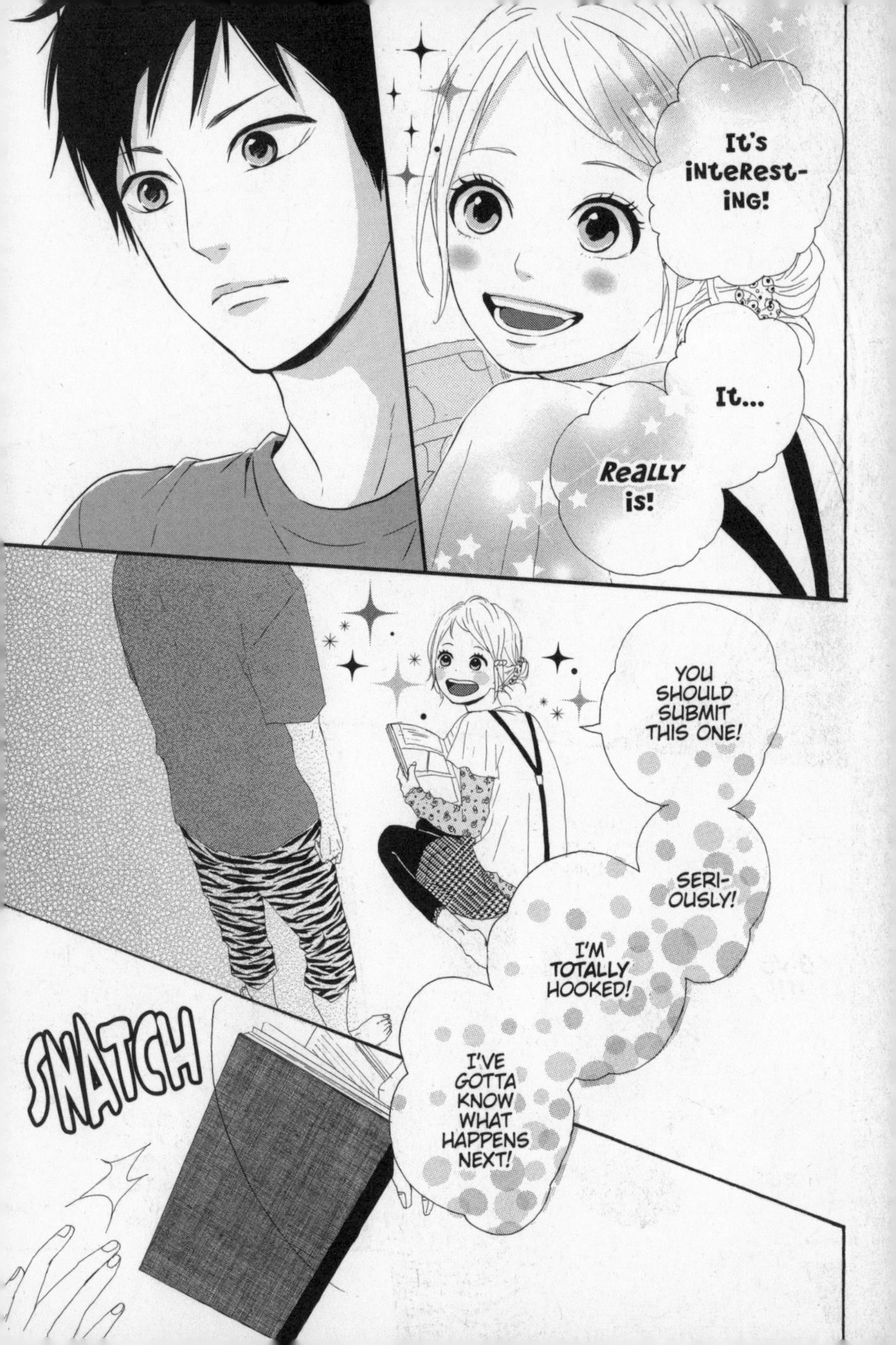
It's interesting!
It...
Really is!
YOU SHOULD SUBMIT THIS ONE!
SERIOUSLY!
I'M TOTALLY HOOKED!
I'VE GOTTA KNOW WHAT HAPPENS NEXT!
SNATCH

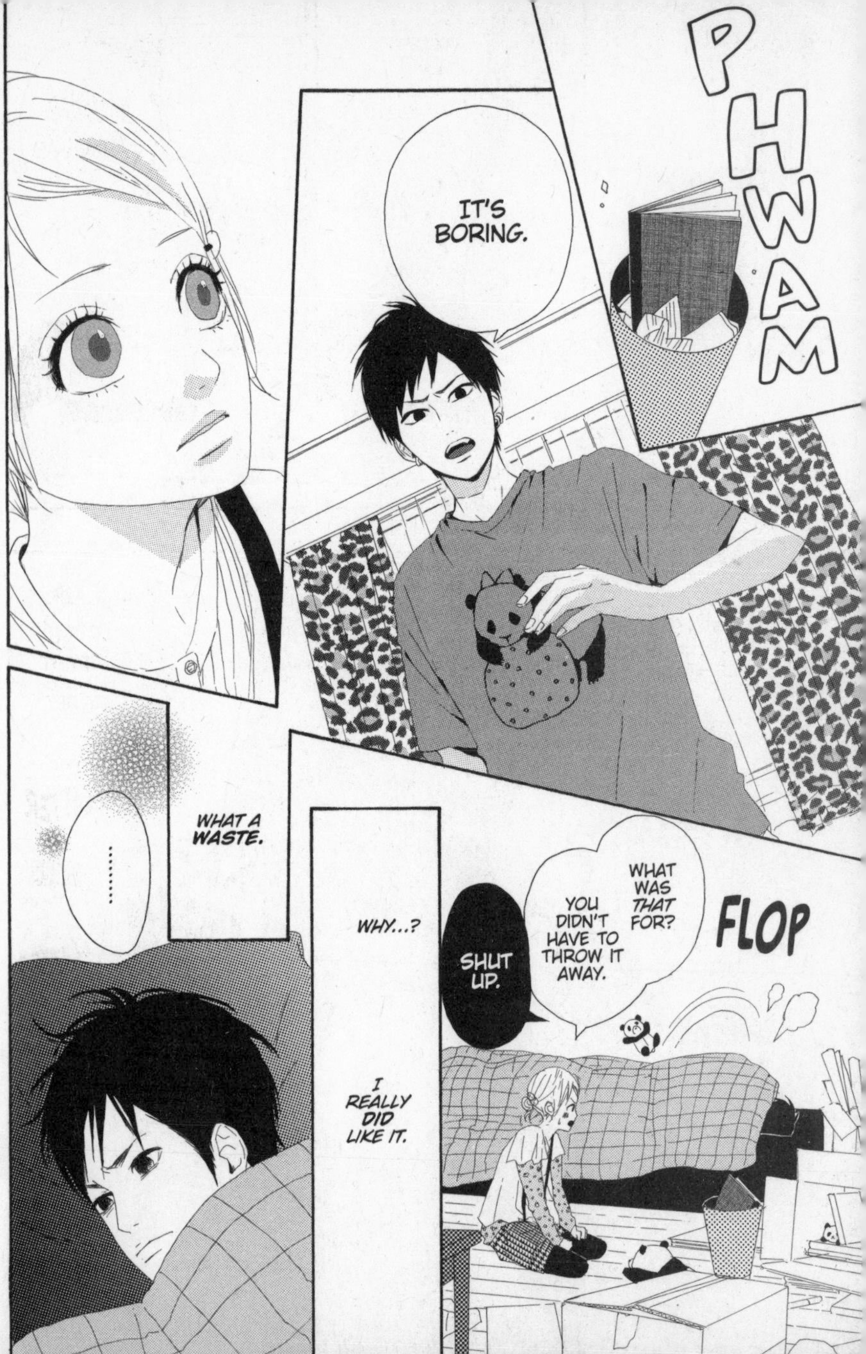
PHWAM
IT'S BORING.
FLOP
WHAT WAS THAT FOR?
YOU DIDN'T HAVE TO THROW IT AWAY.
SHUT UP.
WHY...?
I REALLY DID LIKE IT.
WHAT A WASTE.
......

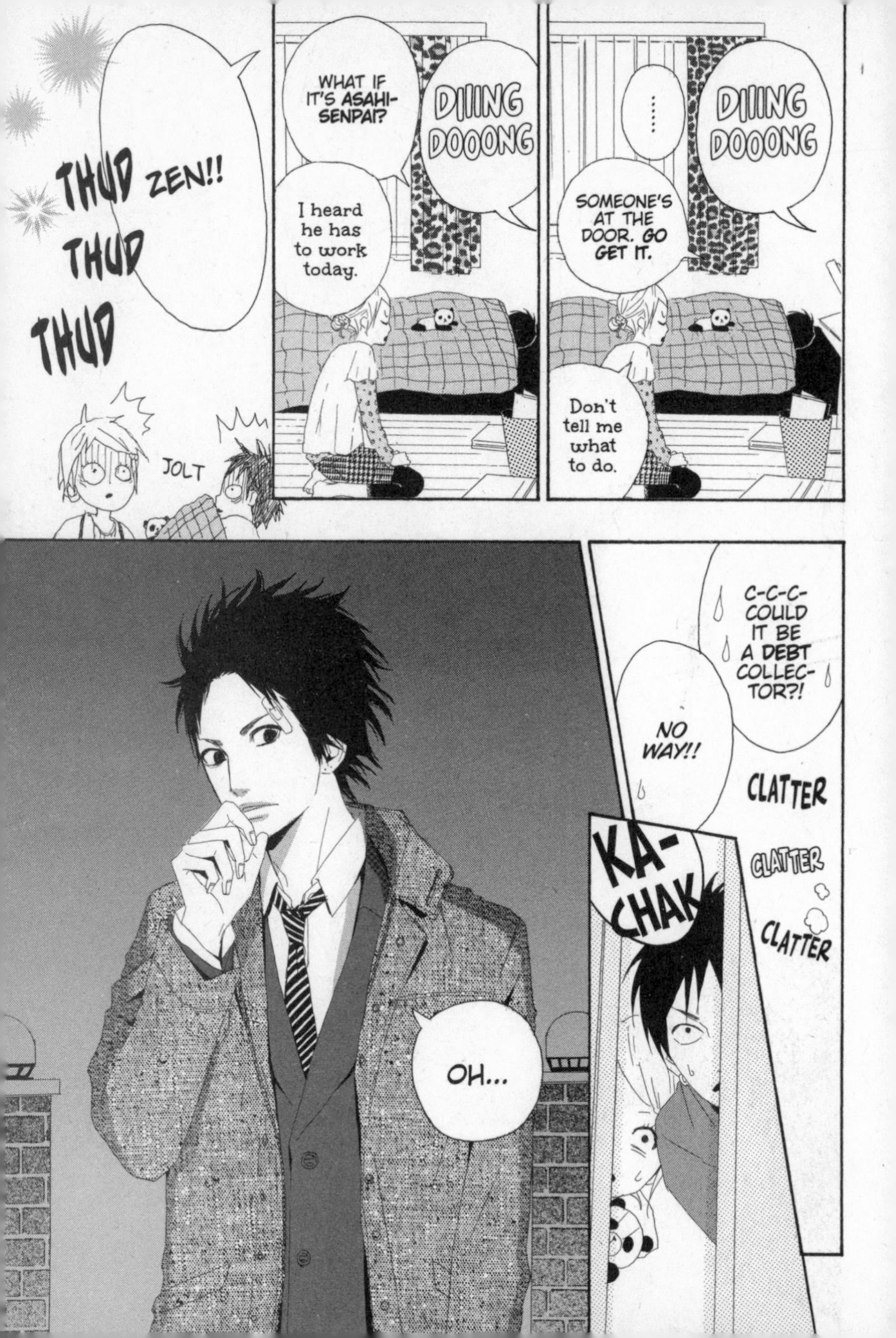
DIIING DOOONG
......
SOMEONE'S AT THE DOOR. GO GET IT.
Don't tell me what to do.
DIIING DOOONG
WHAT IF IT'S ASAHI-SENPAI?
I heard he has to work today.
ZEN!!
THUD THUD THUD
JOLT
C-C-C-COULD IT BE A DEBT COLLECTOR?!
NO WAY!!
CLATTER
CLATTER
CLATTER
KA-CHAK
OH...

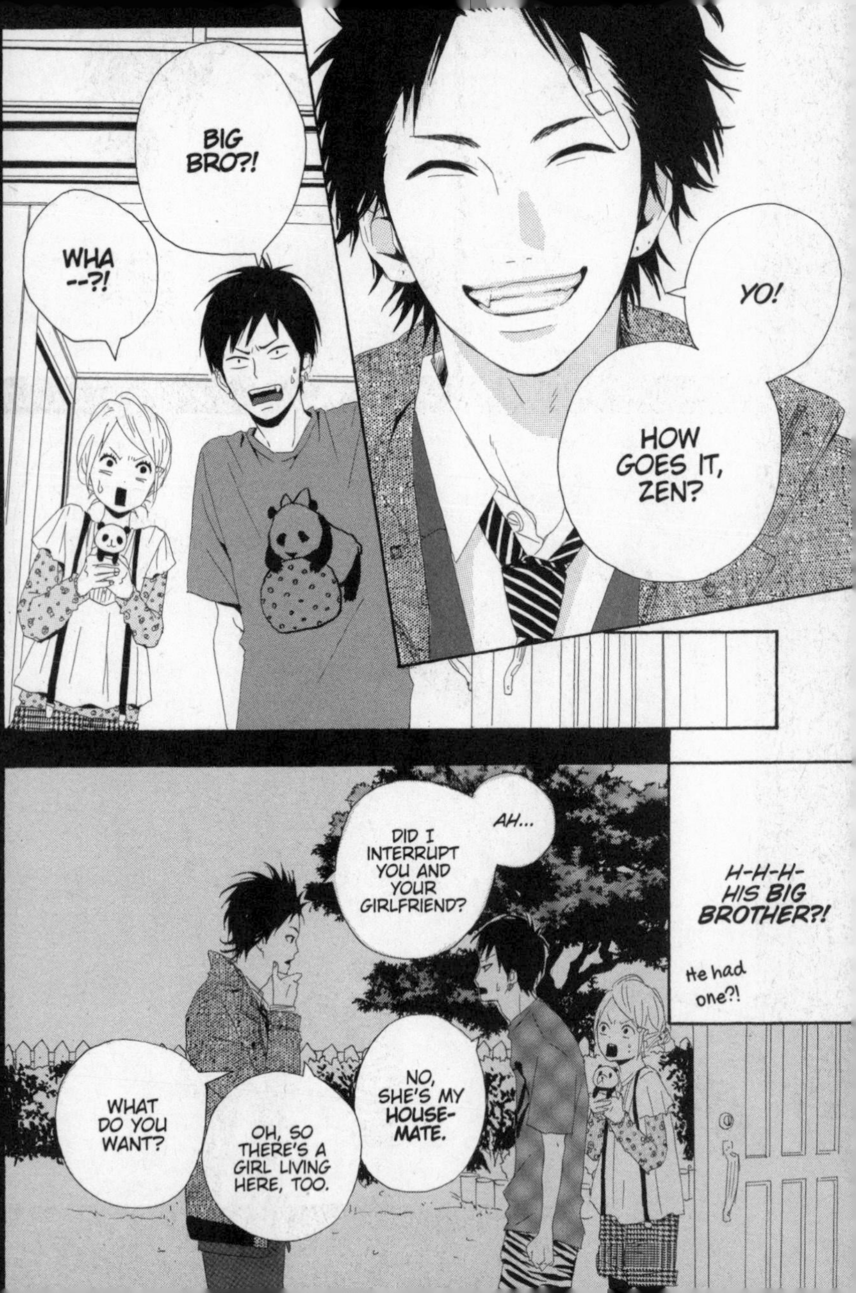
YO!
HOW GOES IT, ZEN?
BIG BRO?!
WHA--?!
H-H-H-HIS BIG BROTHER?!
He had one?!
AH...
DID I INTERRUPT YOU AND YOUR GIRLFRIEND?
NO, SHE'S MY HOUSE-MATE.
OH, SO THERE'S A GIRL LIVING HERE, TOO.
WHAT DO YOU WANT?

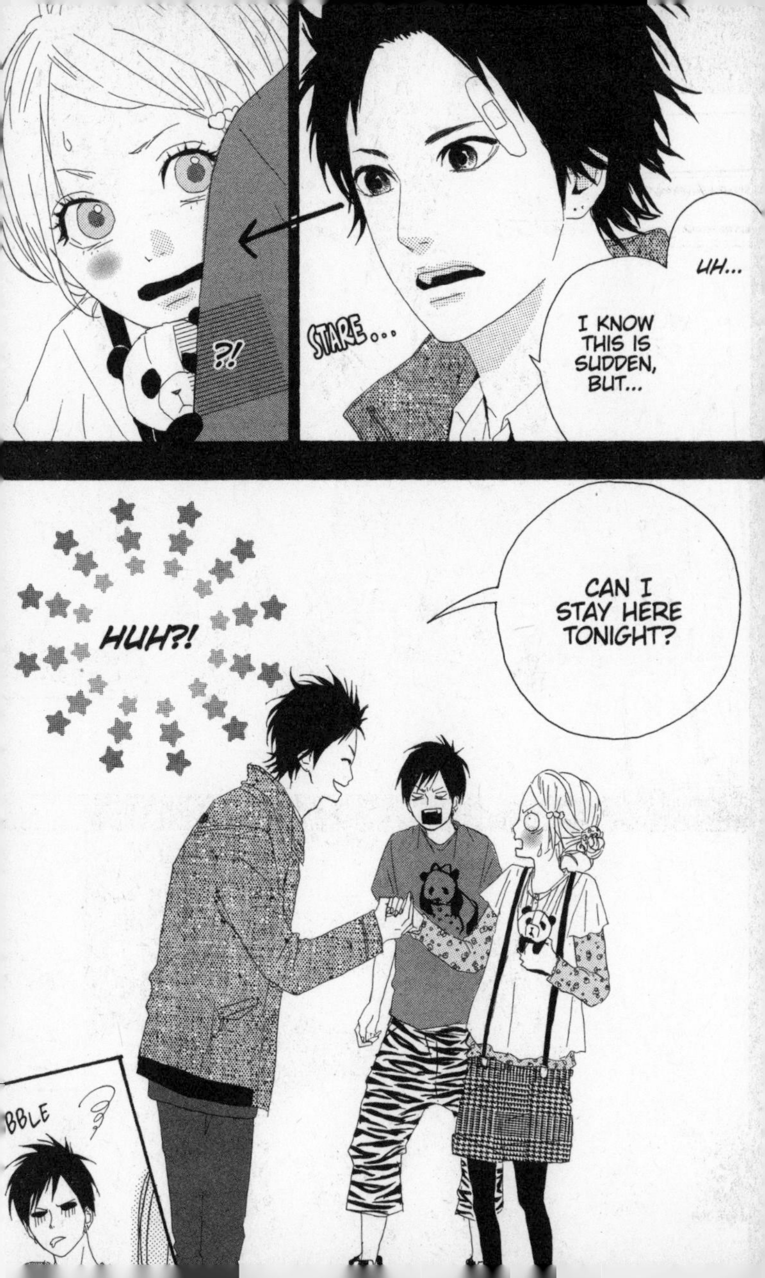
UH...
I KNOW THIS IS SUDDEN, BUT...
STARE...
?!
CAN I STAY HERE TONIGHT?
HUH?!

Before the Realization

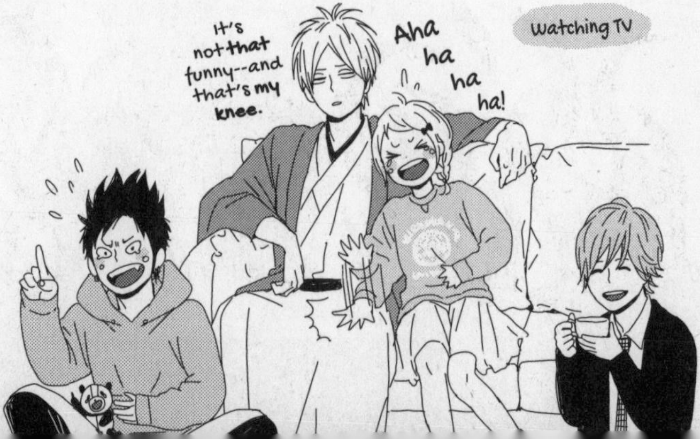
Watching TV
Aha ha ha ha!
It's not that funny--and that's my knee.

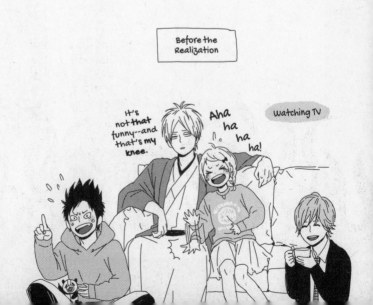

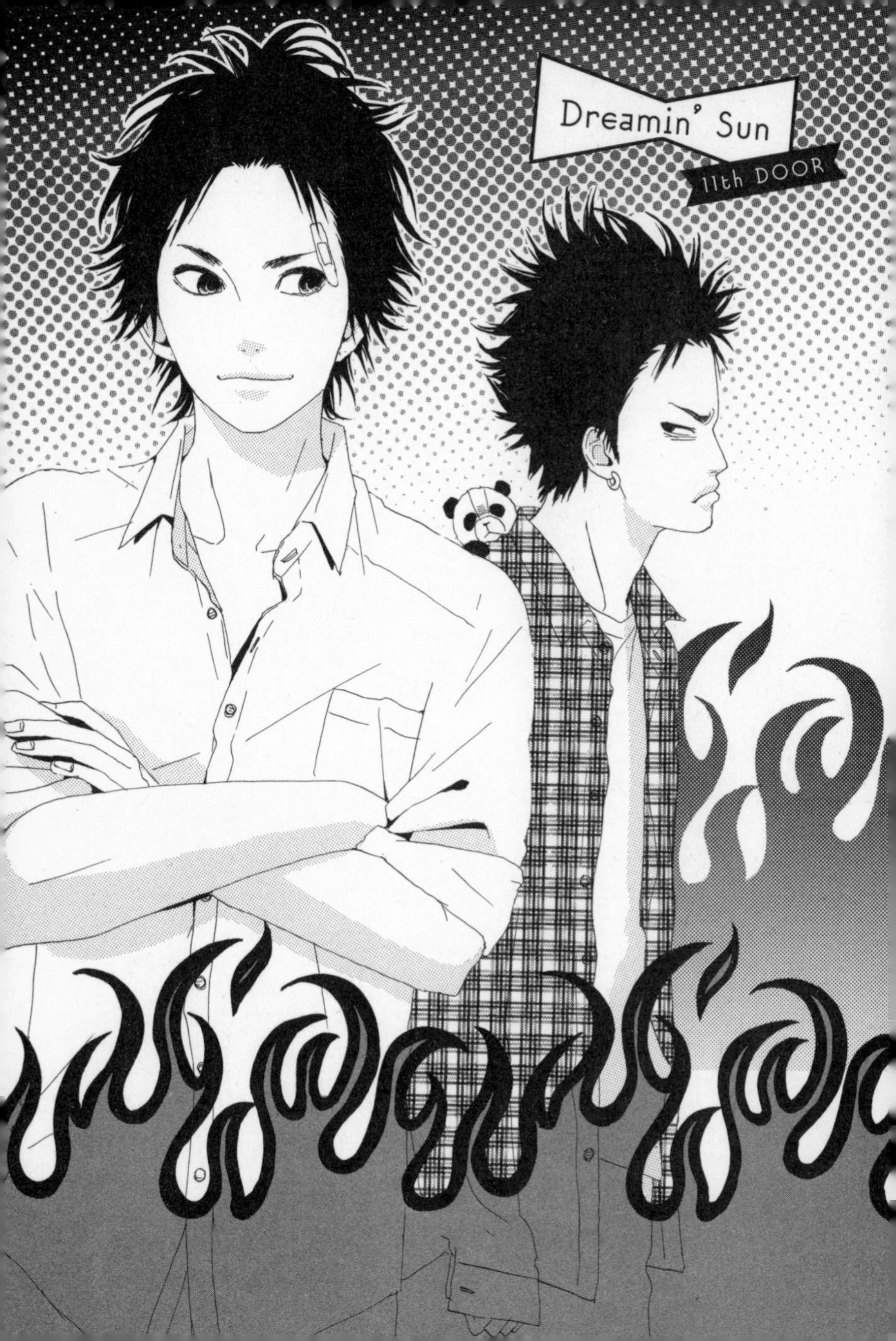
Dreamin' Sun
11th DOOR

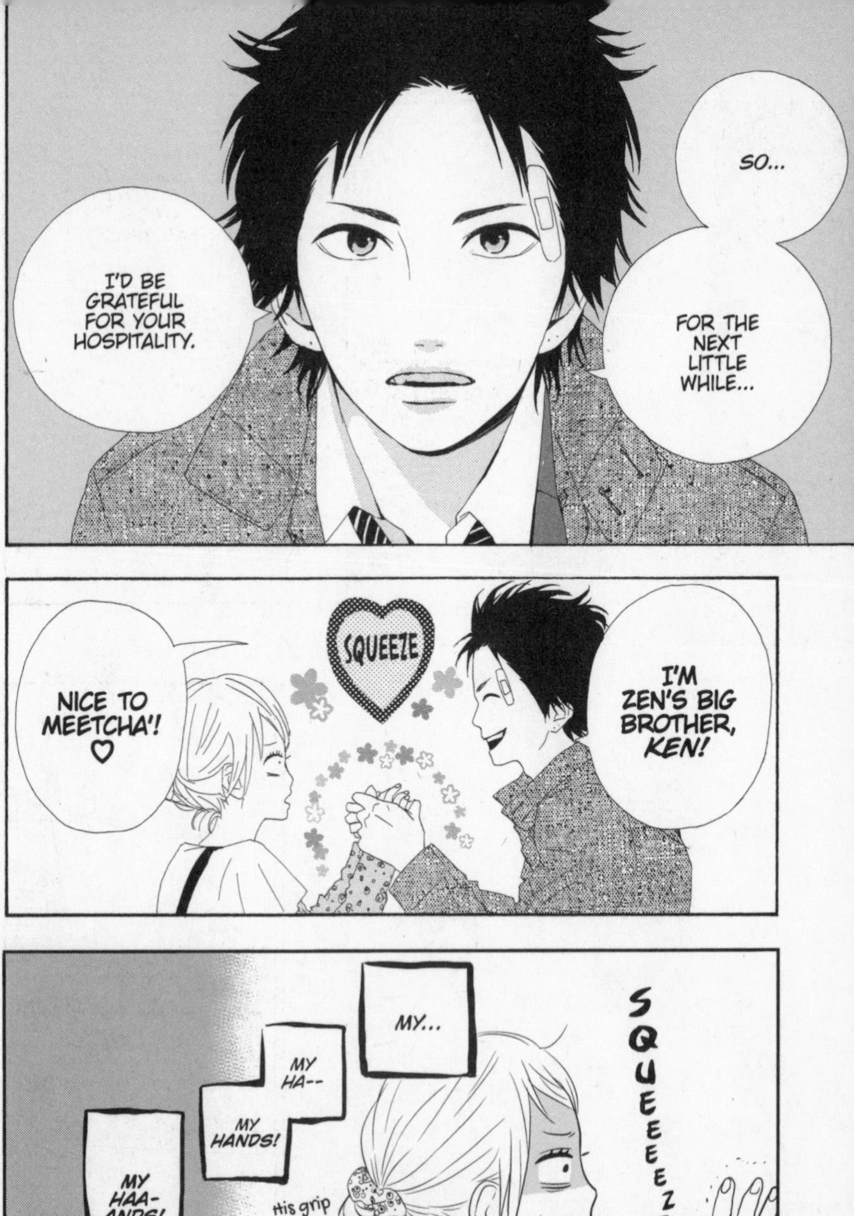
SO...
FOR THE NEXT LITTLE WHILE...
I'D BE GRATEFUL FOR YOUR HOSPITALITY.
I'M ZEN'S BIG BROTHER, KEN!
SQUEEZE
NICE TO MEETCHA'! ♡
SQUEEEEZE
...
MY...
MY HA--
MY HANDS!
His grip is super strong!
MY HAA-ANDS!

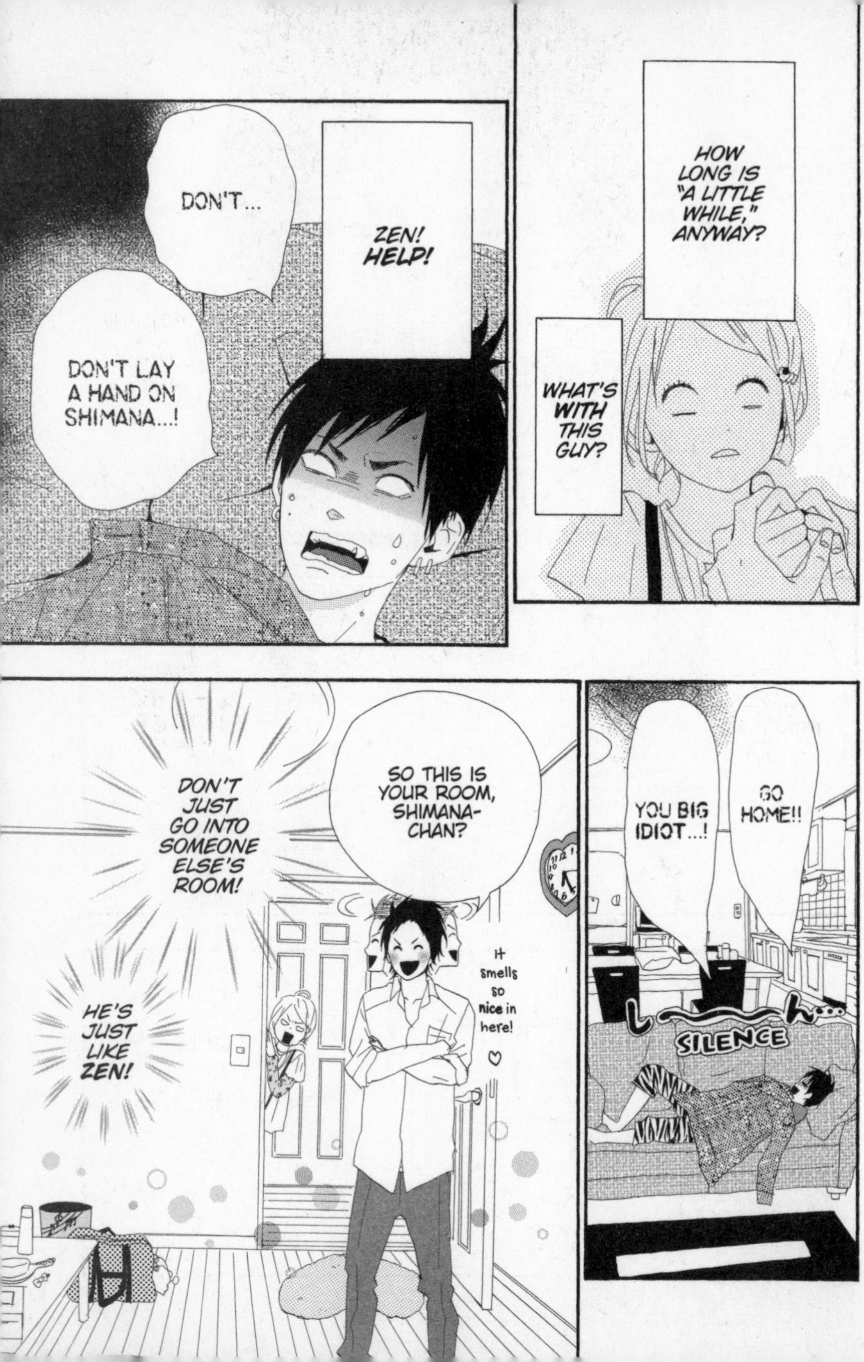
HOW LONG IS "A LITTLE WHILE," ANYWAY?
WHAT'S WITH THIS GUY?
ZEN! HELP!
DON'T...
DON'T LAY A HAND ON SHIMANA...!
GO HOME!!
YOU BIG IDIOT...!
SILENCE
SO THIS IS YOUR ROOM, SHIMANA-CHAN?
It smells so nice in here! ♡
DON'T JUST GO INTO SOMEONE ELSE'S ROOM!
HE'S JUST LIKE ZEN!

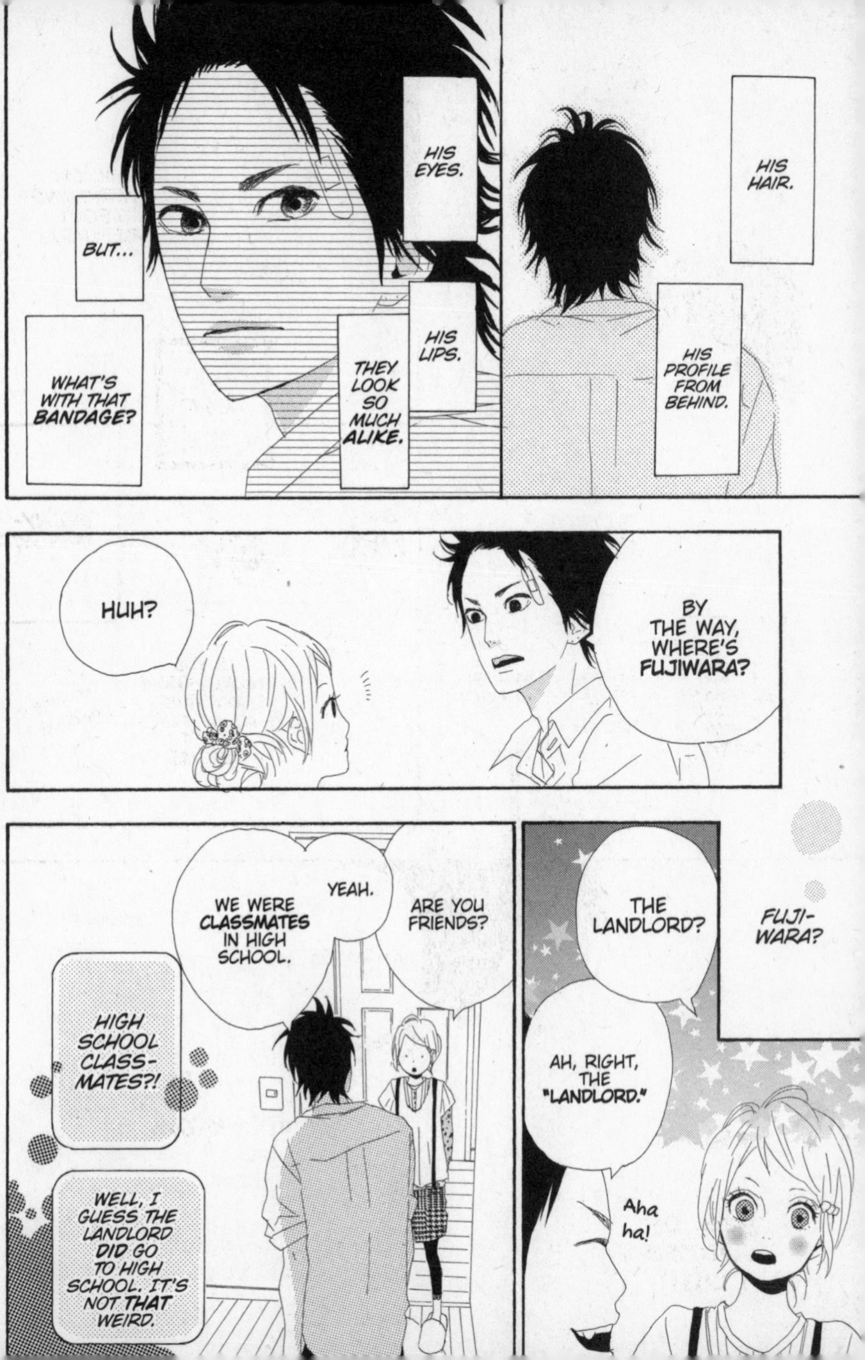
HIS HAIR.
HIS PROFILE FROM BEHIND.
HIS EYES.
HIS LIPS.
THEY LOOK SO MUCH ALIKE.
BUT...
WHAT'S WITH THAT BANDAGE?
BY THE WAY, WHERE'S FUJIWARA?
HUH?
FUJI-WARA?
THE LANDLORD?
AH, RIGHT, THE "LANDLORD."
Aha ha!
ARE YOU FRIENDS?
YEAH.
WE WERE CLASSMATES IN HIGH SCHOOL.
HIGH SCHOOL CLASS-MATES?!
WELL, I GUESS THE LANDLORD DID GO TO HIGH SCHOOL. IT'S NOT THAT WEIRD.

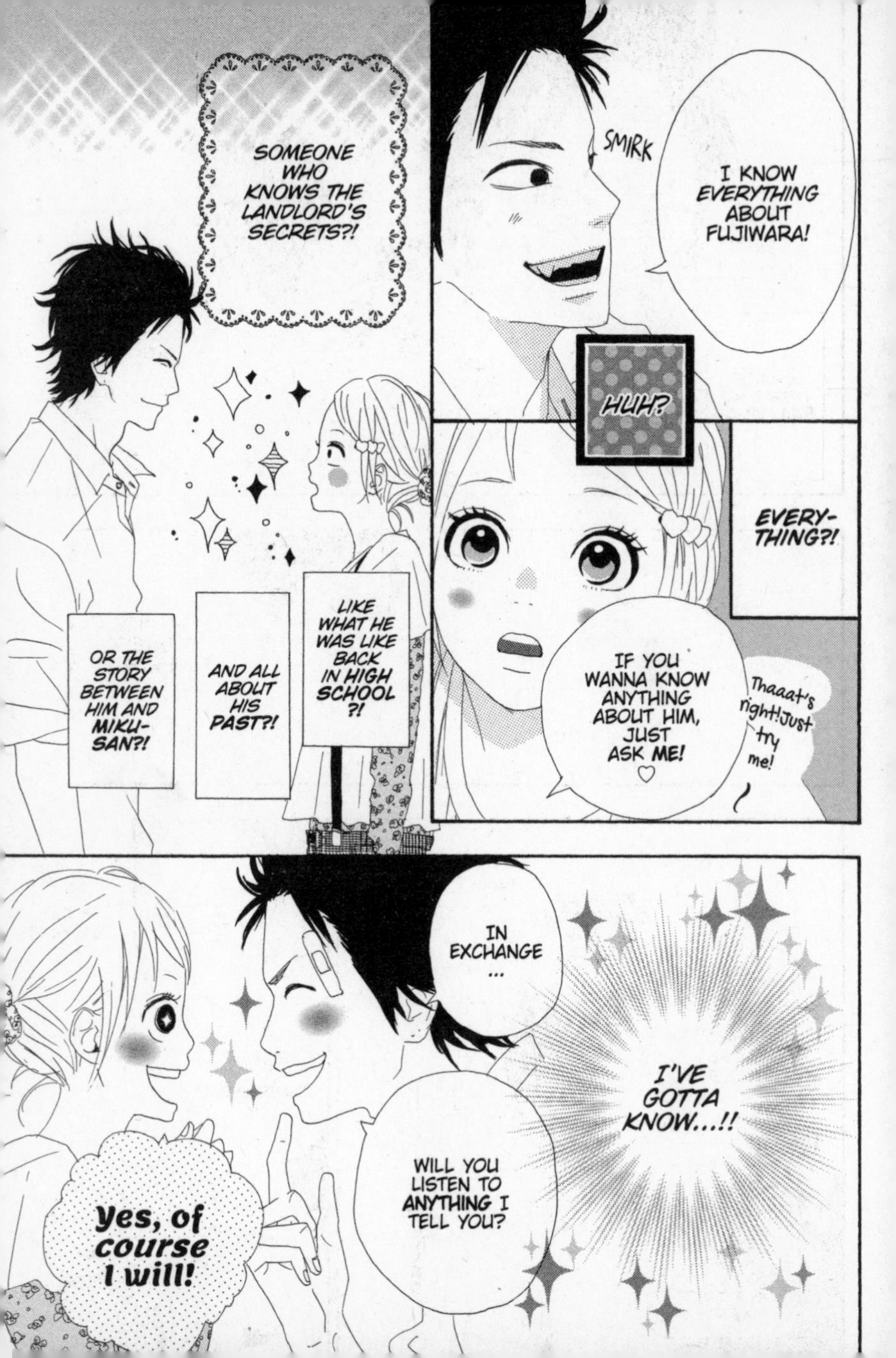
SMIRK
I KNOW EVERYTHING ABOUT FUJIWARA!
HUH?
EVERY-THING?!
IF YOU WANNA KNOW ANYTHING ABOUT HIM, JUST ASK ME! ♡
Thaaat's right! Just try me!
SOMEONE WHO KNOWS THE LANDLORD'S SECRETS?!
LIKE WHAT HE WAS LIKE BACK IN HIGH SCHOOL?!
AND ALL ABOUT HIS PAST?!
OR THE STORY BETWEEN HIM AND MIKU-SAN?!
IN EXCHANGE...
I'VE GOTTA KNOW...!!
WILL YOU LISTEN TO ANYTHING I TELL YOU?
yes, of course I will!

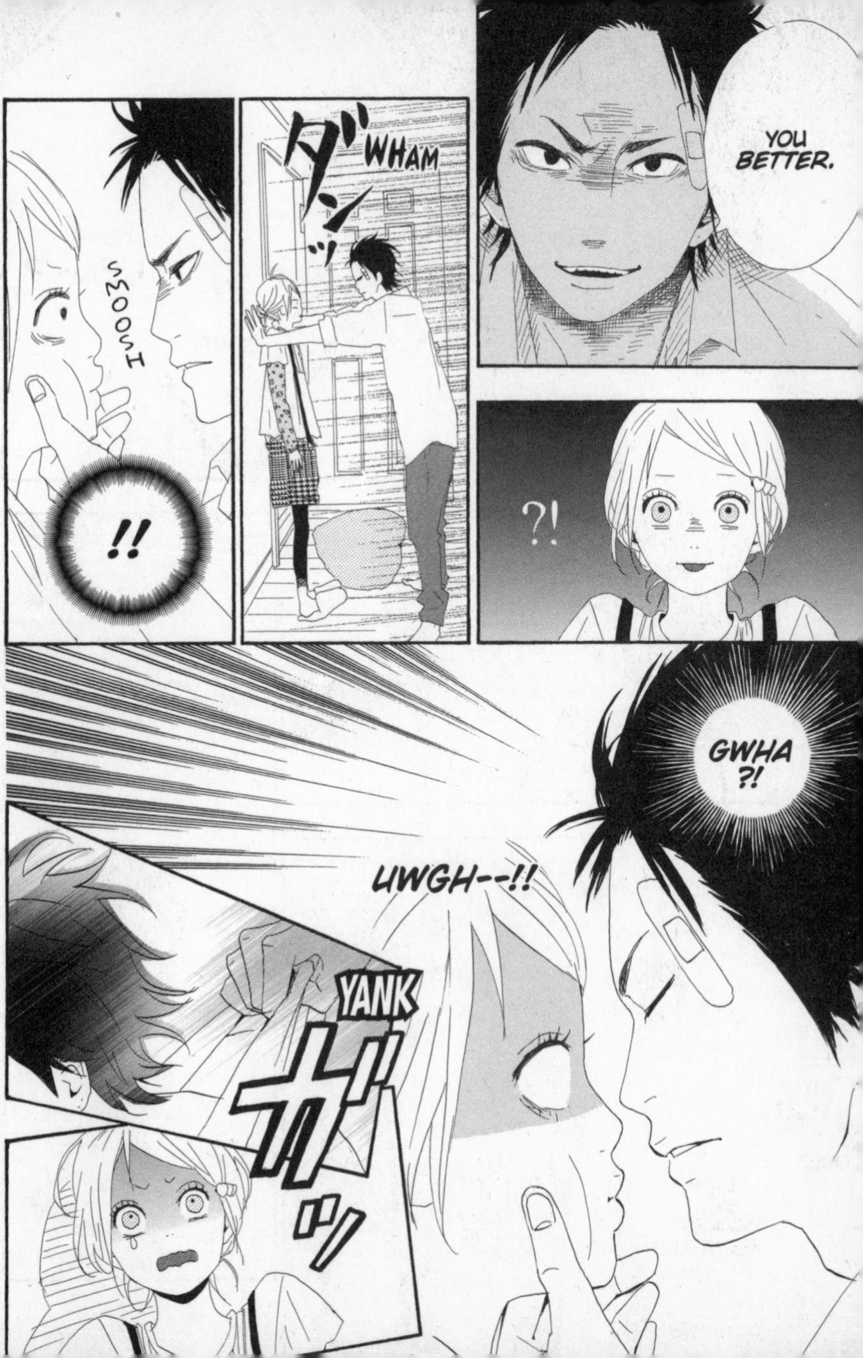
YOU BETTER.
?!
ダンッ
WHAM
SMOOSH
!!
GWHA ?!
UWGH--!!
YANK
ガッ

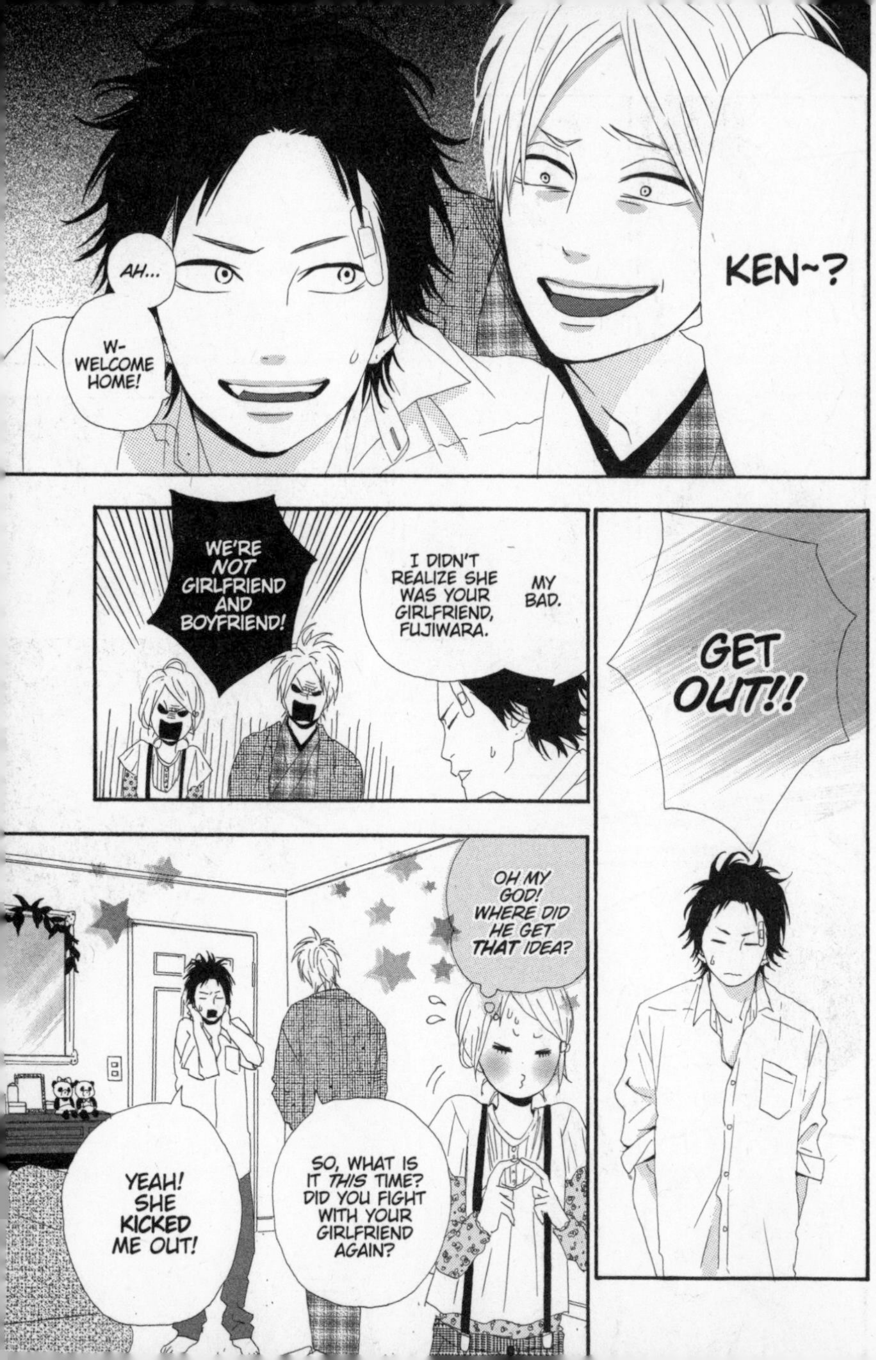
KEN~?
AH...
W- WELCOME HOME!
GET OUT!!
MY BAD.
I DIDN'T REALIZE SHE WAS YOUR GIRLFRIEND, FUJIWARA.
WE'RE NOT GIRLFRIEND AND BOYFRIEND!
OH MY GOD! WHERE DID HE GET THAT IDEA?
SO, WHAT IS IT THIS TIME? DID YOU FIGHT WITH YOUR GIRLFRIEND AGAIN?
YEAH! SHE KICKED ME OUT!

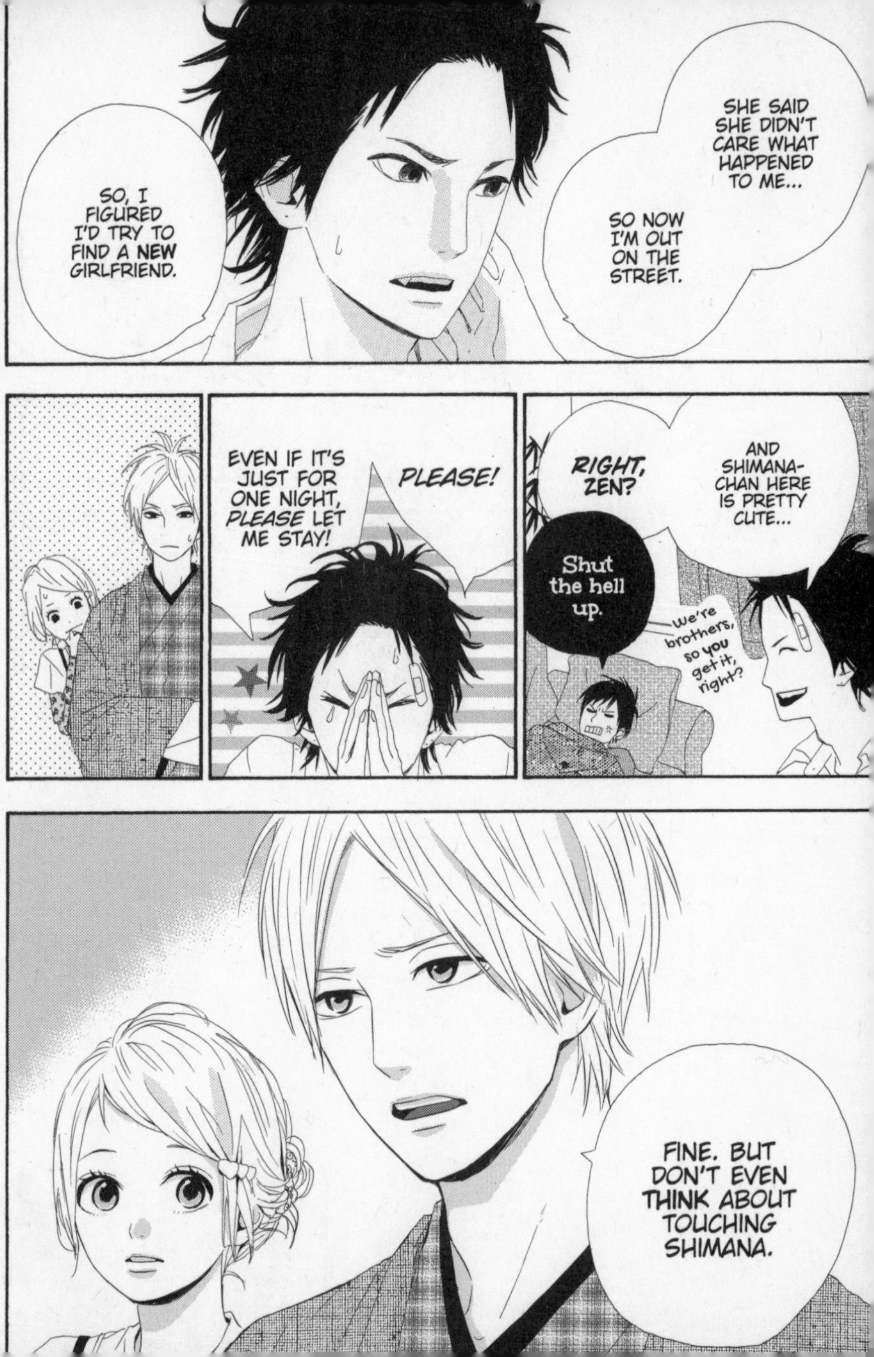
SHE SAID SHE DIDN'T CARE WHAT HAPPENED TO ME...
SO NOW I'M OUT ON THE STREET.
SO, I FIGURED I'D TRY TO FIND A NEW GIRLFRIEND.
AND SHIMANA-CHAN HERE IS PRETTY CUTE...
RIGHT, ZEN?
We're brothers, so you get it, right?
Shut the hell up.
PLEASE!
EVEN IF IT'S JUST FOR ONE NIGHT, PLEASE LET ME STAY!
FINE. BUT DON'T EVEN THINK ABOUT TOUCHING SHIMANA.

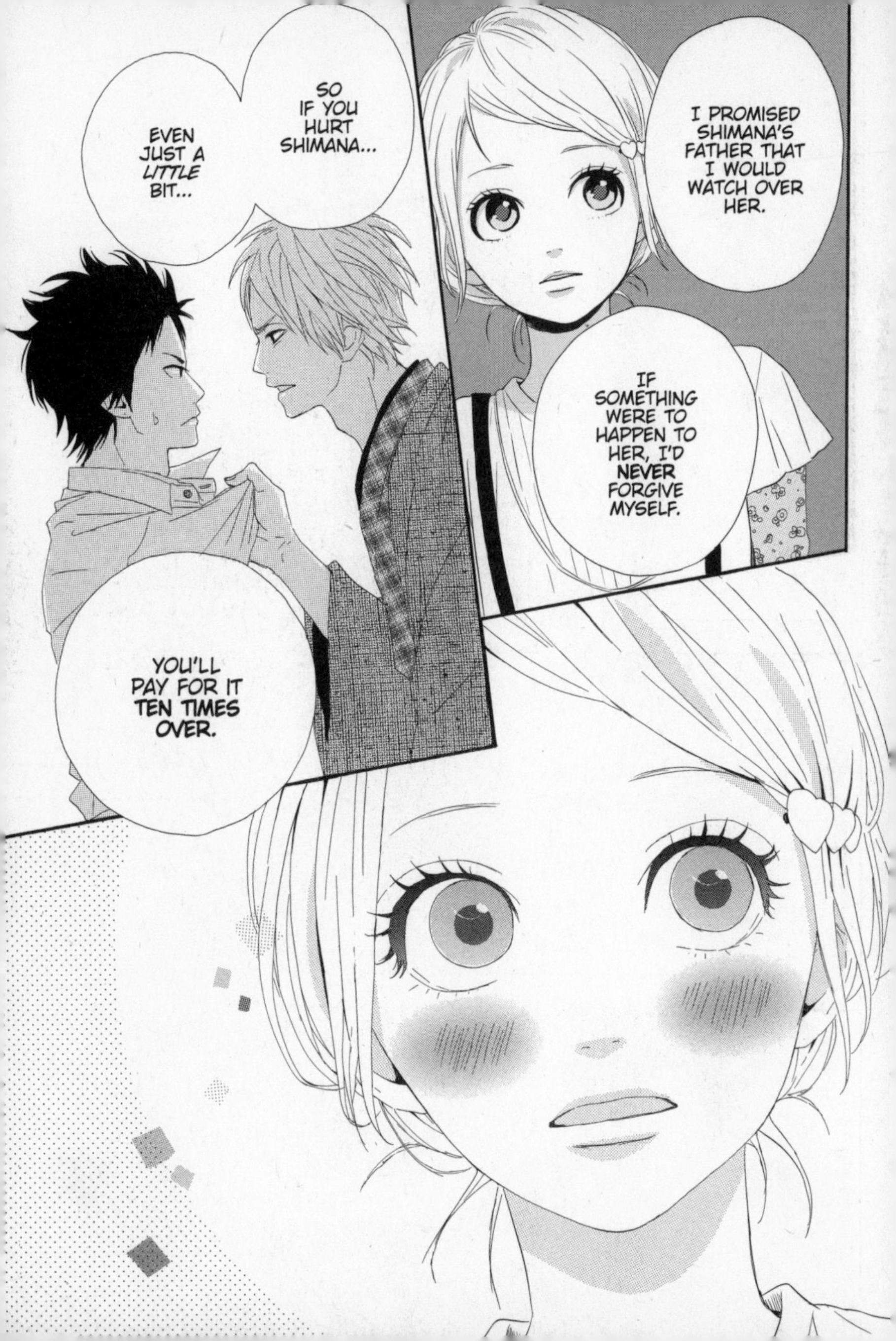
I PROMISED SHIMANA'S FATHER THAT I WOULD WATCH OVER HER.
IF SOMETHING WERE TO HAPPEN TO HER, I'D **NEVER** FORGIVE MYSELF.
SO IF YOU HURT SHIMANA...
EVEN JUST A *LITTLE* BIT...
YOU'LL PAY FOR IT TEN TIMES OVER.

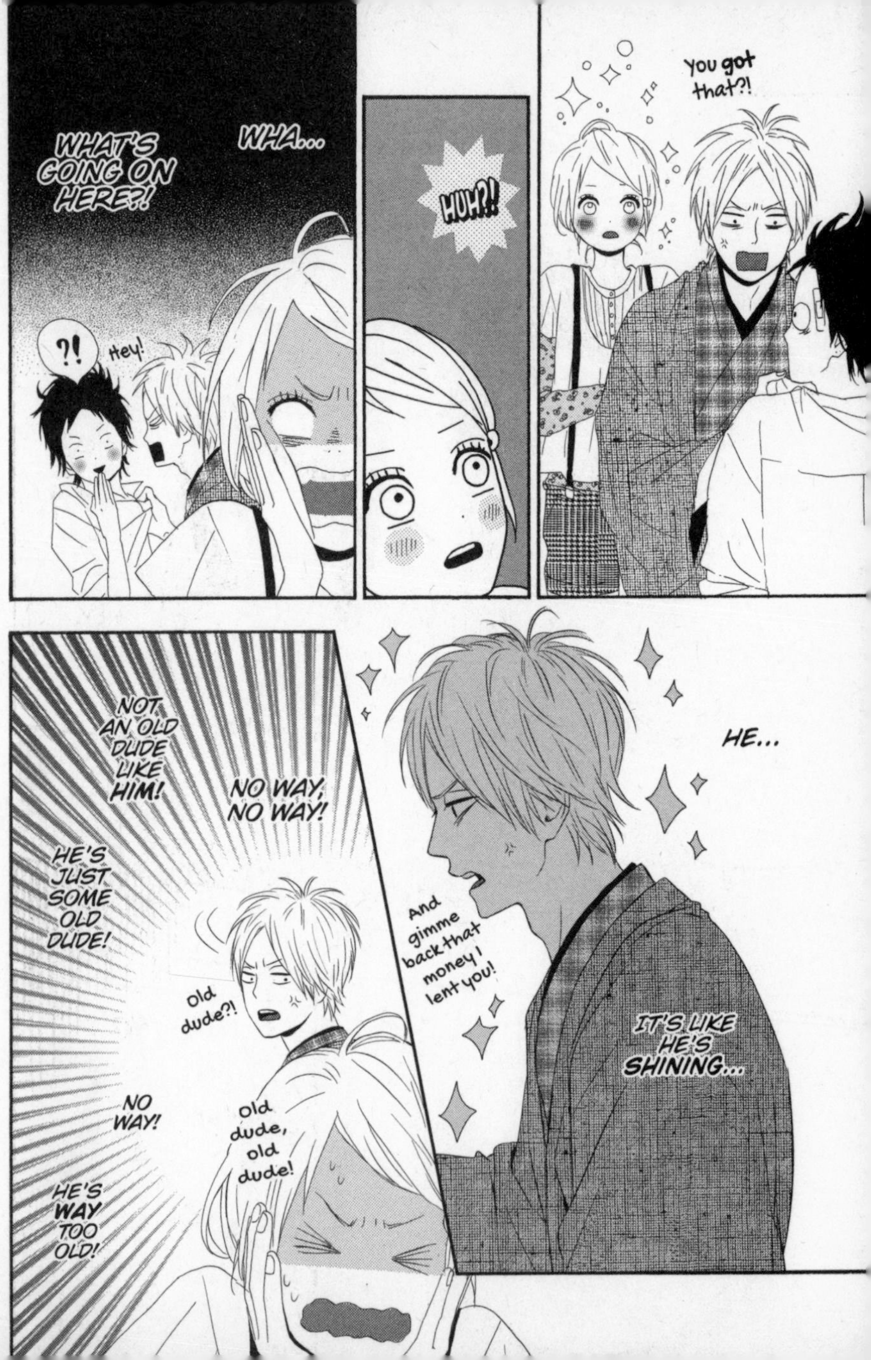
You got that?!
HUH?!
WHA...
WHAT'S GOING ON HERE?!
Hey!
?!
HE...
And gimme back that money I lent you!
IT'S LIKE HE'S SHINING...
NO WAY, NO WAY!
NOT AN OLD DUDE LIKE HIM!
HE'S JUST SOME OLD DUDE!
Old dude?!
Old dude, old dude!
NO WAY!
HE'S WAY TOO OLD!

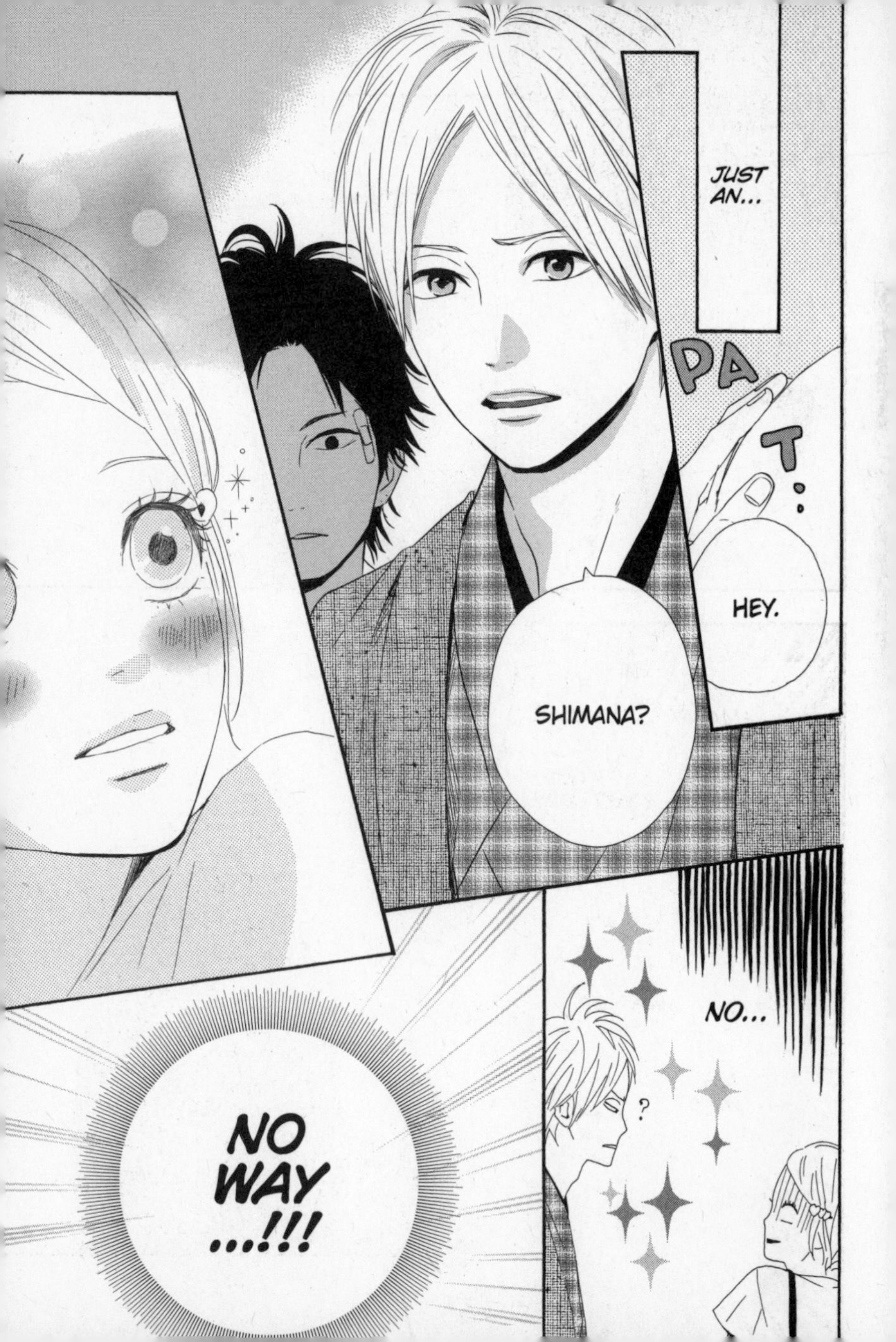
JUST AN...
PAT
HEY.
SHIMANA?
NO...
?
NO WAY ...!!!

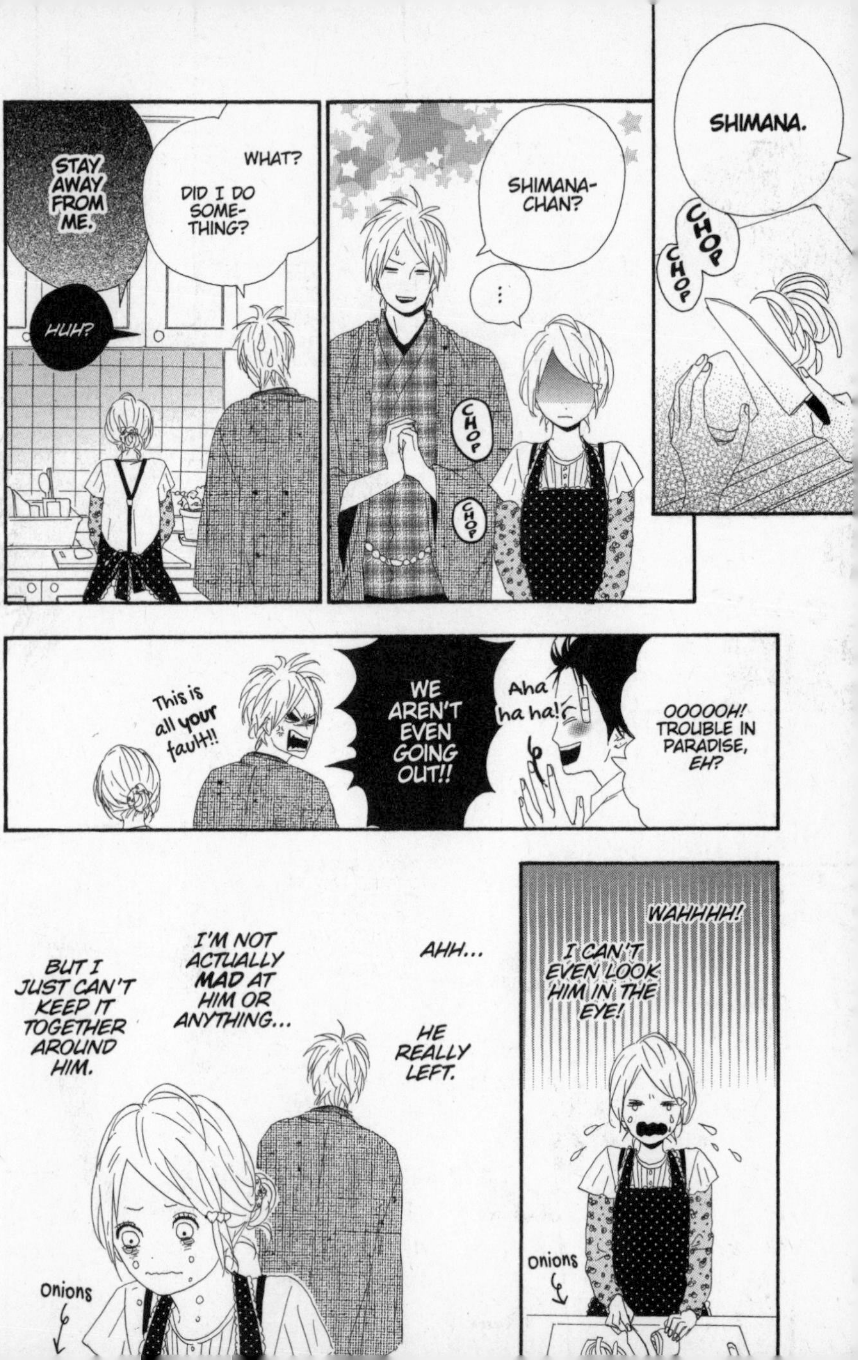
SHIMANA.
CHOP
CHOP
SHIMANA-CHAN?
...
CHOP
CHOP
WHAT?
DID I DO SOMETHING?
STAY AWAY FROM ME.
HUH?
OOOOOH! TROUBLE IN PARADISE, EH?
Aha ha ha!
WE AREN'T EVEN GOING OUT!!
This is all your fault!!
WAHHHH!
I CAN'T EVEN LOOK HIM IN THE EYE!
Onions
AHH...
HE REALLY LEFT.
I'M NOT ACTUALLY MAD AT HIM OR ANYTHING...
BUT I JUST CAN'T KEEP IT TOGETHER AROUND HIM.
Onions

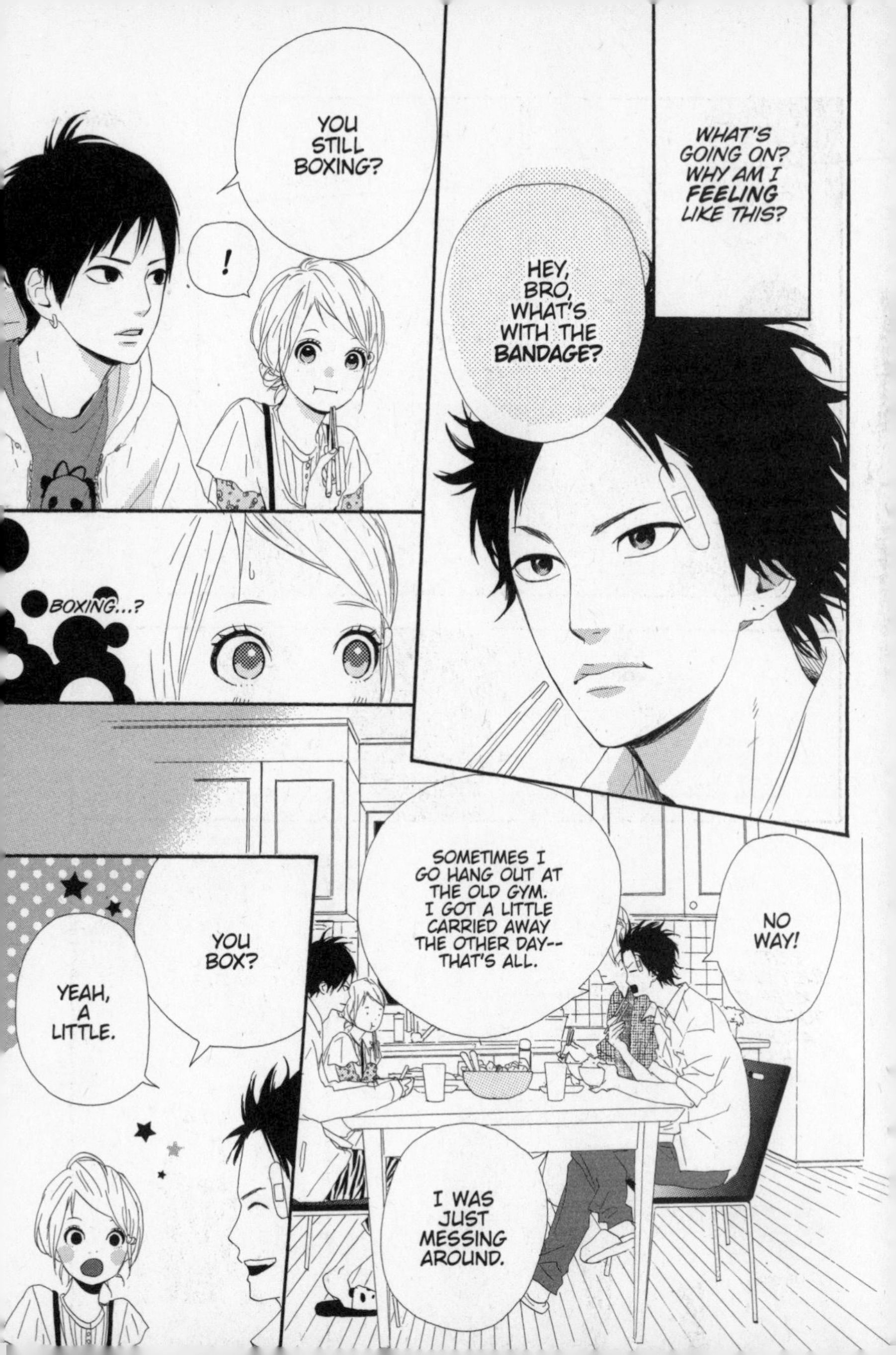
WHAT'S GOING ON? WHY AM I FEELING LIKE THIS?
HEY, BRO, WHAT'S WITH THE BANDAGE?
YOU STILL BOXING?
!
BOXING...?
NO WAY!
SOMETIMES I GO HANG OUT AT THE OLD GYM. I GOT A LITTLE CARRIED AWAY THE OTHER DAY-- THAT'S ALL.
I WAS JUST MESSING AROUND.
YOU BOX?
YEAH, A LITTLE.

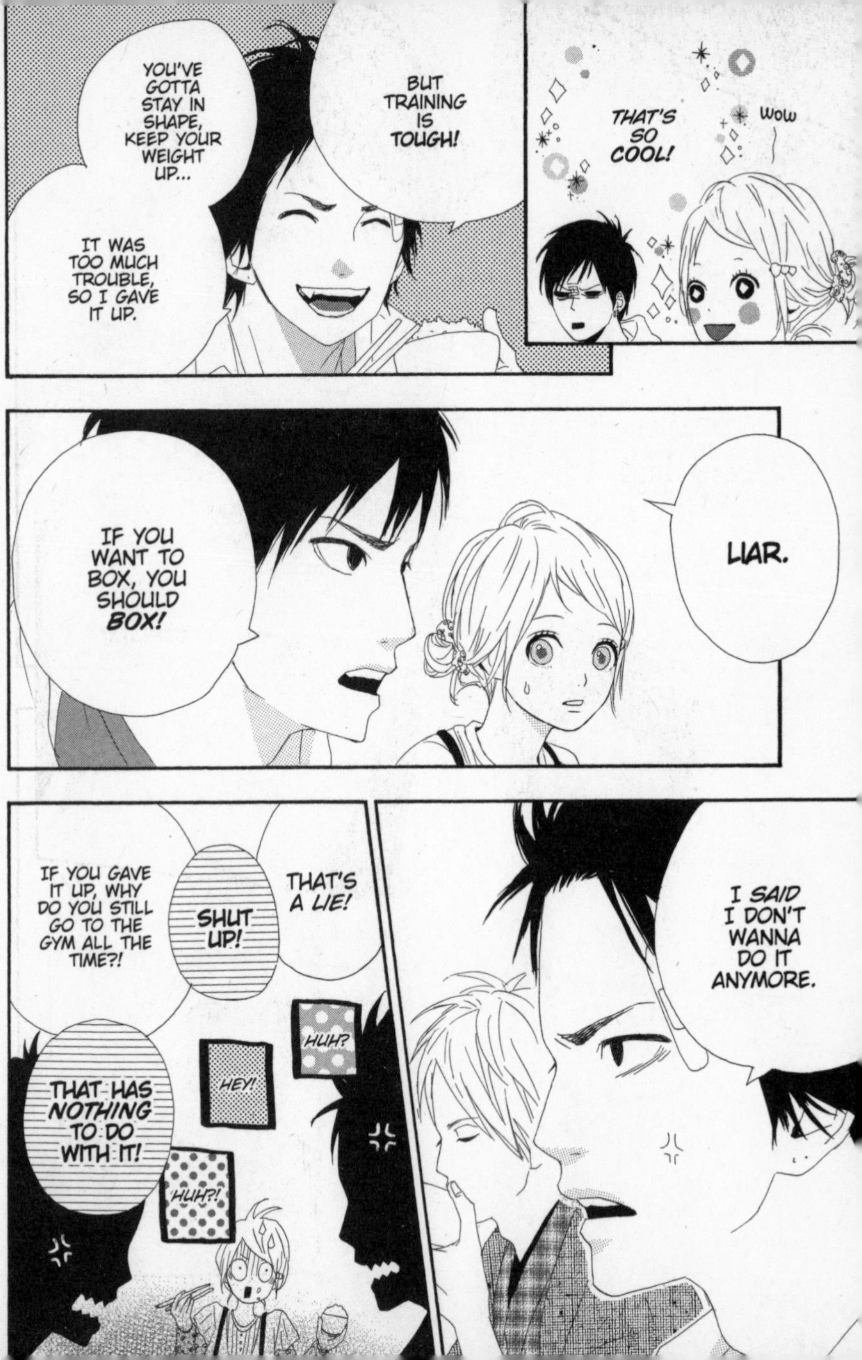
WOW
THAT'S SO COOL!
BUT TRAINING IS TOUGH!
YOU'VE GOTTA STAY IN SHAPE, KEEP YOUR WEIGHT UP...
IT WAS TOO MUCH TROUBLE, SO I GAVE IT UP.
LIAR.
IF YOU WANT TO BOX, YOU SHOULD BOX!
I SAID I DON'T WANNA DO IT ANYMORE.
THAT'S A LIE!
SHUT UP!
IF YOU GAVE IT UP, WHY DO YOU STILL GO TO THE GYM ALL THE TIME?!
HUH?
HEY!
THAT HAS NOTHING TO DO WITH IT!
HUH?!

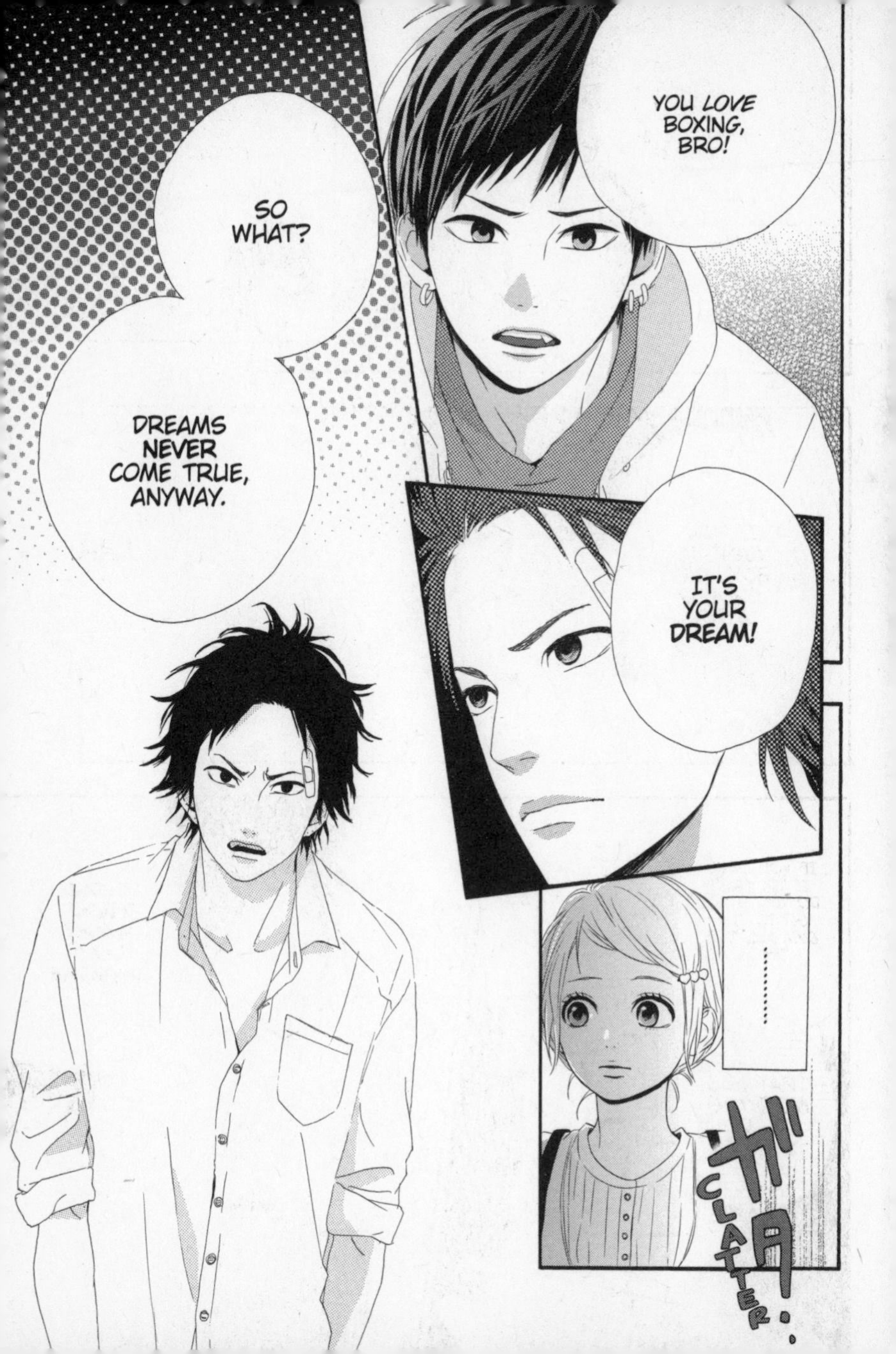
YOU LOVE BOXING, BRO!
IT'S YOUR DREAM!
......
CLATTER!
SO WHAT?
DREAMS NEVER COME TRUE, ANYWAY.

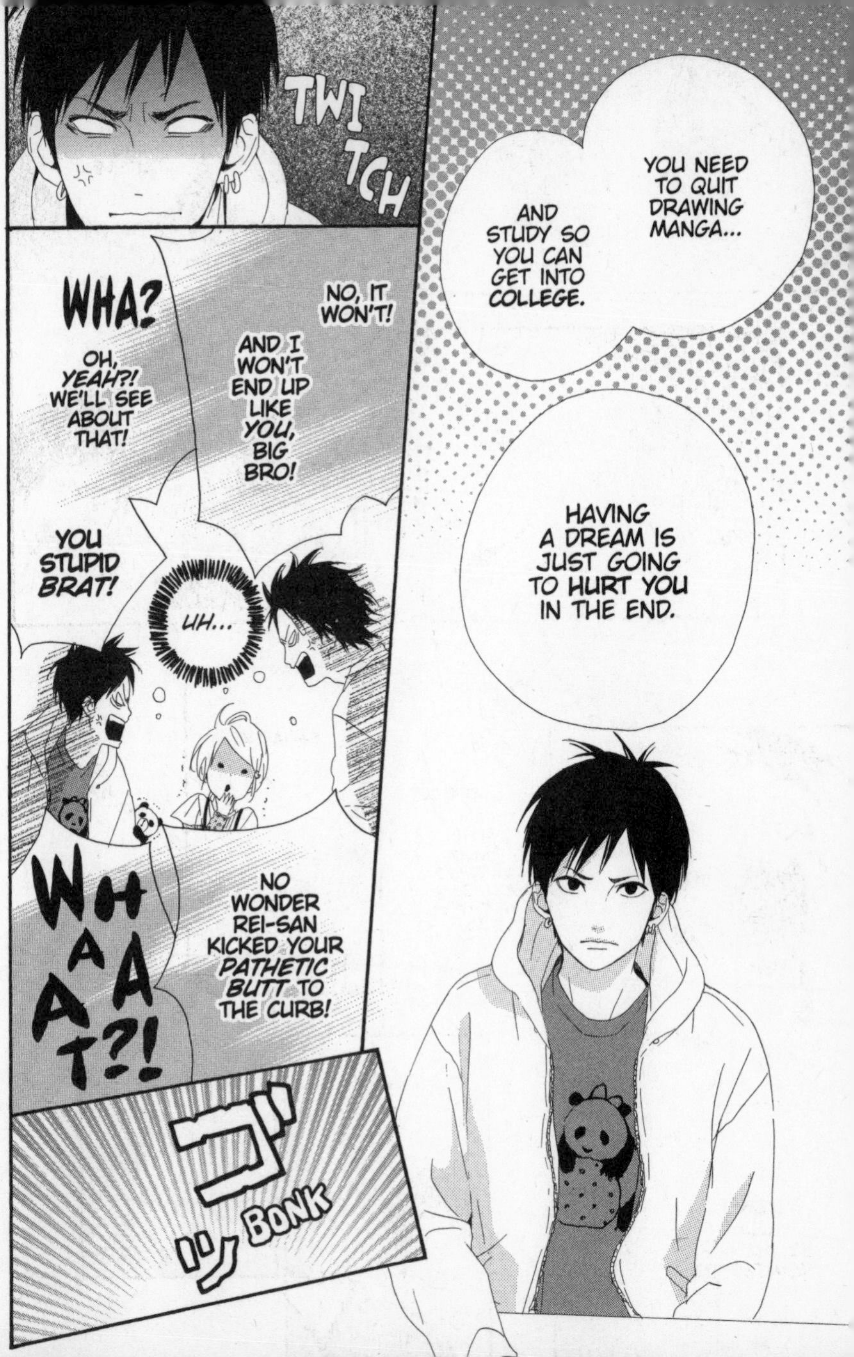
YOU NEED TO QUIT DRAWING MANGA...
AND STUDY SO YOU CAN GET INTO COLLEGE.
HAVING A DREAM IS JUST GOING TO HURT YOU IN THE END.
TWITCH
NO, IT WON'T!
AND I WON'T END UP LIKE YOU, BIG BRO!
WHA?
OH, YEAH?! WE'LL SEE ABOUT THAT!
YOU STUPID BRAT!
UH...
NO WONDER REI-SAN KICKED YOUR PATHETIC BUTT TO THE CURB!
WHAAAT?!
BONK

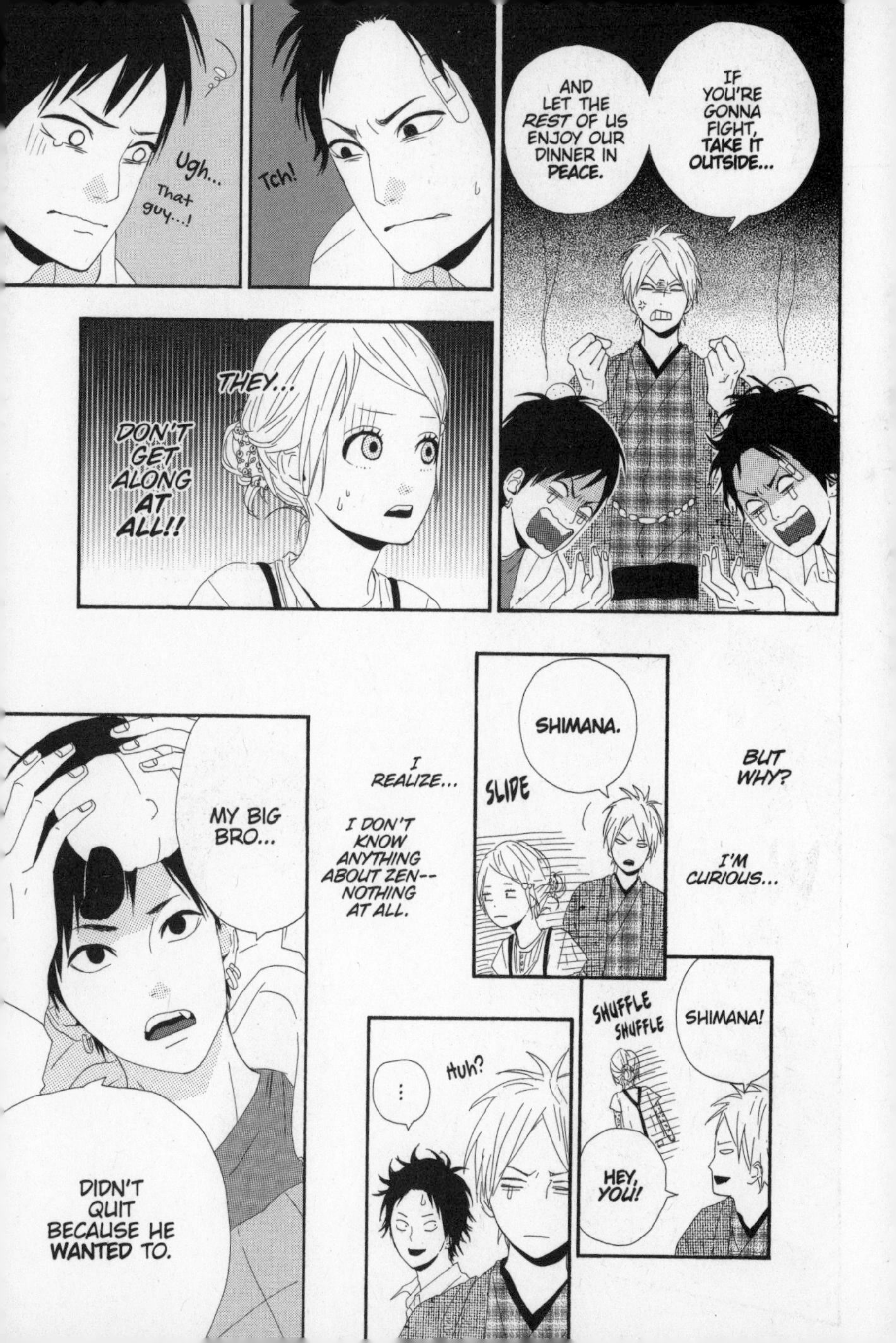
IF YOU'RE GONNA FIGHT, TAKE IT OUTSIDE...
AND LET THE REST OF US ENJOY OUR DINNER IN PEACE.
Tch!
Ugh... That guy...!
THEY...
DON'T GET ALONG AT ALL!!
BUT WHY?
I'M CURIOUS...
SHIMANA.
SLIDE
I REALIZE...
I DON'T KNOW ANYTHING ABOUT ZEN-- NOTHING AT ALL.
SHIMANA!
SHUFFLE SHUFFLE
HEY, YOU!
Huh?
...
MY BIG BRO...
DIDN'T QUIT BECAUSE HE WANTED TO.

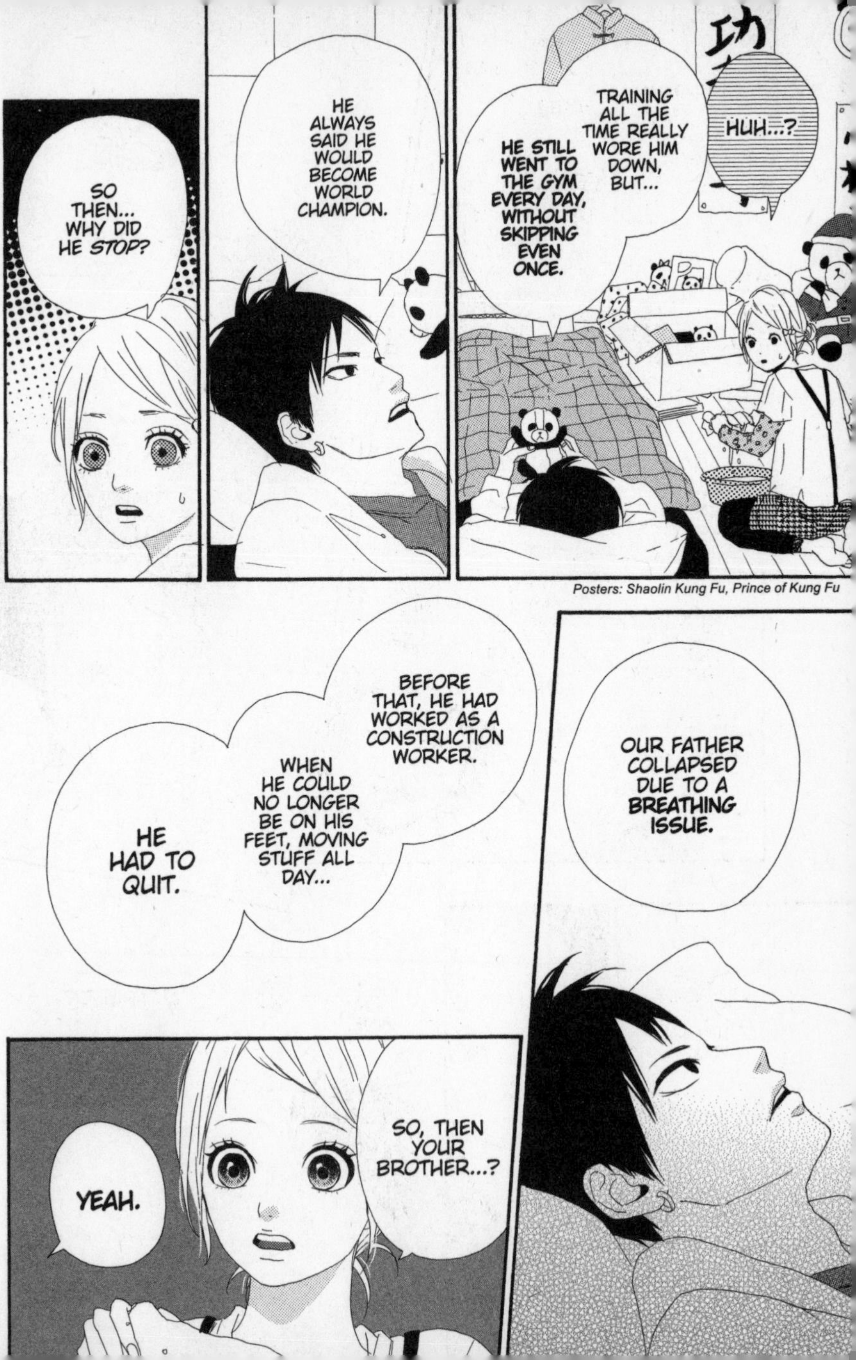
HUH...?
TRAINING ALL THE TIME REALLY WORE HIM DOWN, BUT...
HE STILL WENT TO THE GYM EVERY DAY, WITHOUT SKIPPING EVEN ONCE.
HE ALWAYS SAID HE WOULD BECOME WORLD CHAMPION.
SO THEN... WHY DID HE *STOP*?
OUR FATHER COLLAPSED DUE TO A **BREATHING ISSUE.**
BEFORE THAT, HE HAD WORKED AS A CONSTRUCTION WORKER.
WHEN HE COULD NO LONGER BE ON HIS FEET, MOVING STUFF ALL DAY...
HE HAD TO QUIT.
SO, THEN YOUR BROTHER...?
YEAH.
Posters: Shaolin Kung Fu, Prince of Kung Fu

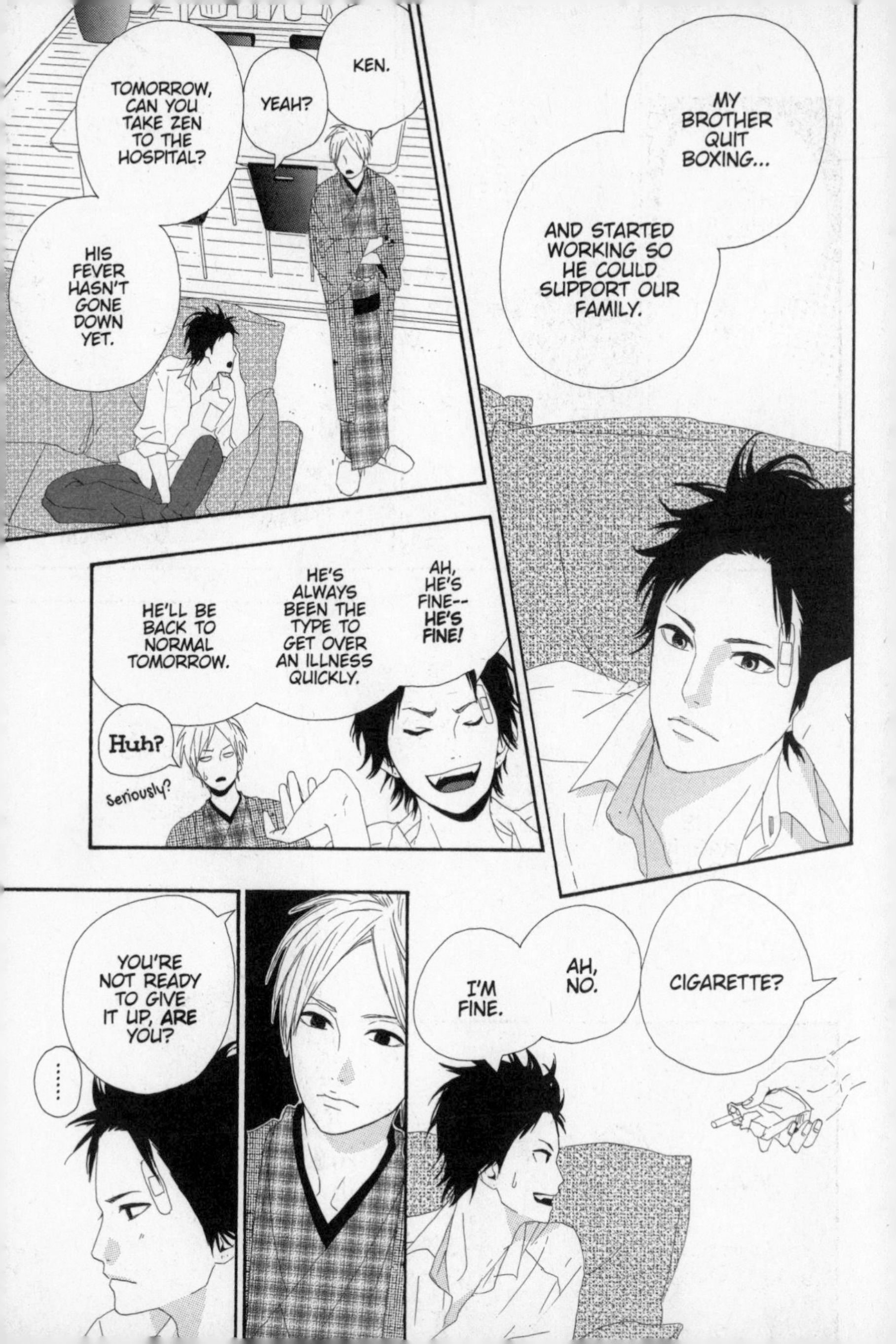
MY BROTHER QUIT BOXING...
AND STARTED WORKING SO HE COULD SUPPORT OUR FAMILY.
KEN.
YEAH?
TOMORROW, CAN YOU TAKE ZEN TO THE HOSPITAL?
HIS FEVER HASN'T GONE DOWN YET.
AH, HE'S FINE--HE'S FINE!
HE'S ALWAYS BEEN THE TYPE TO GET OVER AN ILLNESS QUICKLY.
HE'LL BE BACK TO NORMAL TOMORROW.
Huh?
Seriously?
CIGARETTE?
AH, NO.
I'M FINE.
YOU'RE NOT READY TO GIVE IT UP, ARE YOU?
......

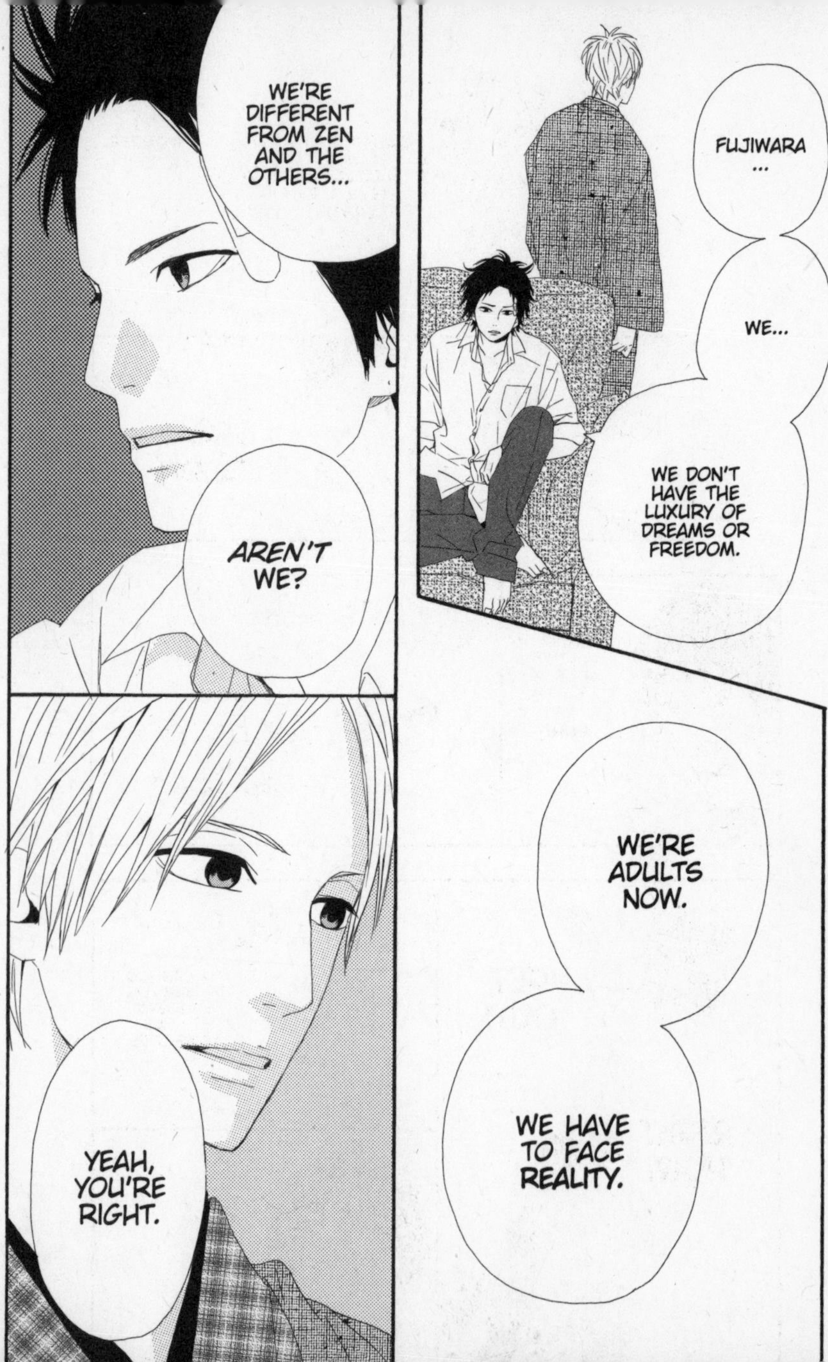
FUJIWARA ...
WE...
WE DON'T HAVE THE LUXURY OF DREAMS OR FREEDOM.
WE'RE DIFFERENT FROM ZEN AND THE OTHERS...
AREN'T WE?
WE'RE ADULTS NOW.
WE HAVE TO FACE REALITY.
YEAH, YOU'RE RIGHT.

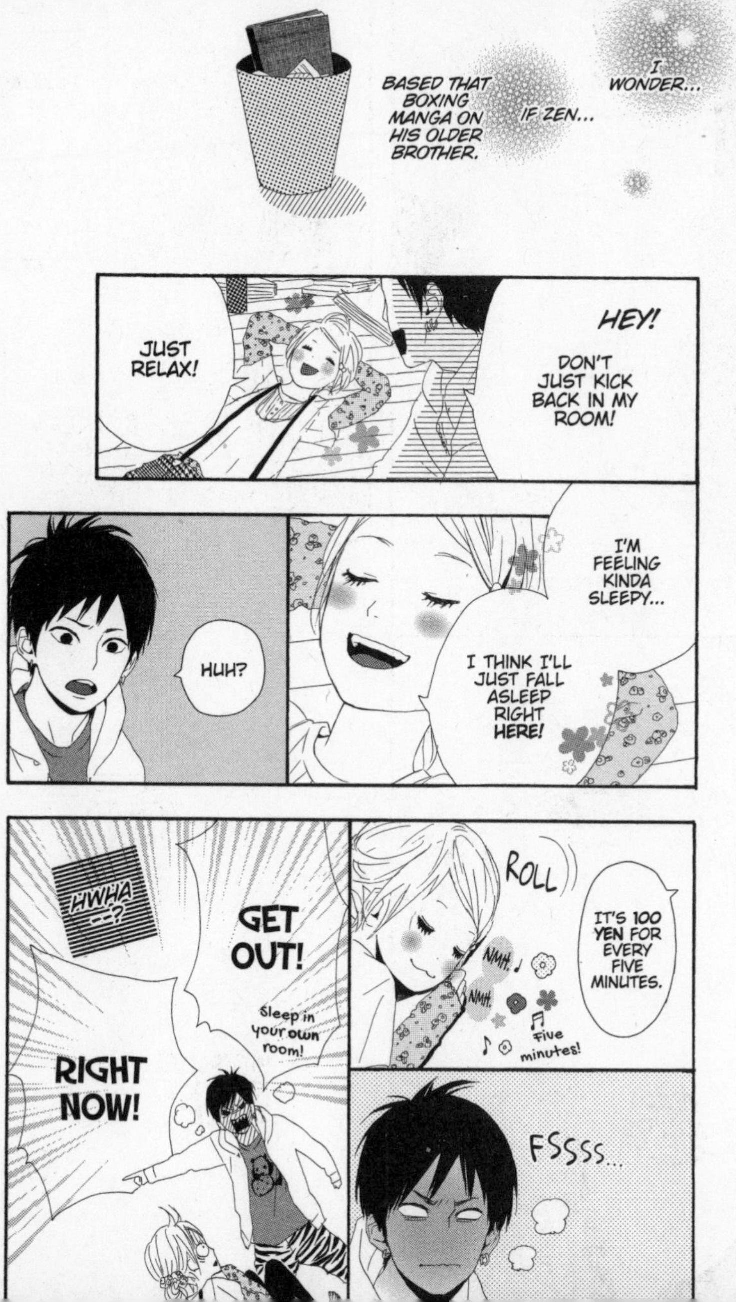
I WONDER...
IF ZEN...
BASED THAT BOXING MANGA ON HIS OLDER BROTHER.
HEY!
DON'T JUST KICK BACK IN MY ROOM!
JUST RELAX!
I'M FEELING KINDA SLEEPY...
I THINK I'LL JUST FALL ASLEEP RIGHT HERE!
HUH?
ROLL
IT'S 100 YEN FOR EVERY FIVE MINUTES.
NMH.
NMH.
Five minutes!
FSSSS...
HWHA--?
GET OUT!
Sleep in your own room!
RIGHT NOW!

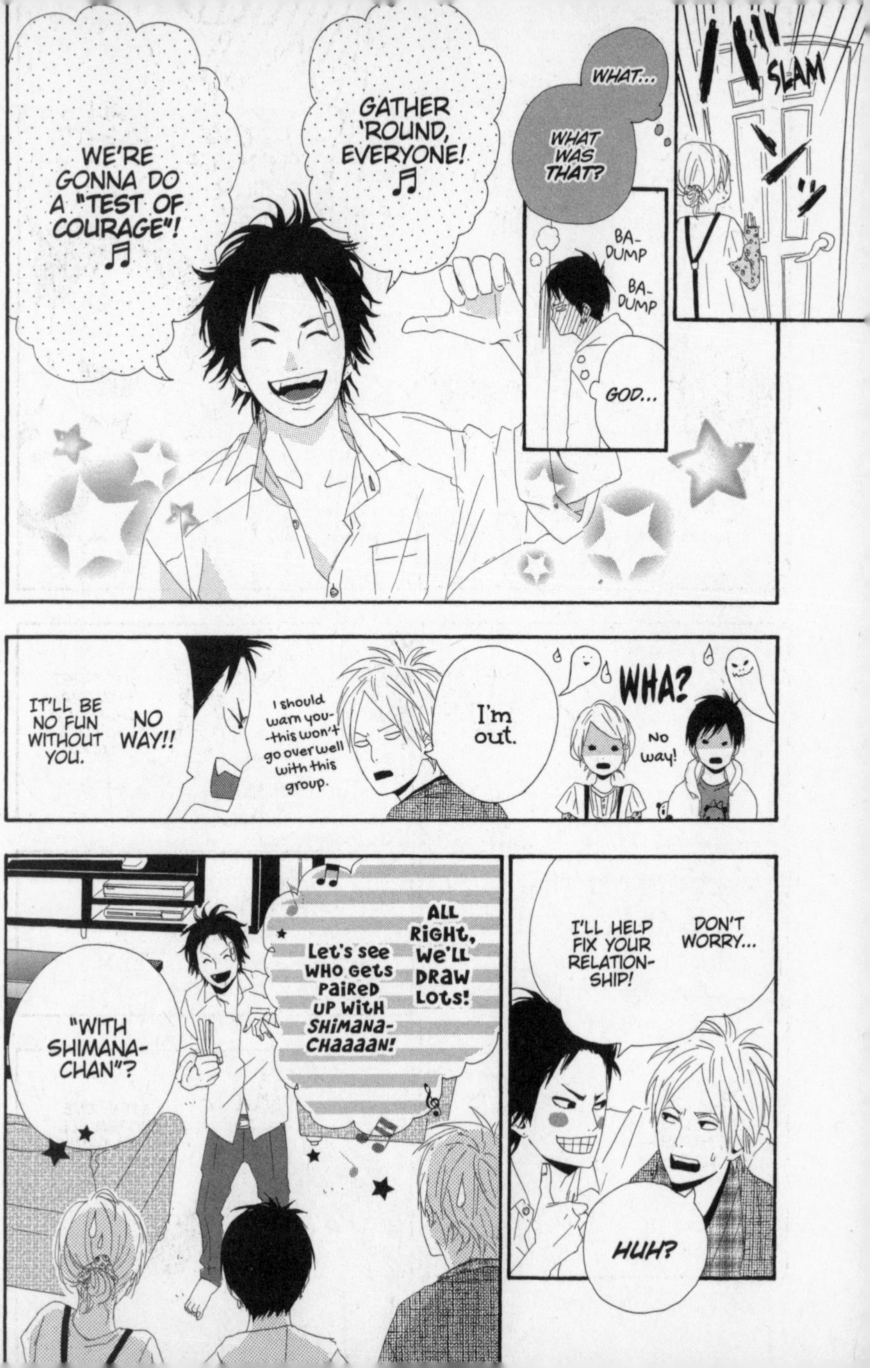
SLAM
WHAT...
WHAT WAS THAT?
BA-DUMP
BA-DUMP
GOD...
GATHER 'ROUND, EVERYONE! ♬
WE'RE GONNA DO A "TEST OF COURAGE"! ♬
WHA?
No way!
I'm out.
I should warn you-this won't go over well with this group.
NO WAY!!
IT'LL BE NO FUN WITHOUT YOU.
DON'T WORRY...
I'LL HELP FIX YOUR RELATION-SHIP!
HUH?
ALL RIGHT, WE'LL DRAW LOTS!
Let's see WHO gets PAIRED UP WITH SHIMANA-CHAAAAN!
"WITH SHIMANA-CHAN"?

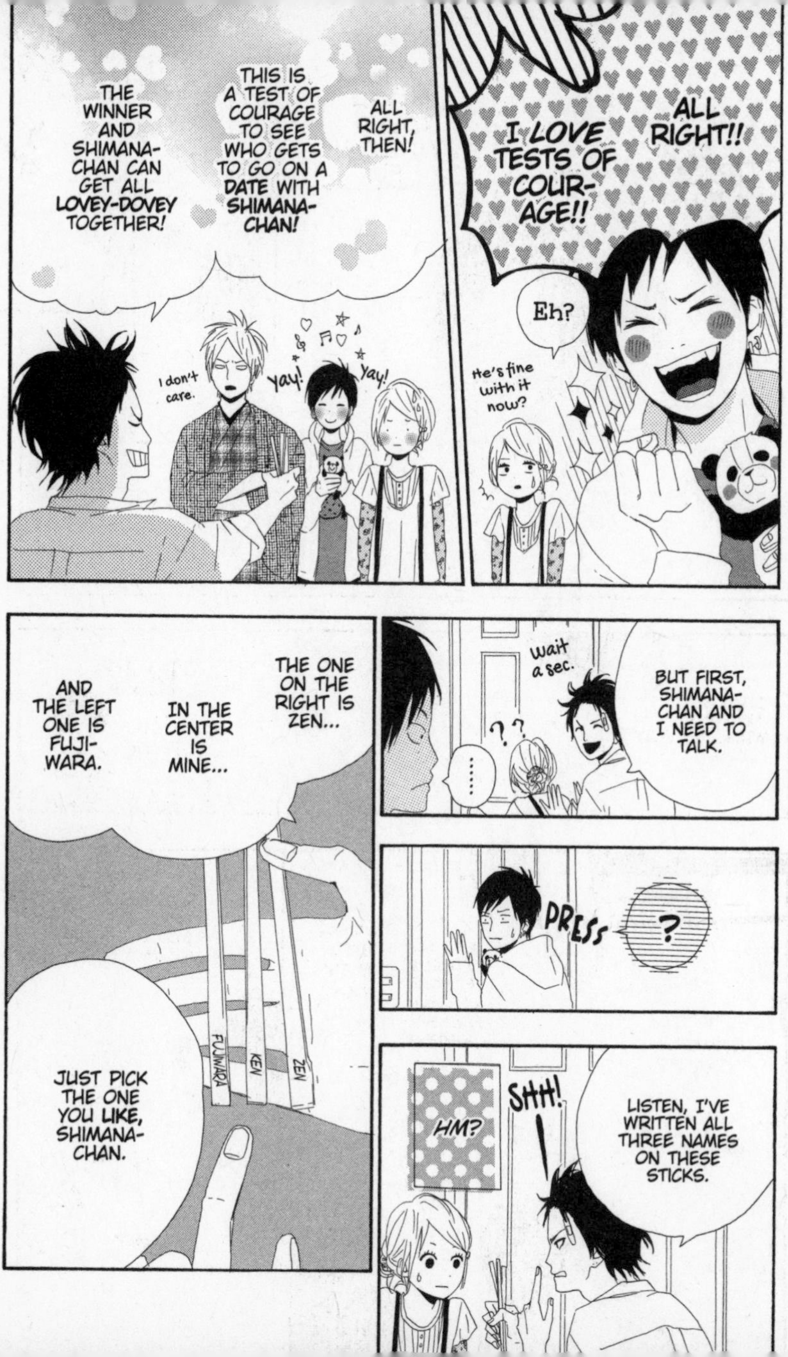
ALL RIGHT!!
I LOVE TESTS OF COURAGE!!
Eh?
He's fine with it now?
ALL RIGHT, THEN!
THIS IS A TEST OF COURAGE TO SEE WHO GETS TO GO ON A DATE WITH SHIMANA-CHAN!
THE WINNER AND SHIMANA-CHAN CAN GET ALL LOVEY-DOVEY TOGETHER!
I don't care.
Yay!
Yay!
BUT FIRST, SHIMANA-CHAN AND I NEED TO TALK.
Wait a sec.
??
......
?
PRESS
LISTEN, I'VE WRITTEN ALL THREE NAMES ON THESE STICKS.
SHH!
HM?
THE ONE ON THE RIGHT IS ZEN...
IN THE CENTER IS MINE...
AND THE LEFT ONE IS FUJI-WARA.
ZEN
KEN
FUJIWARA
JUST PICK THE ONE YOU LIKE, SHIMANA-CHAN.

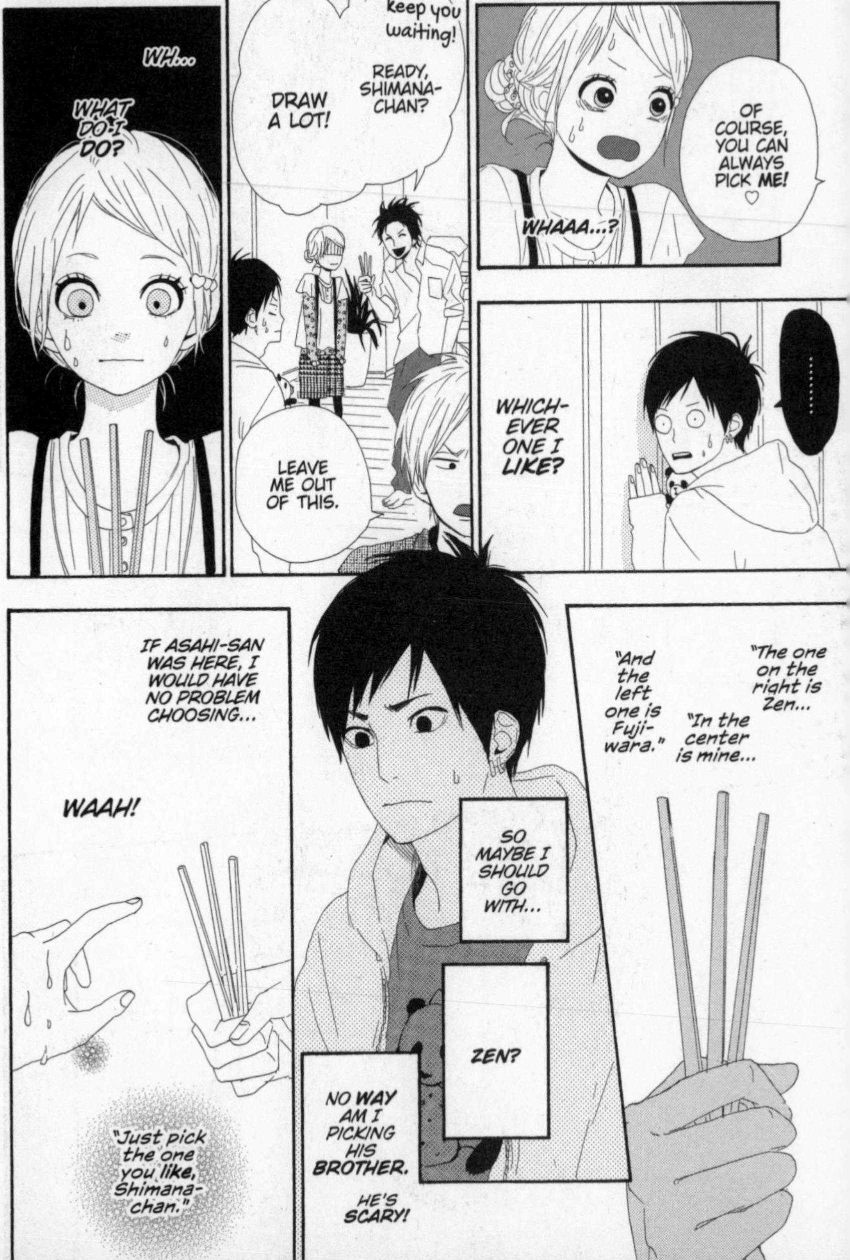
OF COURSE, YOU CAN ALWAYS PICK ME! ♡
WHAAA...?
......
WHICH-EVER ONE I LIKE?
Sorry to keep you waiting!
READY, SHIMANA-CHAN?
DRAW A LOT!
LEAVE ME OUT OF THIS.
WH...
WHAT DO I DO?
"The one on the right is Zen...
"In the center is mine...
"And the left one is Fuji-wara."
SO MAYBE I SHOULD GO WITH...
ZEN?
NO WAY AM I PICKING HIS BROTHER.
HE'S SCARY!
IF ASAHI-SAN WAS HERE, I WOULD HAVE NO PROBLEM CHOOSING...
WAAH!
"Just pick the one you like, Shimana-chan."

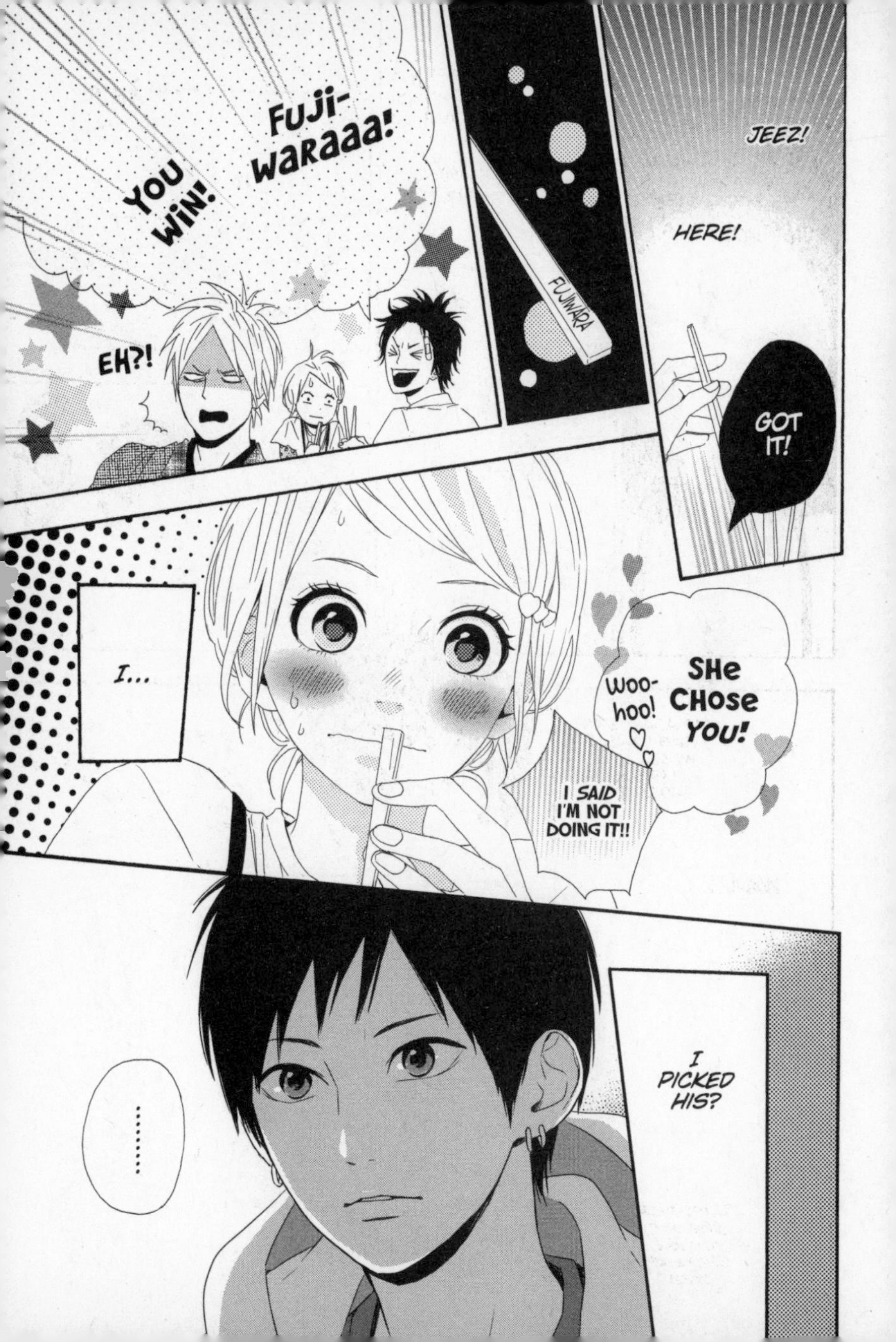
JEEZ!
HERE!
GOT IT!
FUJIWARA
Fuji-waraaa!
YOU WIN!
EH?!
SHe CHOSE YOU!
Woo-hoo!
I SAID I'M NOT DOING IT!!
I...
I PICKED HIS?
......

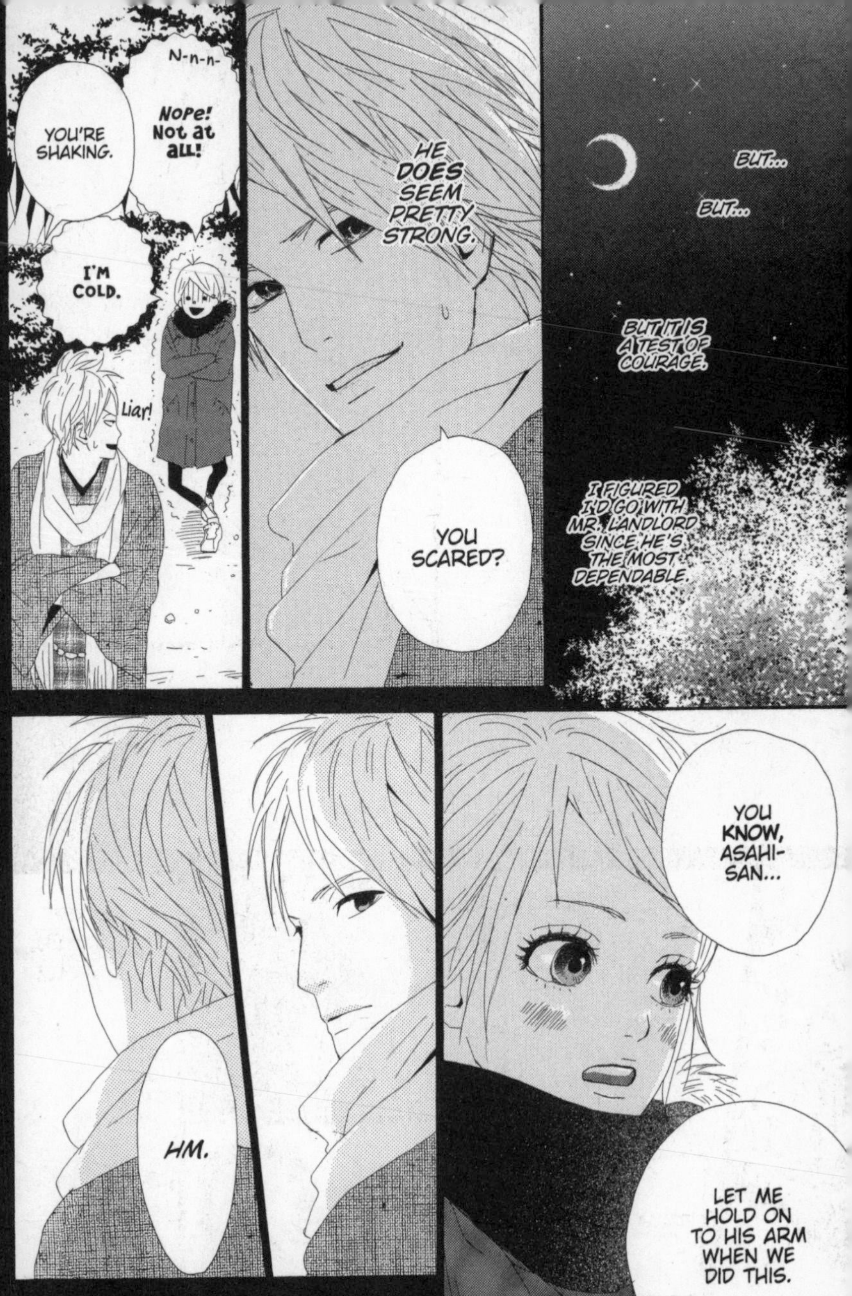
BUT...
BUT...
BUT IT IS A TEST OF COURAGE.
I FIGURED I'D GO WITH MR. LANDLORD SINCE HE'S THE MOST DEPENDABLE.
HE DOES SEEM PRETTY STRONG.
YOU SCARED?
N-n-n-
Nope! Not at all!
YOU'RE SHAKING.
I'M COLD.
Liar!
YOU KNOW, ASAHI-SAN...
LET ME HOLD ON TO HIS ARM WHEN WE DID THIS.
HM.

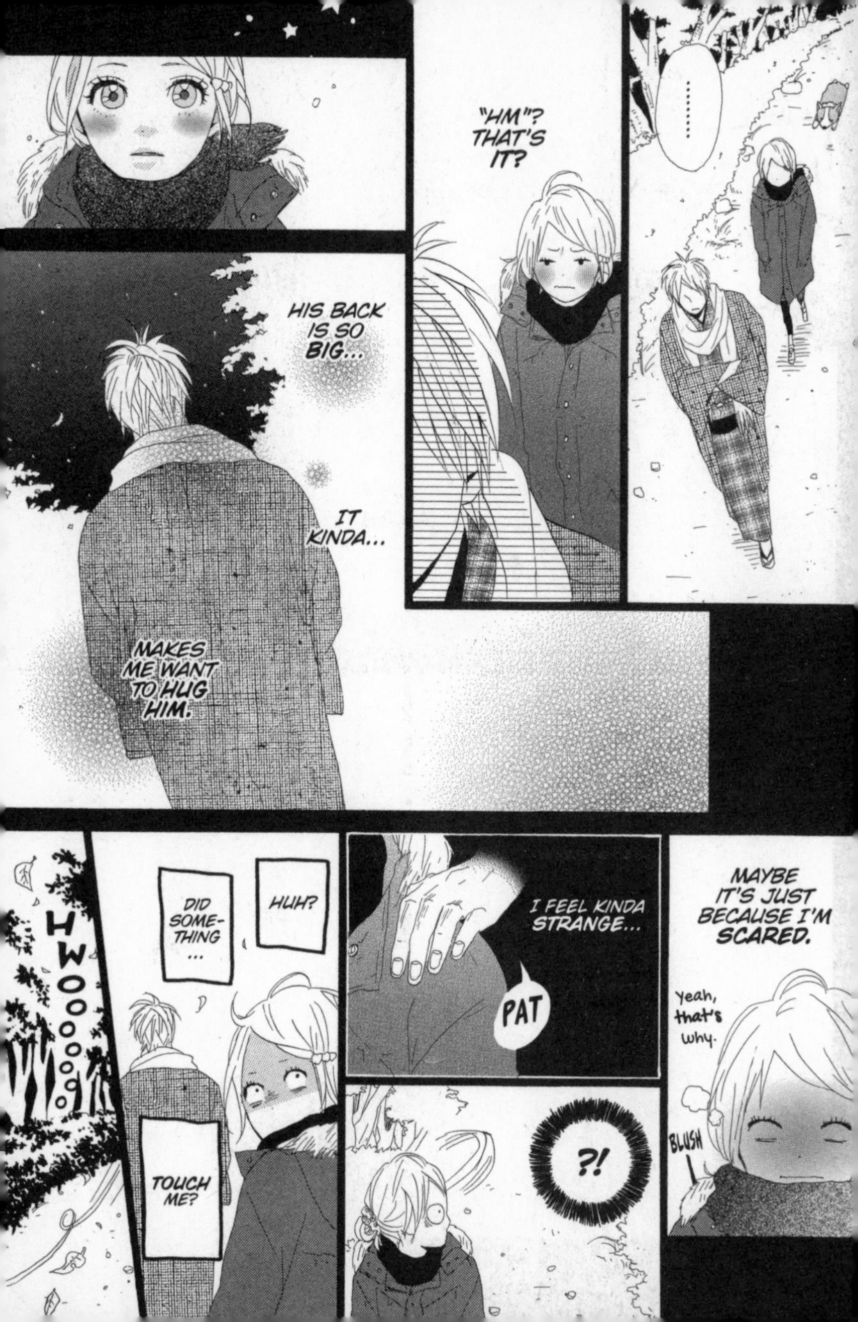
......
"HM"? THAT'S IT?
HIS BACK IS SO BIG...
IT KINDA...
MAKES ME WANT TO HUG HIM.
MAYBE IT'S JUST BECAUSE I'M SCARED.
Yeah, that's why.
BLUSH
I FEEL KINDA STRANGE...
PAT
?!
HUH?
DID SOMETHING ...
TOUCH ME?
HWOOOOOOO

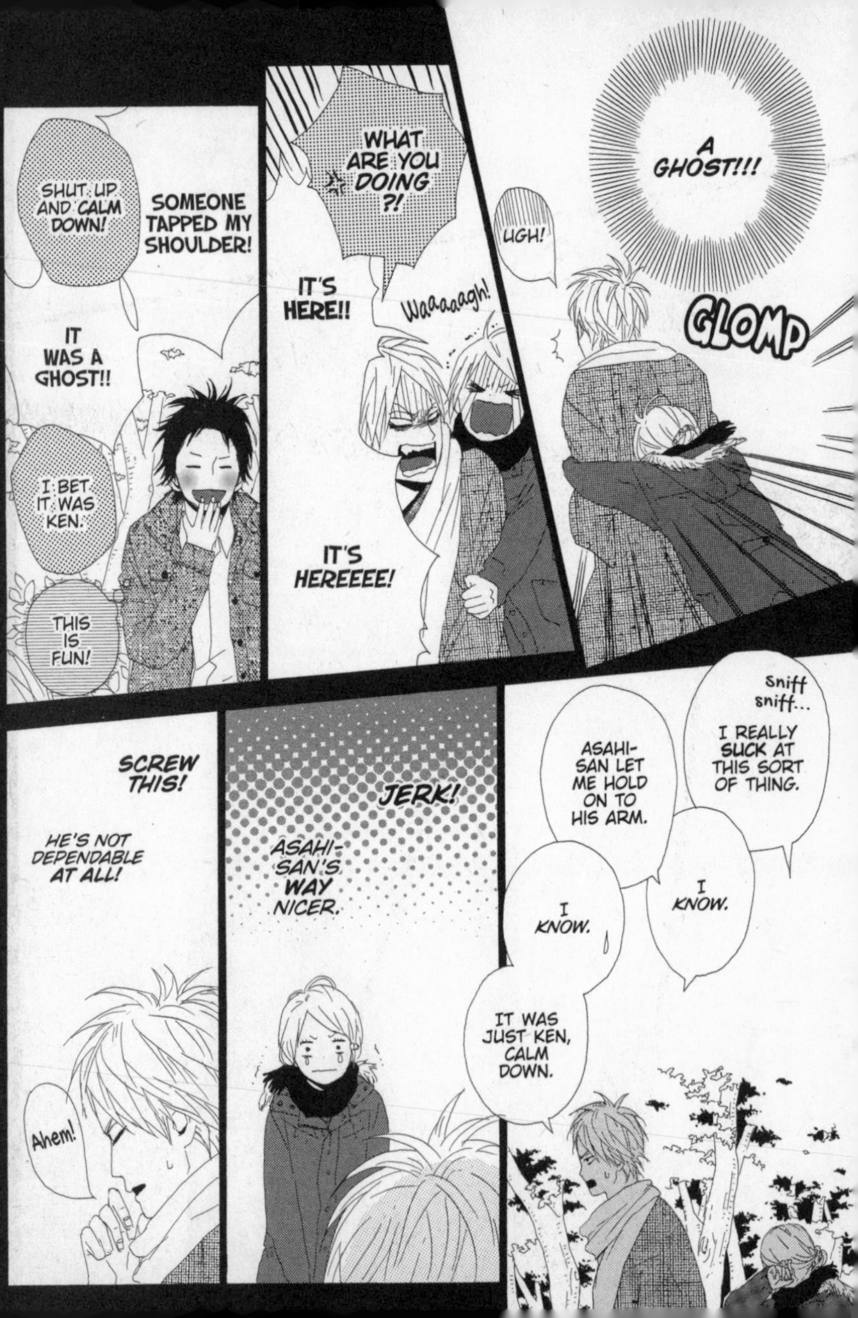
A GHOST!!!
GLOMP
UGH!
WHAT ARE YOU DOING ?!
IT'S HERE!!
Waaaaaagh!
IT'S HEREEEE!
SOMEONE TAPPED MY SHOULDER!
SHUT UP AND CALM DOWN!
IT WAS A GHOST!!
I BET IT WAS KEN.
THIS IS FUN!
Sniff sniff...
I REALLY SUCK AT THIS SORT OF THING.
ASAHI-SAN LET ME HOLD ON TO HIS ARM.
I KNOW.
I KNOW.
IT WAS JUST KEN, CALM DOWN.
JERK!
ASAHI-SAN'S WAY NICER.
SCREW THIS!
HE'S NOT DEPENDABLE AT ALL!
Ahem!

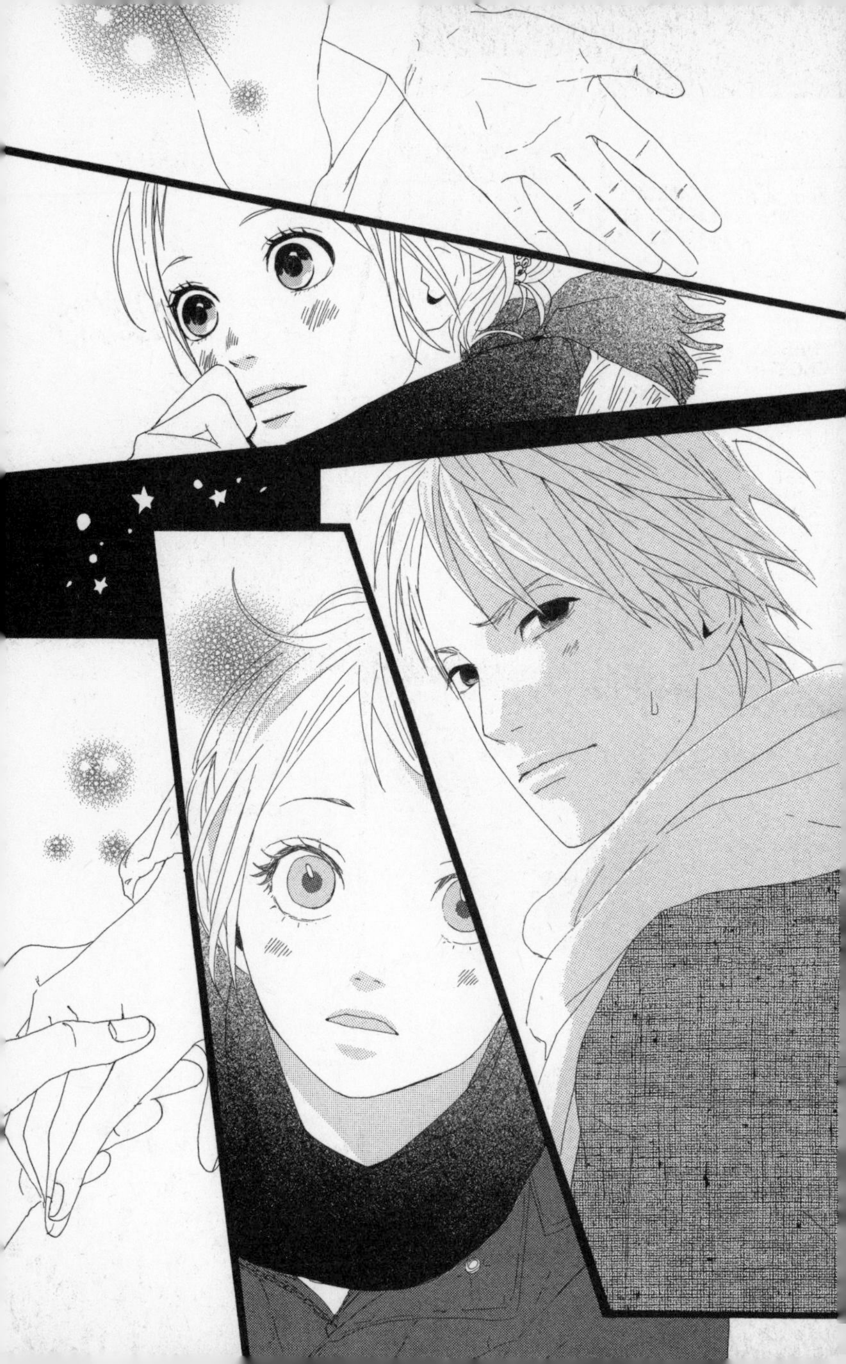

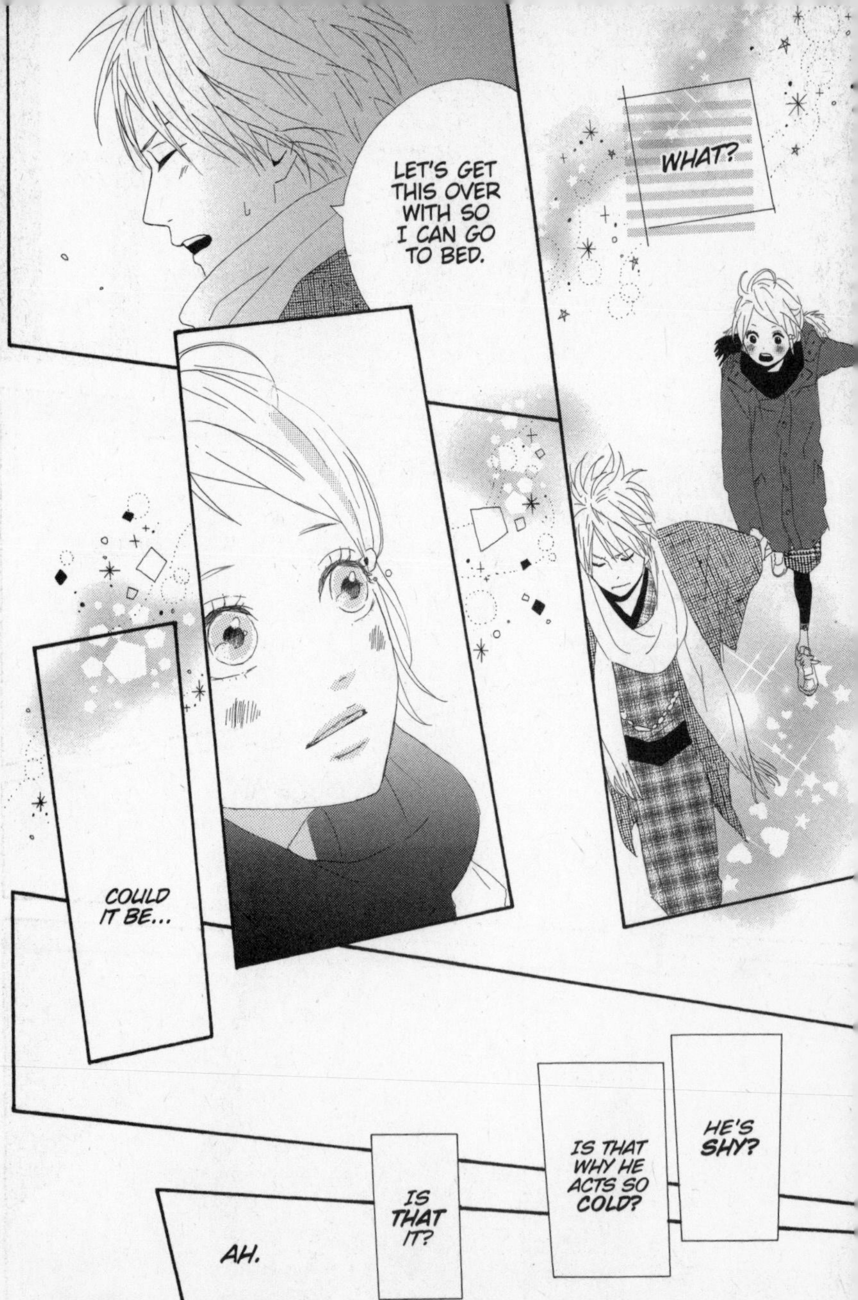
WHAT?
LET'S GET THIS OVER WITH SO I CAN GO TO BED.
COULD IT BE...
HE'S SHY?
IS THAT WHY HE ACTS SO COLD?
IS THAT IT?
AH.

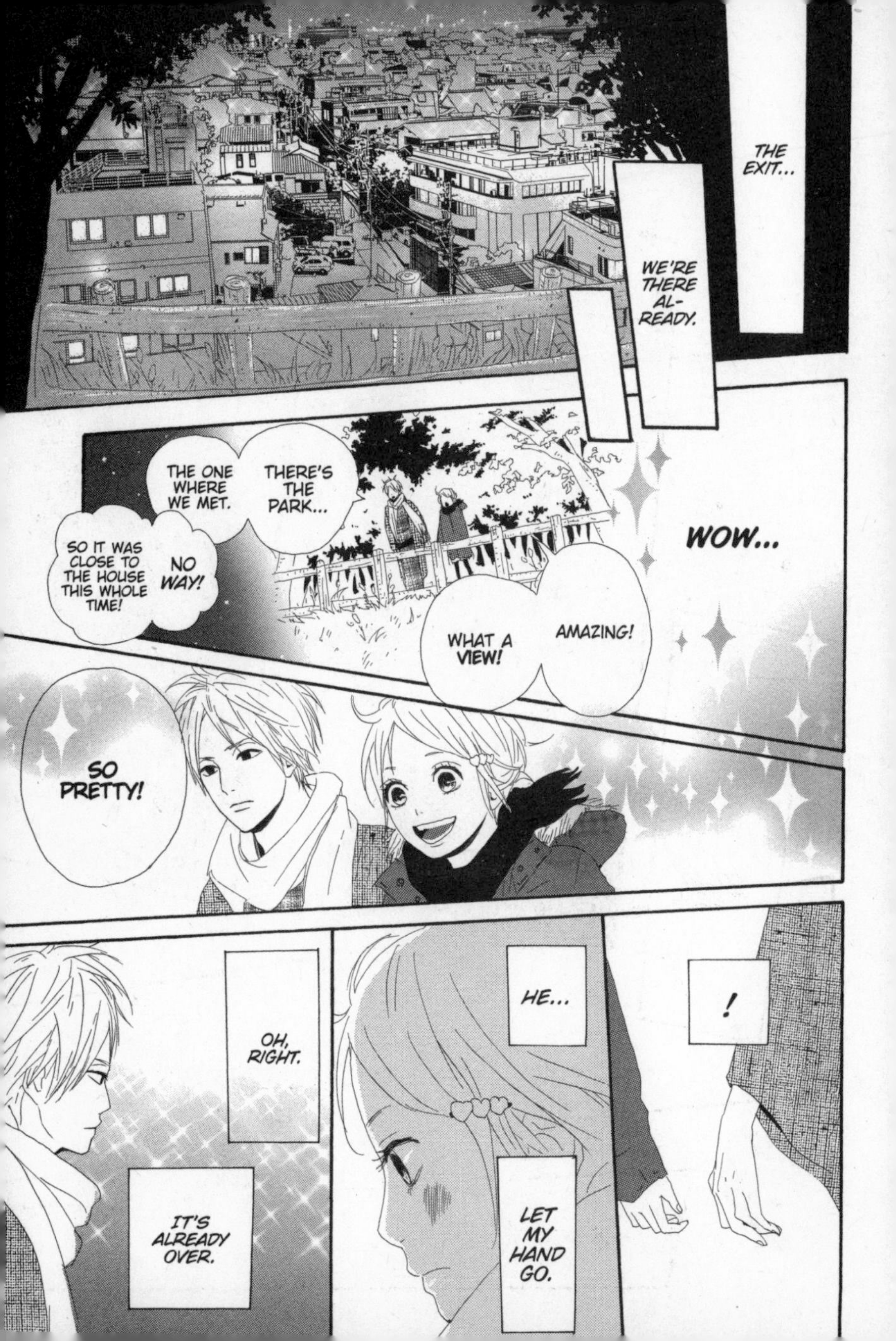
THE EXIT...
WE'RE THERE AL-READY.
WOW...
AMAZING!
WHAT A VIEW!
THERE'S THE PARK...
THE ONE WHERE WE MET.
NO WAY!
SO IT WAS CLOSE TO THE HOUSE THIS WHOLE TIME!
SO PRETTY!
!
HE...
LET MY HAND GO.
OH, RIGHT.
IT'S ALREADY OVER.

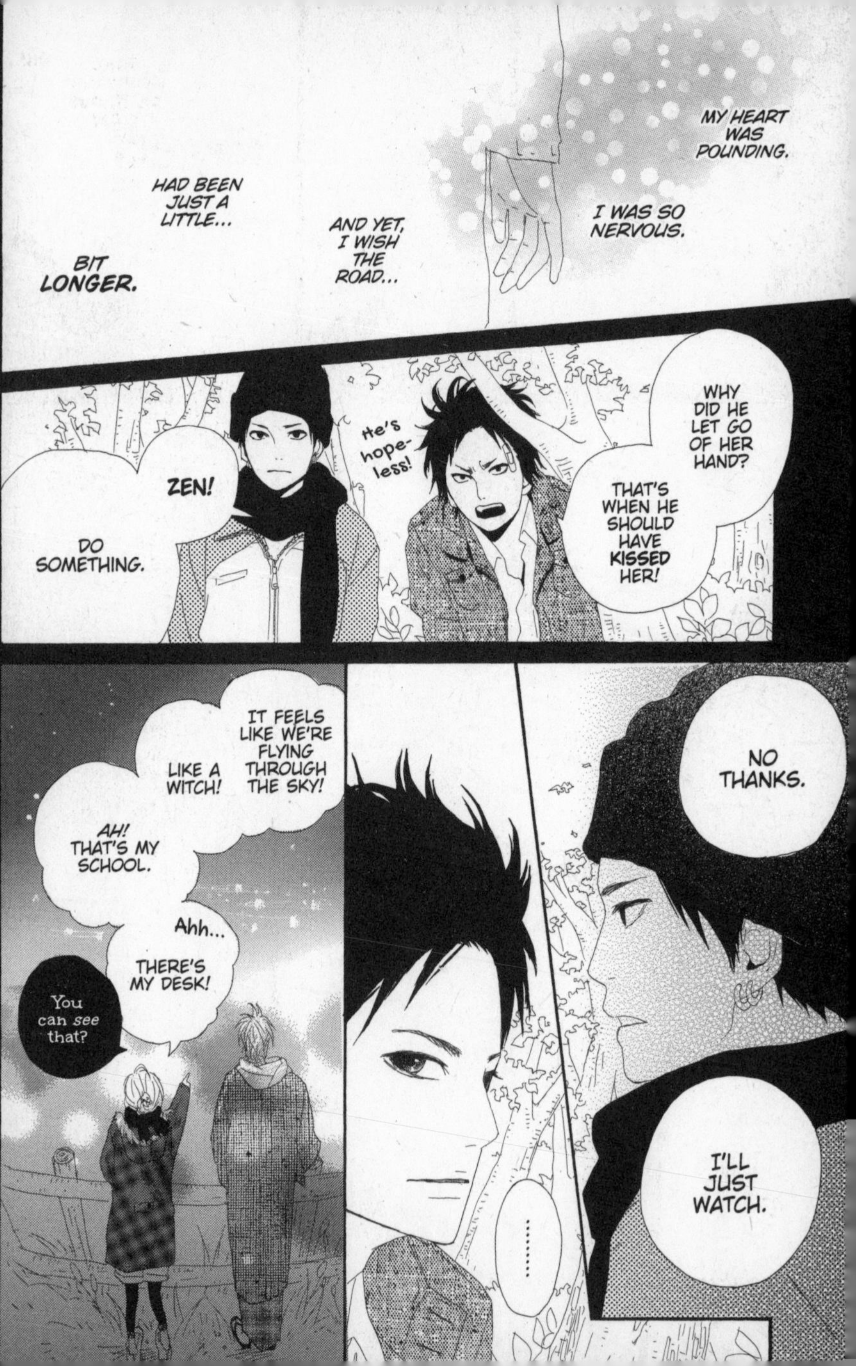
MY HEART WAS POUNDING.
I WAS SO NERVOUS.
AND YET, I WISH THE ROAD...
HAD BEEN JUST A LITTLE...
BIT LONGER.
WHY DID HE LET GO OF HER HAND?
THAT'S WHEN HE SHOULD HAVE KISSED HER!
He's hopeless!
ZEN!
DO SOMETHING.
NO THANKS.
I'LL JUST WATCH.
......
IT FEELS LIKE WE'RE FLYING THROUGH THE SKY!
LIKE A WITCH!
AH! THAT'S MY SCHOOL.
Ahh...
THERE'S MY DESK!
You can see that?

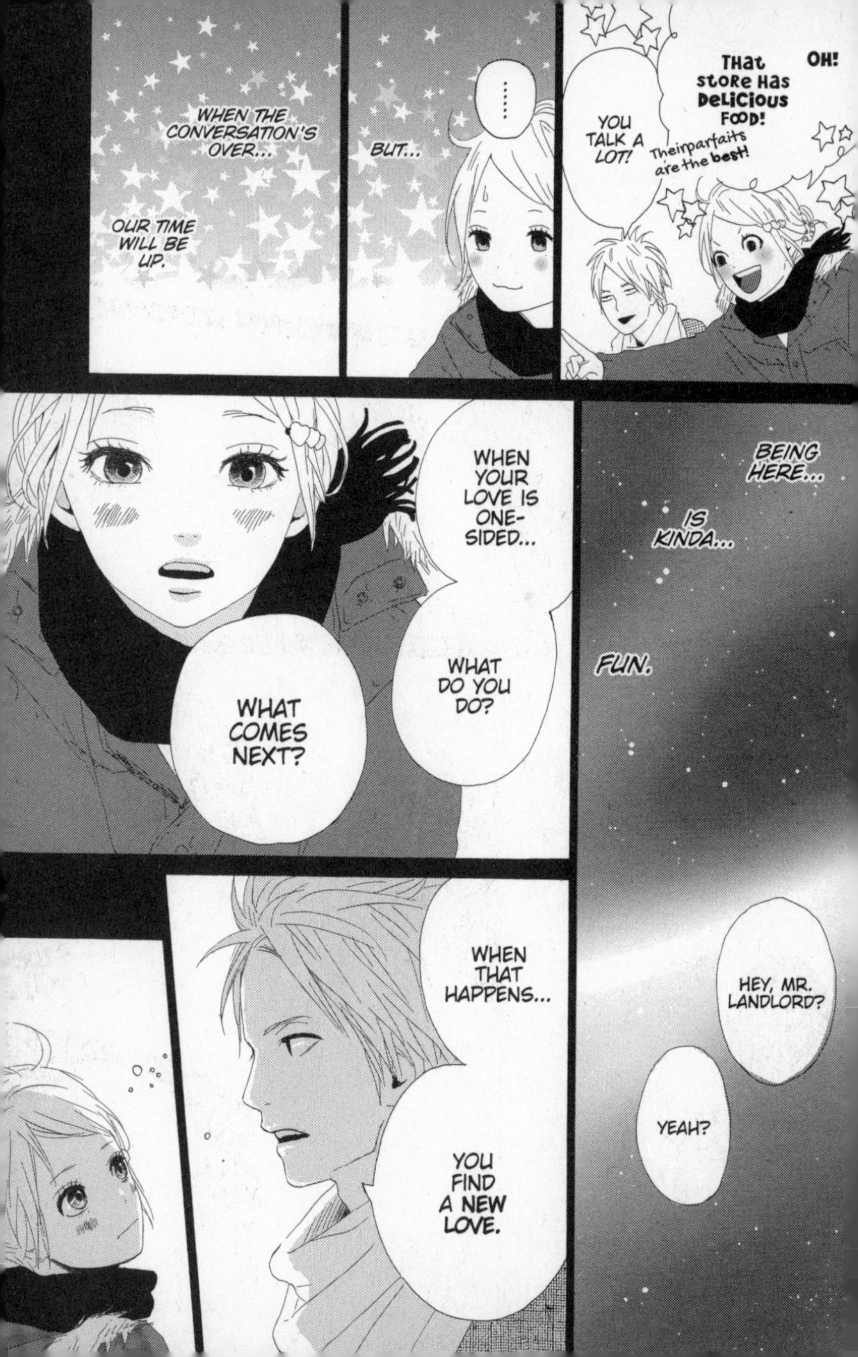
OH!
That store has Delicious Food!
Theirparfaits are the best!
YOU TALK A LOT!
......
BUT...
WHEN THE CONVERSATION'S OVER...
OUR TIME WILL BE UP.
BEING HERE...
IS KINDA...
FUN.
HEY, MR. LANDLORD?
YEAH?
WHEN YOUR LOVE IS ONE-SIDED...
WHAT DO YOU DO?
WHAT COMES NEXT?
WHEN THAT HAPPENS...
YOU FIND A NEW LOVE.

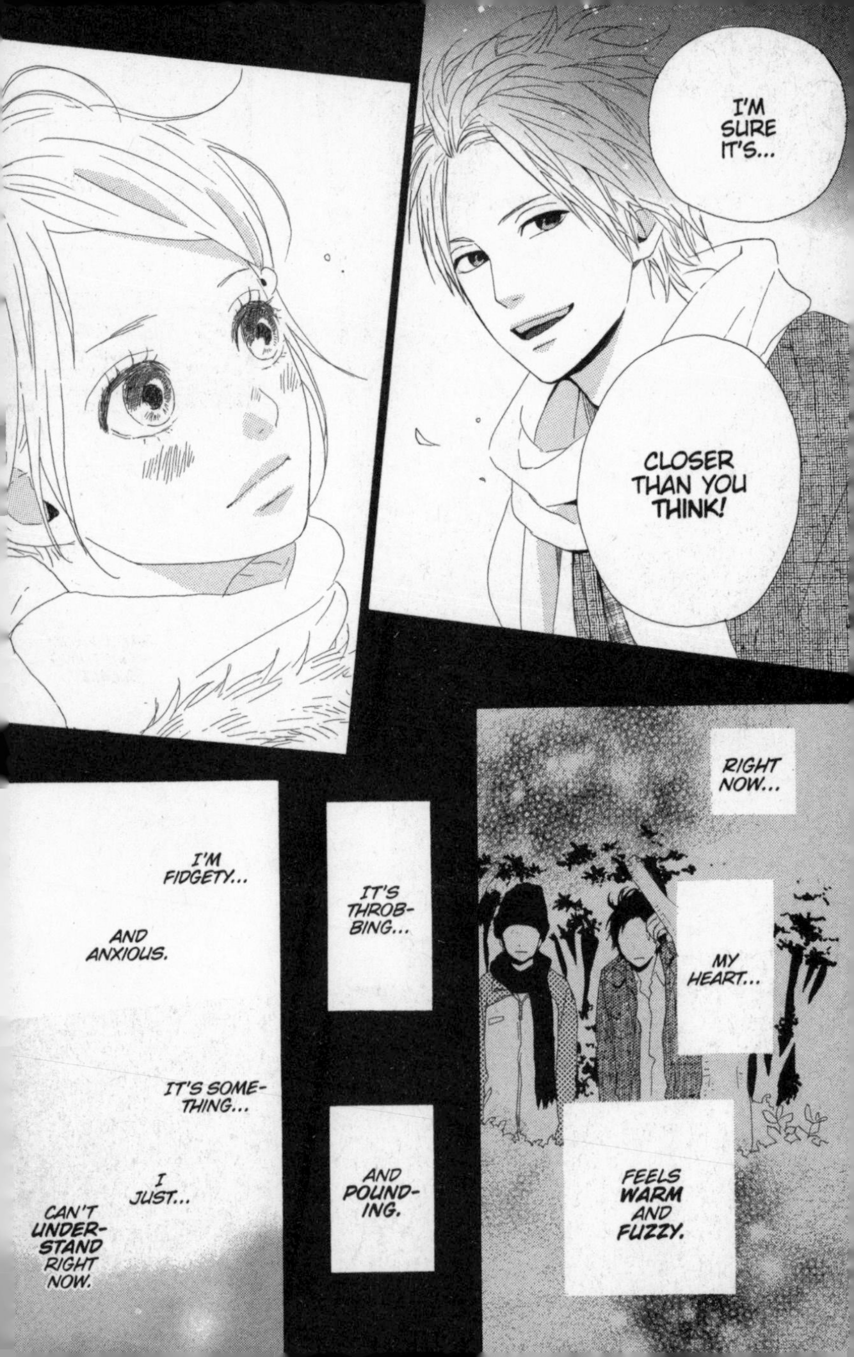
I'M SURE IT'S...
CLOSER THAN YOU THINK!
RIGHT NOW...
MY HEART...
FEELS WARM AND FUZZY.
IT'S THROBBING...
AND POUNDING.
I'M FIDGETY...
AND ANXIOUS.
IT'S SOMETHING...
I JUST...
CAN'T UNDERSTAND RIGHT NOW.

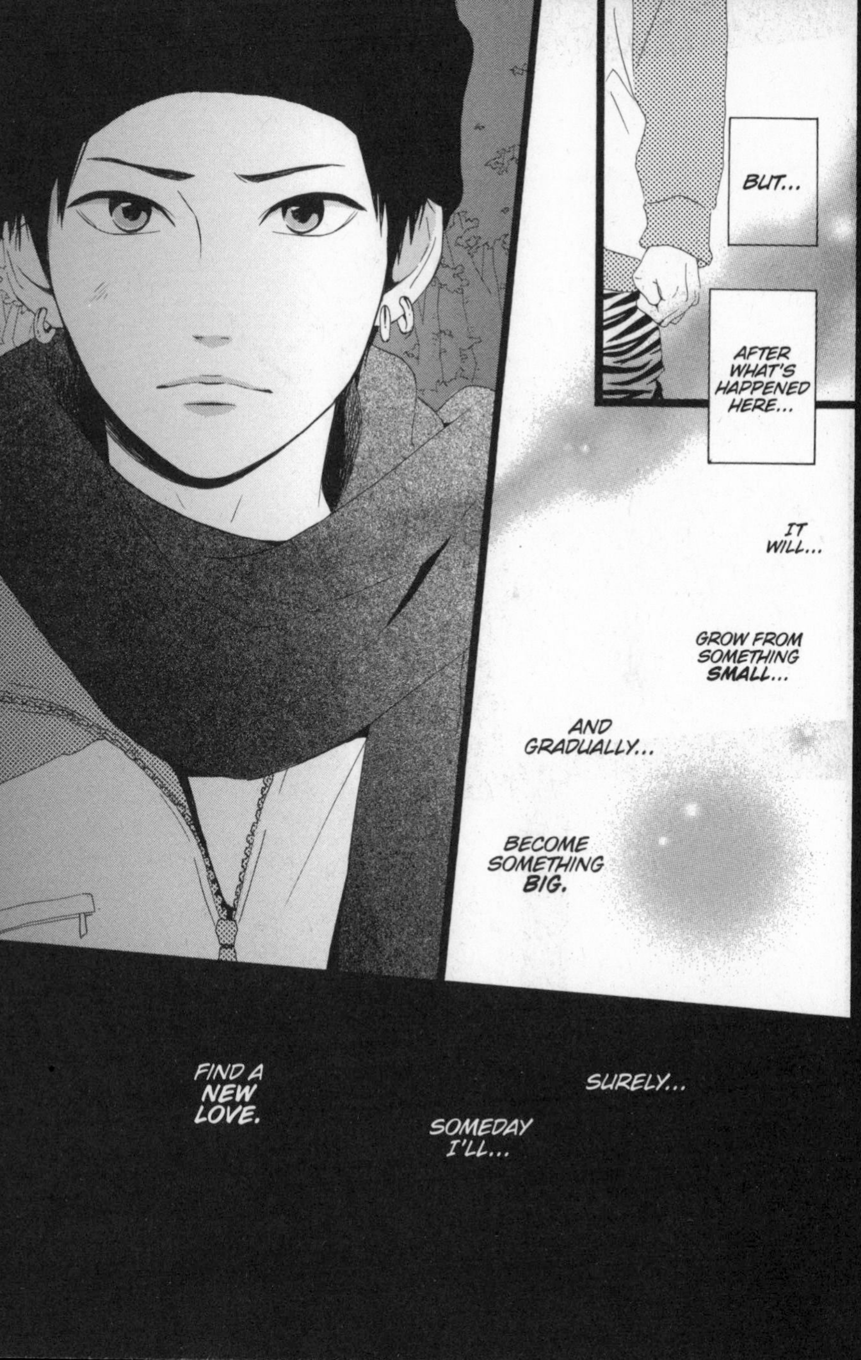
BUT...
AFTER WHAT'S HAPPENED HERE...
IT WILL...
GROW FROM SOMETHING SMALL...
AND GRADUALLY...
BECOME SOMETHING BIG.
SURELY...
SOMEDAY I'LL...
FIND A NEW LOVE.

Before the Realization

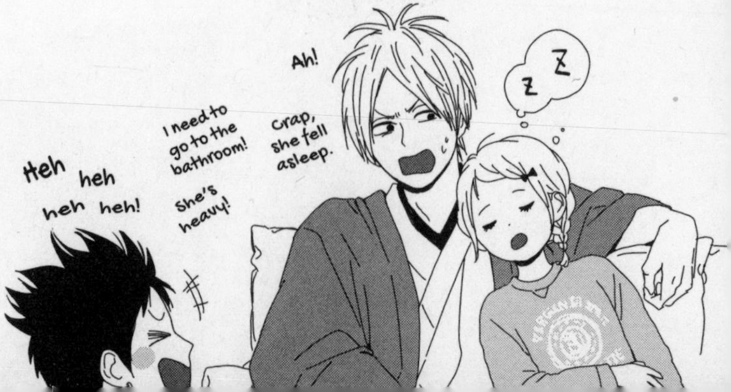
Z Z
Ah!
Crap, she fell asleep.
I need to go to the bathroom!
She's heavy!
Heh heh heh heh!

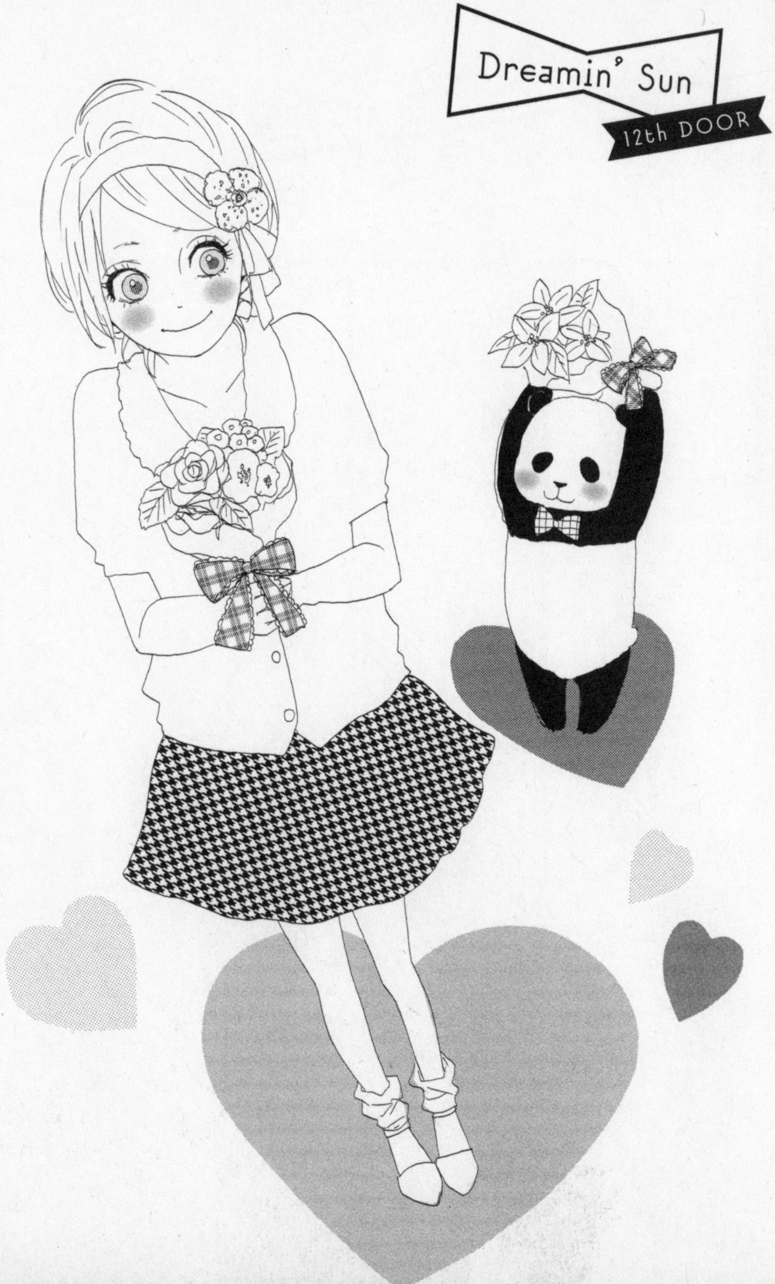
Dreamin' Sun
12th DOOR

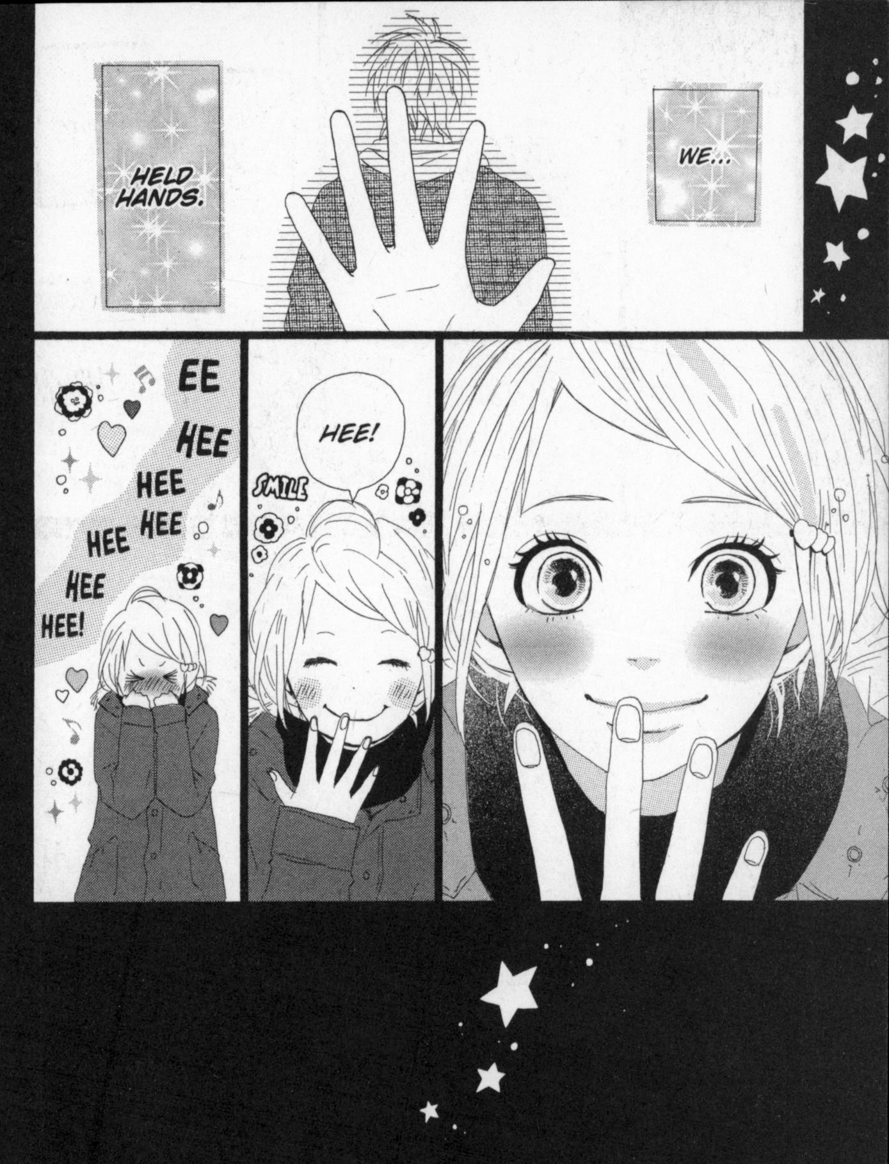
WE...
HELD HANDS.
HEE!
SMILE
EE HEE HEE HEE HEE HEE HEE!

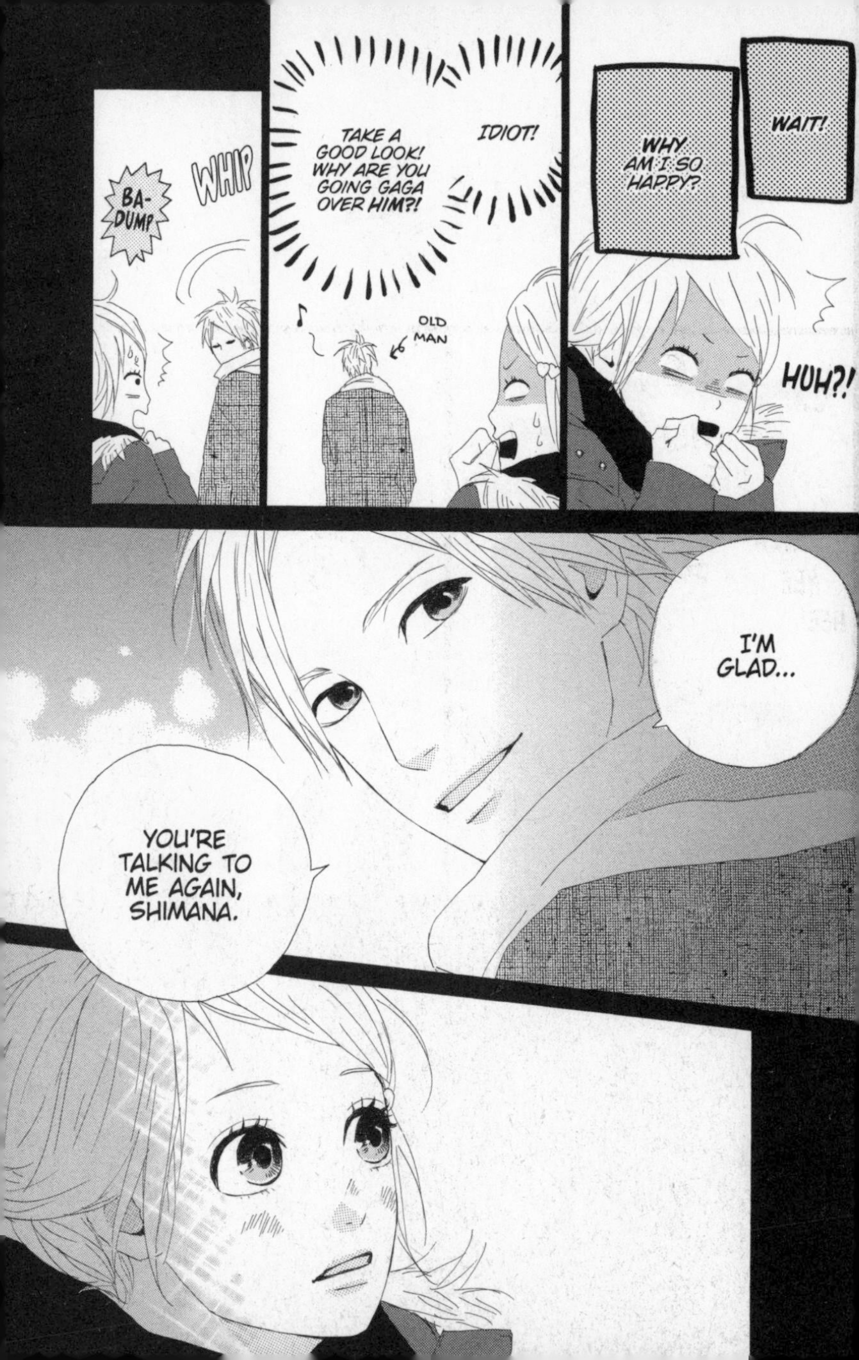
WAIT!
WHY AM I SO HAPPY?
HUH?!
IDIOT!
TAKE A GOOD LOOK! WHY ARE YOU GOING GAGA OVER HIM?!
OLD MAN
WHIP
BA-DUMP
I'M GLAD...
YOU'RE TALKING TO ME AGAIN, SHIMANA.

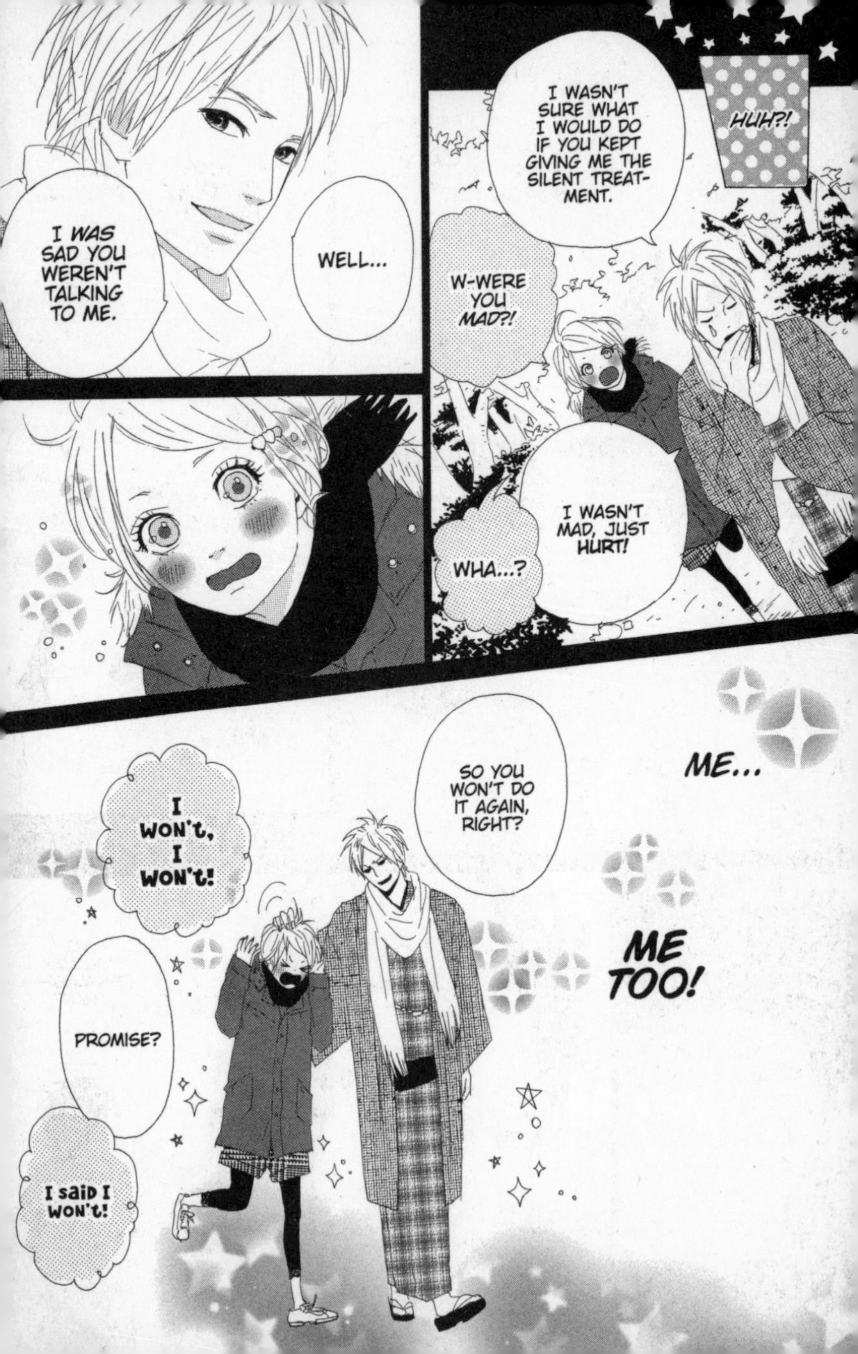
HUH?!
I WASN'T SURE WHAT I WOULD DO IF YOU KEPT GIVING ME THE SILENT TREAT-MENT.
W-WERE YOU MAD?!
I WASN'T MAD, JUST HURT!
WHA...?
WELL...
I WAS SAD YOU WEREN'T TALKING TO ME.
ME...
SO YOU WON'T DO IT AGAIN, RIGHT?
I WON'T, I WON'T!
ME TOO!
PROMISE?
I said I WON'T!

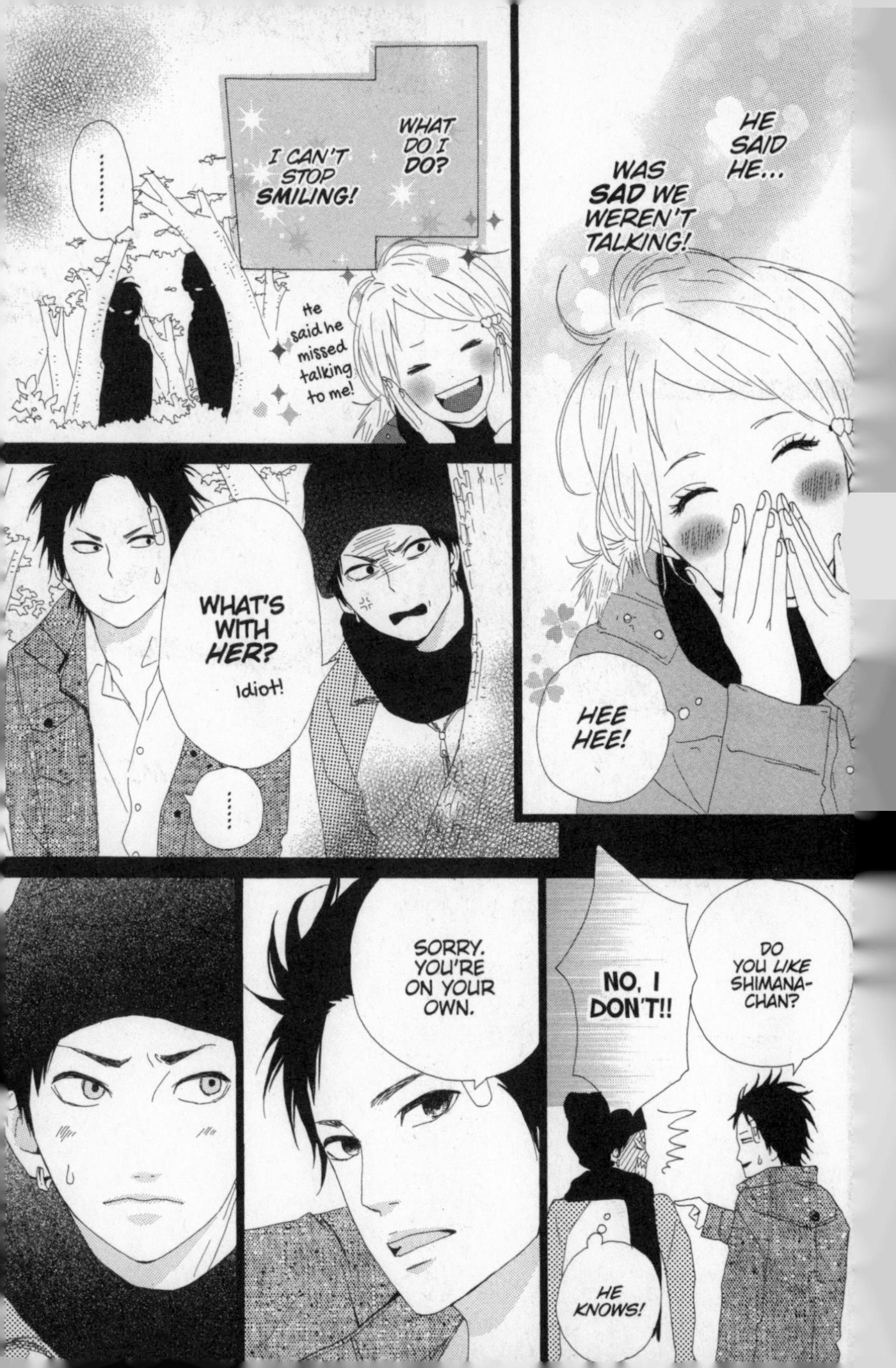
HE SAID HE...
WAS SAD WE WEREN'T TALKING!
HEE HEE!
WHAT DO I DO?
I CAN'T STOP SMILING!
He said he missed talking to me!
......
WHAT'S WITH HER?
Idiot!
......
DO YOU LIKE SHIMANA-CHAN?
NO, I DON'T!!
HE KNOWS!
SORRY. YOU'RE ON YOUR OWN.

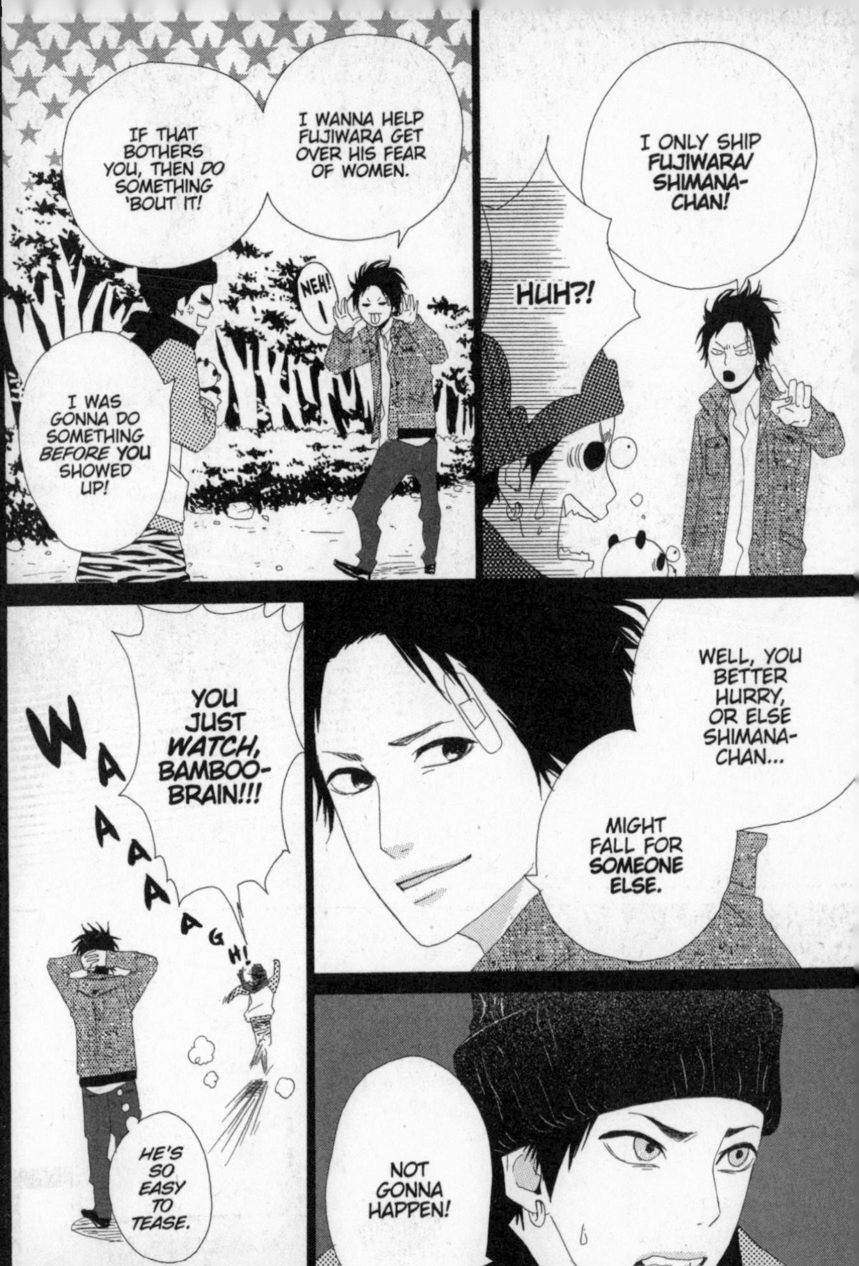
I ONLY SHIP FUJIWARA/ SHIMANA-CHAN!
HUH?!
I WANNA HELP FUJIWARA GET OVER HIS FEAR OF WOMEN.
IF THAT BOTHERS YOU, THEN DO SOMETHING 'BOUT IT!
NEH!
I WAS GONNA DO SOMETHING BEFORE YOU SHOWED UP!
WELL, YOU BETTER HURRY, OR ELSE SHIMANA-CHAN...
MIGHT FALL FOR SOMEONE ELSE.
NOT GONNA HAPPEN!
YOU JUST WATCH, BAMBOO-BRAIN!!!
WAAAAAAGH!
HE'S SO EASY TO TEASE.

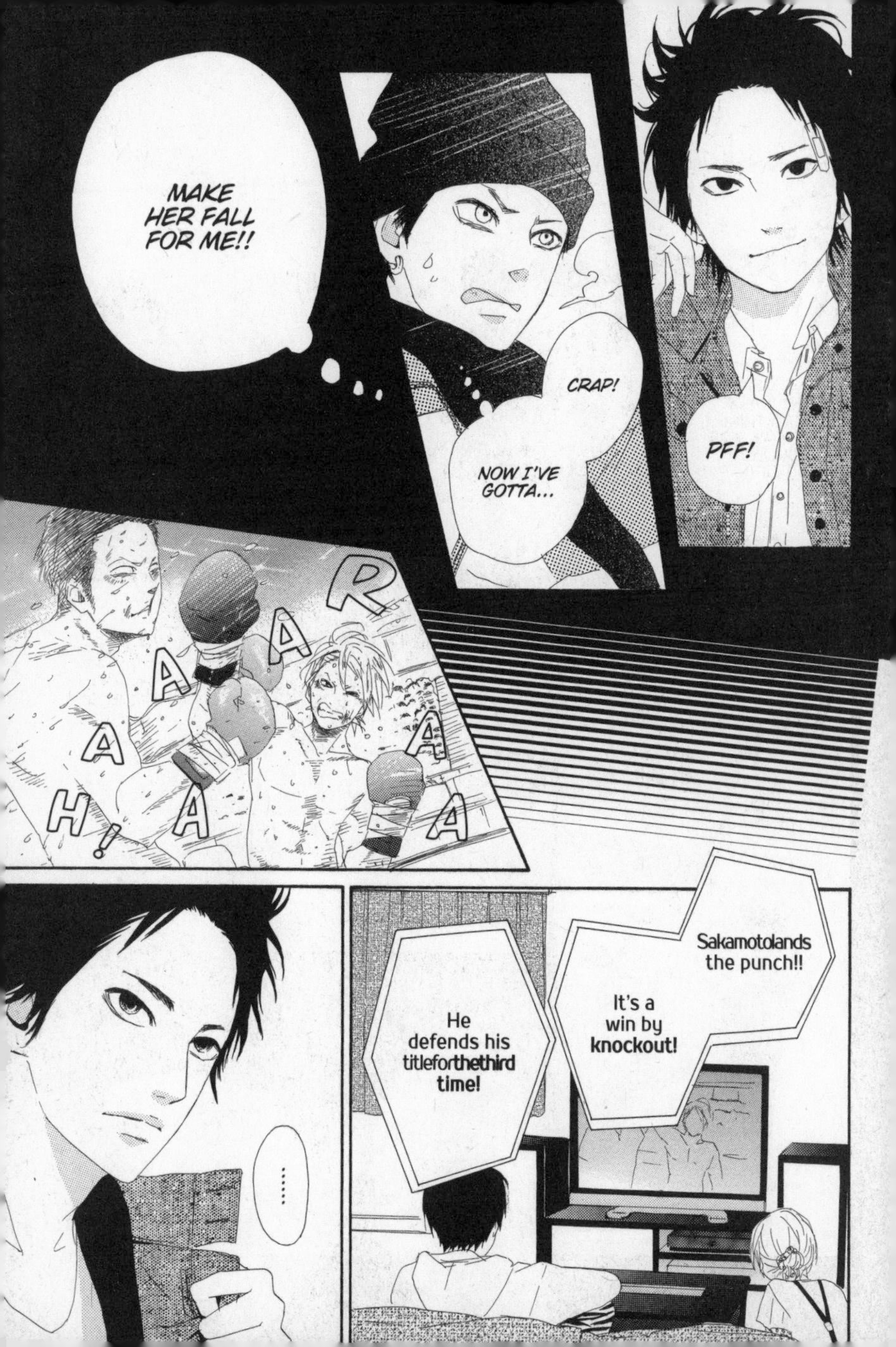
PFF!
CRAP!
NOW I'VE GOTTA...
MAKE HER FALL FOR ME!!
RAAAAAAH!
Sakamoto lands the punch!!
It's a win by knockout!
He defends his title for the third time!
......

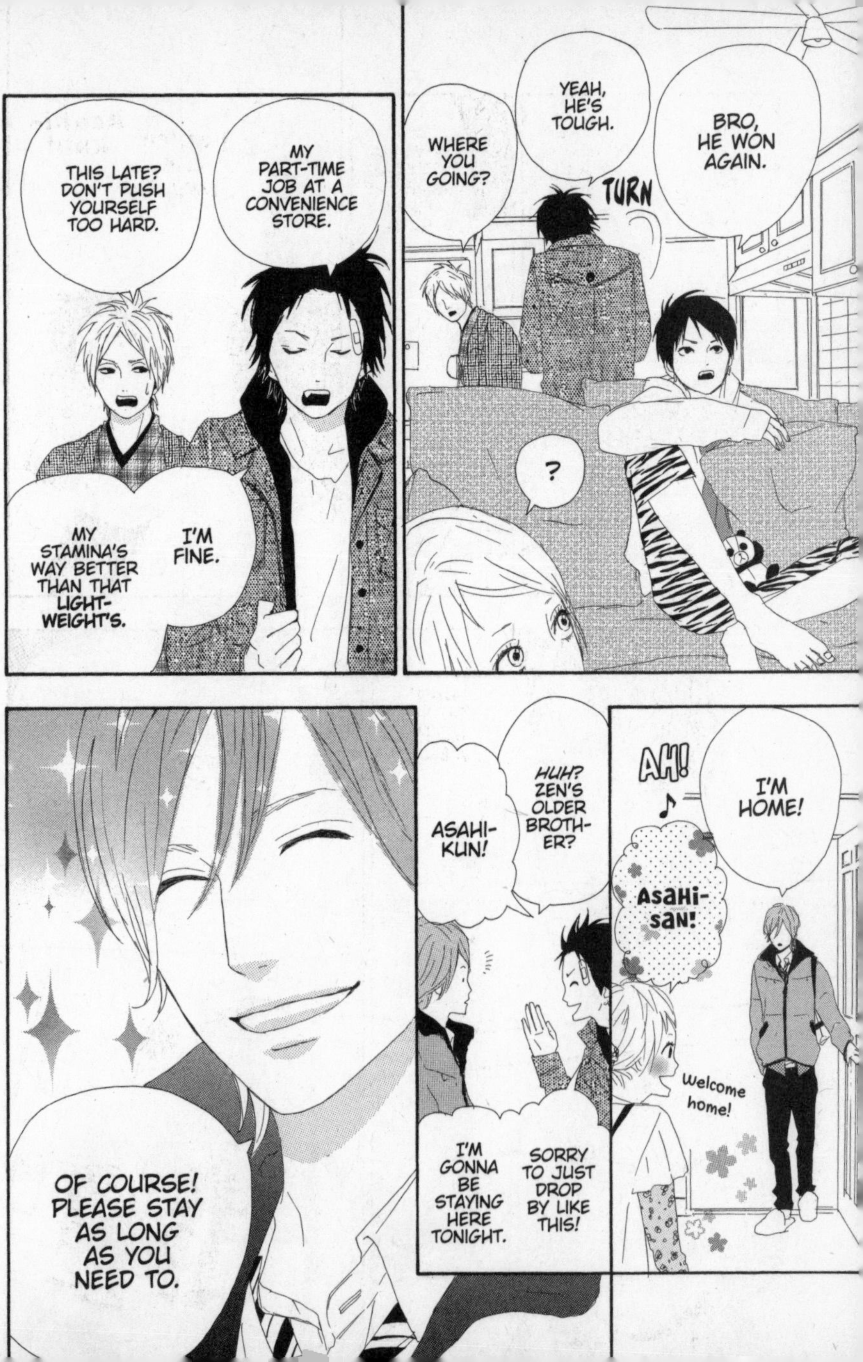
BRO, HE WON AGAIN.
YEAH, HE'S TOUGH.
TURN
WHERE YOU GOING?
?
MY PART-TIME JOB AT A CONVENIENCE STORE.
THIS LATE? DON'T PUSH YOURSELF TOO HARD.
I'M FINE.
MY STAMINA'S WAY BETTER THAN THAT LIGHT-WEIGHT'S.
I'M HOME!
AH!
Asahi-san!
Welcome home!
HUH? ZEN'S OLDER BROTHER?
ASAHI-KUN!
SORRY TO JUST DROP BY LIKE THIS!
I'M GONNA BE STAYING HERE TONIGHT.
OF COURSE! PLEASE STAY AS LONG AS YOU NEED TO.

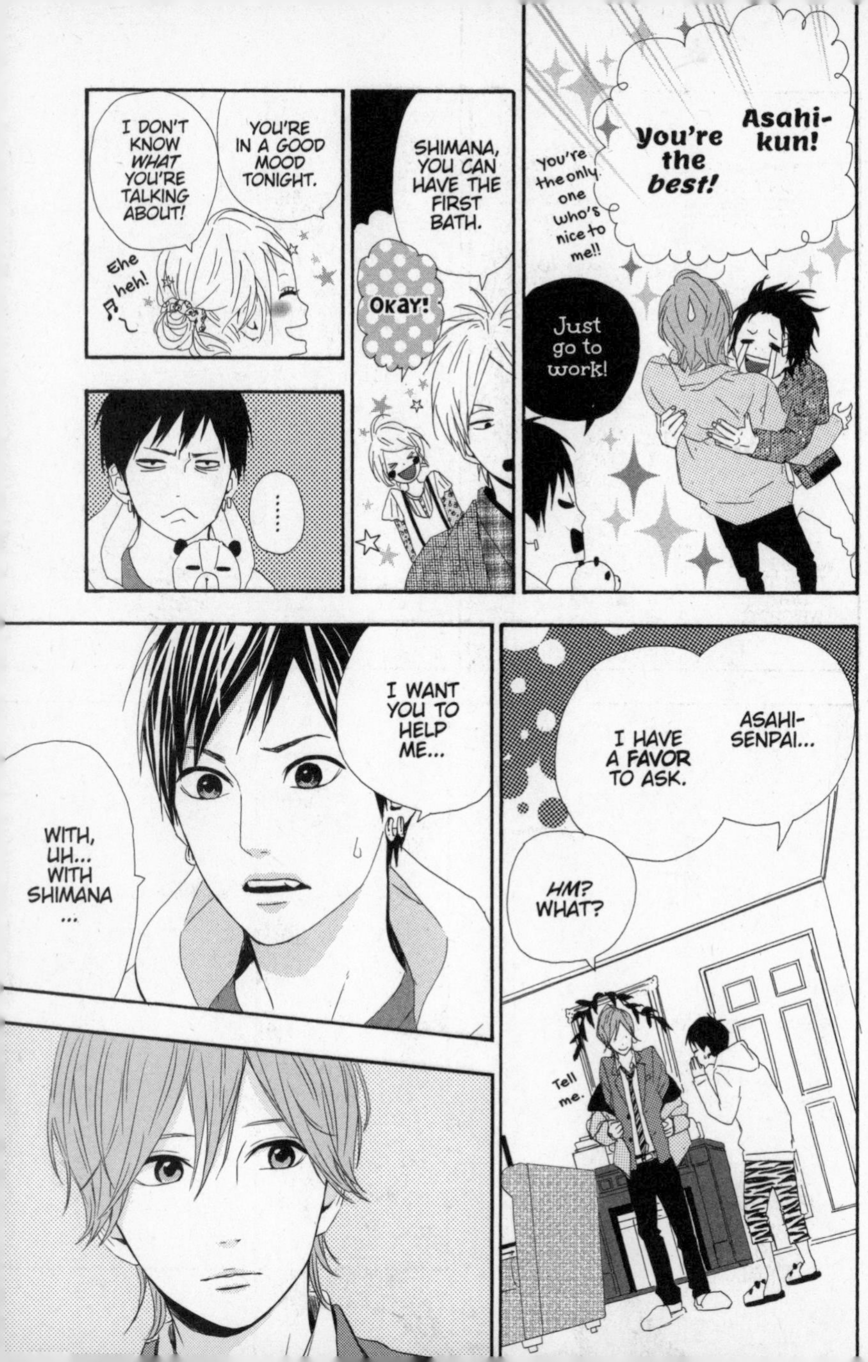
Asahi-kun! You're the best!
You're the only one who's nice to me!!
Just go to work!
SHIMANA, YOU CAN HAVE THE FIRST BATH.
OKAY!
YOU'RE IN A GOOD MOOD TONIGHT.
I DON'T KNOW WHAT YOU'RE TALKING ABOUT!
Ehe heh!
......
ASAHI-SENPAI...
I HAVE A FAVOR TO ASK.
HM? WHAT?
Tell me.
I WANT YOU TO HELP ME...
WITH, UH... WITH SHIMANA...

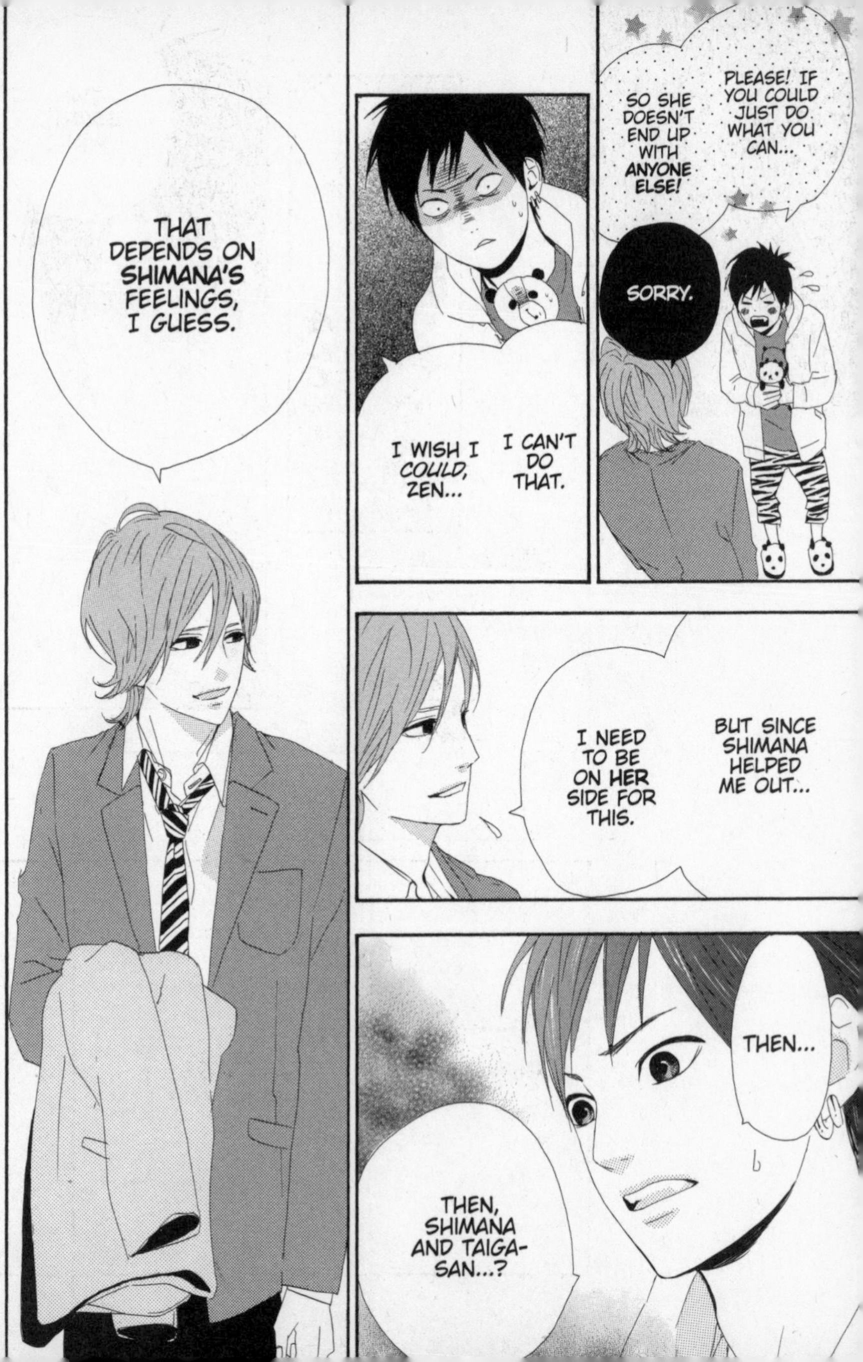
PLEASE! IF YOU COULD JUST DO WHAT YOU CAN...
SO SHE DOESN'T END UP WITH ANYONE ELSE!
SORRY.
I CAN'T DO THAT.
I WISH I COULD, ZEN...
BUT SINCE SHIMANA HELPED ME OUT...
I NEED TO BE ON HER SIDE FOR THIS.
THEN...
THEN, SHIMANA AND TAIGA-SAN...?
THAT DEPENDS ON SHIMANA'S FEELINGS, I GUESS.

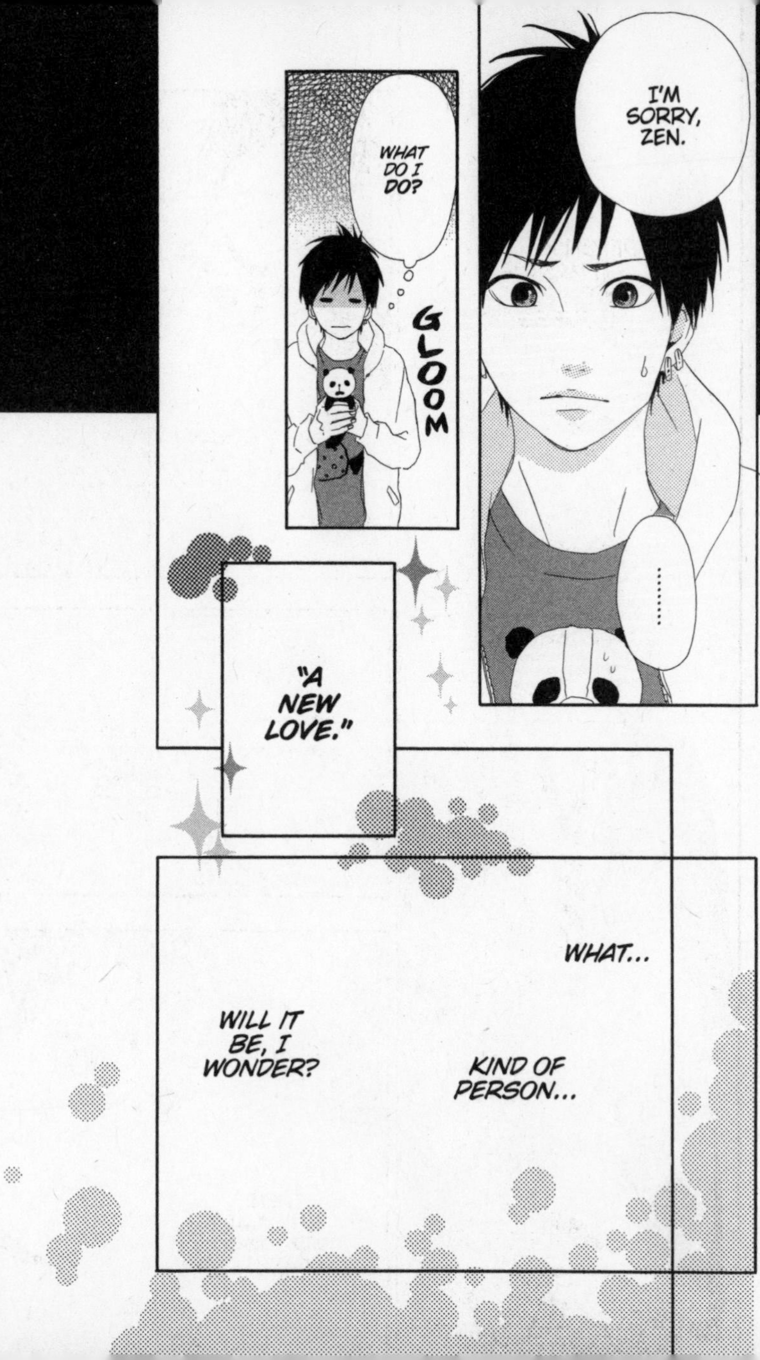
I'M SORRY, ZEN.
WHAT DO I DO?
GLOOM
......
"A NEW LOVE."
WHAT...
KIND OF PERSON...
WILL IT BE, I WONDER?

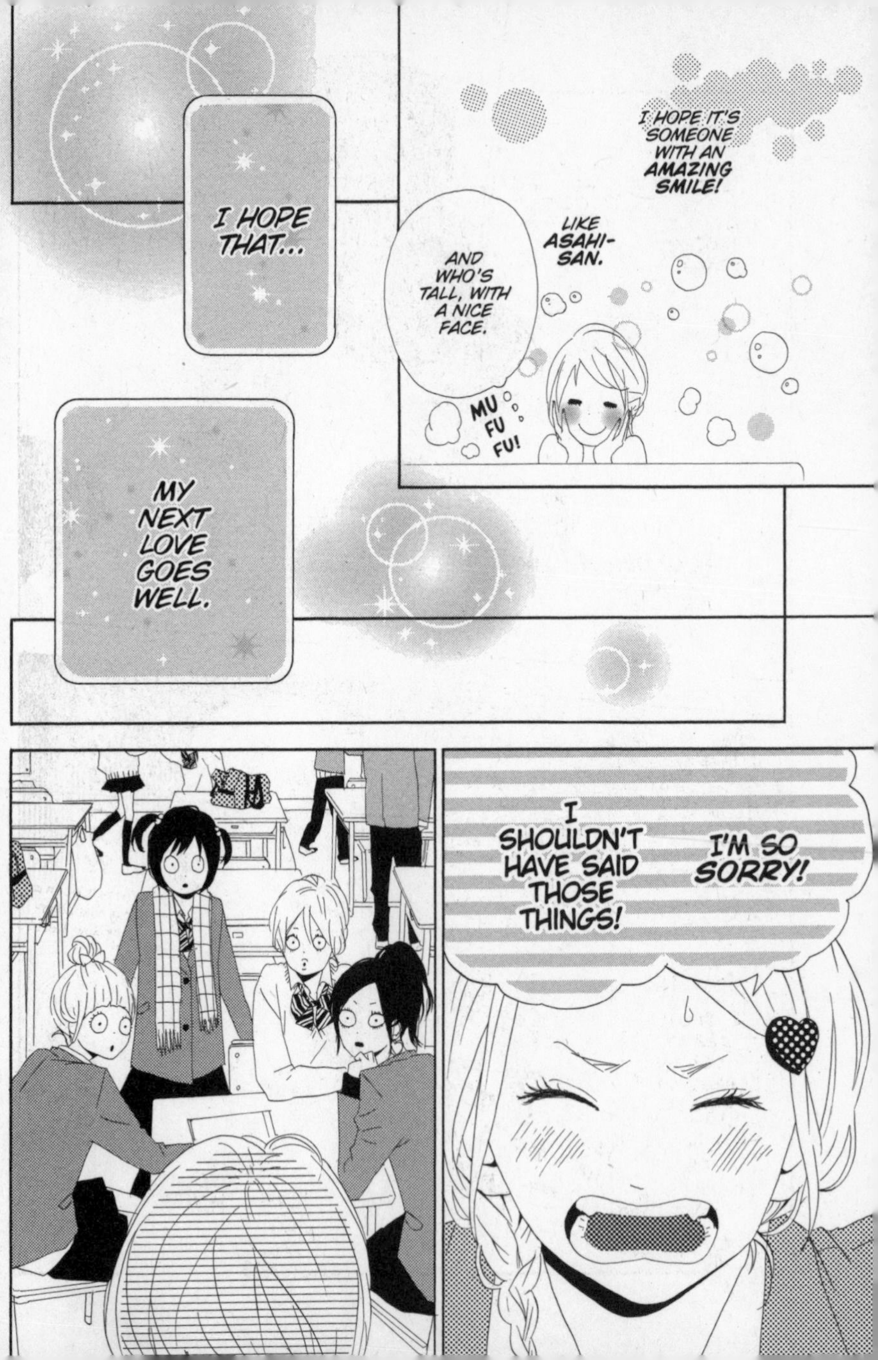
I HOPE IT'S SOMEONE WITH AN AMAZING SMILE!
LIKE ASAHI-SAN.
AND WHO'S TALL, WITH A NICE FACE.
MU FU FU!
I HOPE THAT...
MY NEXT LOVE GOES WELL.
I SHOULDN'T HAVE SAID THOSE THINGS!
I'M SO SORRY!

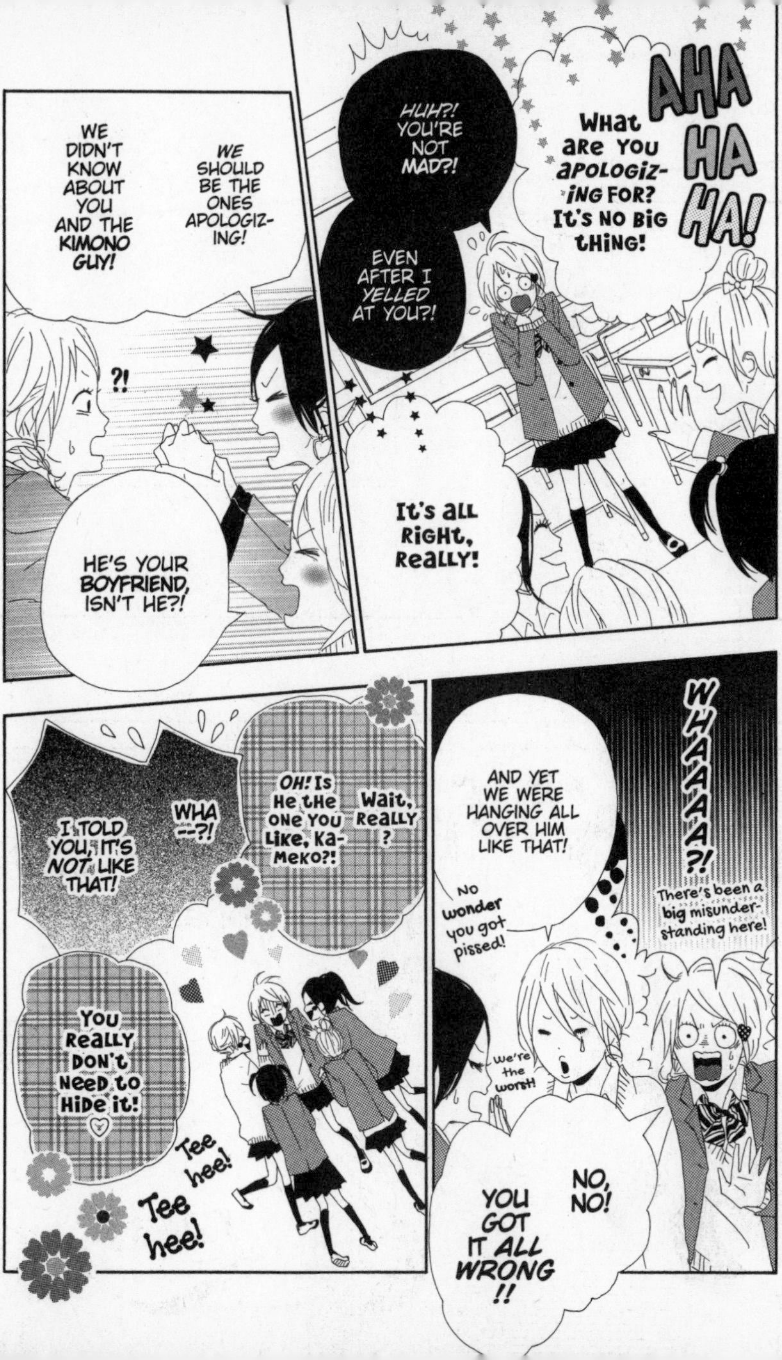
AHA HA HA!
What are you apologizing for? It's no big thing!
HUH?! YOU'RE NOT MAD?!
EVEN AFTER I YELLED AT YOU?!
It's all right, really!
WE SHOULD BE THE ONES APOLOGIZING!
WE DIDN'T KNOW ABOUT YOU AND THE KIMONO GUY!
?!
HE'S YOUR BOYFRIEND, ISN'T HE?!
WHAAAAA?!
There's been a big misunderstanding here!
AND YET WE WERE HANGING ALL OVER HIM LIKE THAT!
No wonder you got pissed!
We're the worst!
NO, NO!
YOU GOT IT ALL WRONG!!
Wait, really?
OH! Is he the one you like, Kameko?!
WHA--?!
I TOLD YOU, IT'S NOT LIKE THAT!
You really don't need to hide it!
Tee hee!
Tee hee!

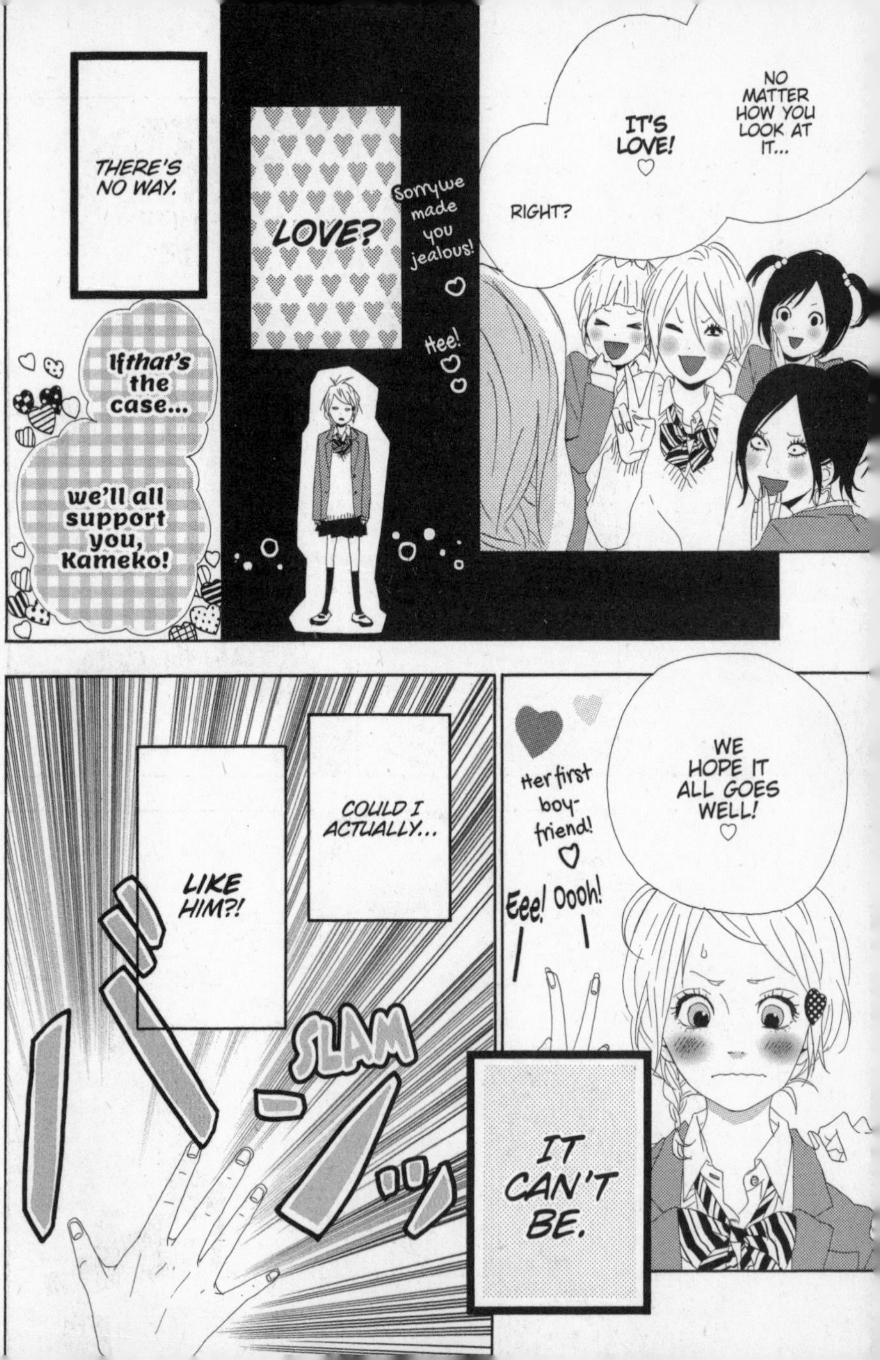
NO MATTER HOW YOU LOOK AT IT...
IT'S LOVE! ♡
RIGHT?
LOVE?
Sorry we made you jealous! ♡
Hee! ♡
THERE'S NO WAY.
If that's the case...
we'll all support you, Kameko!
WE HOPE IT ALL GOES WELL! ♡
Her first boy-friend! ♡
Oooh!
Eee!
IT CAN'T BE.
COULD I ACTUALLY...
LIKE HIM?!
SLAM

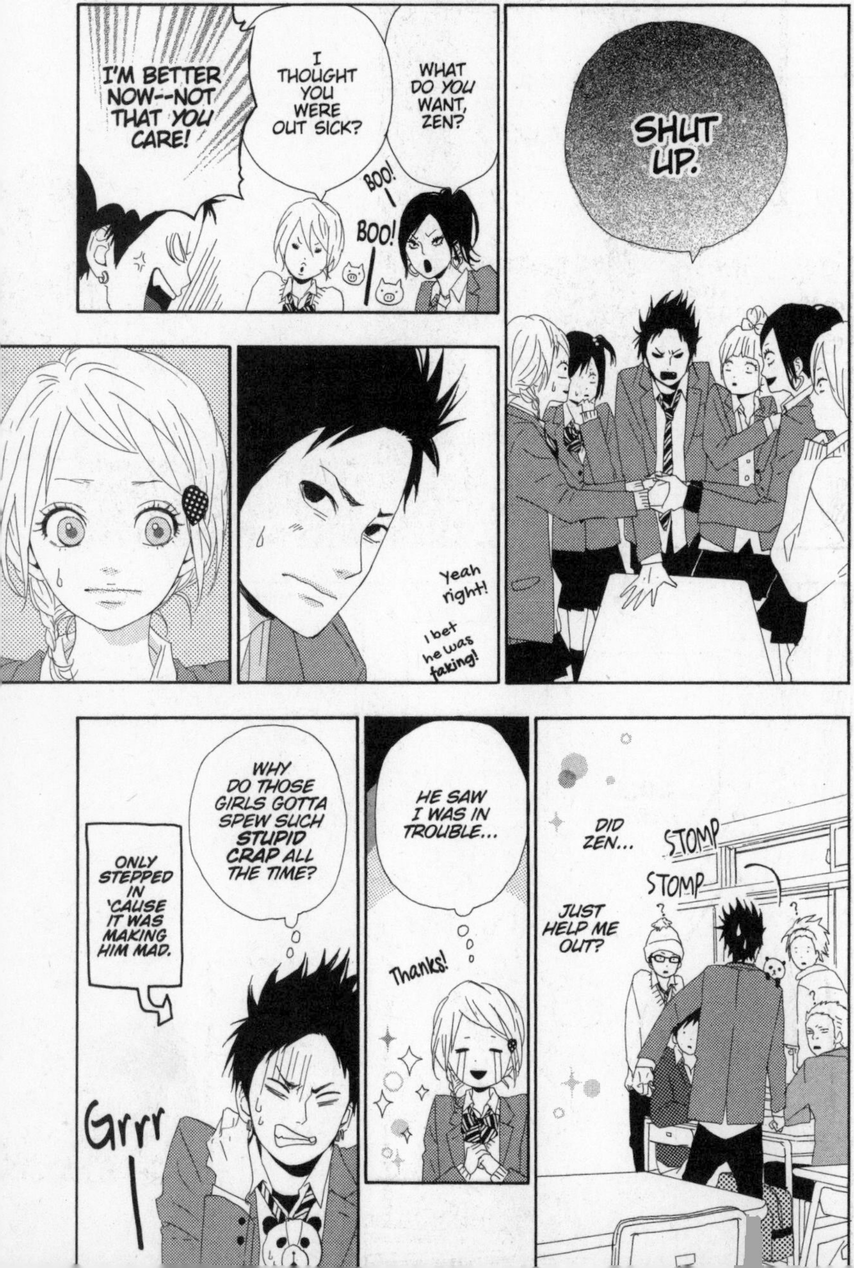
SHUT UP.
WHAT DO YOU WANT, ZEN?
I THOUGHT YOU WERE OUT SICK?
BOO!
BOO!
I'M BETTER NOW--NOT THAT YOU CARE!
Yeah right!
I bet he was faking!
DID ZEN...
STOMP
STOMP
JUST HELP ME OUT?
HE SAW I WAS IN TROUBLE...
Thanks!
WHY DO THOSE GIRLS GOTTA SPEW SUCH STUPID CRAP ALL THE TIME?
ONLY STEPPED IN 'CAUSE IT WAS MAKING HIM MAD.
Grrr

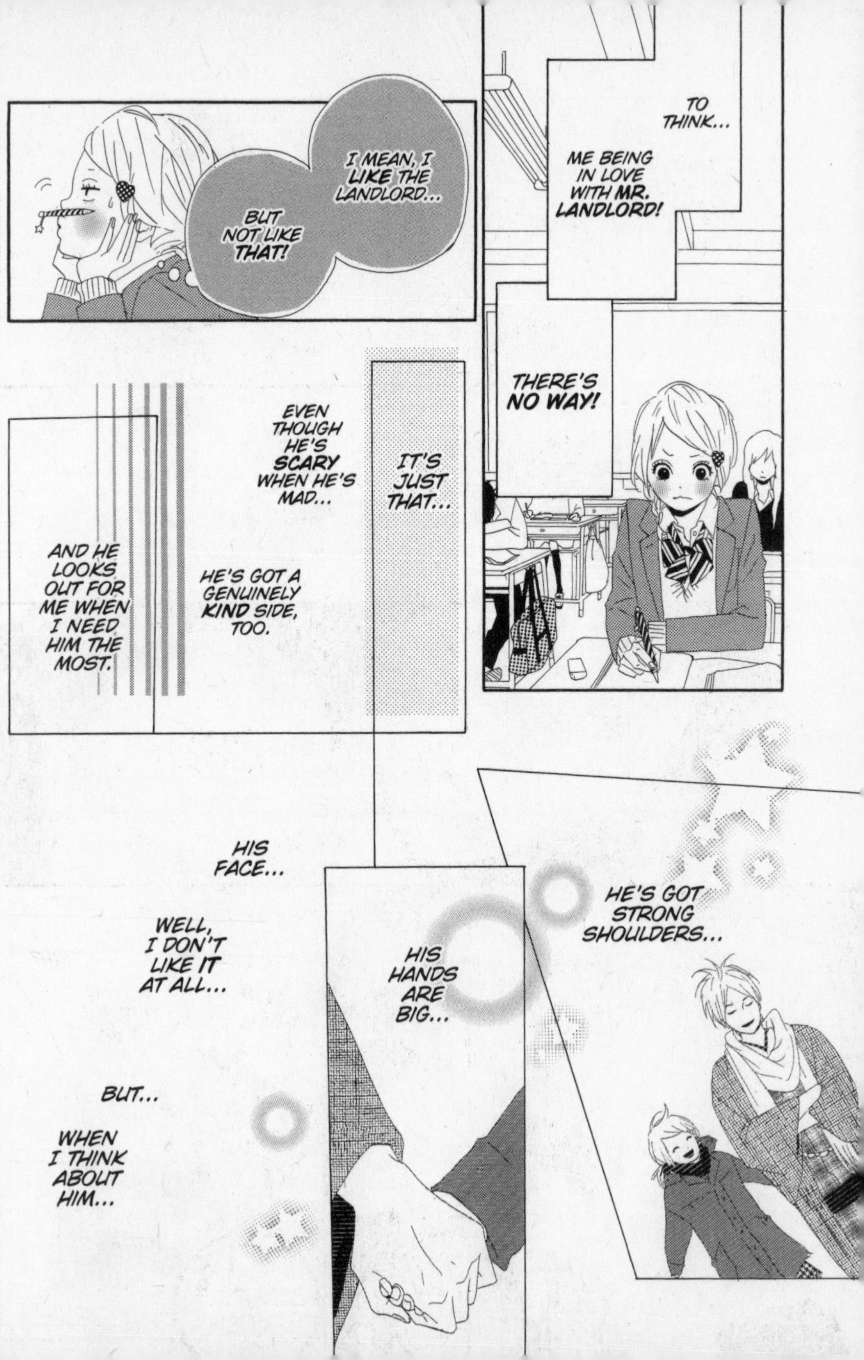
TO THINK...
ME BEING IN LOVE WITH MR. LANDLORD!
THERE'S NO WAY!
I MEAN, I LIKE THE LANDLORD...
BUT NOT LIKE THAT!
IT'S JUST THAT...
EVEN THOUGH HE'S SCARY WHEN HE'S MAD...
HE'S GOT A GENUINELY KIND SIDE, TOO.
AND HE LOOKS OUT FOR ME WHEN I NEED HIM THE MOST.
HE'S GOT STRONG SHOULDERS...
HIS HANDS ARE BIG...
HIS FACE...
WELL, I DON'T LIKE IT AT ALL...
BUT...
WHEN I THINK ABOUT HIM...

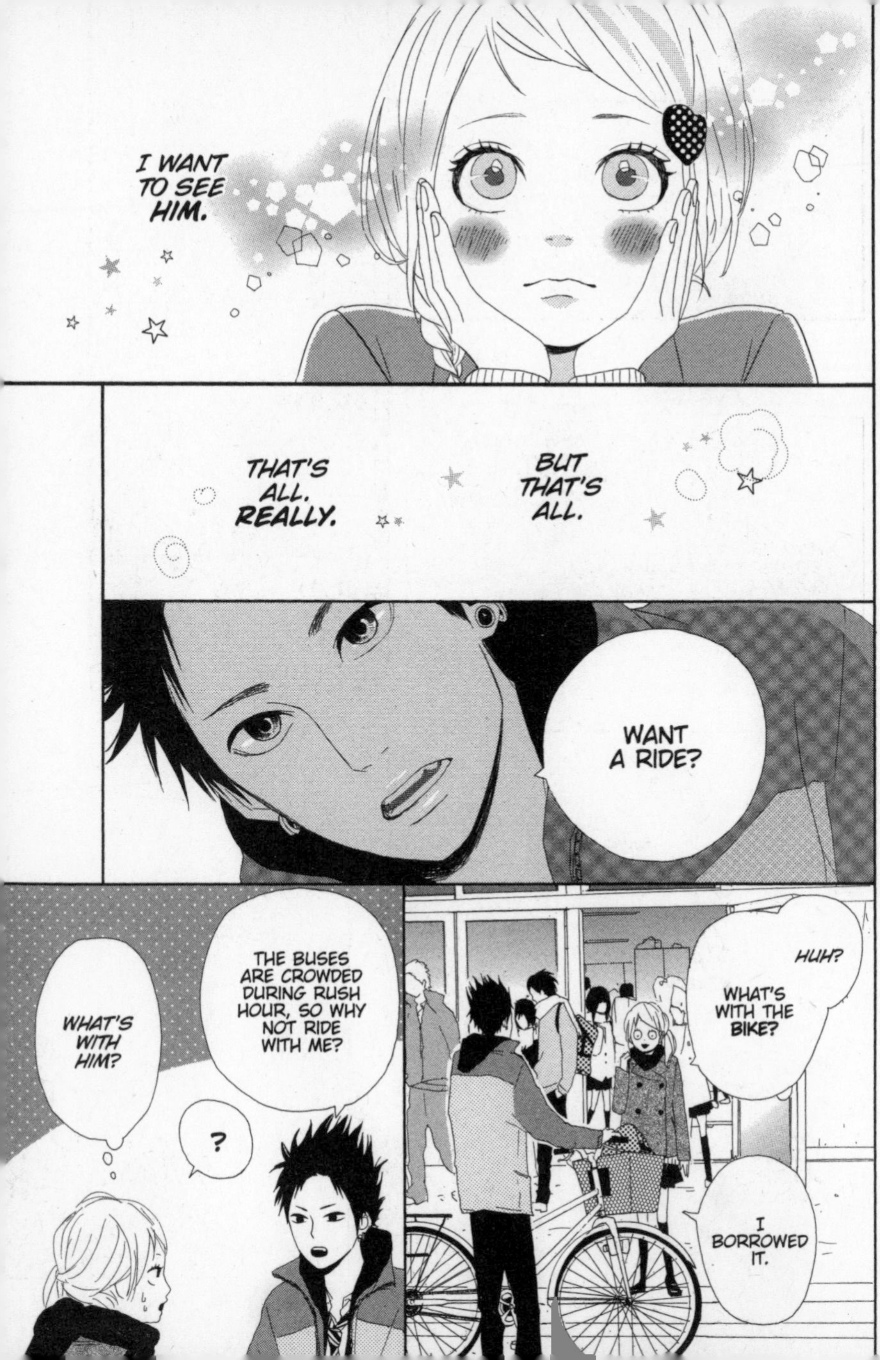
I WANT TO SEE HIM.
BUT THAT'S ALL.
THAT'S ALL. REALLY.
WANT A RIDE?
HUH?
WHAT'S WITH THE BIKE?
I BORROWED IT.
THE BUSES ARE CROWDED DURING RUSH HOUR, SO WHY NOT RIDE WITH ME?
WHAT'S WITH HIM?
?

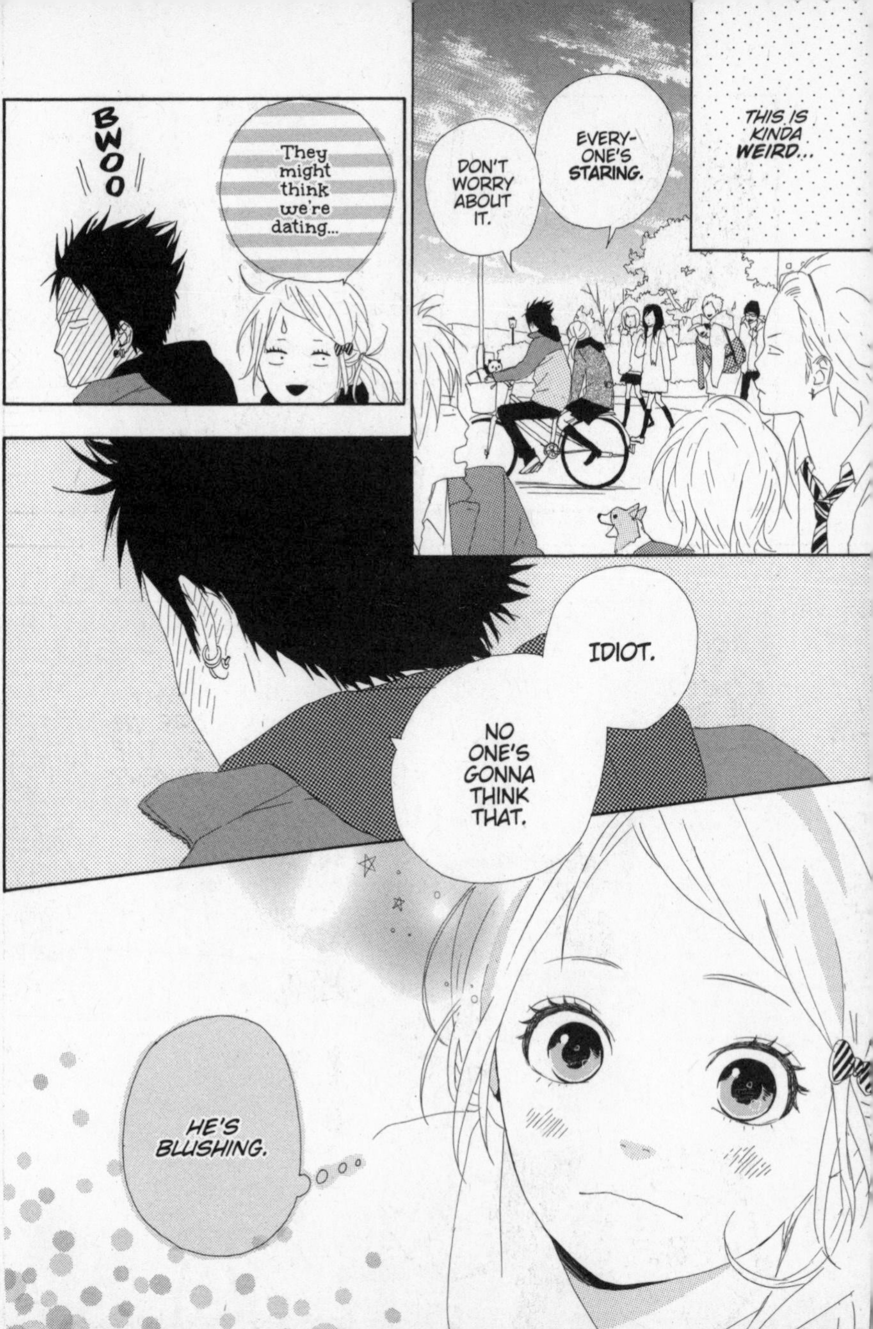
THIS IS KINDA WEIRD...
EVERY-ONE'S STARING.
DON'T WORRY ABOUT IT.
They might think we're dating...
BWOO
IDIOT.
NO ONE'S GONNA THINK THAT.
HE'S BLUSHING.

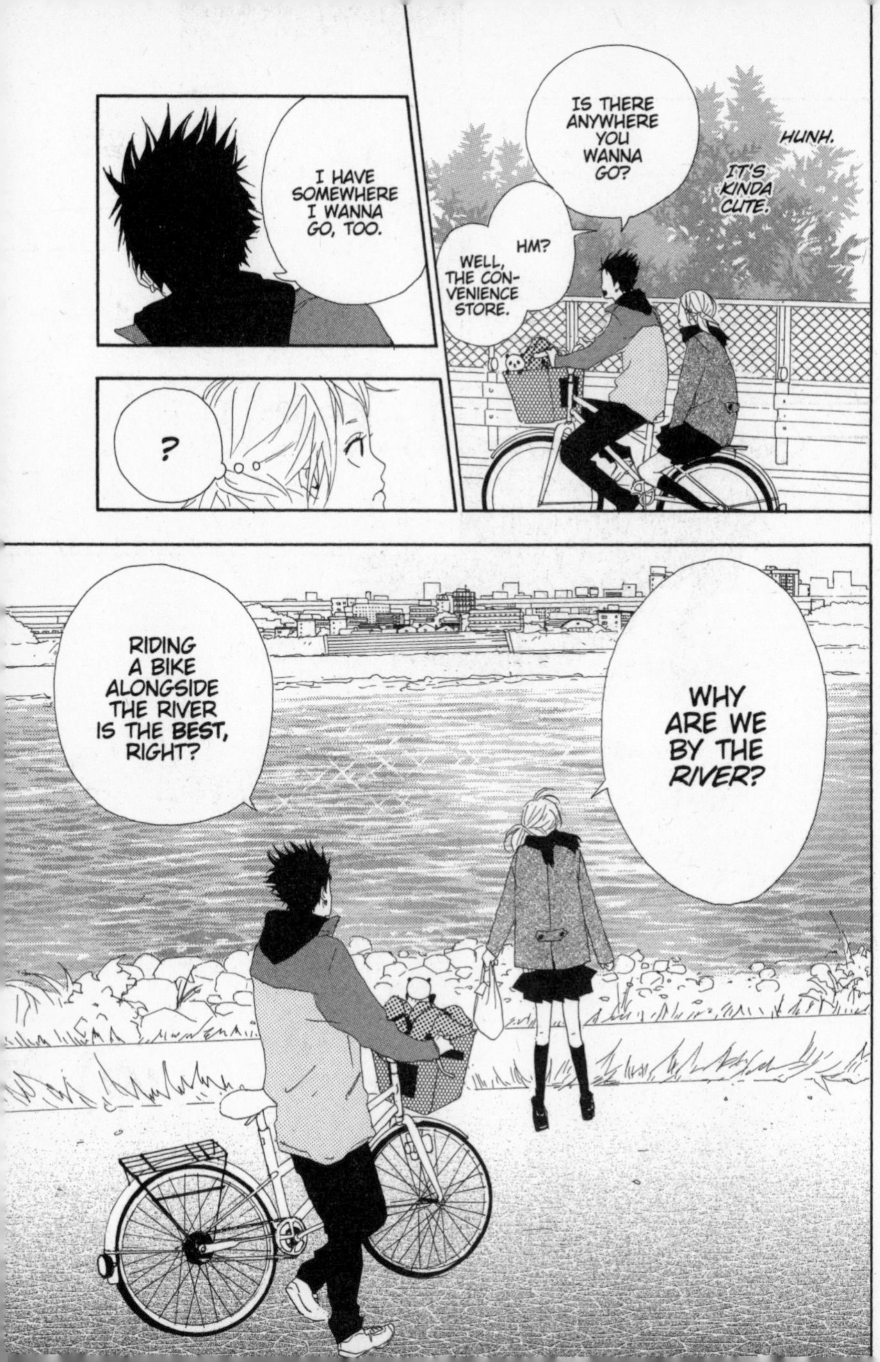
IS THERE ANYWHERE YOU WANNA GO?
HM? WELL, THE CON-VENIENCE STORE.
HUNH. IT'S KINDA CUTE.
I HAVE SOMEWHERE I WANNA GO, TOO.
?
WHY ARE WE BY THE *RIVER*?
RIDING A BIKE ALONGSIDE THE RIVER IS THE BEST, RIGHT?

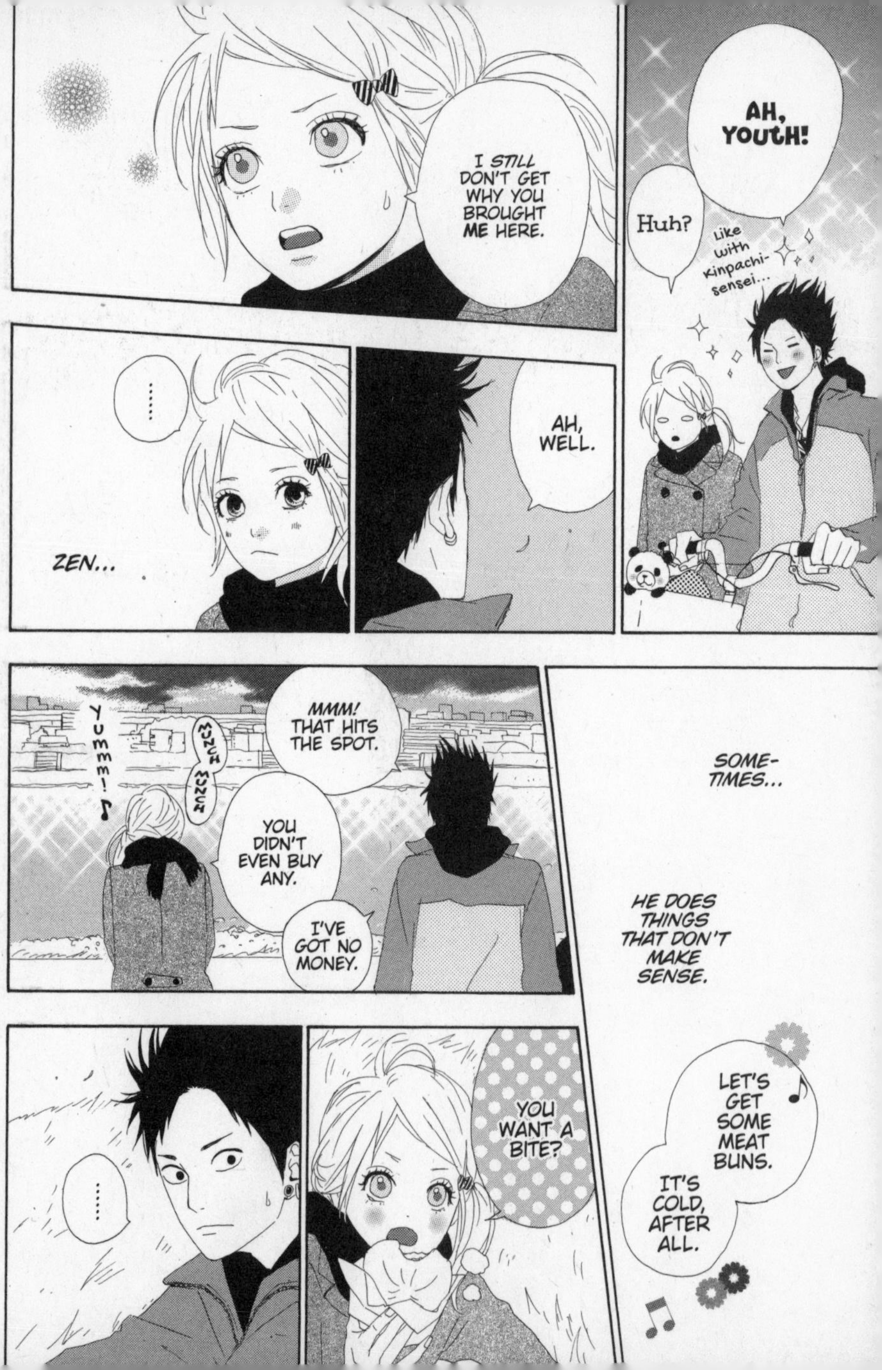
AH, YOUTH!
Like with Kinpachi-sensei...
Huh?
I STILL DON'T GET WHY YOU BROUGHT ME HERE.
AH, WELL.
......
ZEN...
SOME-TIMES...
HE DOES THINGS THAT DON'T MAKE SENSE.
LET'S GET SOME MEAT BUNS.
IT'S COLD, AFTER ALL.
MMM! THAT HITS THE SPOT.
MUNCH MUNCH
YUMMM!
YOU DIDN'T EVEN BUY ANY.
I'VE GOT NO MONEY.
YOU WANT A BITE?
......

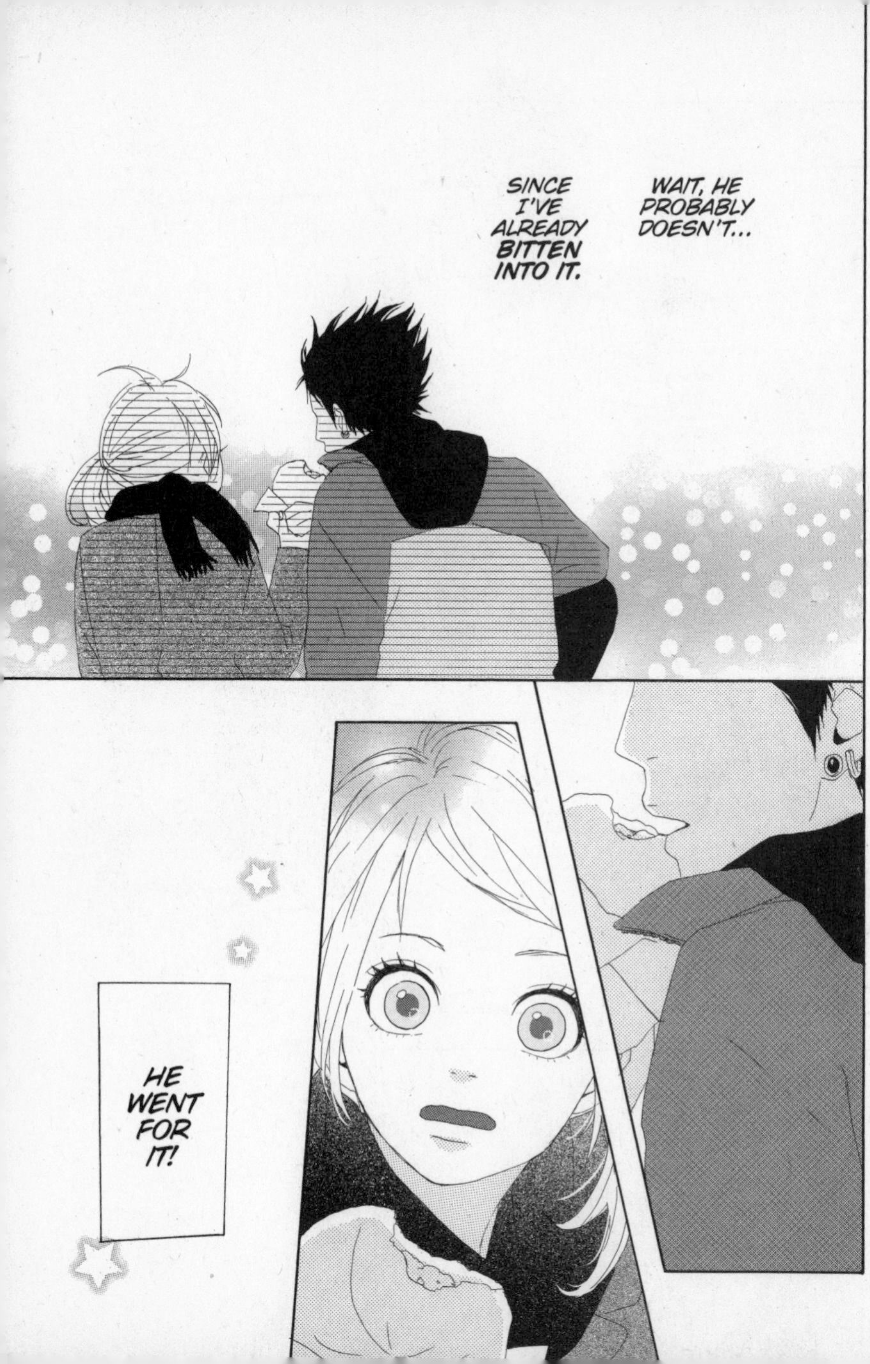
WAIT, HE PROBABLY DOESN'T...
SINCE I'VE ALREADY BITTEN INTO IT.
HE WENT FOR IT!

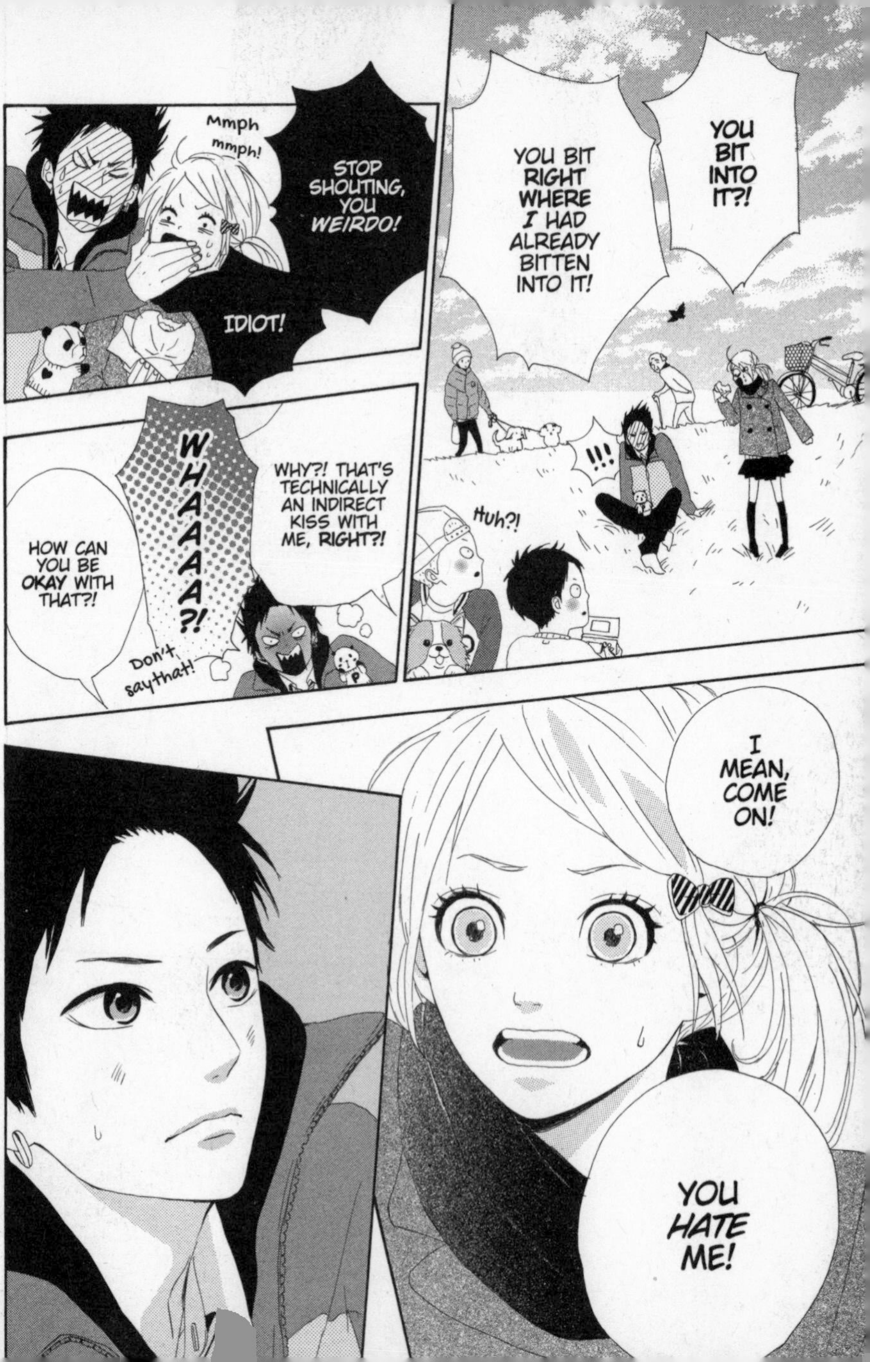
YOU BIT INTO IT?!
YOU BIT RIGHT WHERE I HAD ALREADY BITTEN INTO IT!
!!!
Huh?!
Mmph mmph!
STOP SHOUTING, YOU WEIRDO!
IDIOT!
WHY?! THAT'S TECHNICALLY AN INDIRECT KISS WITH ME, RIGHT?!
WHAAAAA?!
Don't say that!
HOW CAN YOU BE OKAY WITH THAT?!
I MEAN, COME ON!
YOU HATE ME!

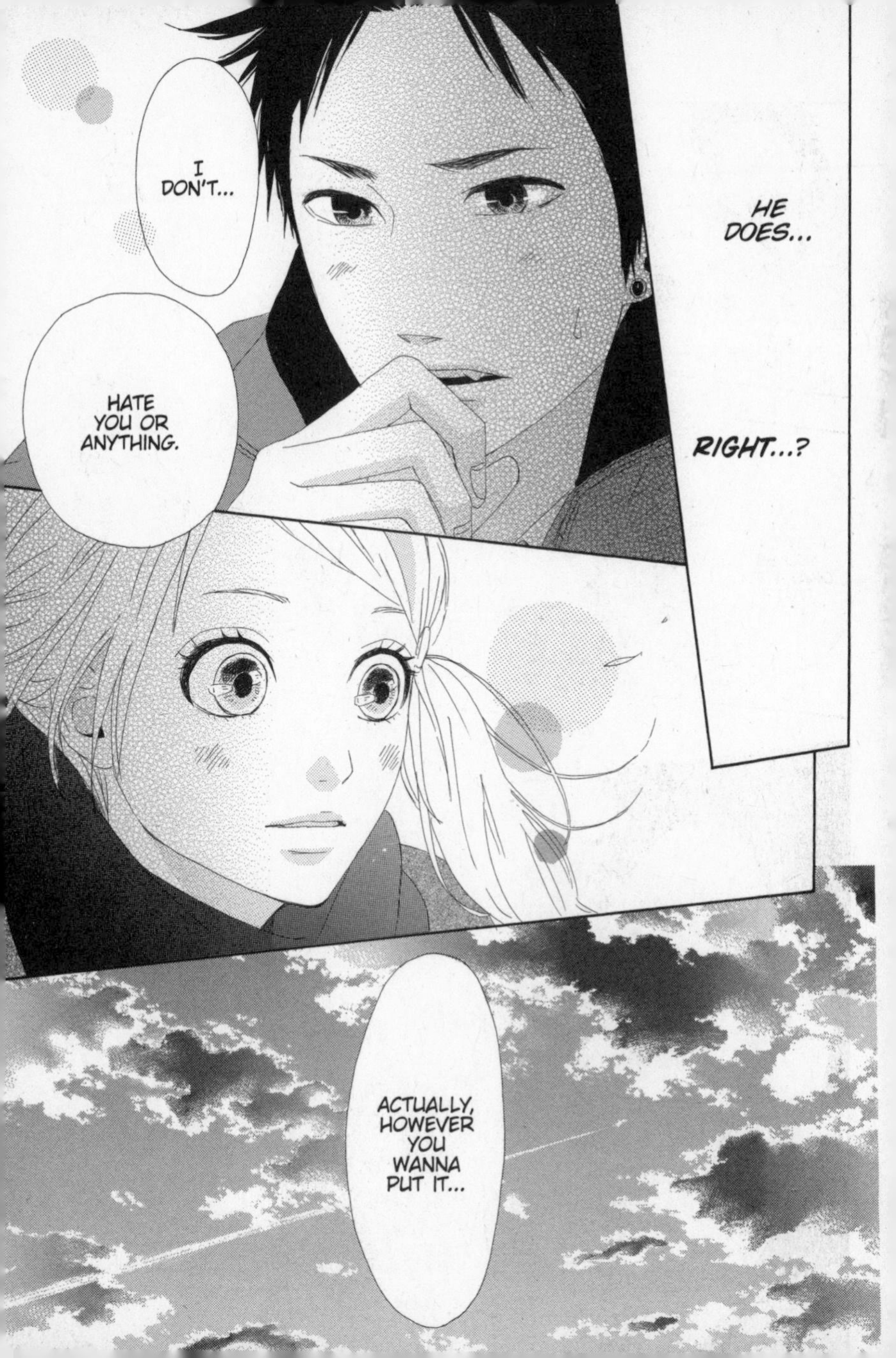
HE DOES...
RIGHT...?
I DON'T...
HATE YOU OR ANYTHING.
ACTUALLY, HOWEVER YOU WANNA PUT IT...

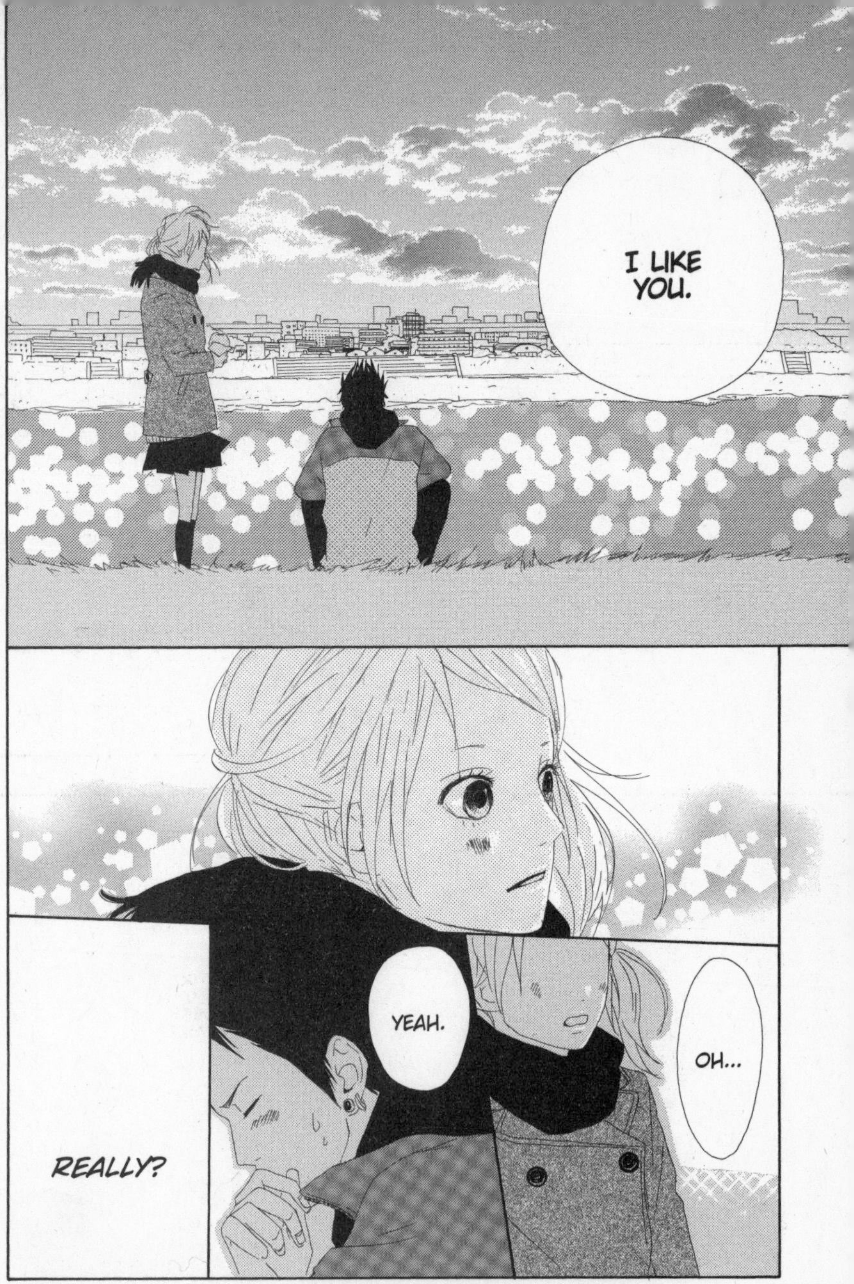
I LIKE YOU.
OH...
YEAH.
REALLY?

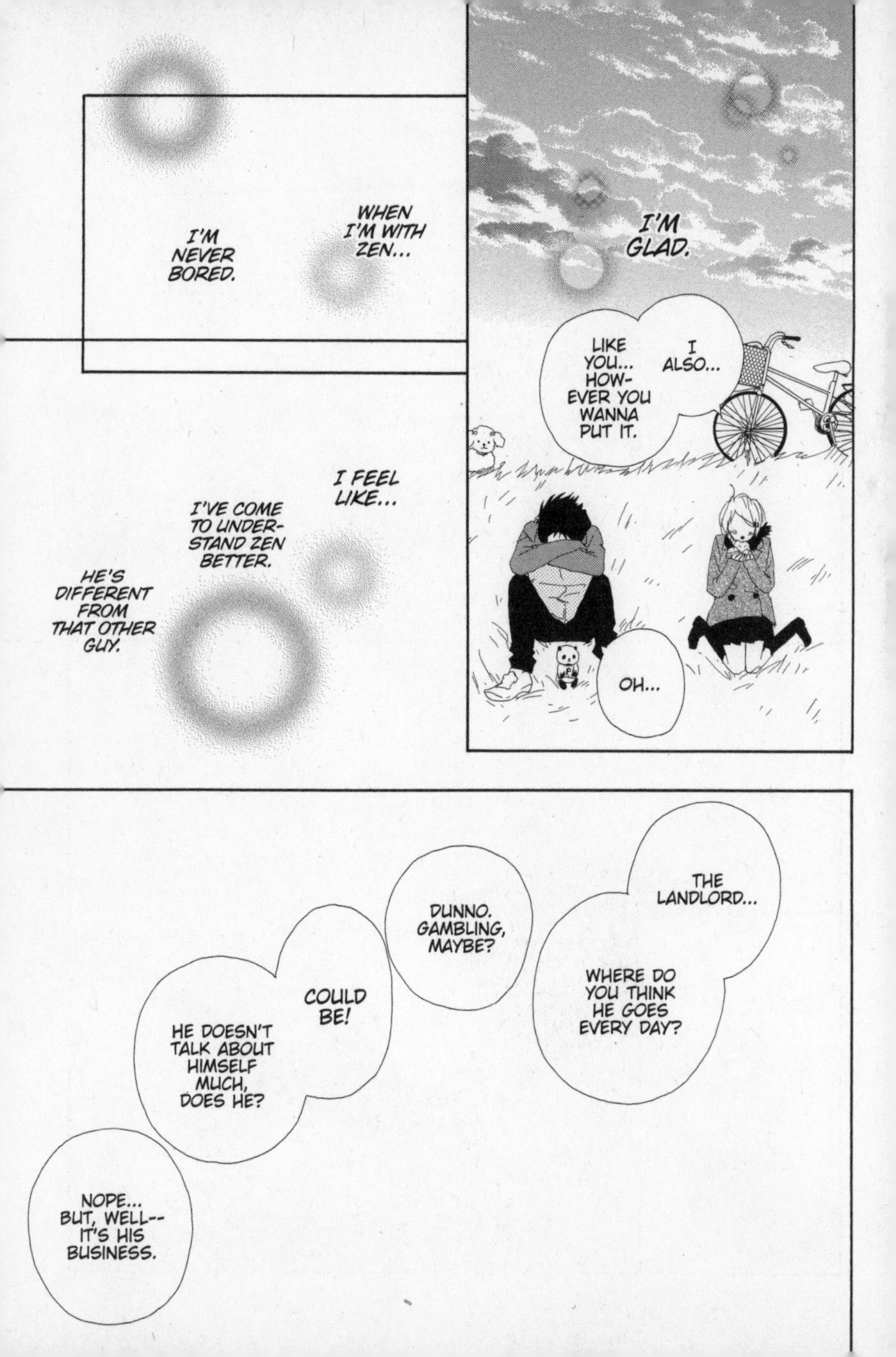
I'M GLAD.
I ALSO... LIKE YOU... HOW-EVER YOU WANNA PUT IT.
OH...
WHEN I'M WITH ZEN...
I'M NEVER BORED.
I FEEL LIKE...
I'VE COME TO UNDER-STAND ZEN BETTER.
HE'S DIFFERENT FROM THAT OTHER GUY.
THE LANDLORD...
WHERE DO YOU THINK HE GOES EVERY DAY?
DUNNO. GAMBLING, MAYBE?
COULD BE!
HE DOESN'T TALK ABOUT HIMSELF MUCH, DOES HE?
NOPE... BUT, WELL-- IT'S HIS BUSINESS.

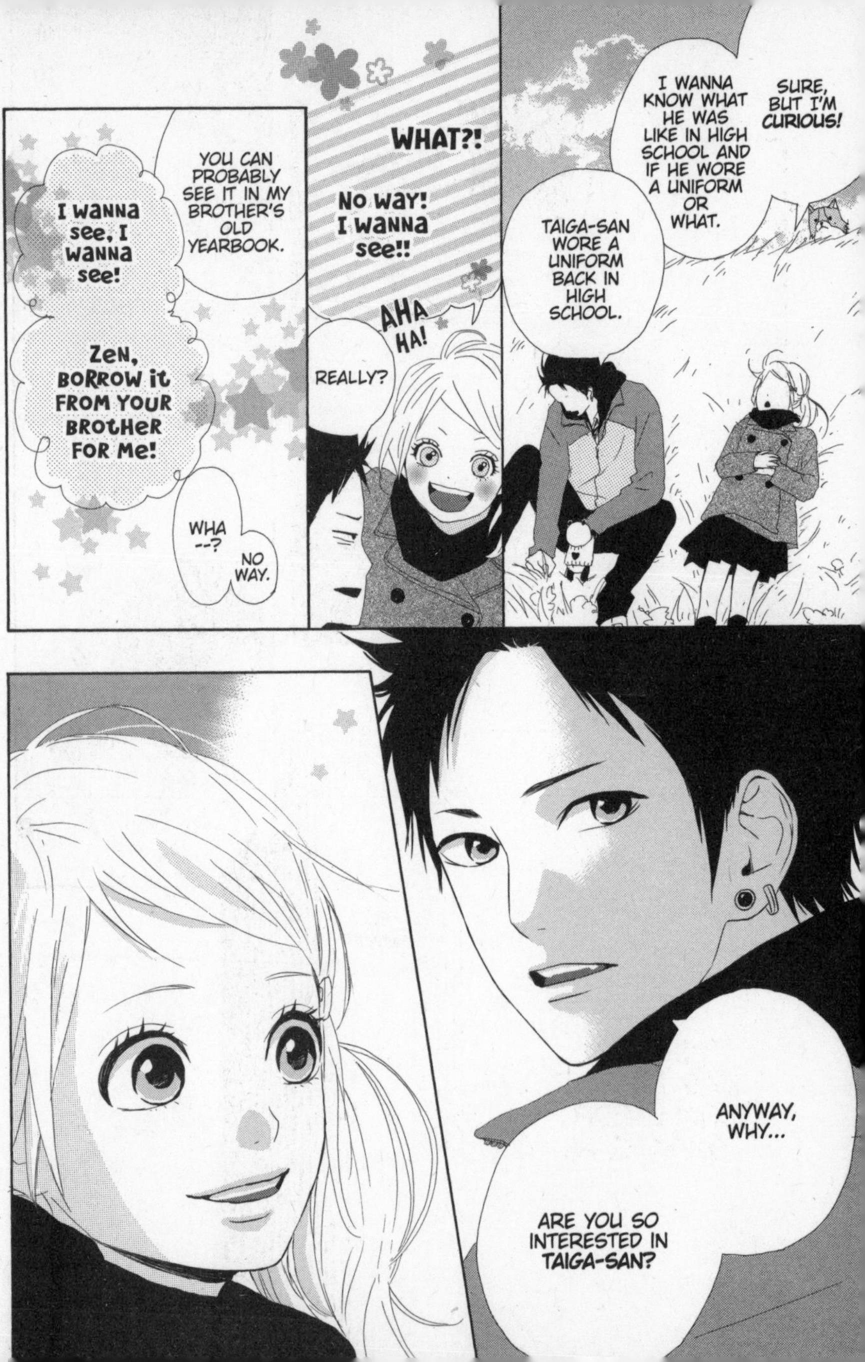
SURE, BUT I'M CURIOUS!
I WANNA KNOW WHAT HE WAS LIKE IN HIGH SCHOOL AND IF HE WORE A UNIFORM OR WHAT.
TAIGA-SAN WORE A UNIFORM BACK IN HIGH SCHOOL.
WHAT?!
No way! I wanna see!!
AHA HA!
REALLY?
YOU CAN PROBABLY SEE IT IN MY BROTHER'S OLD YEARBOOK.
I wanna see, I wanna see!
Zen, BORROW it FROM YOUR BROTHER FOR Me!
WHA--?
NO WAY.
ANYWAY, WHY...
ARE YOU SO INTERESTED IN TAIGA-SAN?

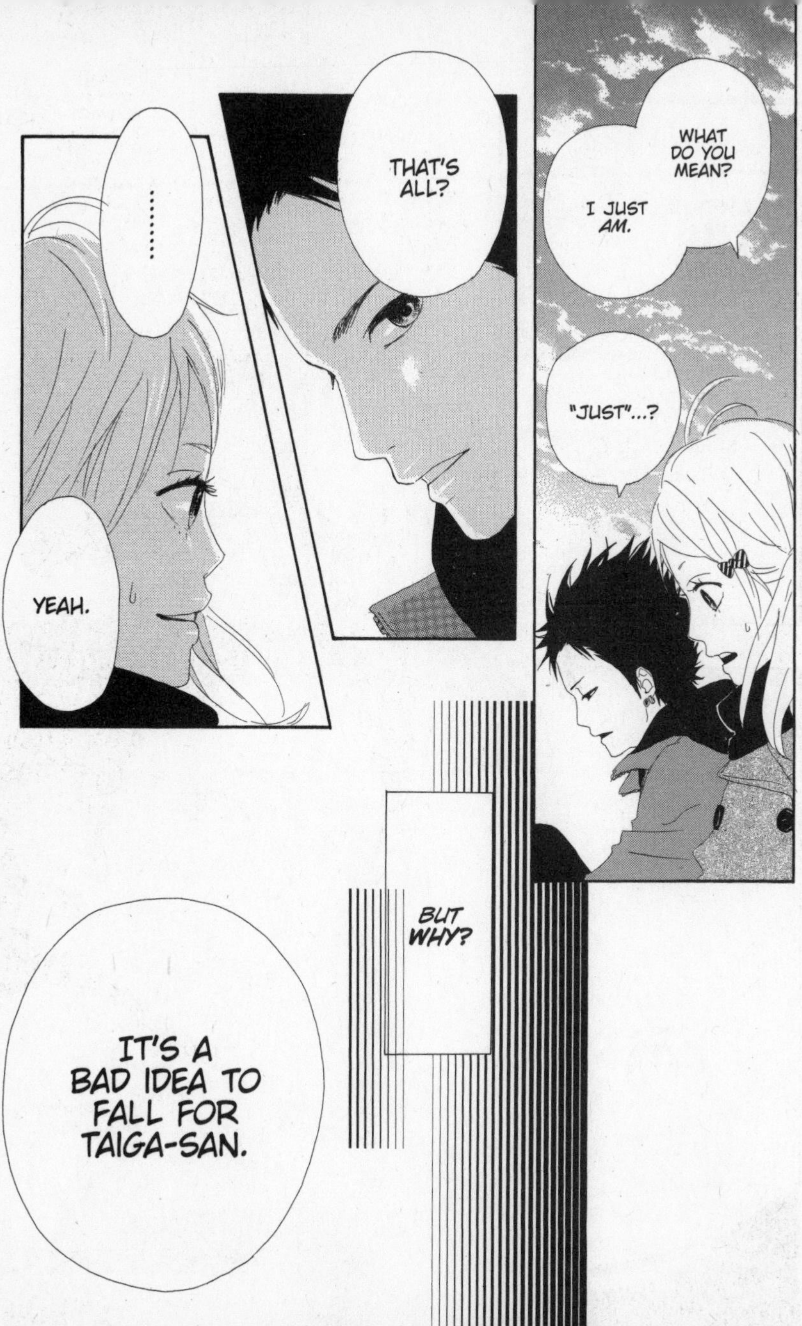
WHAT DO YOU MEAN?
I JUST AM.
"JUST"...?
THAT'S ALL?
......
YEAH.
BUT WHY?
IT'S A BAD IDEA TO FALL FOR TAIGA-SAN.

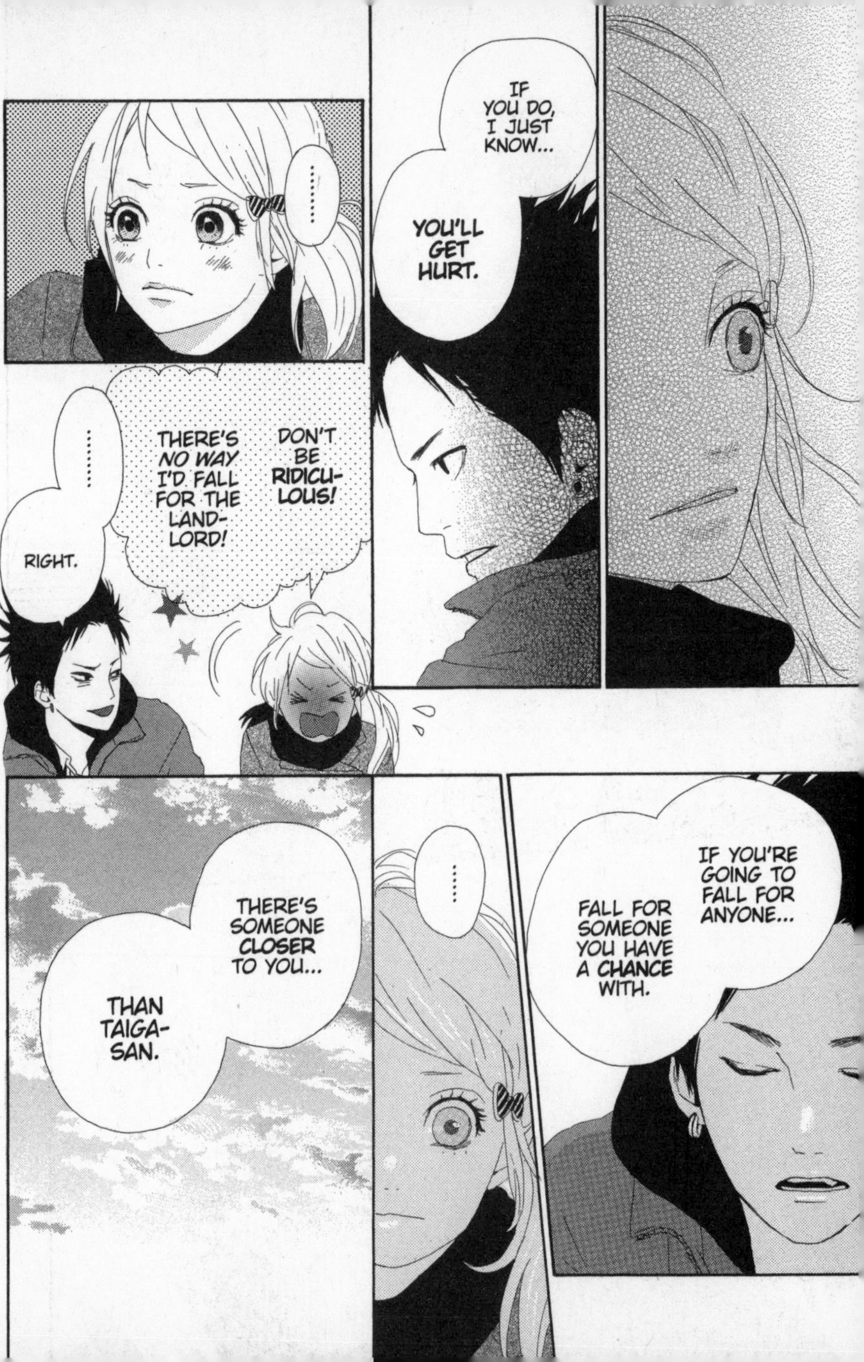
IF YOU DO, I JUST KNOW...
YOU'LL GET HURT.
......
DON'T BE RIDICULOUS!
THERE'S NO WAY I'D FALL FOR THE LANDLORD!
......
RIGHT.
IF YOU'RE GOING TO FALL FOR ANYONE...
FALL FOR SOMEONE YOU HAVE A CHANCE WITH.
......
THERE'S SOMEONE CLOSER TO YOU...
THAN TAIGA-SAN.

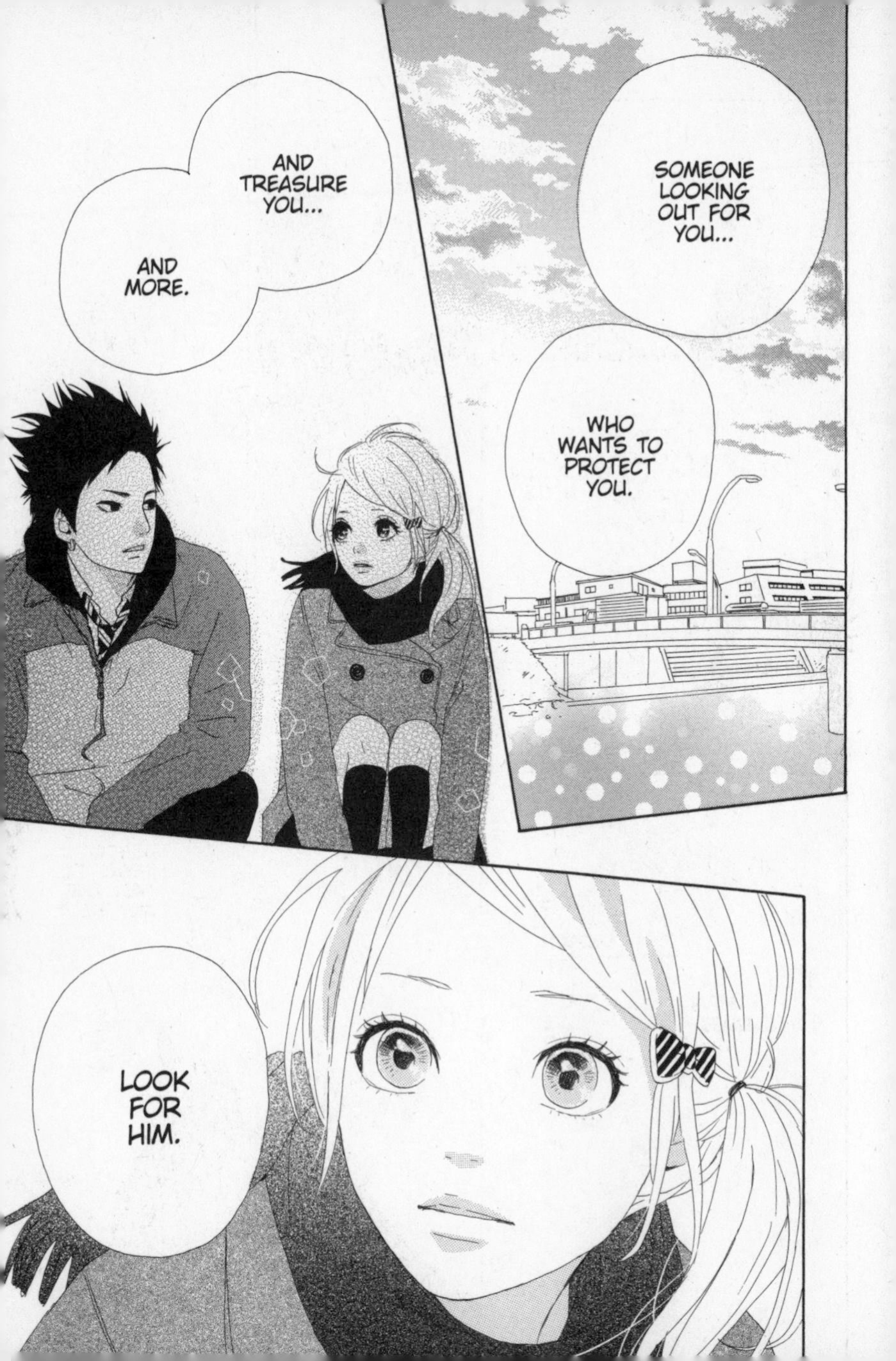
SOMEONE LOOKING OUT FOR YOU...
WHO WANTS TO PROTECT YOU.
AND TREASURE YOU...
AND MORE.
LOOK FOR HIM.

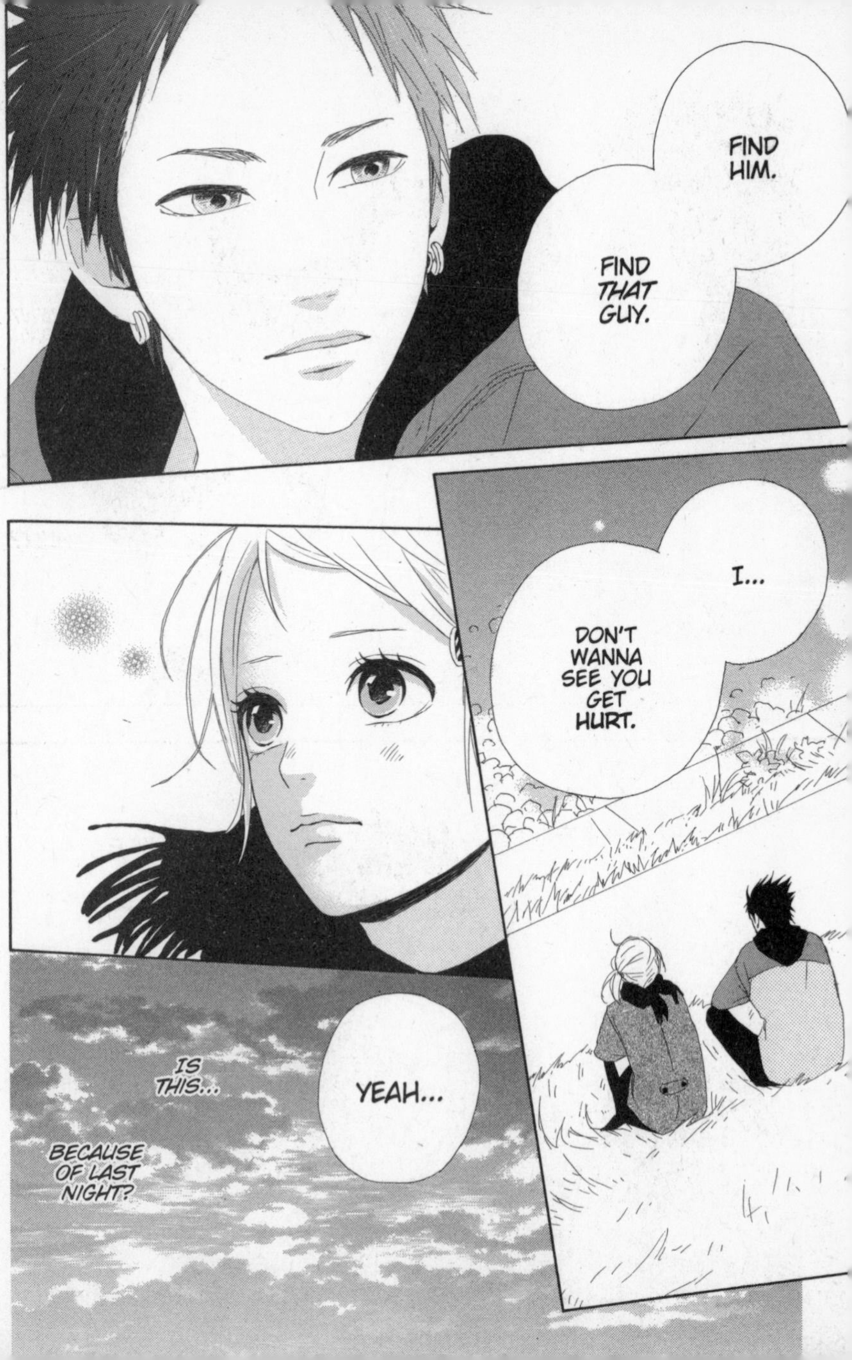
FIND HIM.
FIND *THAT* GUY.
I...
DON'T WANNA SEE YOU GET HURT.
YEAH...
IS THIS...
BECAUSE OF LAST NIGHT?

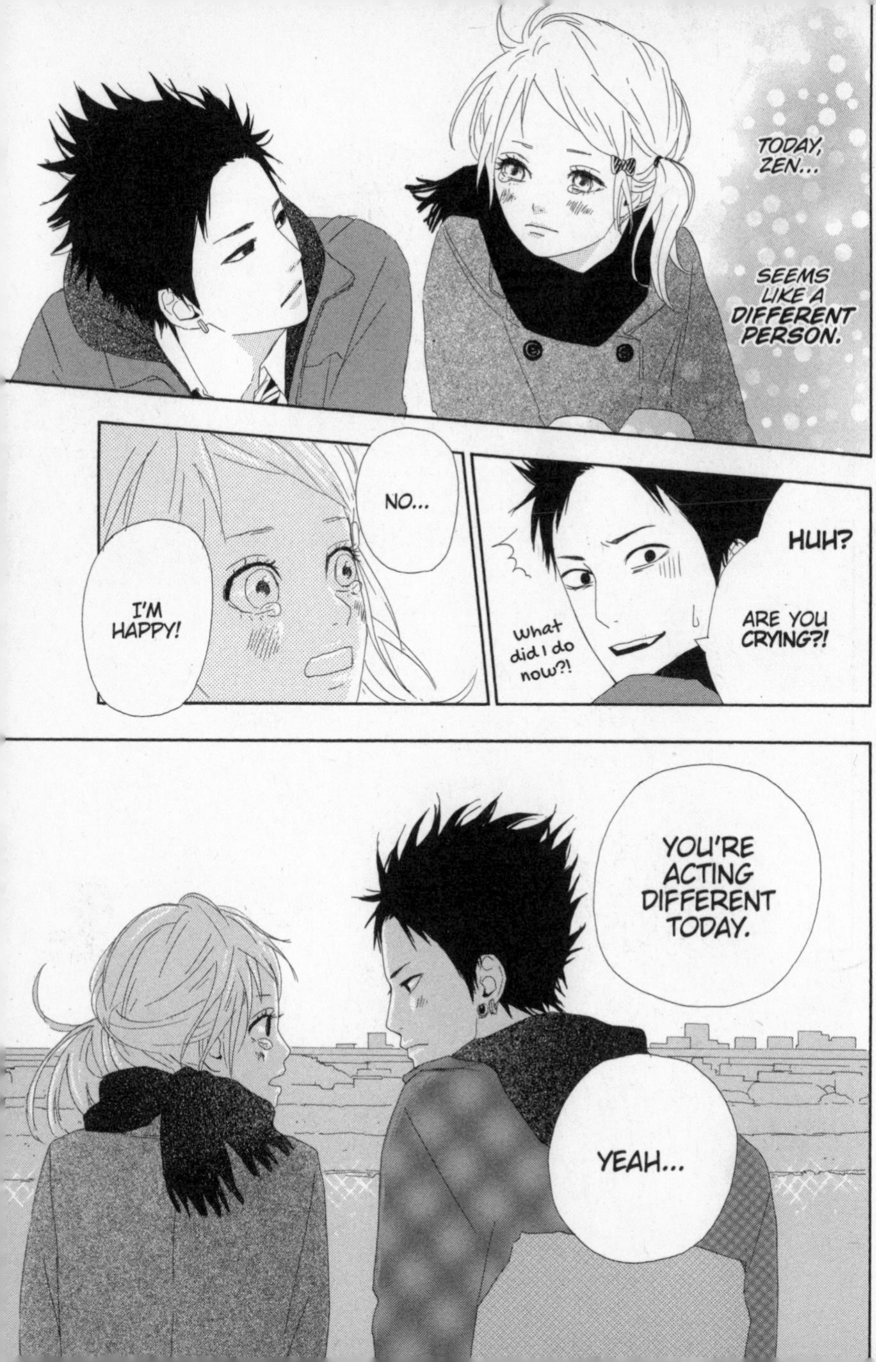
TODAY, ZEN...
SEEMS LIKE A DIFFERENT PERSON.
HUH?
ARE YOU CRYING?!
What did I do now?!
NO...
I'M HAPPY!
YOU'RE ACTING DIFFERENT TODAY.
YEAH...

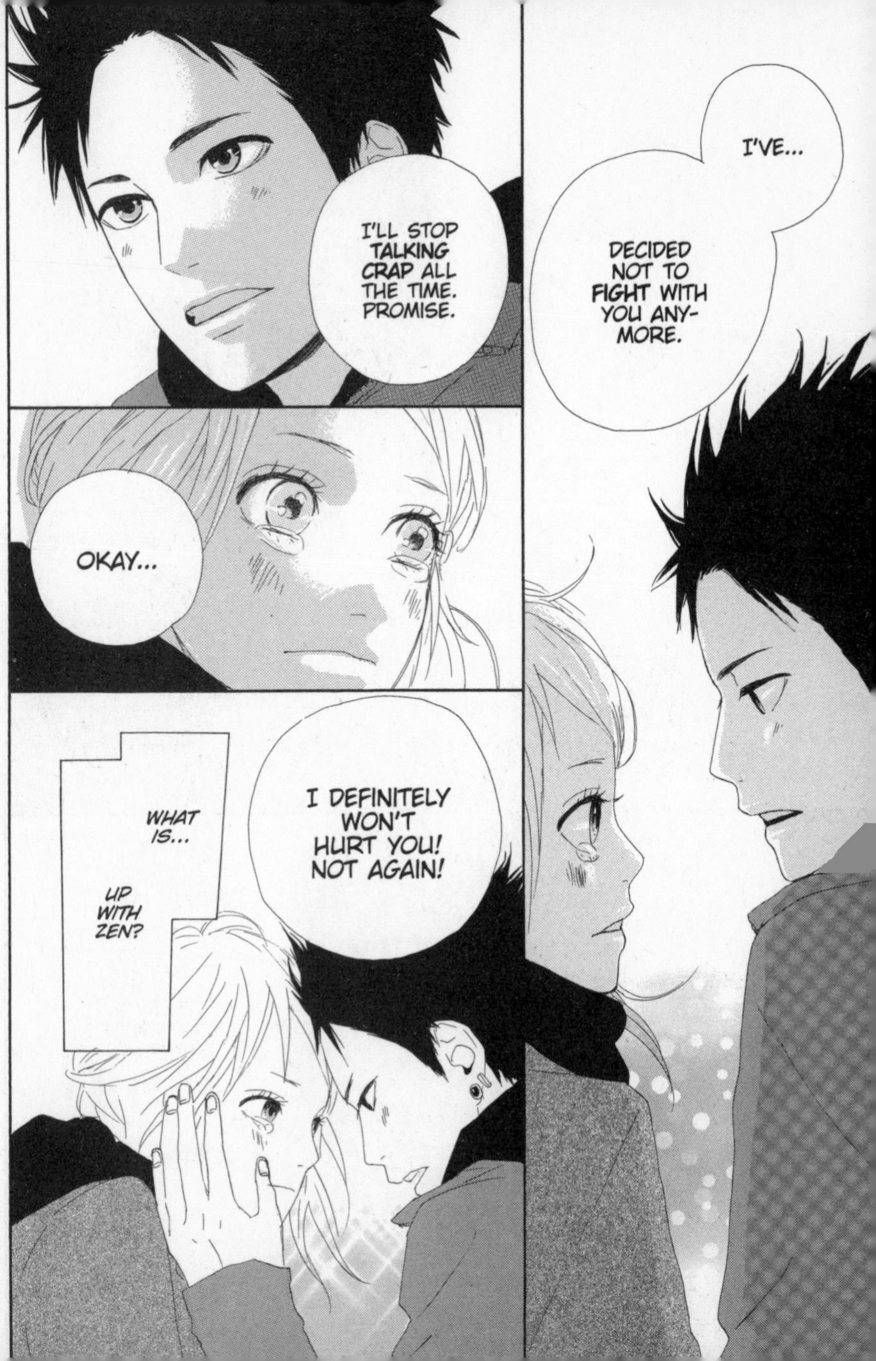
I'VE...
DECIDED NOT TO FIGHT WITH YOU ANY-MORE.
I'LL STOP TALKING CRAP ALL THE TIME. PROMISE.
OKAY...
I DEFINITELY WON'T HURT YOU! NOT AGAIN!
WHAT IS...
UP WITH ZEN?

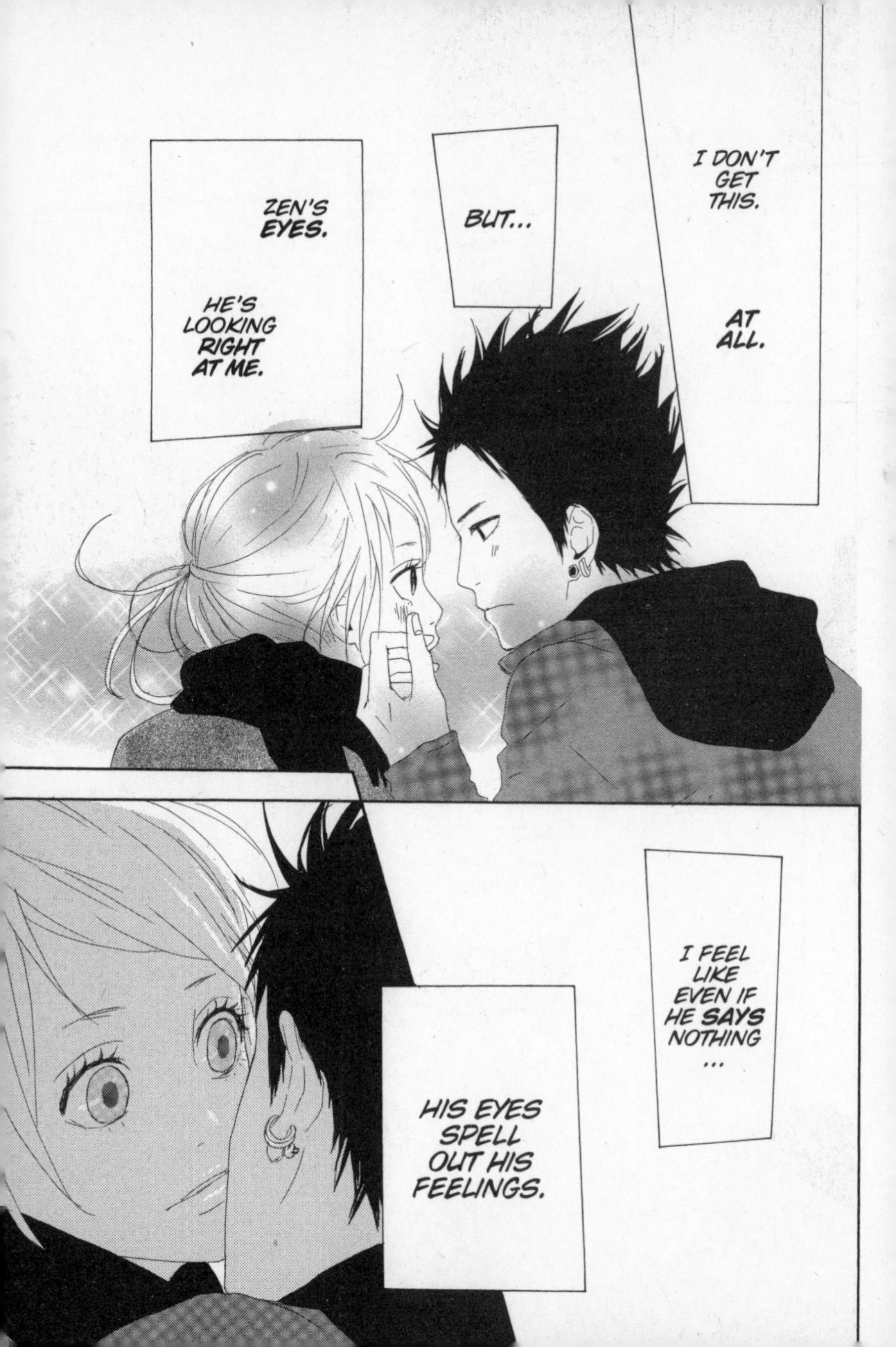
I DON'T GET THIS.
AT ALL.
BUT...
ZEN'S EYES.
HE'S LOOKING RIGHT AT ME.
I FEEL LIKE EVEN IF HE SAYS NOTHING...
HIS EYES SPELL OUT HIS FEELINGS.

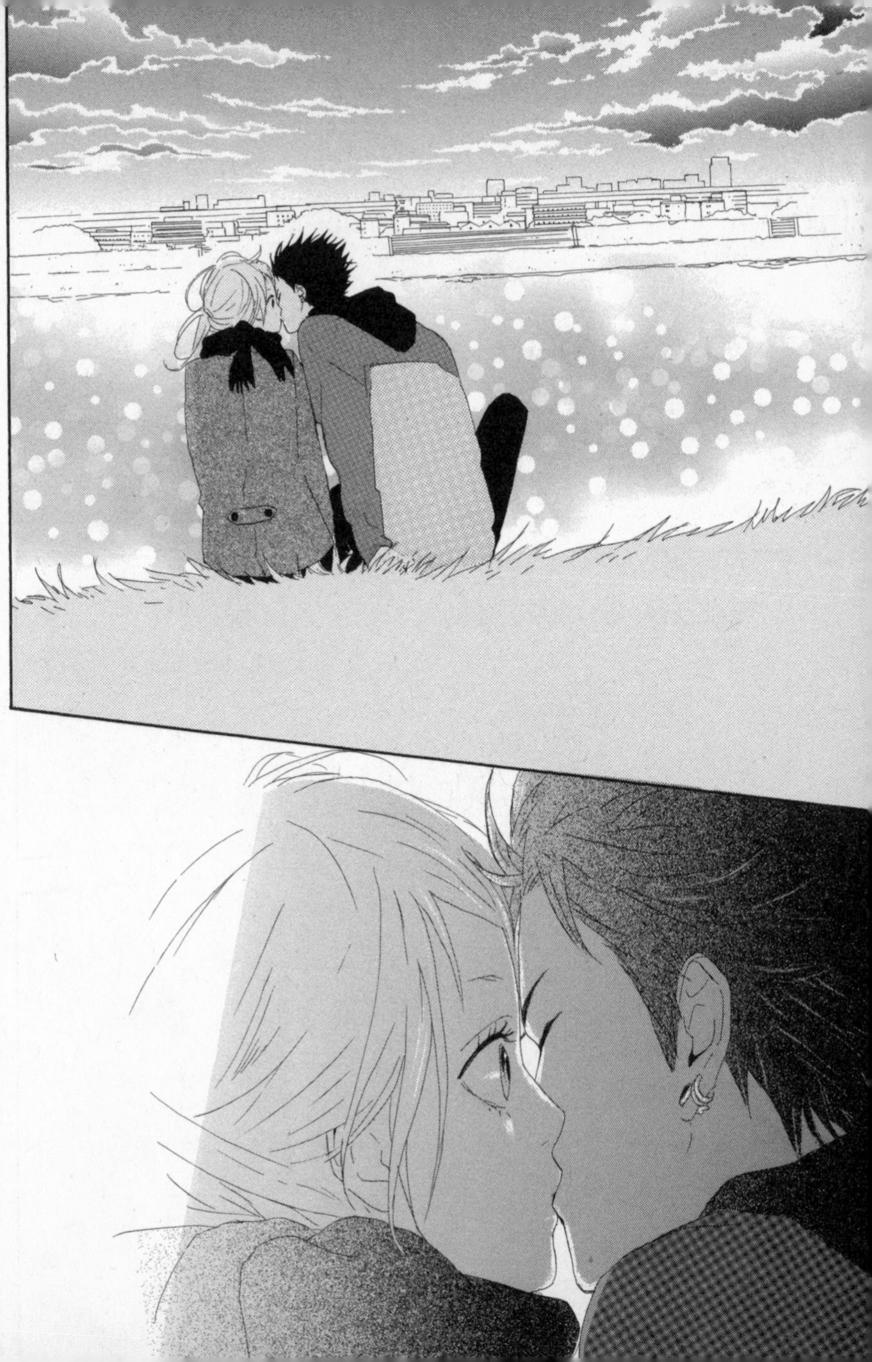

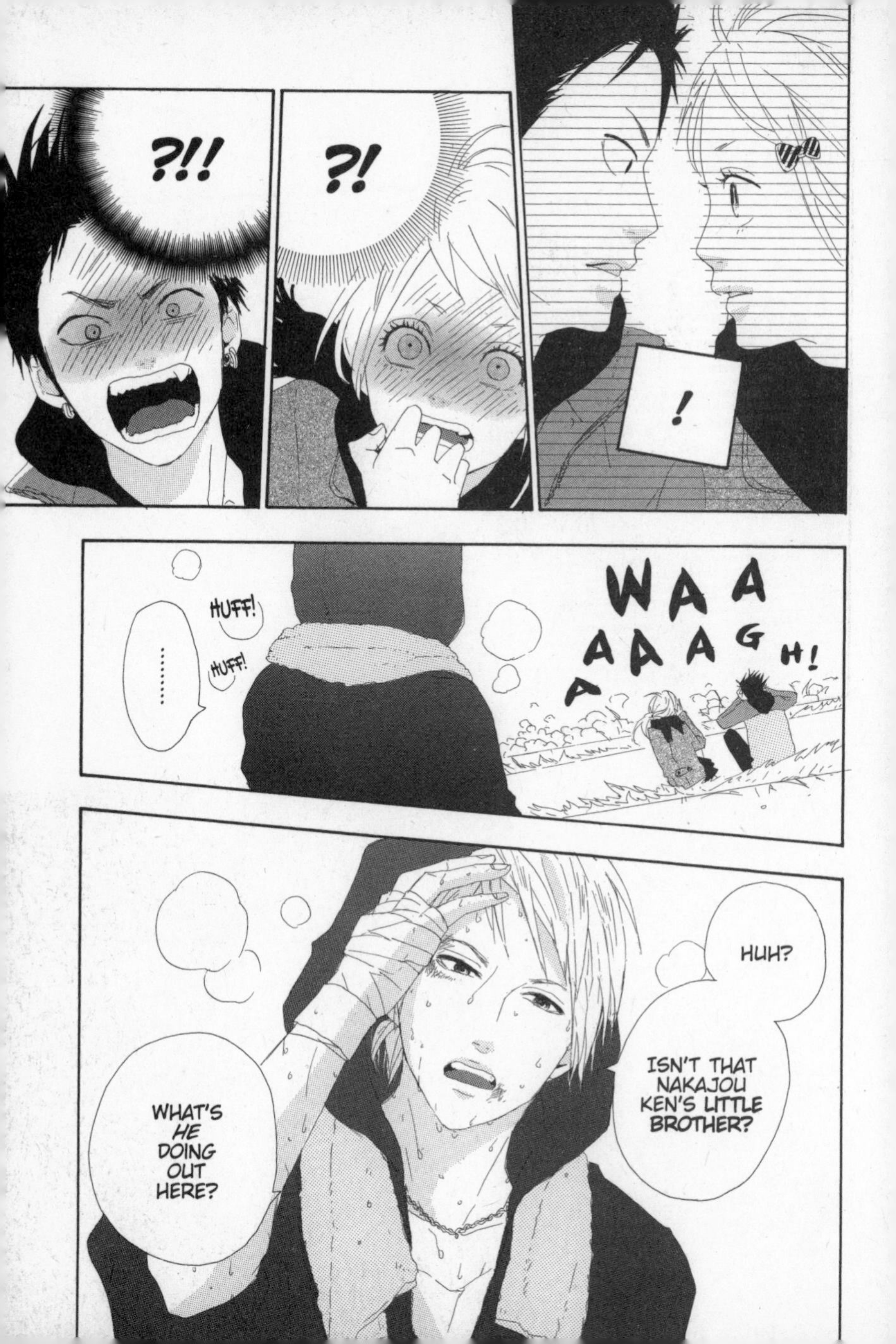
!
?!
?!!
WAAAAAAGH!
HUFF!
HUFF!
......
HUH?
ISN'T THAT NAKAJOU KEN'S LITTLE BROTHER?
WHAT'S *HE* DOING OUT HERE?

After The Realization

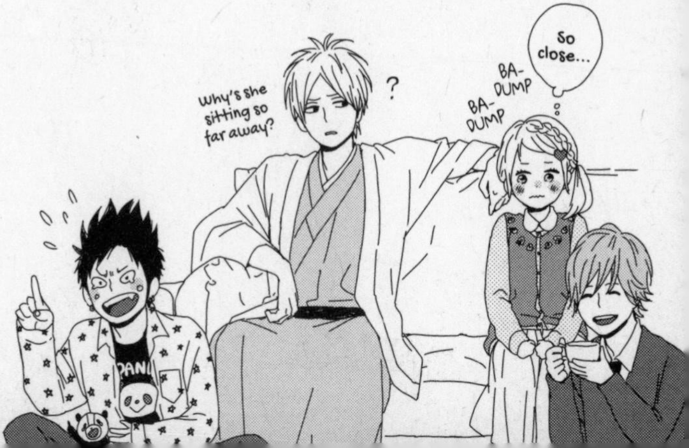
So close...
BA-DUMP
BA-DUMP
?
Why's she sitting so far away?

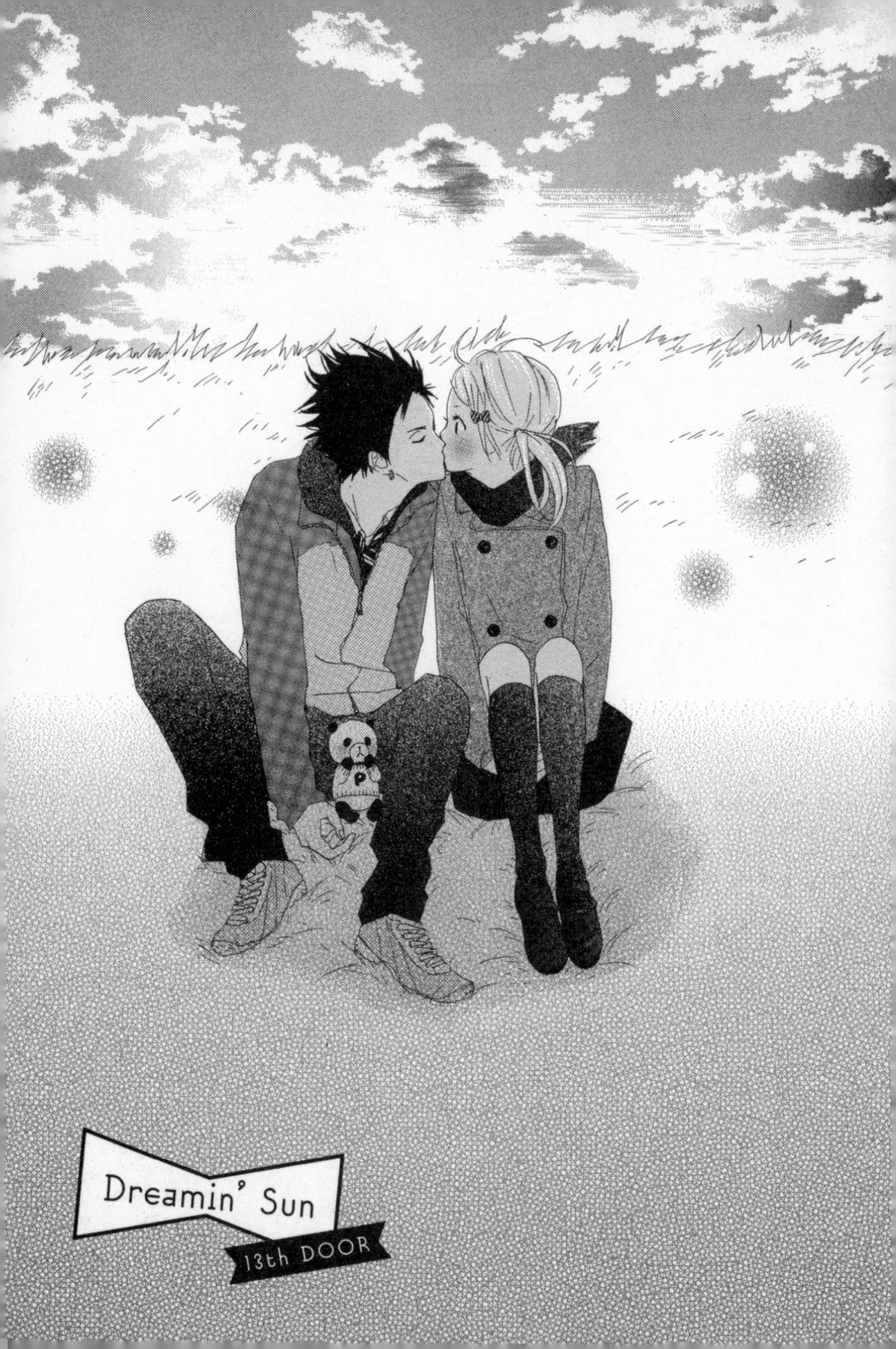
Dreamin' Sun
13th DOOR

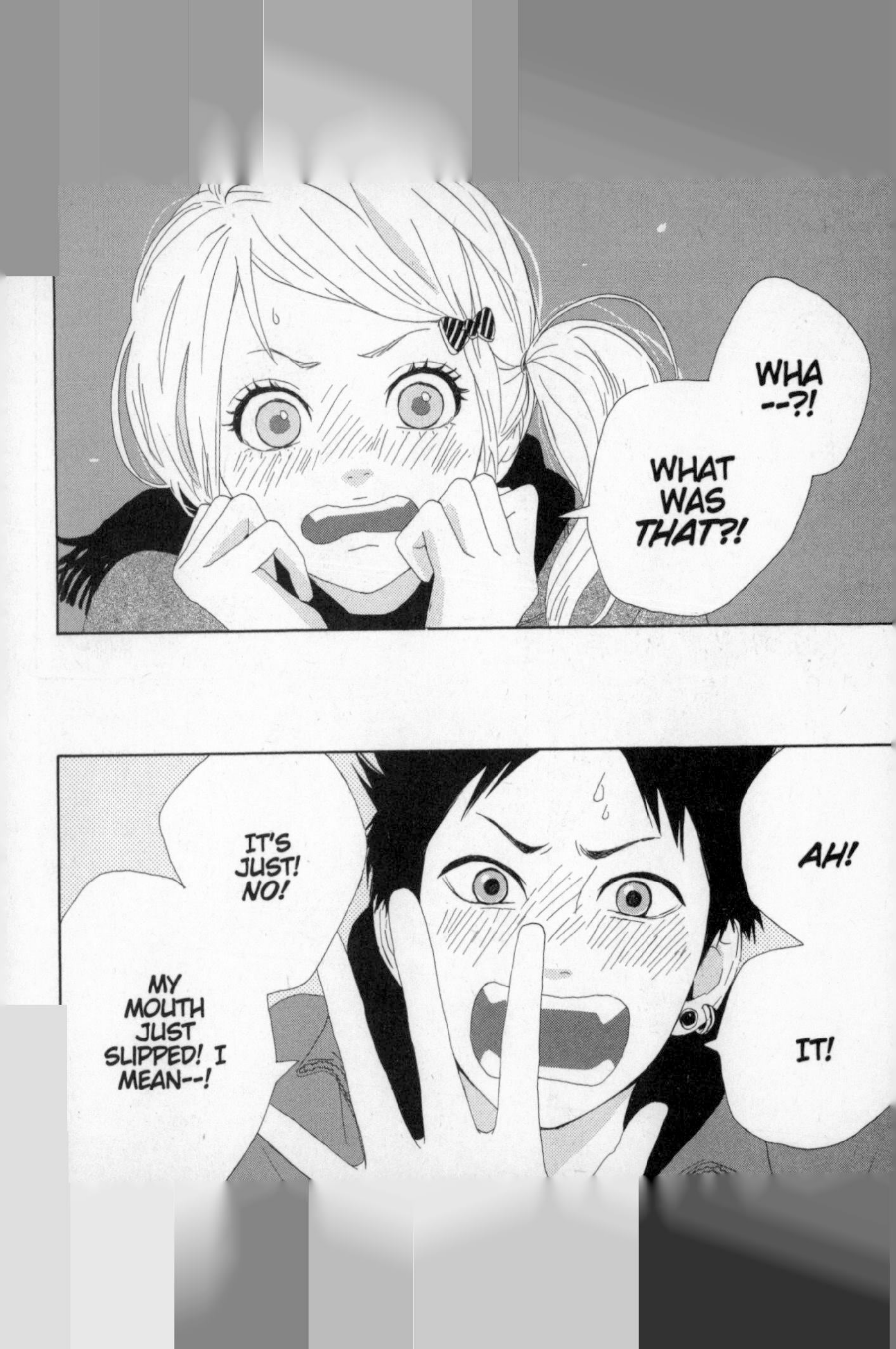
WHA --?!
WHAT WAS THAT?!
AH!
IT!
IT'S JUST! NO!
MY MOUTH JUST SLIPPED! I MEAN--!

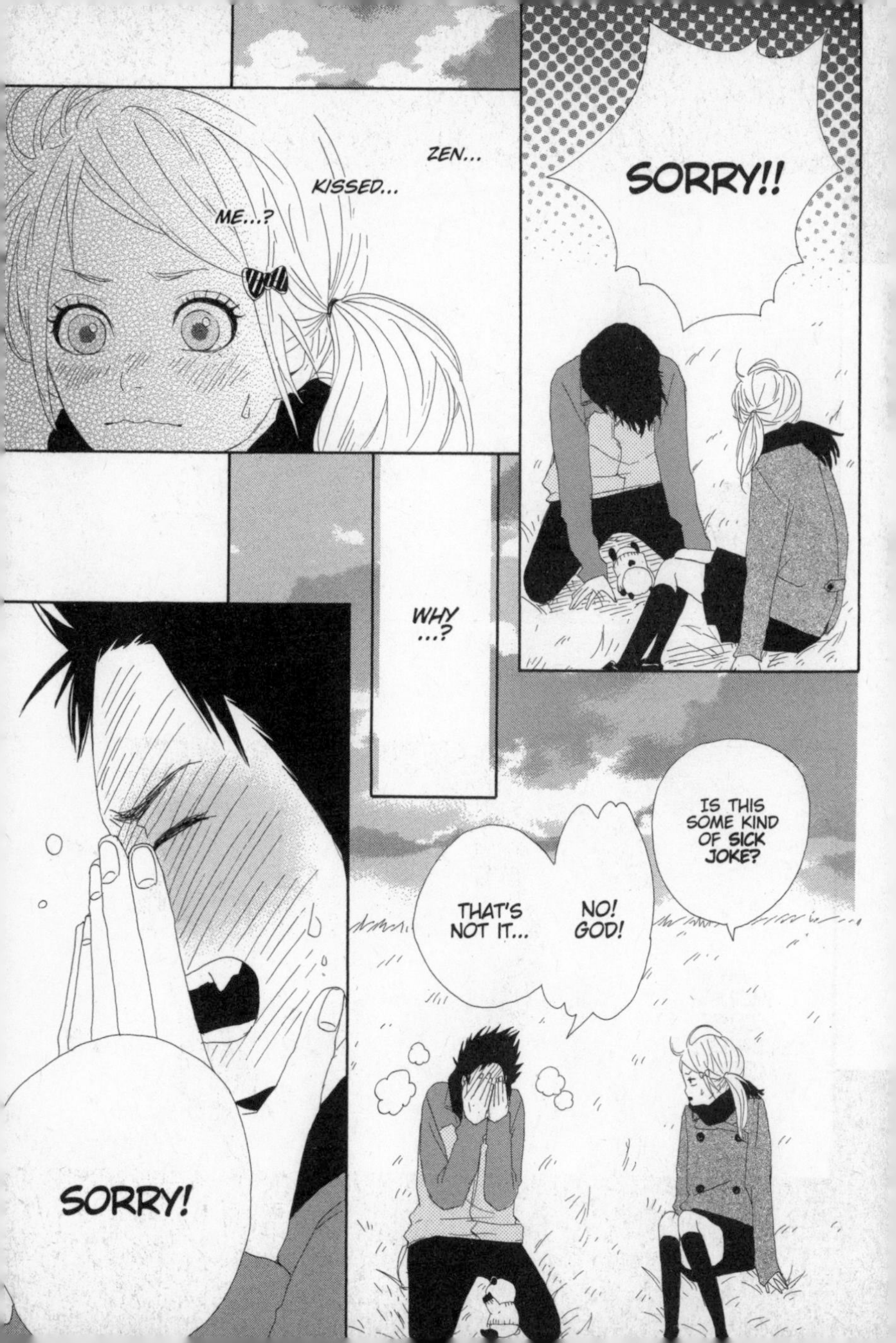
SORRY!!
ZEN...
KISSED...
ME...?
WHY ...?
IS THIS SOME KIND OF SICK JOKE?
NO! GOD!
THAT'S NOT IT...
SORRY!

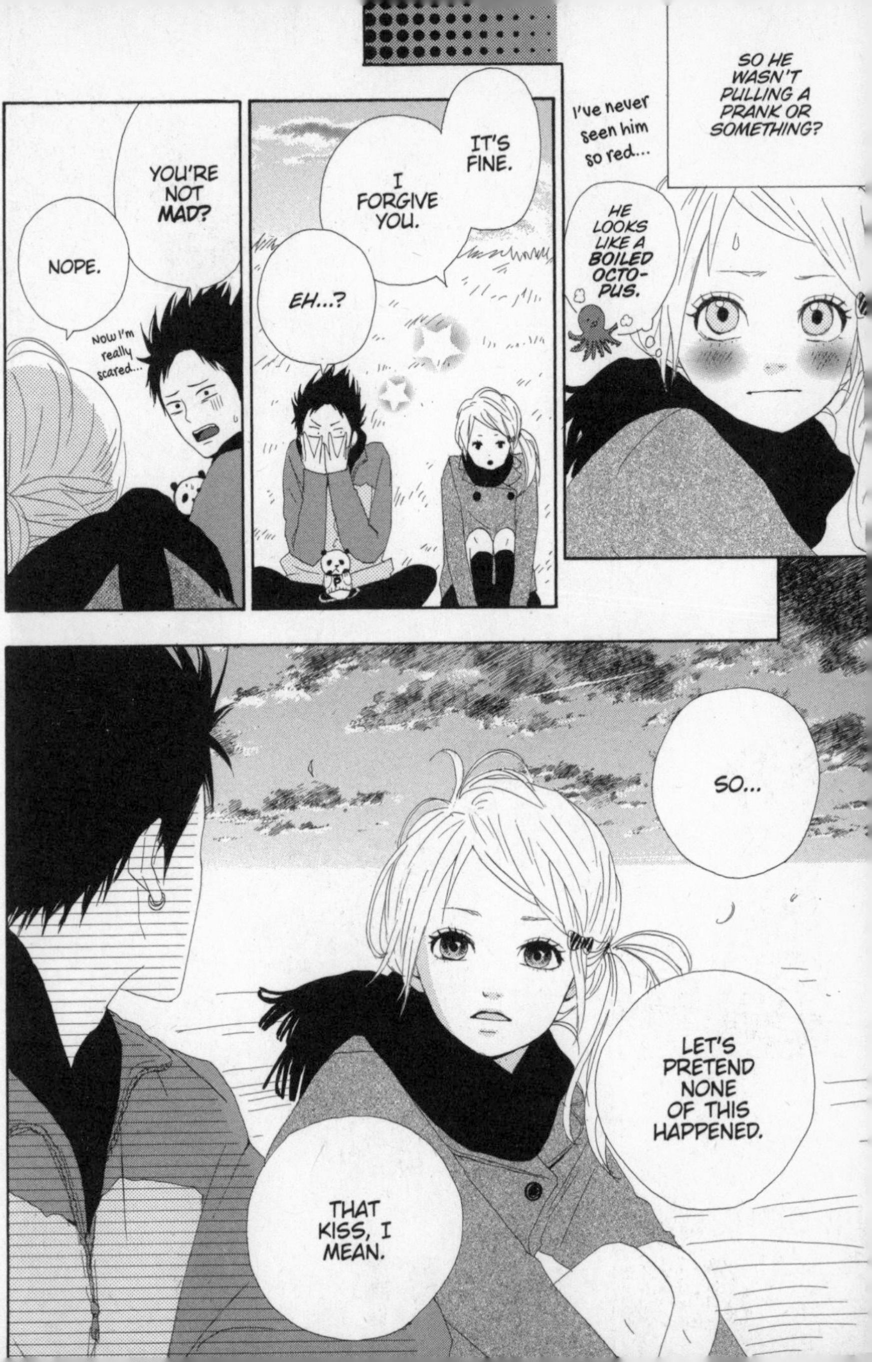
SO HE WASN'T PULLING A PRANK OR SOMETHING?
I've never seen him so red...
HE LOOKS LIKE A BOILED OCTO-PUS.
IT'S FINE.
I FORGIVE YOU.
EH...?
YOU'RE NOT MAD?
NOPE.
Now I'm really scared...
SO...
LET'S PRETEND NONE OF THIS HAPPENED.
THAT KISS, I MEAN.

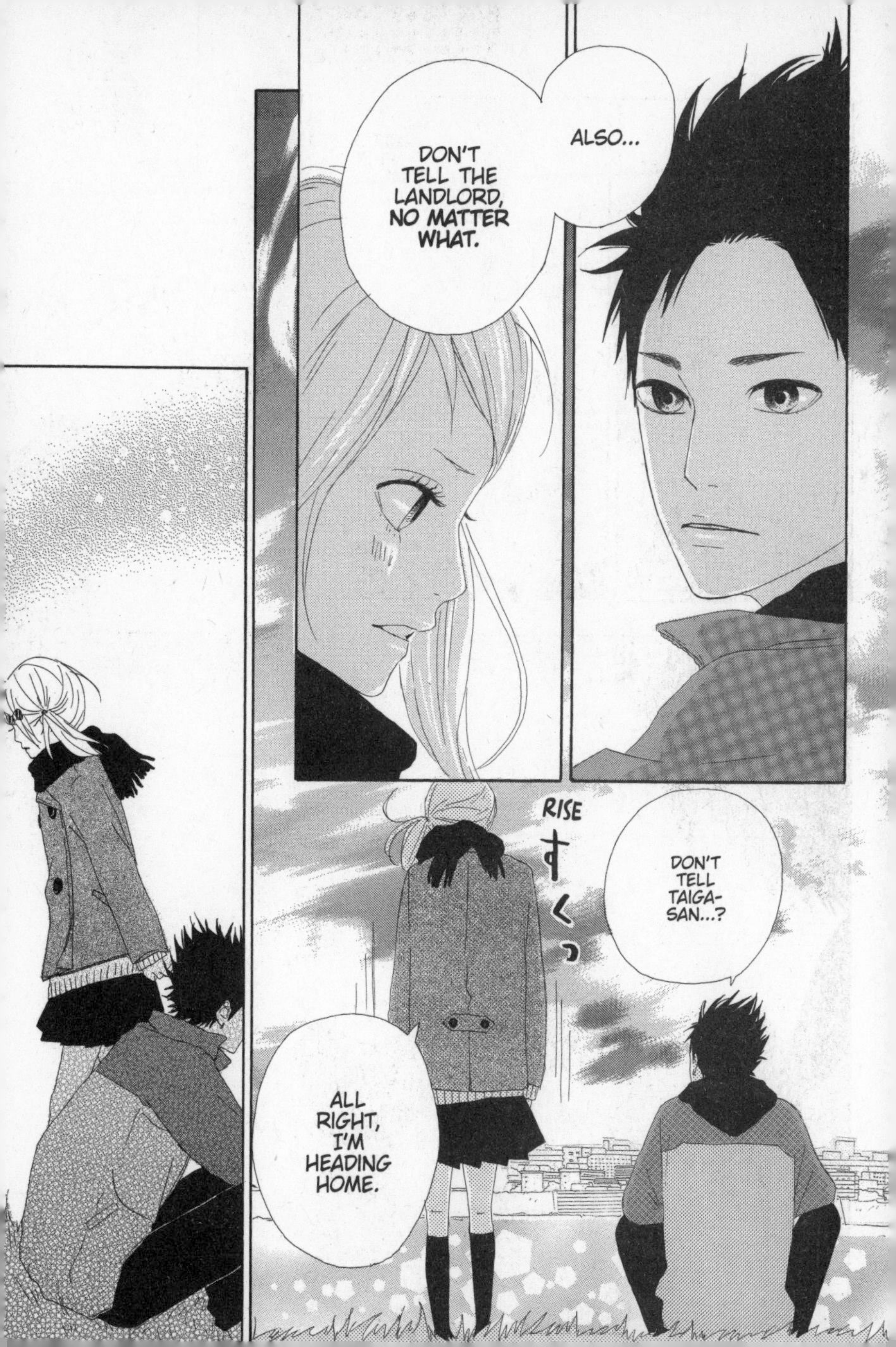
ALSO...
DON'T TELL THE LANDLORD, NO MATTER WHAT.
RISE
すくっ
DON'T TELL TAIGA-SAN...?
ALL RIGHT, I'M HEADING HOME.

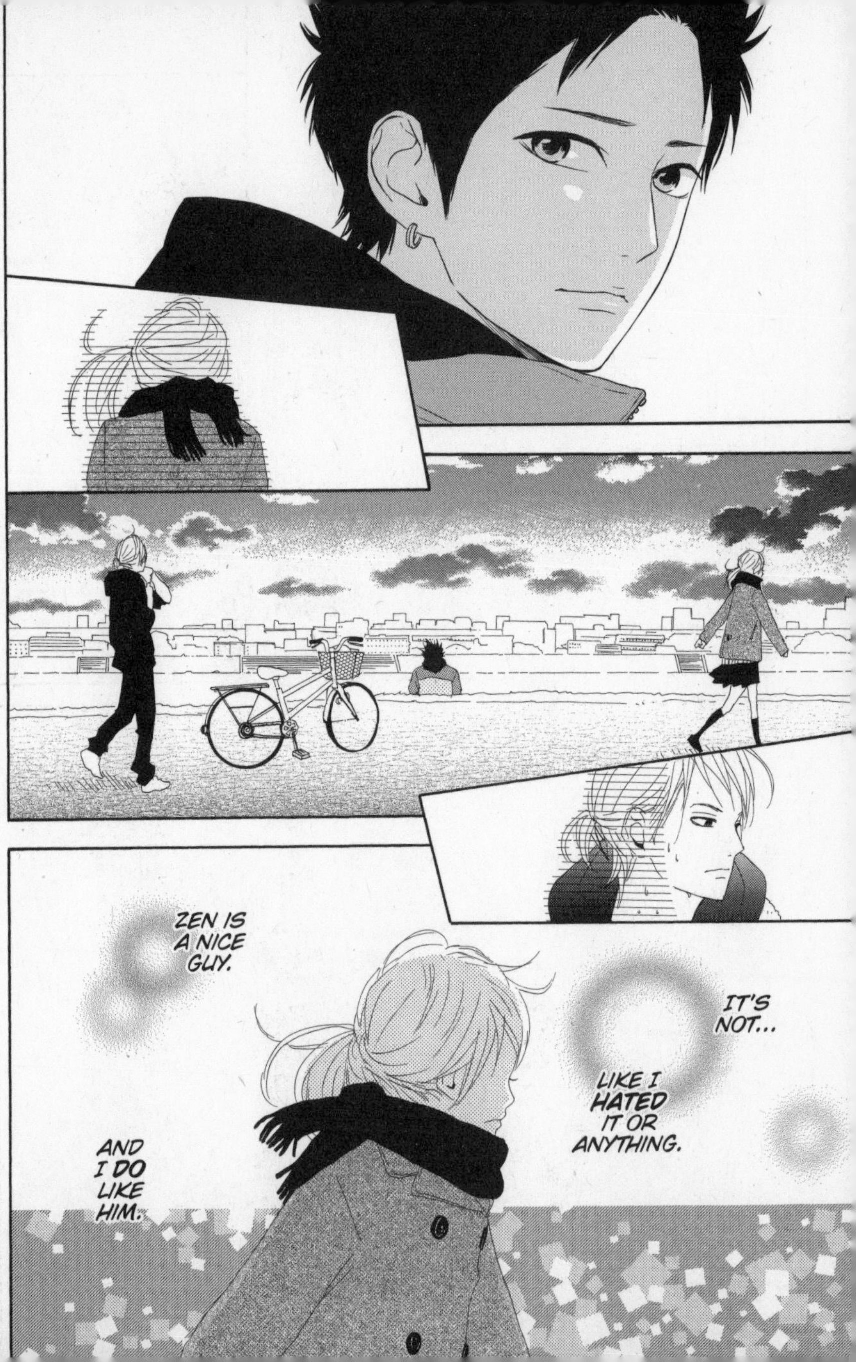
IT'S NOT...
LIKE I HATED IT OR ANYTHING.
ZEN IS A NICE GUY.
AND I DO LIKE HIM.

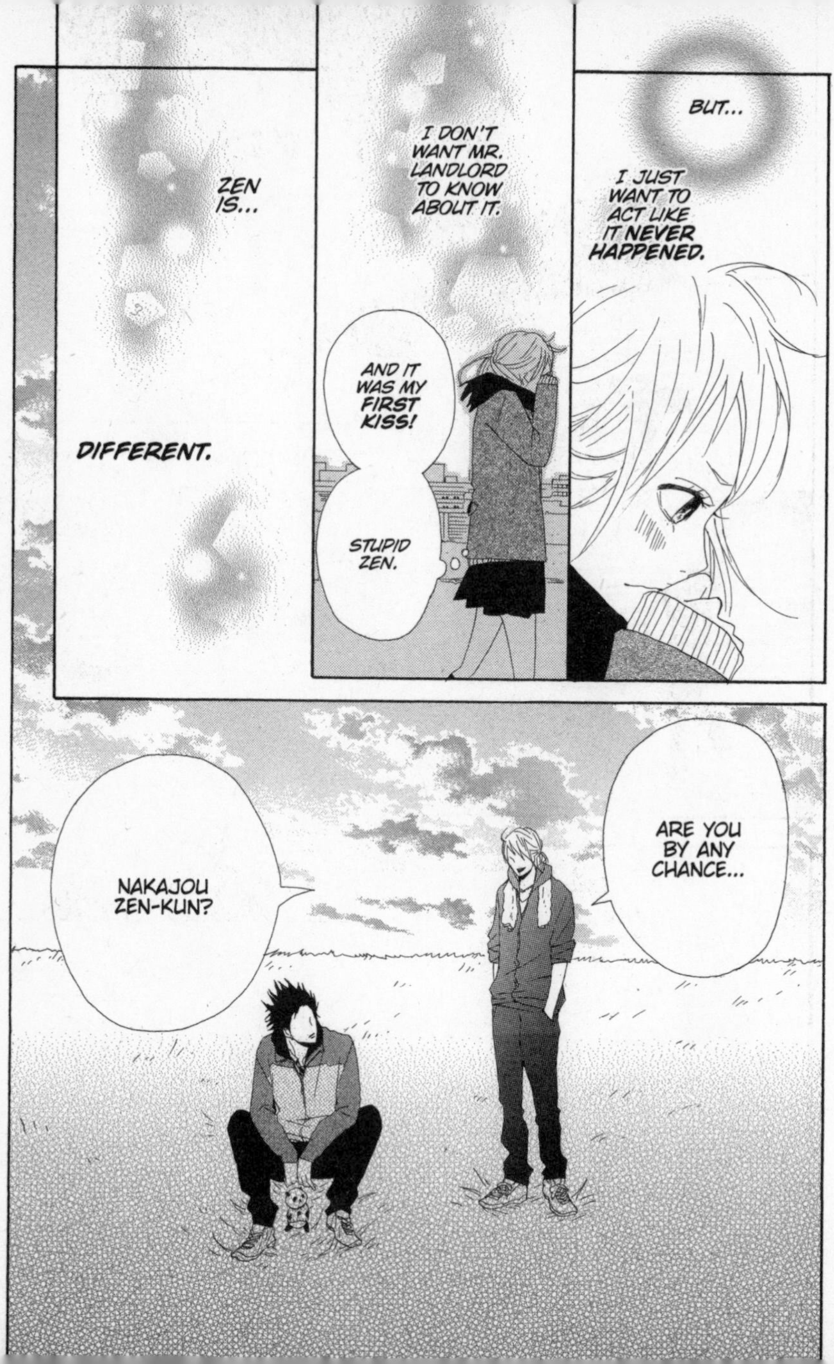
BUT...
I JUST WANT TO ACT LIKE IT NEVER HAPPENED.
I DON'T WANT MR. LANDLORD TO KNOW ABOUT IT.
AND IT WAS MY FIRST KISS!
STUPID ZEN.
ZEN IS...
DIFFERENT.
ARE YOU BY ANY CHANCE...
NAKAJOU ZEN-KUN?

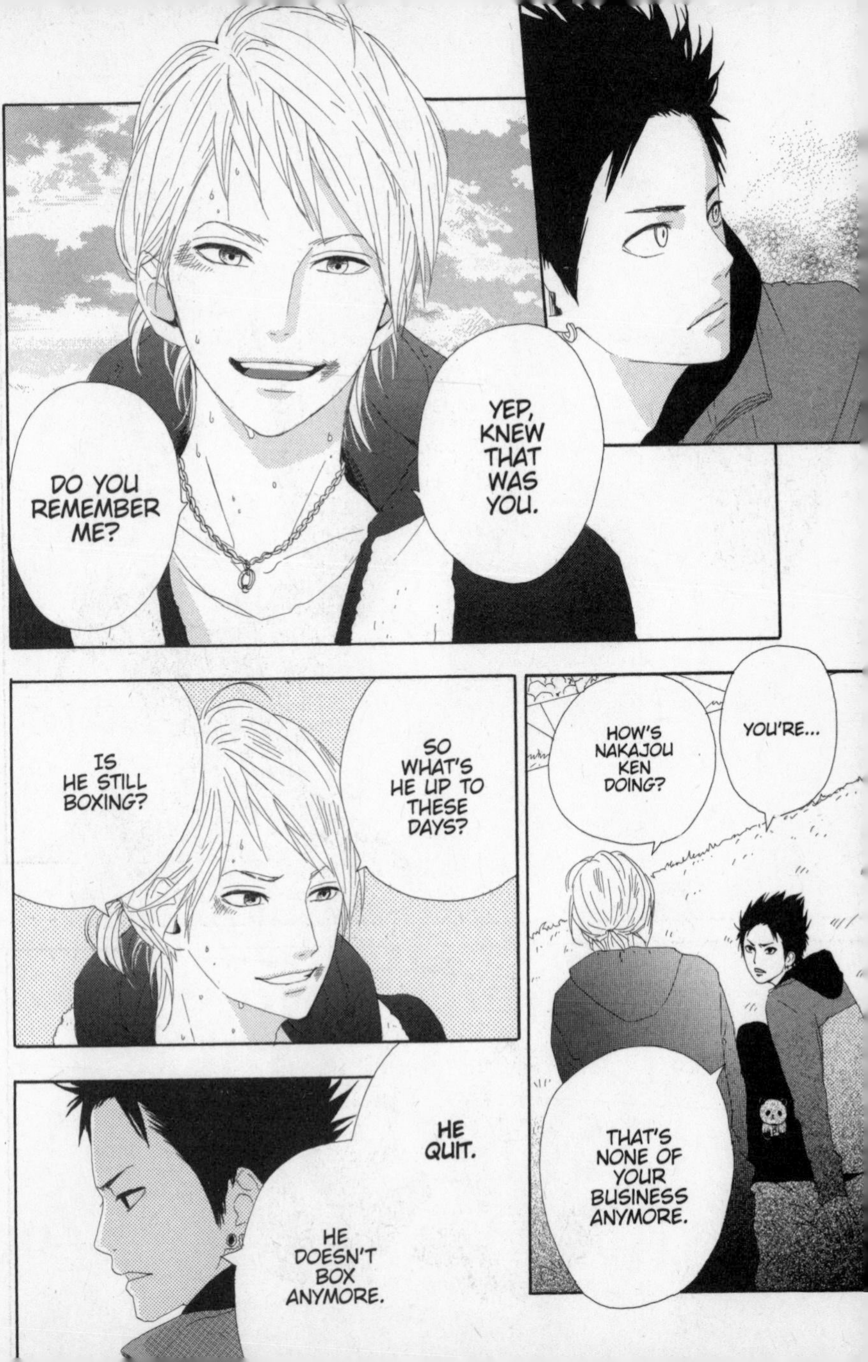
YEP, KNEW THAT WAS YOU.
DO YOU REMEMBER ME?
YOU'RE...
HOW'S NAKAJOU KEN DOING?
THAT'S NONE OF YOUR BUSINESS ANYMORE.
SO WHAT'S HE UP TO THESE DAYS?
IS HE STILL BOXING?
HE QUIT.
HE DOESN'T BOX ANYMORE.

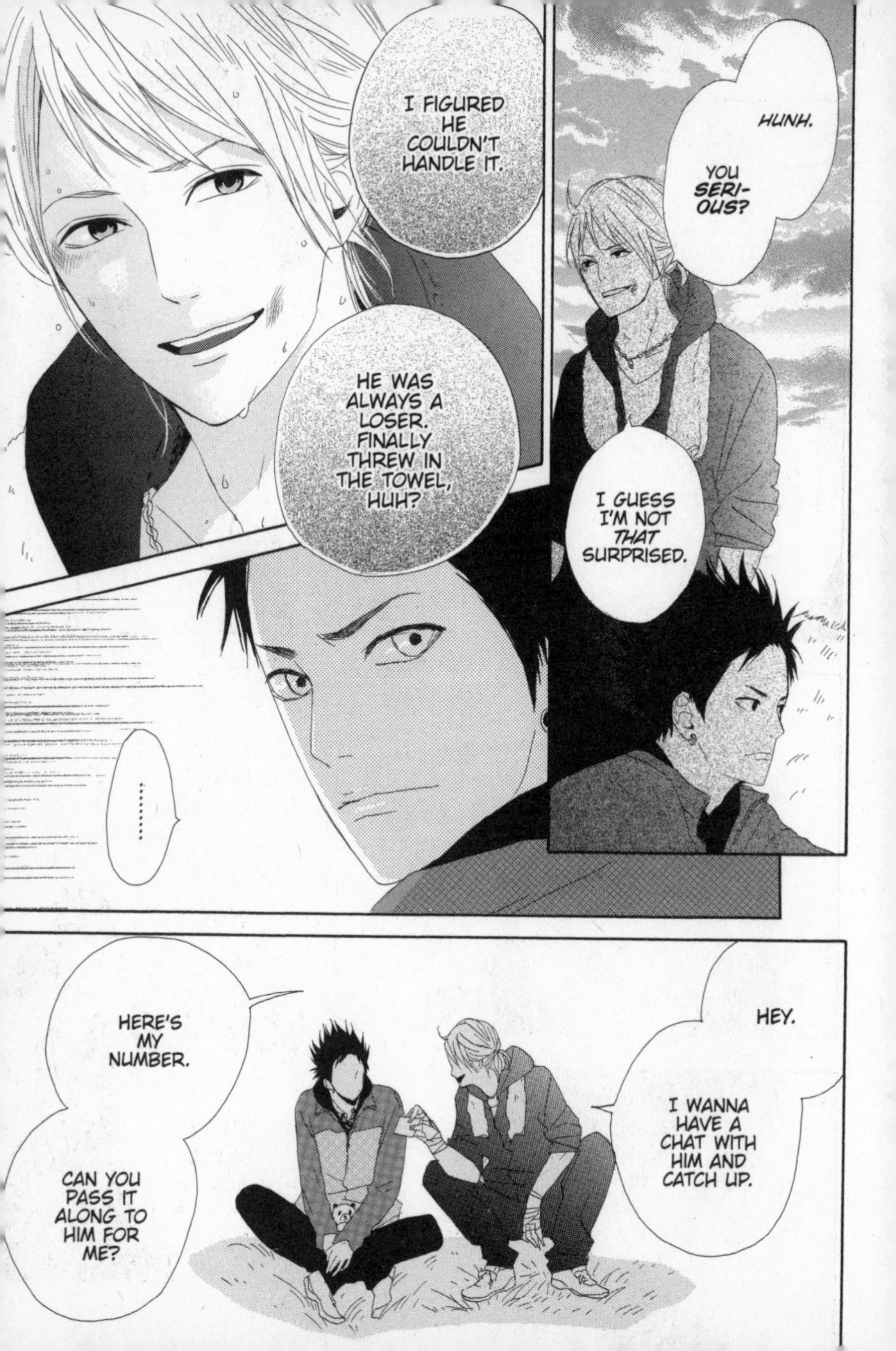
HUNH.
YOU SERI-OUS?
I GUESS I'M NOT *THAT* SURPRISED.
I FIGURED HE COULDN'T HANDLE IT.
HE WAS ALWAYS A LOSER. FINALLY THREW IN THE TOWEL, HUH?
......
HEY.
I WANNA HAVE A CHAT WITH HIM AND CATCH UP.
HERE'S MY NUMBER.
CAN YOU PASS IT ALONG TO HIM FOR ME?

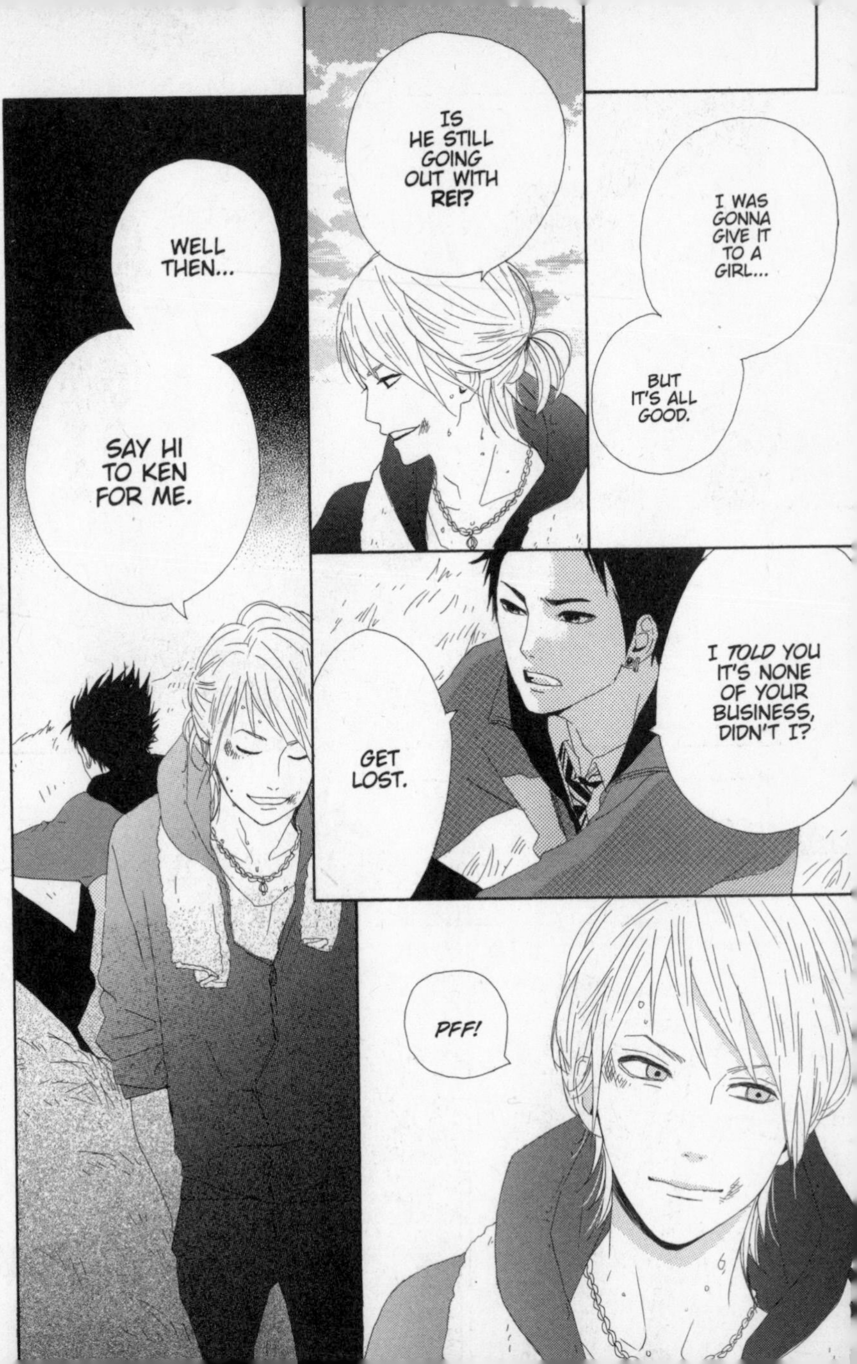
I WAS GONNA GIVE IT TO A GIRL...
BUT IT'S ALL GOOD.
IS HE STILL GOING OUT WITH REI?
I *TOLD* YOU IT'S NONE OF YOUR BUSINESS, DIDN'T I?
GET LOST.
PFF!
WELL THEN...
SAY HI TO KEN FOR ME.

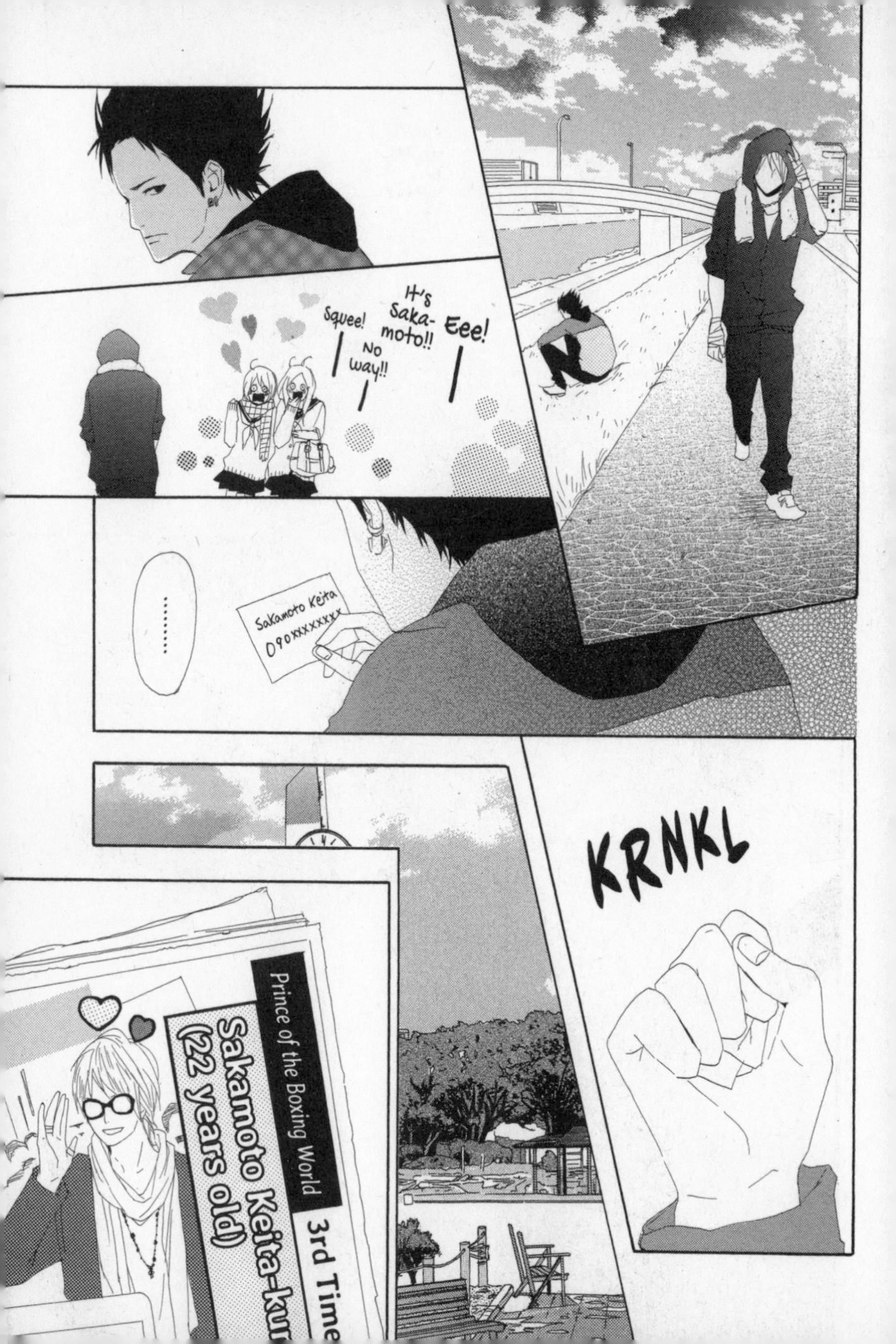
Eee!
It's Saka-moto!!
No way!!
Squee!
……
Sakamoto Keita
090xxxxxxxx
KRNKL
3rd Time
Prince of the Boxing World
Sakamoto Keita-ku
(22 years old)

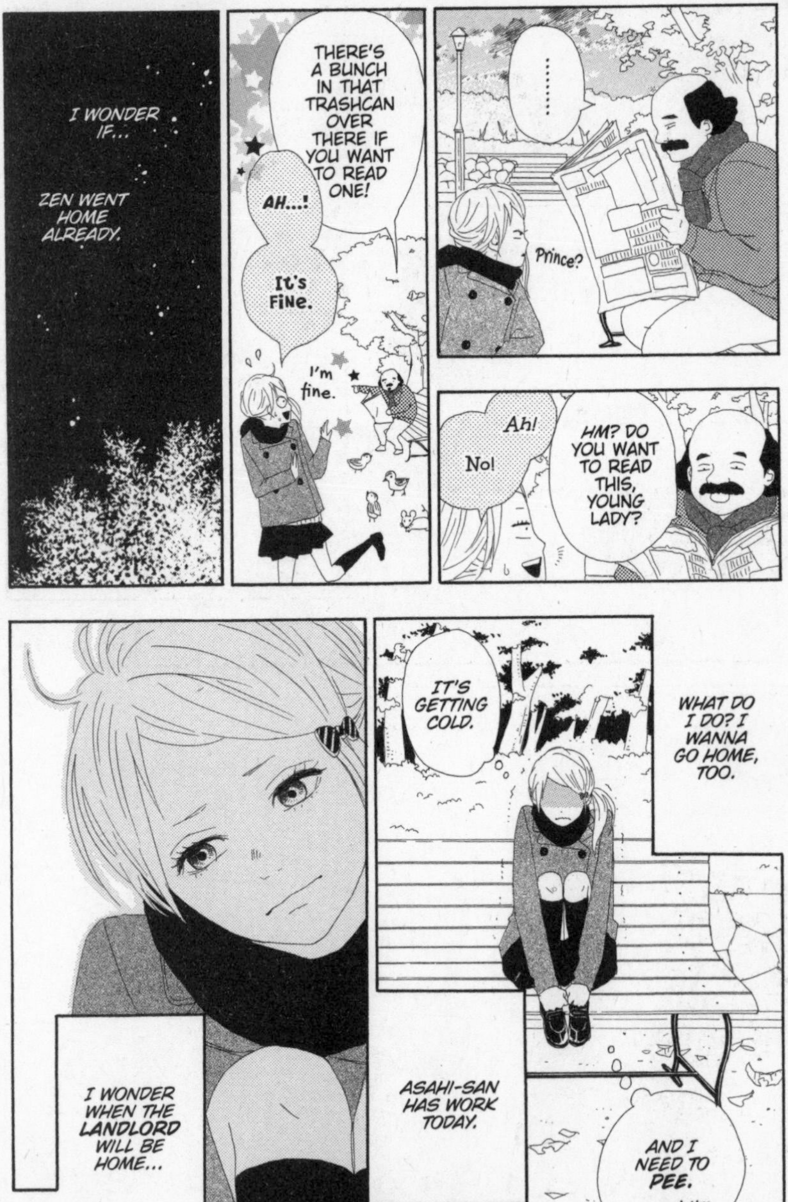

......
Prince?
HM? DO YOU WANT TO READ THIS, YOUNG LADY?
Ah! No!
THERE'S A BUNCH IN THAT TRASHCAN OVER THERE IF YOU WANT TO READ ONE!
AH...!
It's Fine.
I'm fine.
I WONDER IF...
ZEN WENT HOME ALREADY.
IT'S GETTING COLD.
WHAT DO I DO? I WANNA GO HOME, TOO.
ASAHI-SAN HAS WORK TODAY.
AND I NEED TO PEE.
But I'm scared.
I WONDER WHEN THE LANDLORD WILL BE HOME...

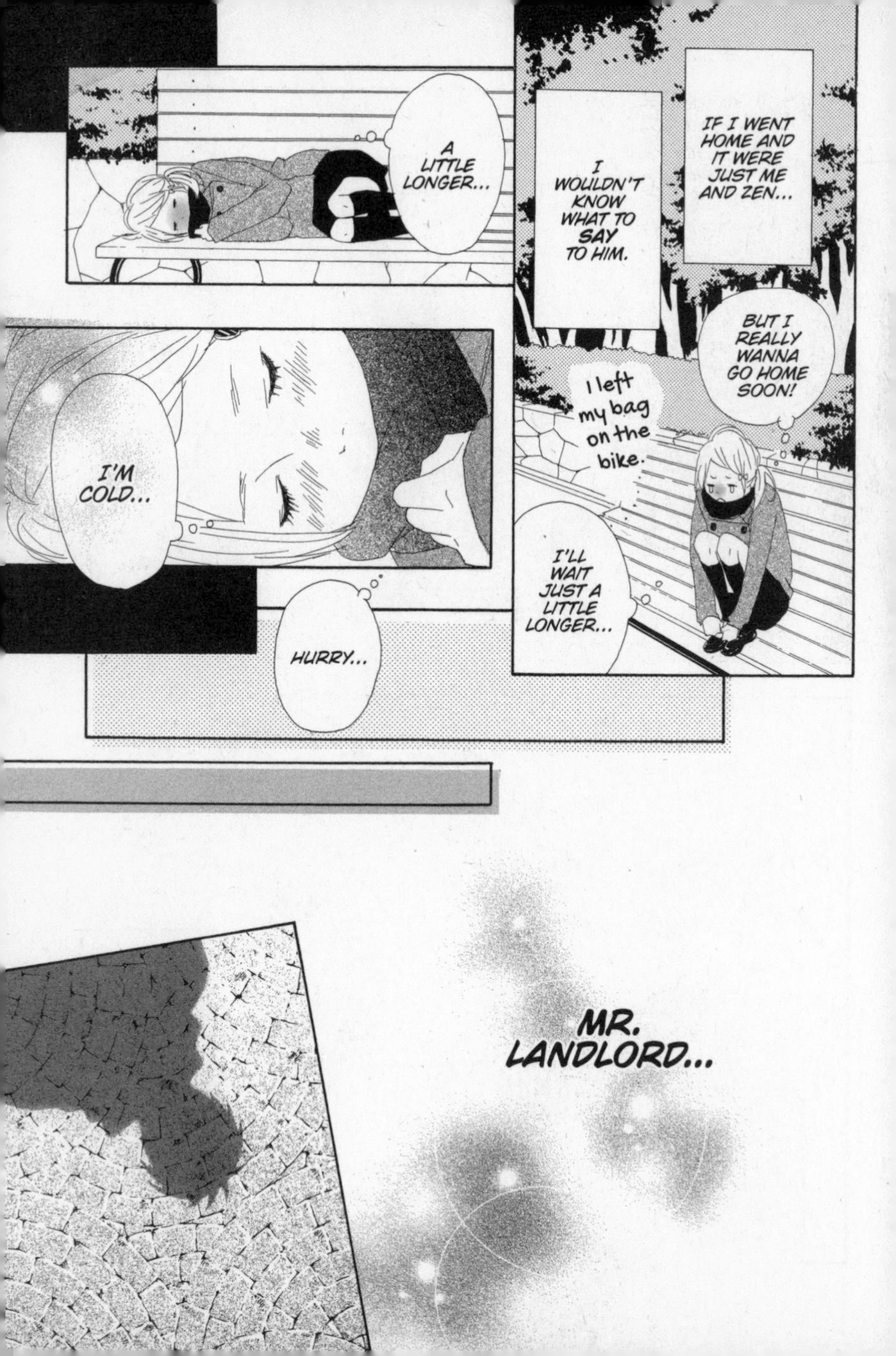
IF I WENT HOME AND IT WERE JUST ME AND ZEN...
I WOULDN'T KNOW WHAT TO SAY TO HIM.
BUT I REALLY WANNA GO HOME SOON!
I left my bag on the bike.
I'LL WAIT JUST A LITTLE LONGER...
A LITTLE LONGER...
I'M COLD...
HURRY...
MR. LANDLORD...

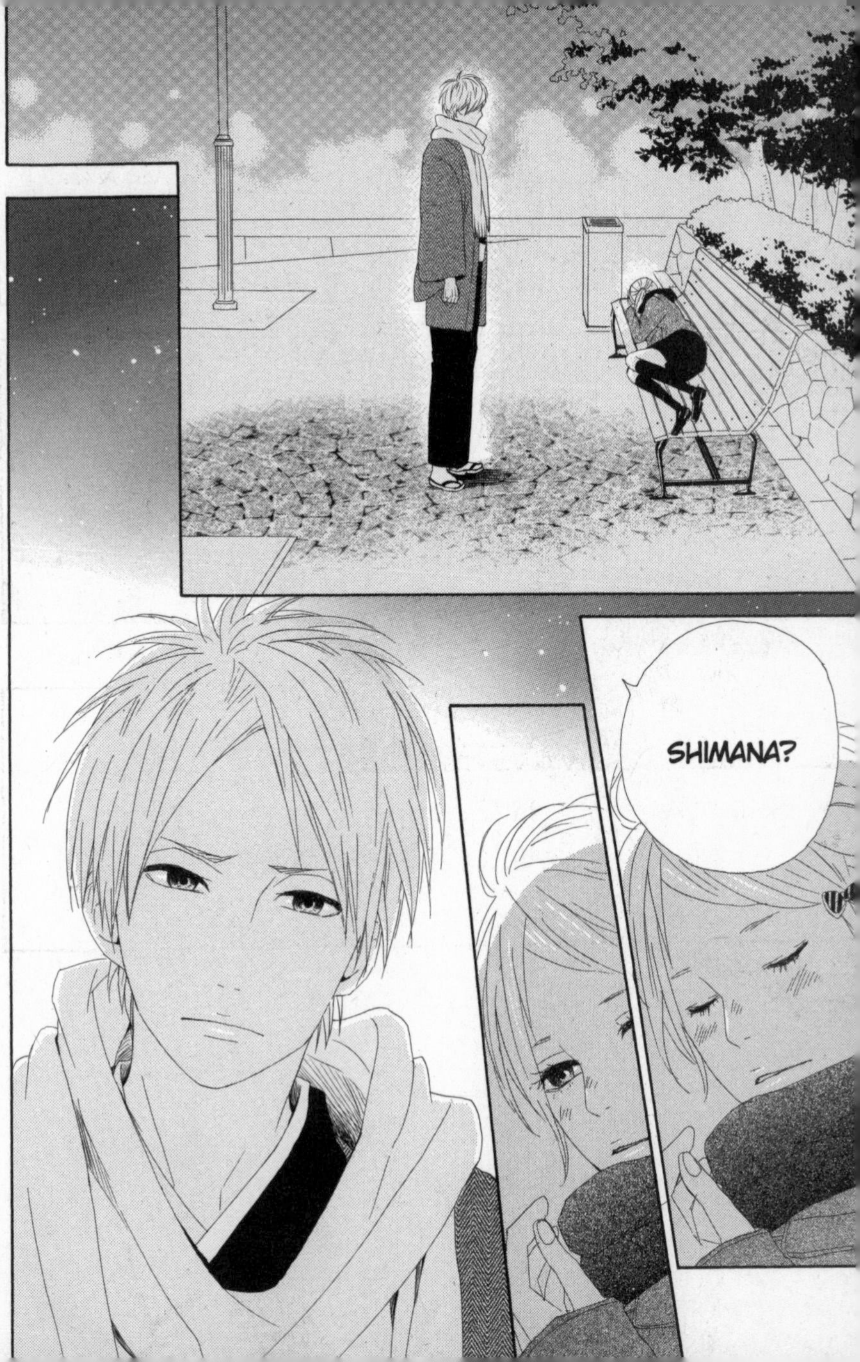
SHIMANA?

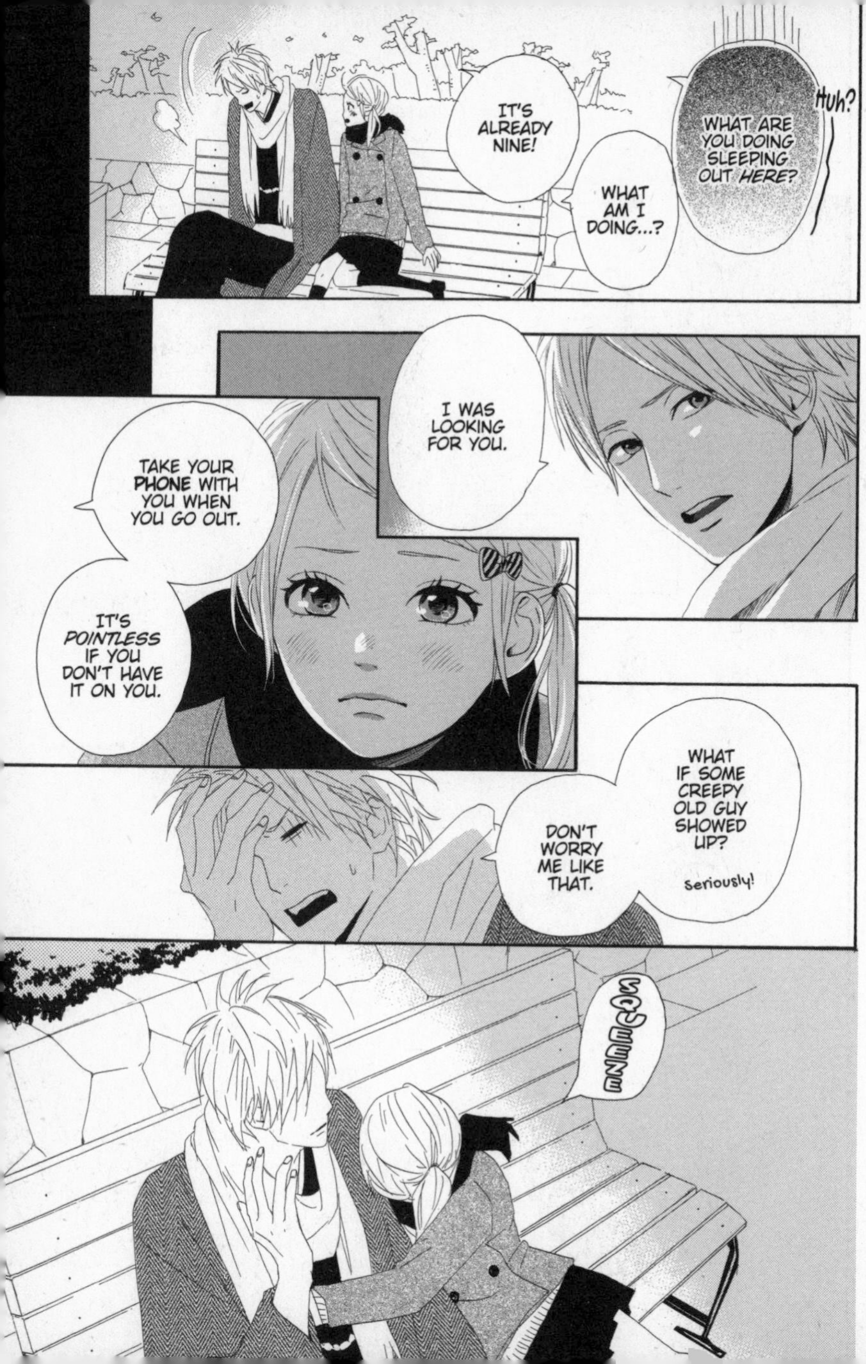
Huh?
WHAT ARE YOU DOING SLEEPING OUT HERE?
WHAT AM I DOING...?
IT'S ALREADY NINE!
I WAS LOOKING FOR YOU.
TAKE YOUR PHONE WITH YOU WHEN YOU GO OUT.
IT'S POINTLESS IF YOU DON'T HAVE IT ON YOU.
WHAT IF SOME CREEPY OLD GUY SHOWED UP?
Seriously!
DON'T WORRY ME LIKE THAT.
SQUEEEZE

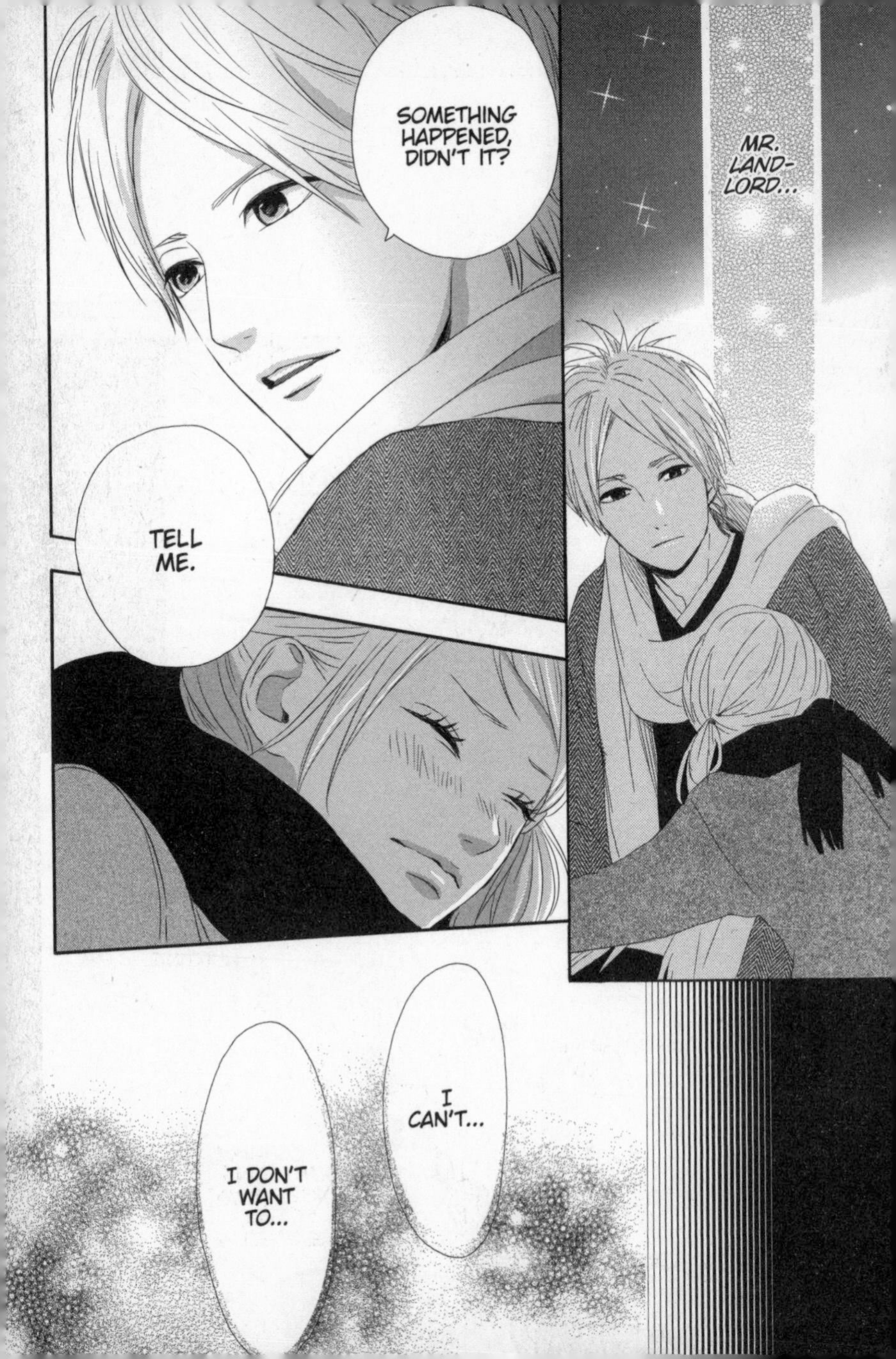
MR. LAND-LORD...
SOMETHING HAPPENED, DIDN'T IT?
TELL ME.
I CAN'T...
I DON'T WANT TO...

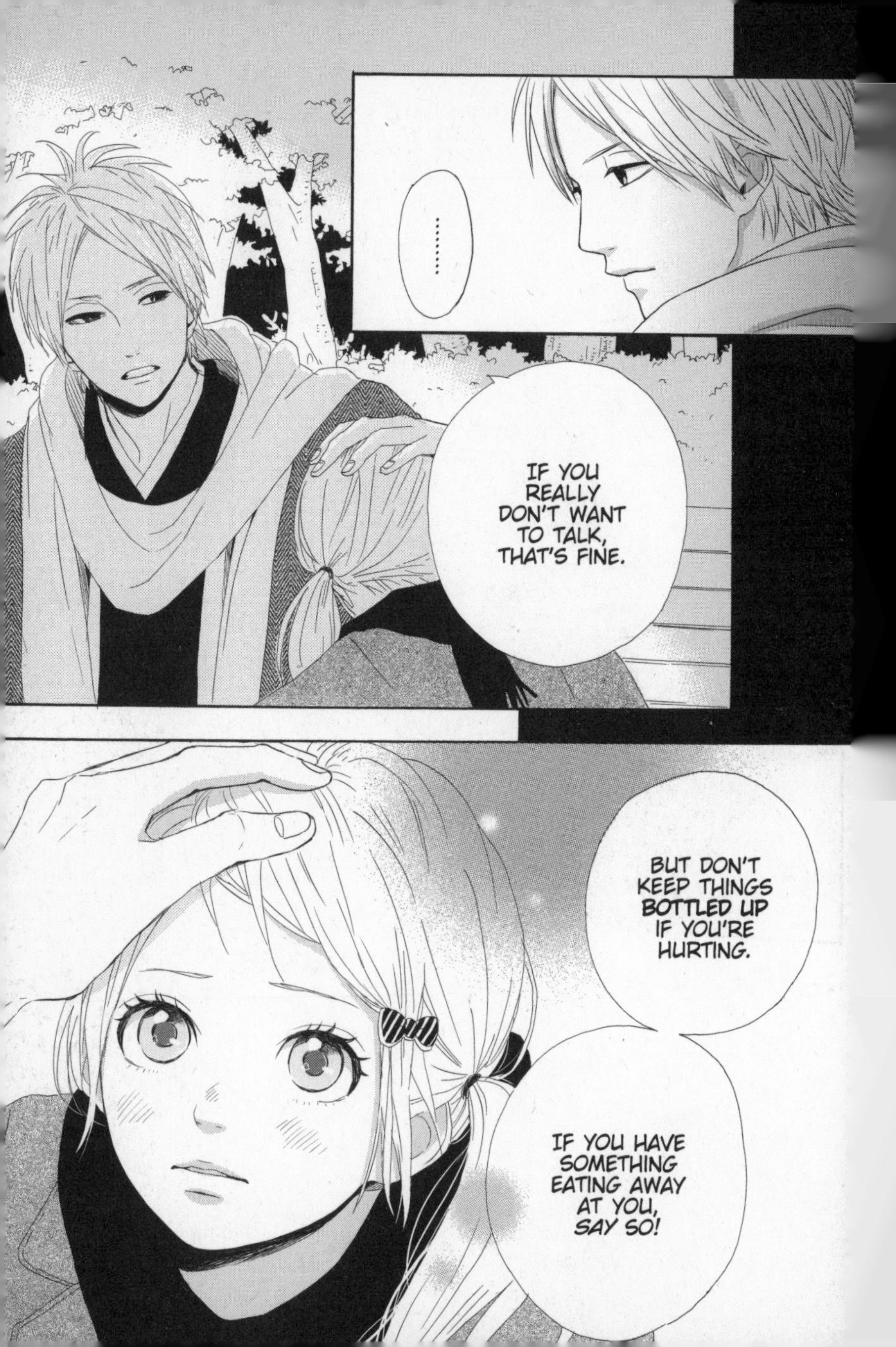
......
IF YOU REALLY DON'T WANT TO TALK, THAT'S FINE.
BUT DON'T KEEP THINGS BOTTLED UP IF YOU'RE HURTING.
IF YOU HAVE SOMETHING EATING AWAY AT YOU, SAY SO!

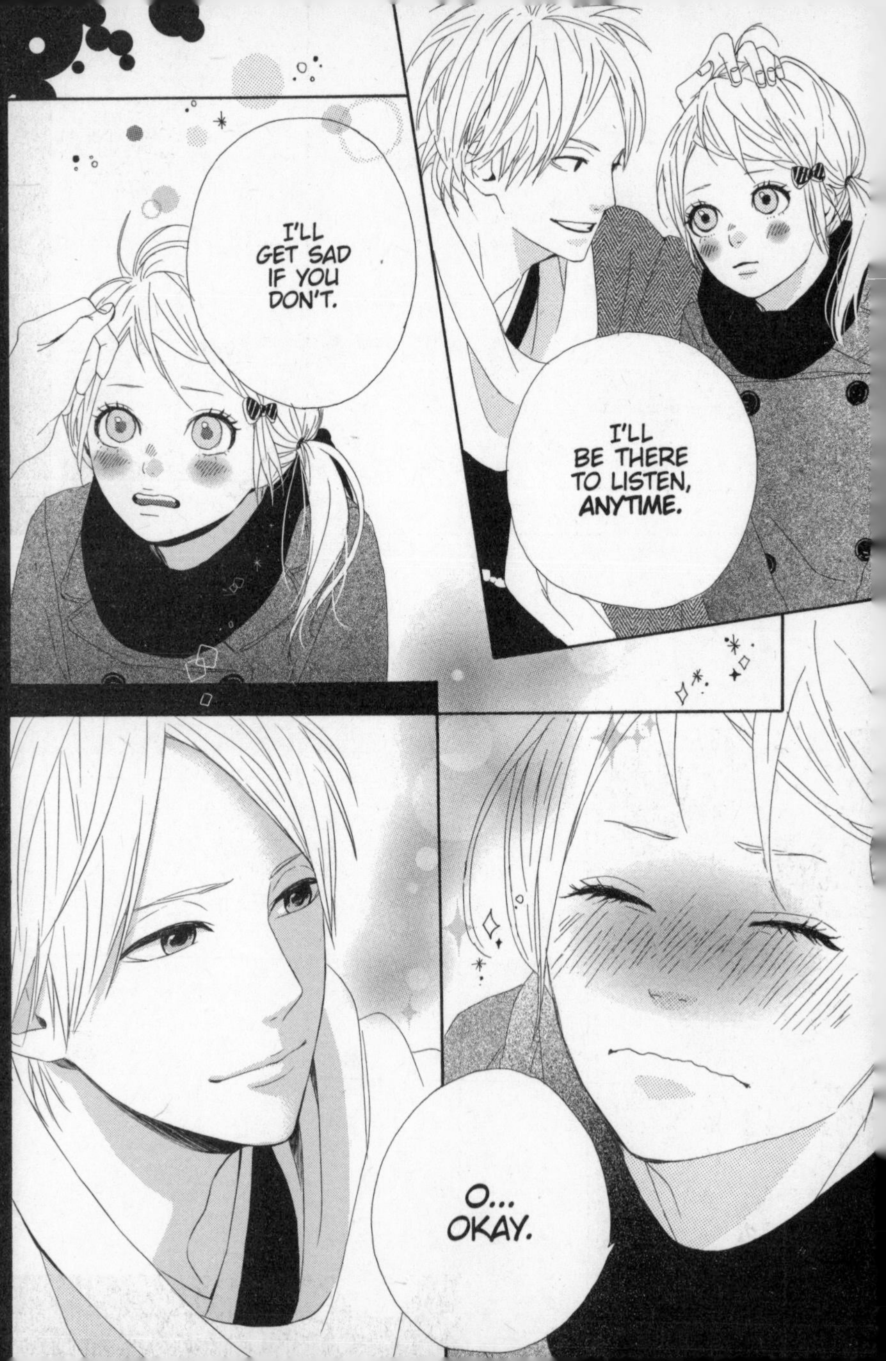
I'LL BE THERE TO LISTEN, ANYTIME.
I'LL GET SAD IF YOU DON'T.
O... OKAY.

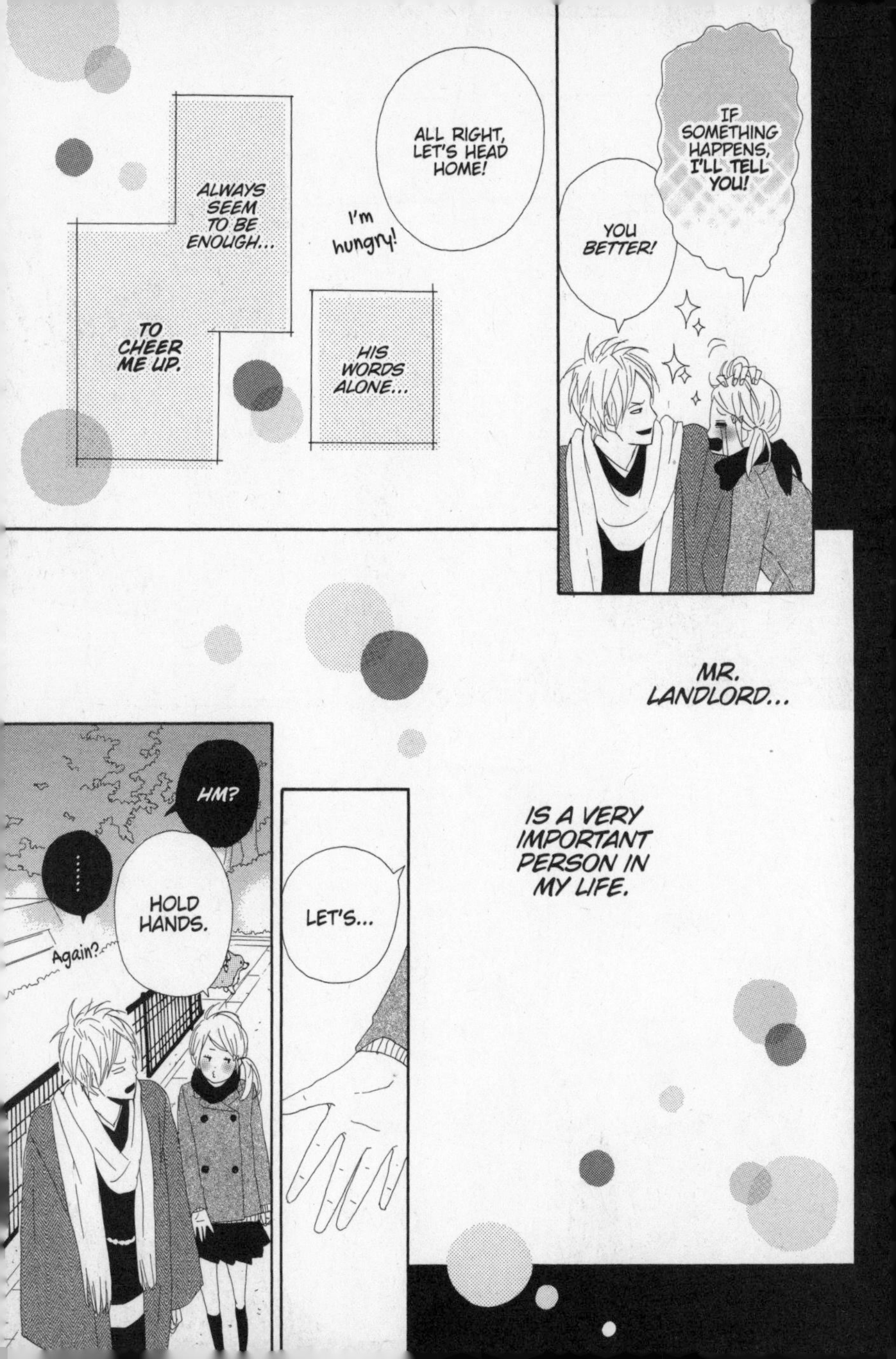
IF SOMETHING HAPPENS, I'LL TELL YOU!
YOU BETTER!
ALL RIGHT, LET'S HEAD HOME!
I'm hungry!
HIS WORDS ALONE...
ALWAYS SEEM TO BE ENOUGH...
TO CHEER ME UP.
MR. LANDLORD...
IS A VERY IMPORTANT PERSON IN MY LIFE.
LET'S...
HM?
HOLD HANDS.
......
Again?

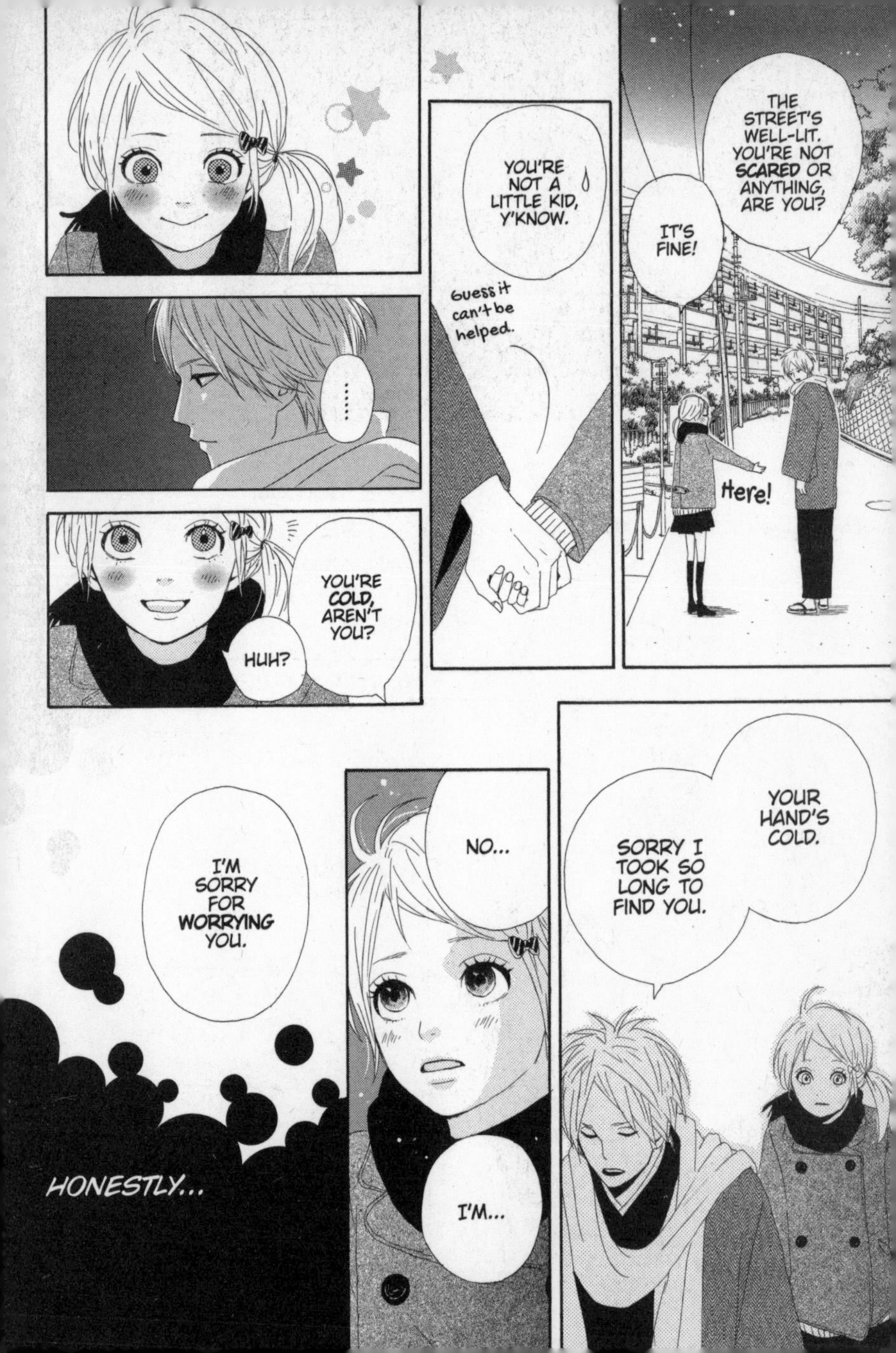
THE STREET'S WELL-LIT. YOU'RE NOT SCARED OR ANYTHING, ARE YOU?
IT'S FINE!
Here!
YOU'RE NOT A LITTLE KID, Y'KNOW.
Guess it can't be helped.
......
YOU'RE COLD, AREN'T YOU?
HUH?
YOUR HAND'S COLD.
SORRY I TOOK SO LONG TO FIND YOU.
NO...
I'M...
I'M SORRY FOR WORRYING YOU.
HONESTLY...

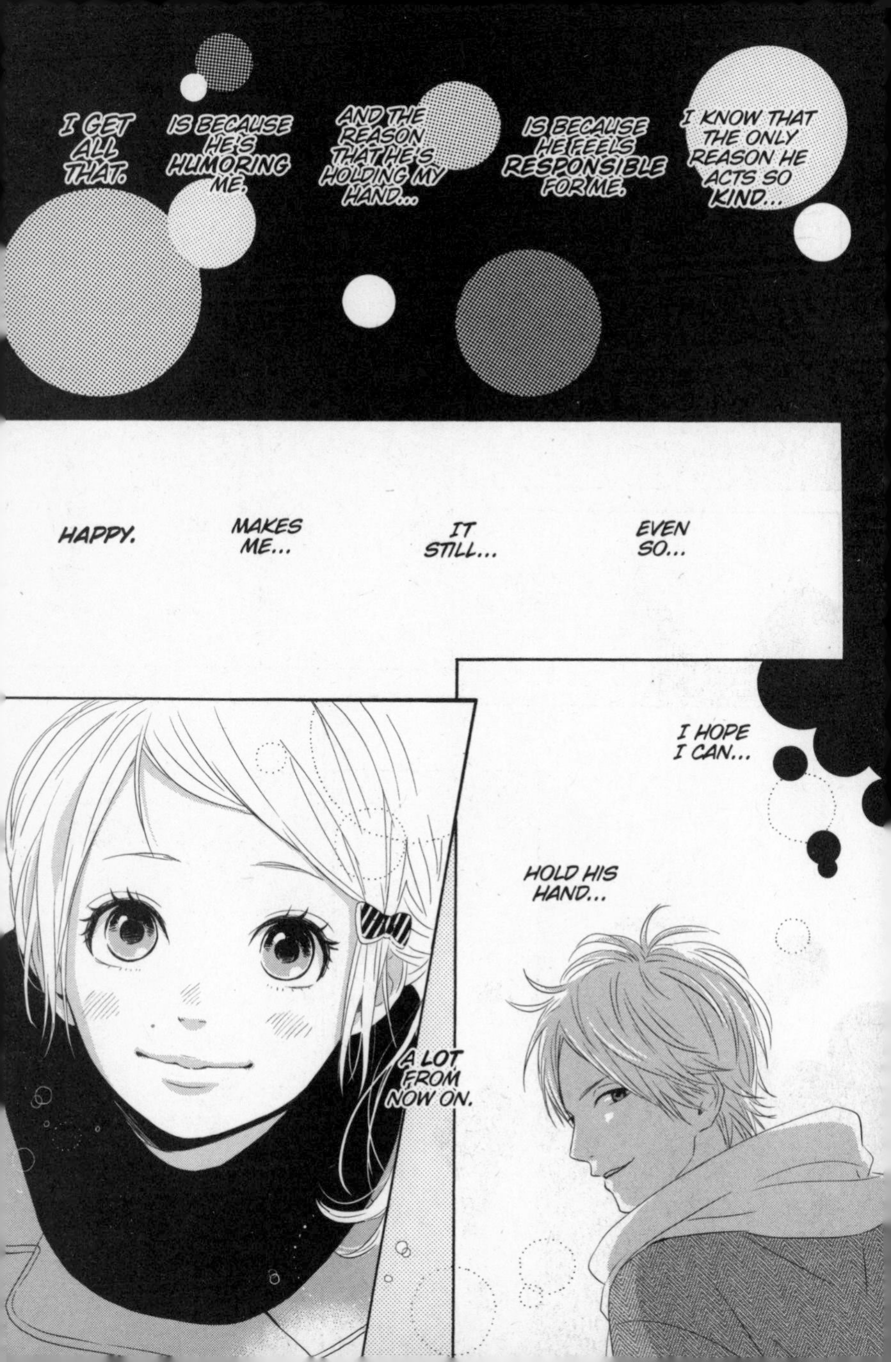
I KNOW THAT THE ONLY REASON HE ACTS SO KIND...
IS BECAUSE HE FEELS RESPONSIBLE FOR ME.
AND THE REASON THAT HE'S HOLDING MY HAND...
IS BECAUSE HE'S HUMORING ME.
I GET ALL THAT.
EVEN SO...
IT STILL...
MAKES ME...
HAPPY.
I HOPE I CAN...
HOLD HIS HAND...
A LOT FROM NOW ON.

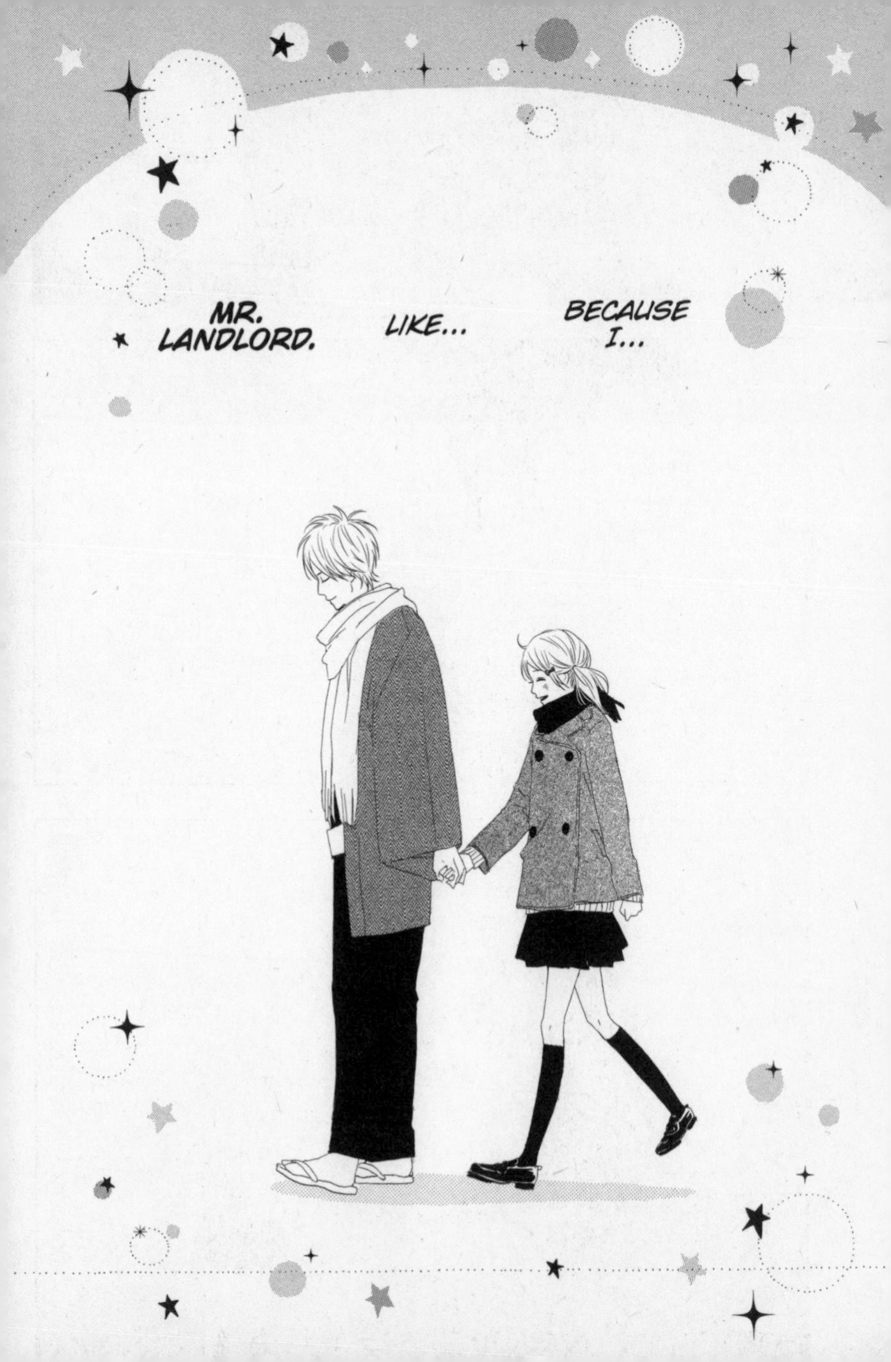
BECAUSE I...
LIKE...
MR. LANDLORD.

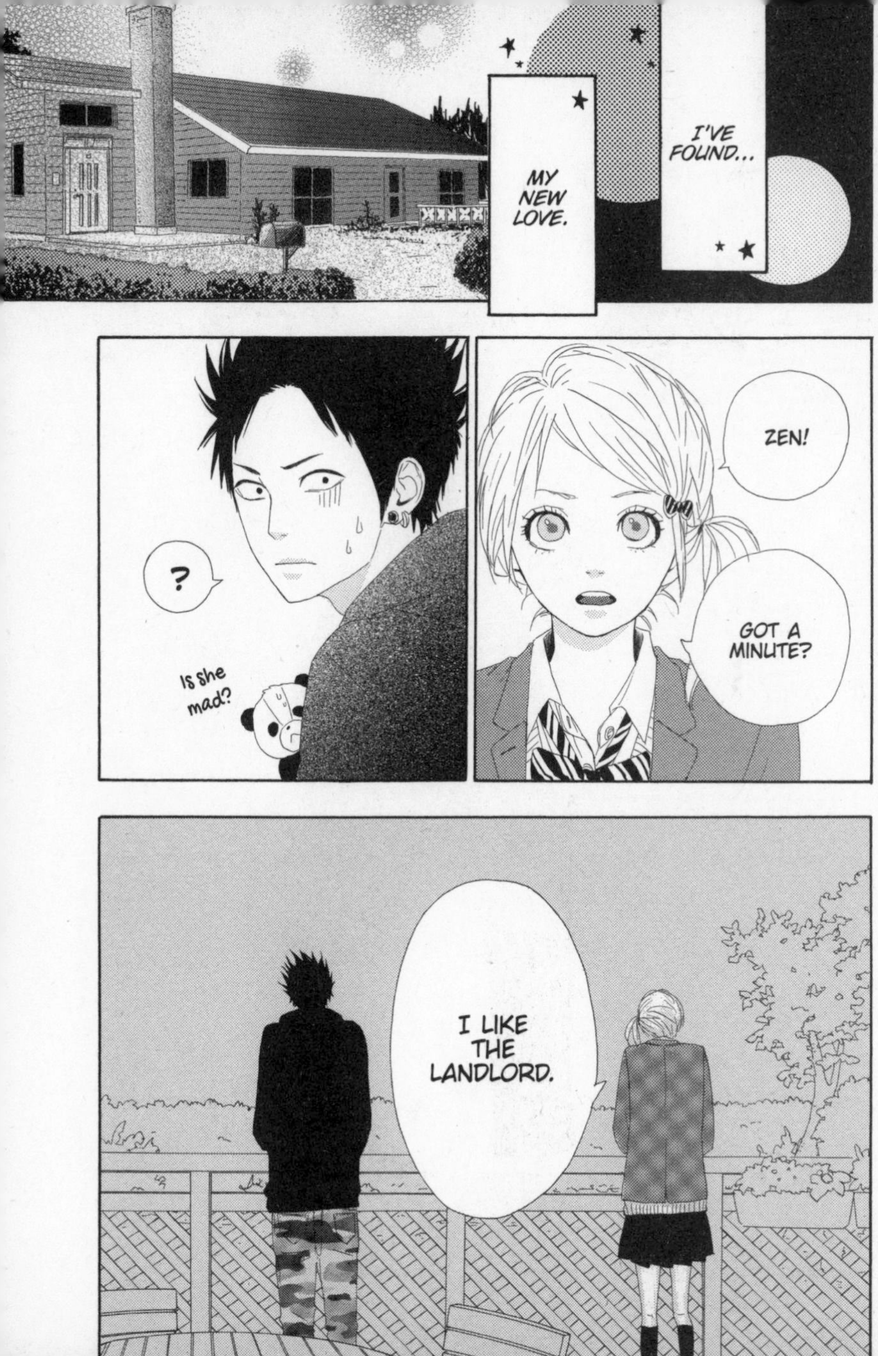
I'VE FOUND...
MY NEW LOVE.
ZEN!
GOT A MINUTE?
?
Is she mad?
I LIKE THE LANDLORD.

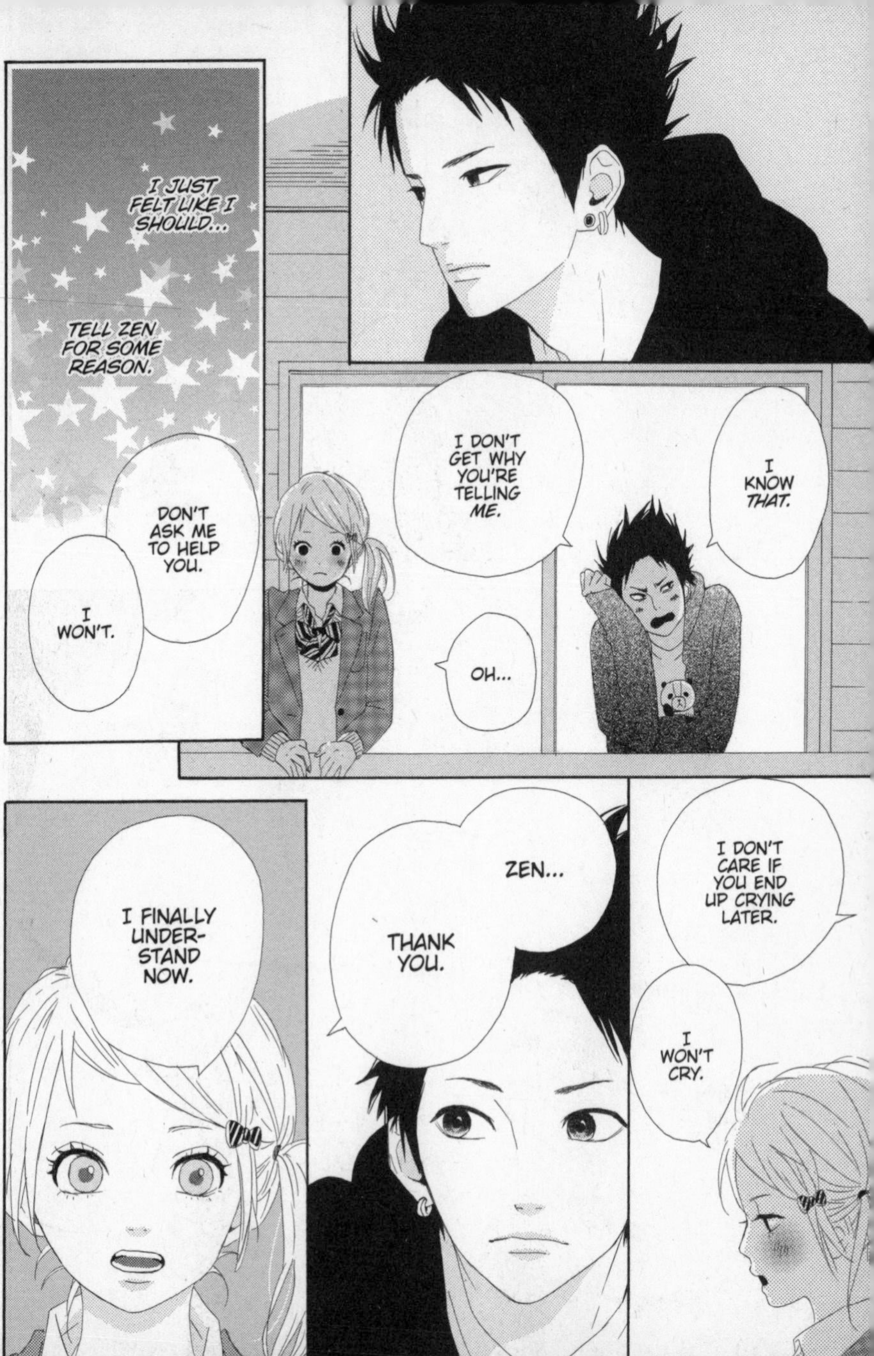
I KNOW THAT.
I DON'T GET WHY YOU'RE TELLING ME.
OH...
I JUST FELT LIKE I SHOULD...
TELL ZEN FOR SOME REASON.
DON'T ASK ME TO HELP YOU.
I WON'T.
I DON'T CARE IF YOU END UP CRYING LATER.
I WON'T CRY.
ZEN...
THANK YOU.
I FINALLY UNDER-STAND NOW.

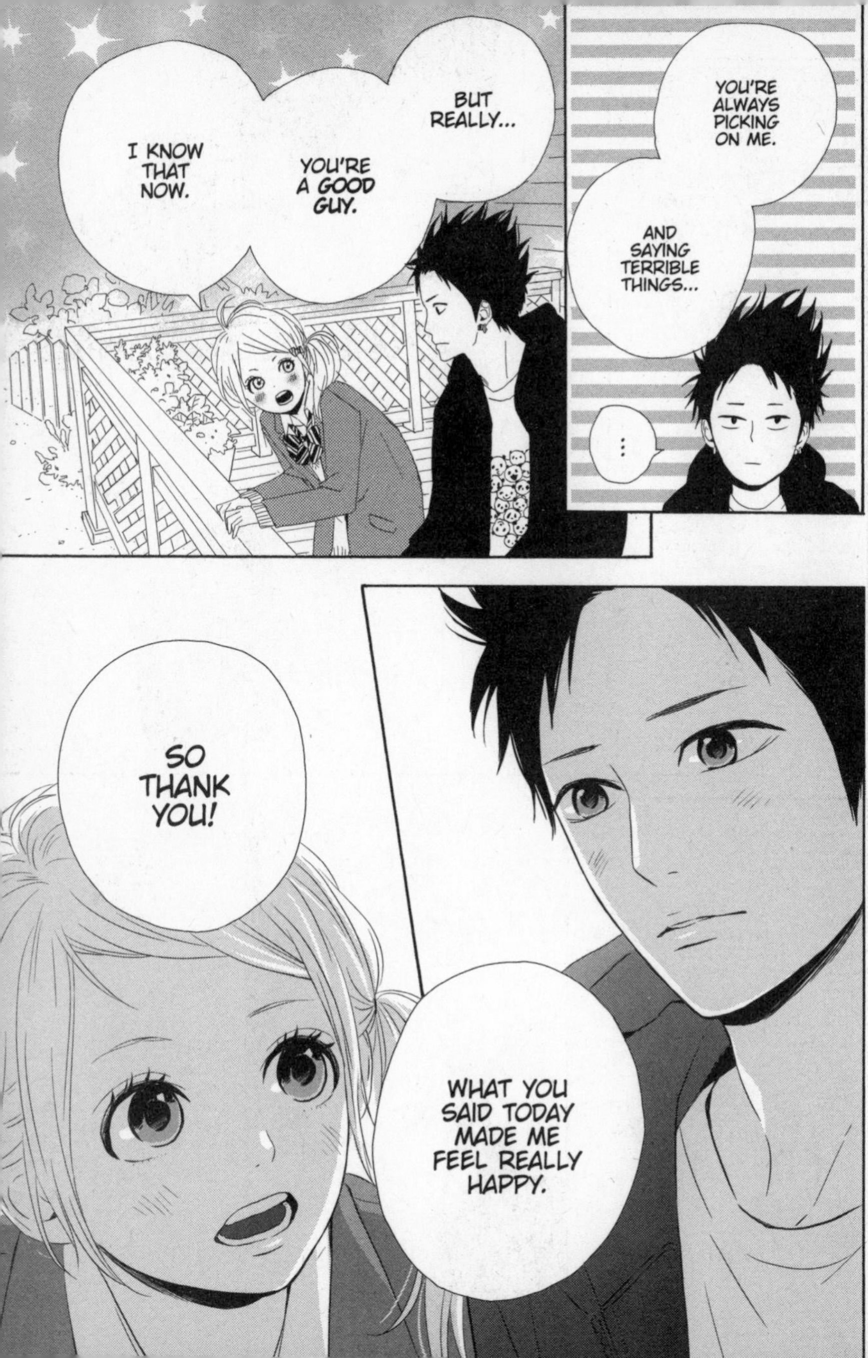
YOU'RE ALWAYS PICKING ON ME.
AND SAYING TERRIBLE THINGS...
...
BUT REALLY...
YOU'RE A GOOD GUY.
I KNOW THAT NOW.
SO THANK YOU!
WHAT YOU SAID TODAY MADE ME FEEL REALLY HAPPY.

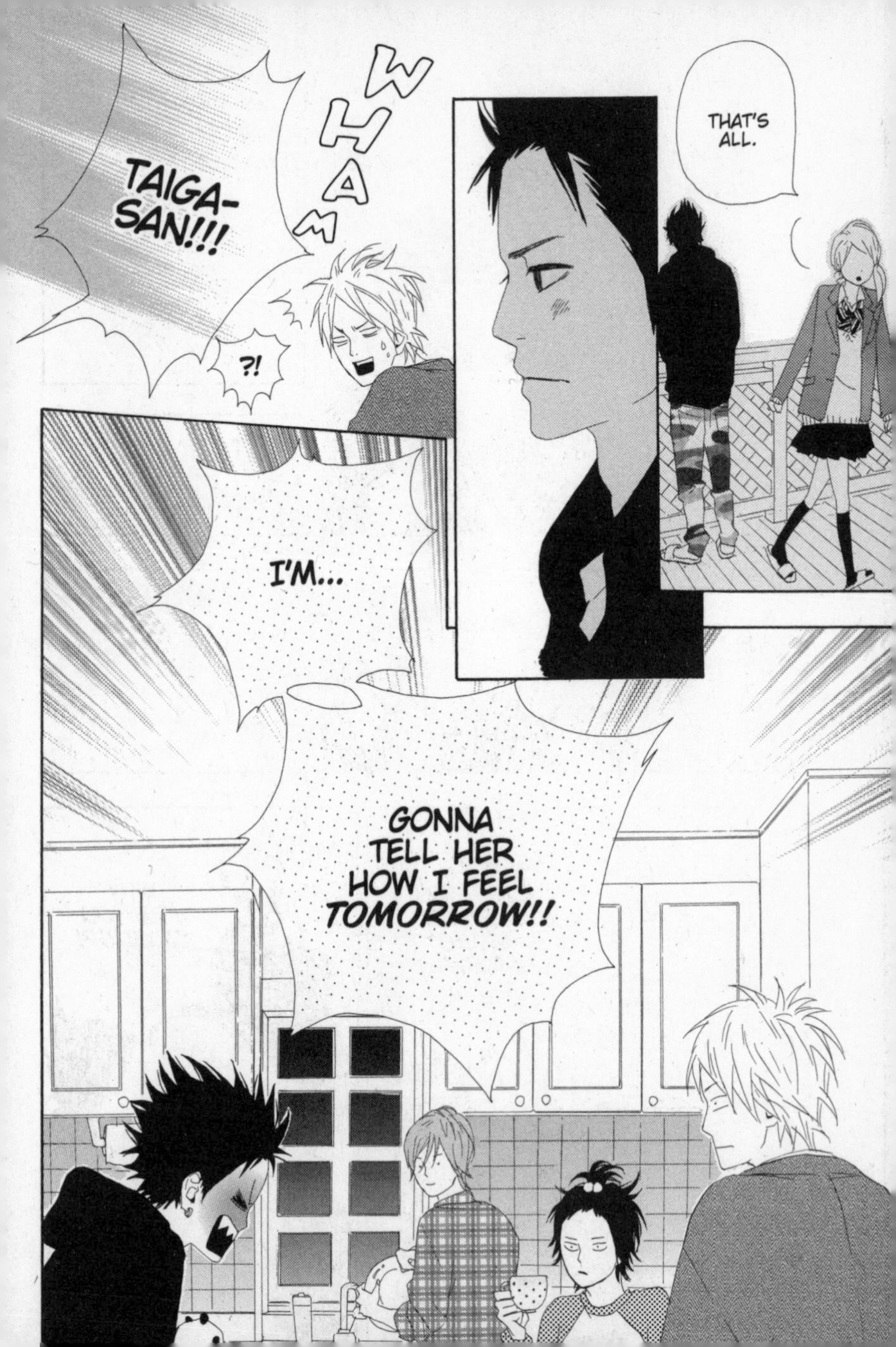
THAT'S ALL.
WHAM
TAIGA-SAN!!!
?!
I'M...
GONNA TELL HER HOW I FEEL TOMORROW!!

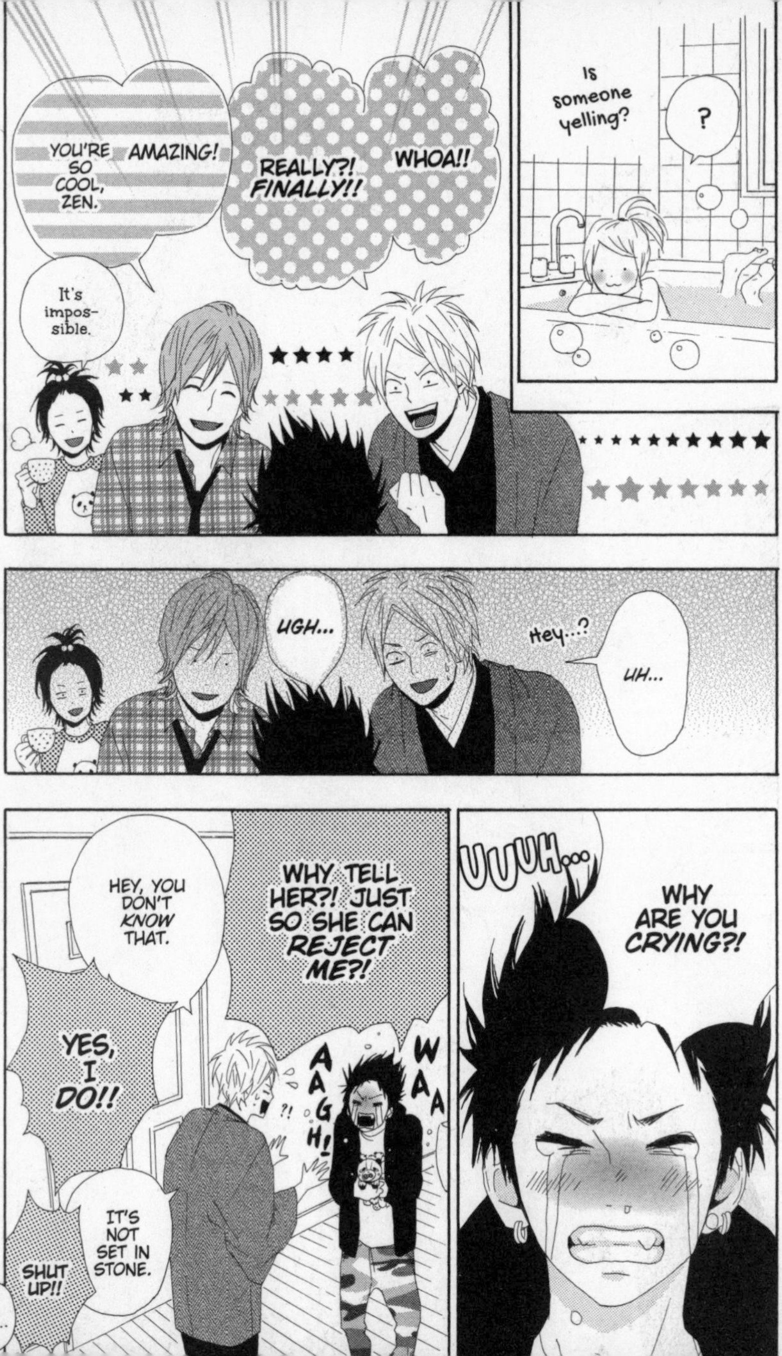
Is someone yelling?
?
WHOA!!
REALLY?! FINALLY!!
AMAZING!
YOU'RE SO COOL, ZEN.
It's impossible.
Hey...?
UH...
UGH...
UUUH...
WHY ARE YOU CRYING?!
WHY TELL HER?! JUST SO SHE CAN REJECT ME?!
WAA
AAGH!
?!
HEY, YOU DON'T KNOW THAT.
YES, I DO!!
IT'S NOT SET IN STONE.
SHUT UP!!
oh boy...

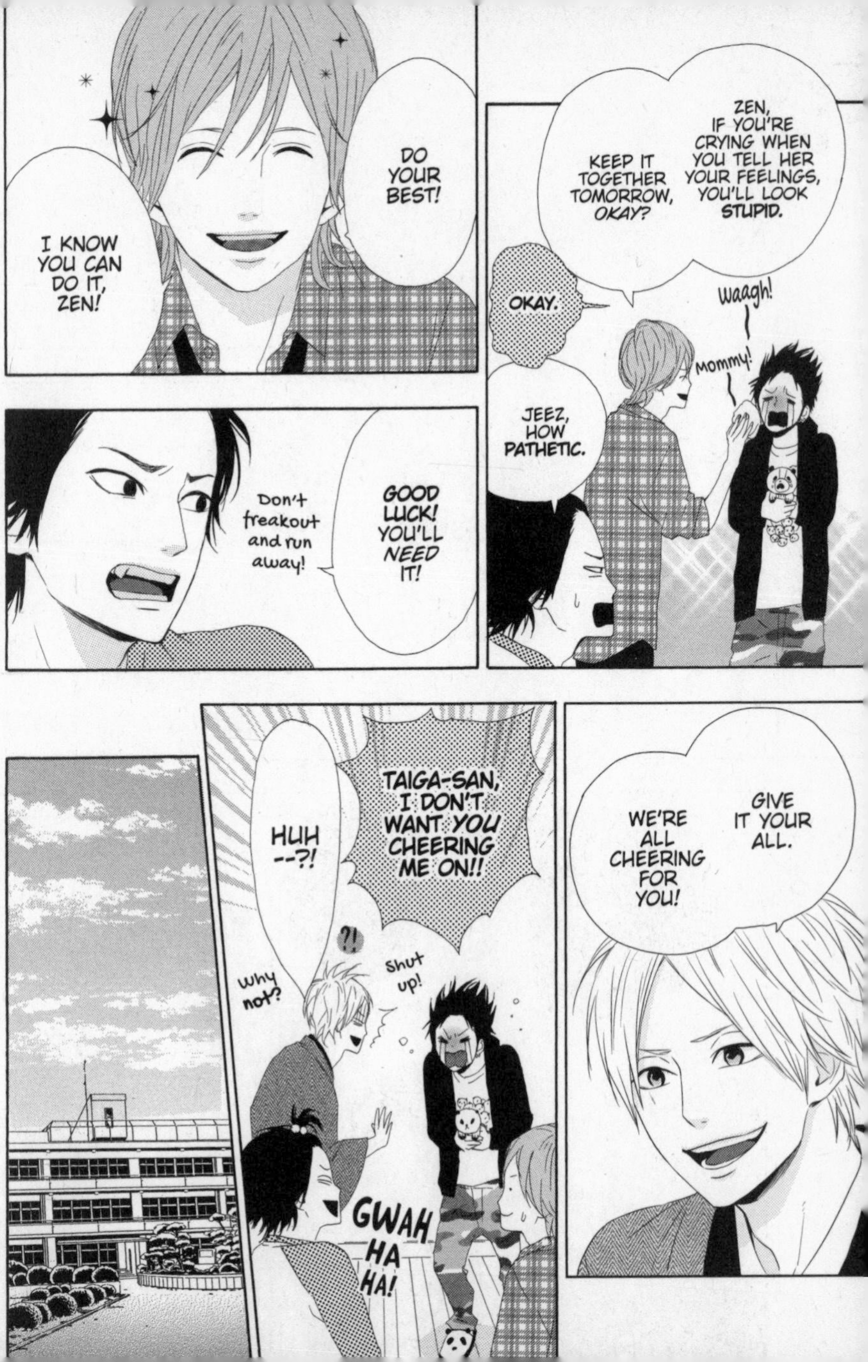

ZEN, IF YOU'RE CRYING WHEN YOU TELL HER YOUR FEELINGS, YOU'LL LOOK STUPID.
KEEP IT TOGETHER TOMORROW, OKAY?
Waagh!
Mommy!
OKAY.
JEEZ, HOW PATHETIC.
DO YOUR BEST!
I KNOW YOU CAN DO IT, ZEN!
GOOD LUCK! YOU'LL NEED IT!
Don't freakout and run away!
GIVE IT YOUR ALL.
WE'RE ALL CHEERING FOR YOU!
TAIGA-SAN, I DON'T WANT YOU CHEERING ME ON!!
HUH --?!
?!
Shut up!
Why not?
GWAH HA HA!

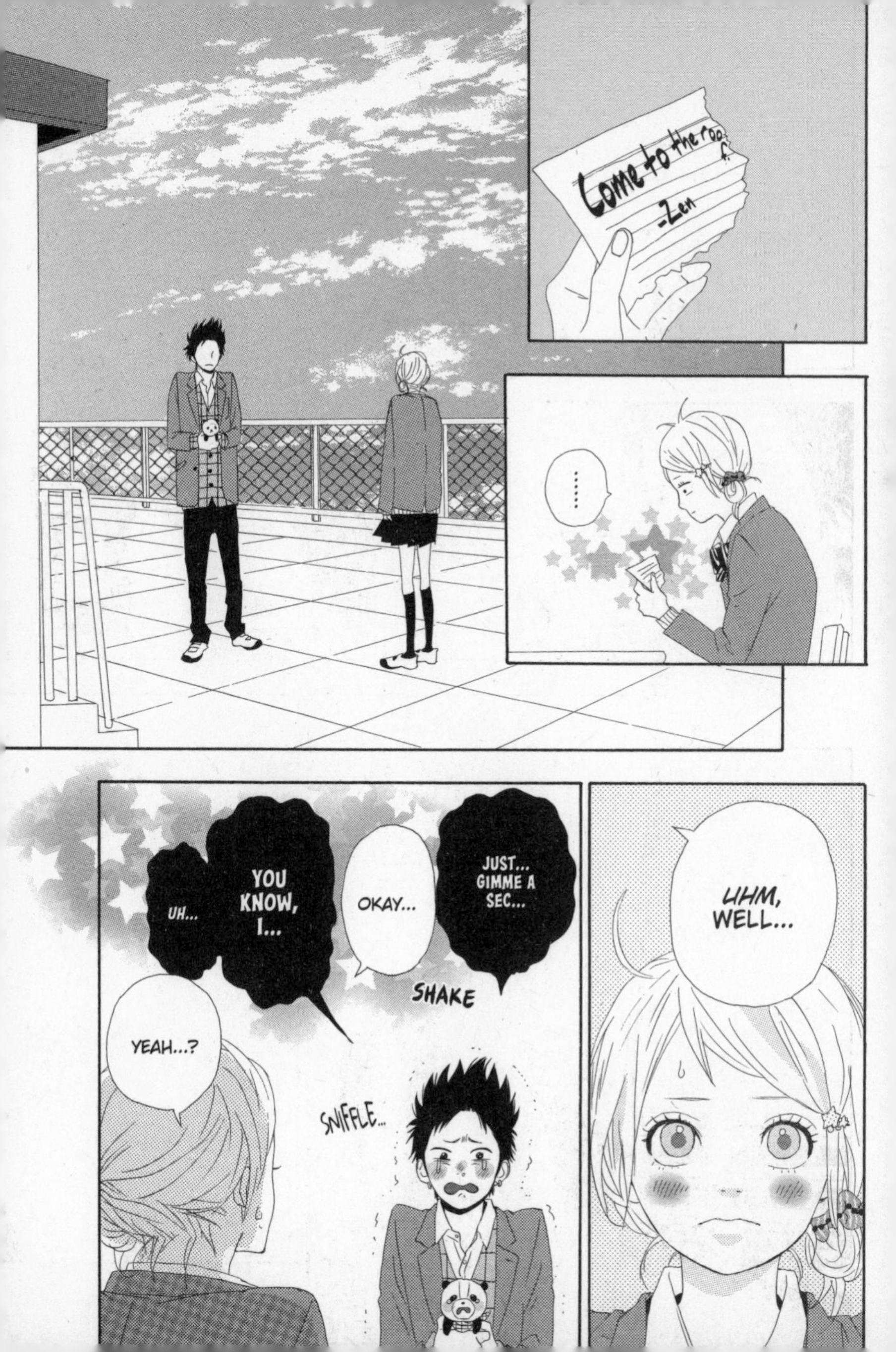
Come to the roof.
-Zen
......
UHM, WELL...
JUST... GIMME A SEC...
OKAY...
YOU KNOW, I...
UH...
SHAKE
YEAH...?
SNIFFLE...

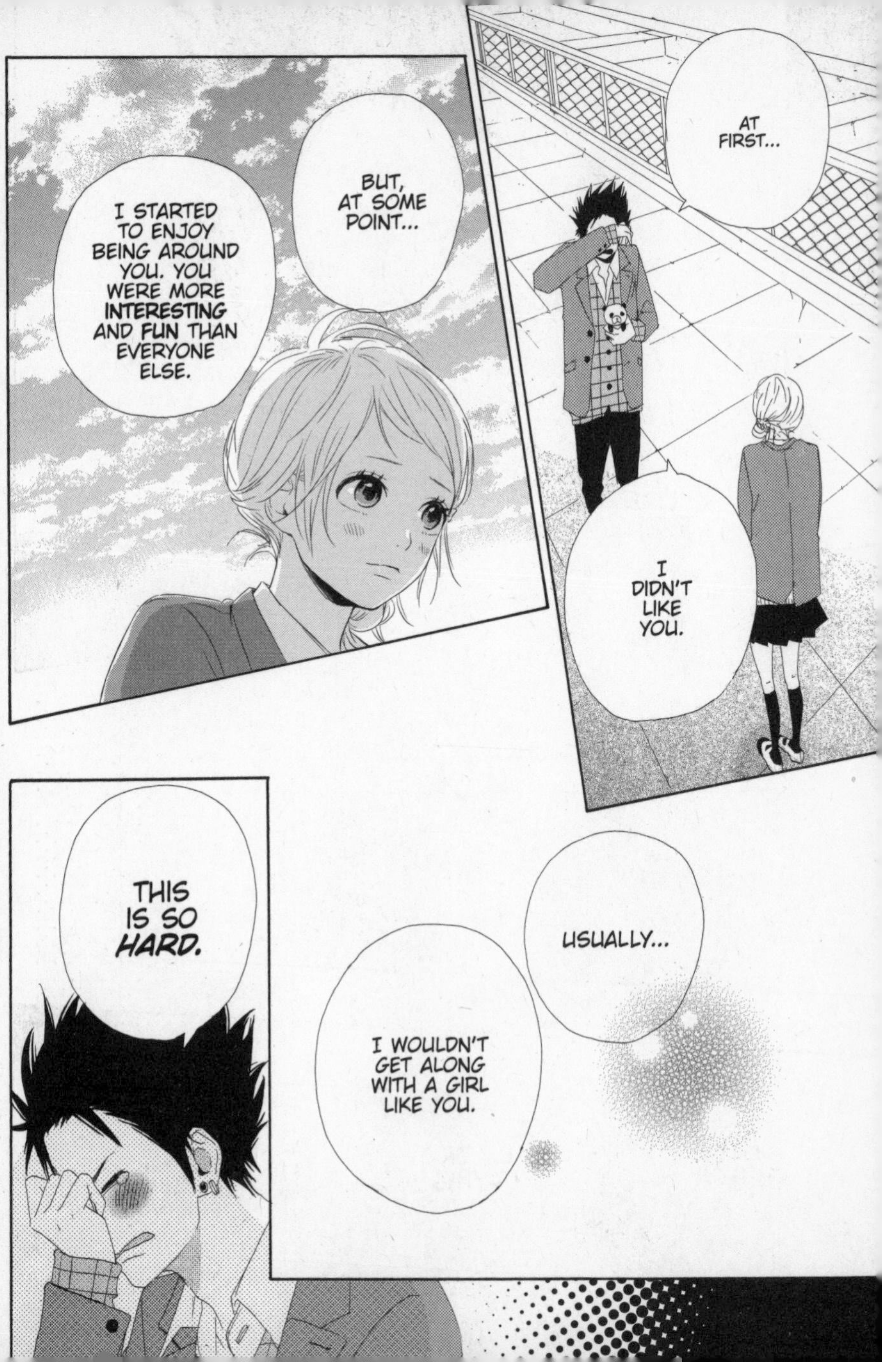
AT FIRST...
I DIDN'T LIKE YOU.
BUT, AT SOME POINT...
I STARTED TO ENJOY BEING AROUND YOU. YOU WERE MORE **INTERESTING** AND **FUN** THAN EVERYONE ELSE.
USUALLY...
I WOULDN'T GET ALONG WITH A GIRL LIKE YOU.
THIS IS SO ***HARD.***

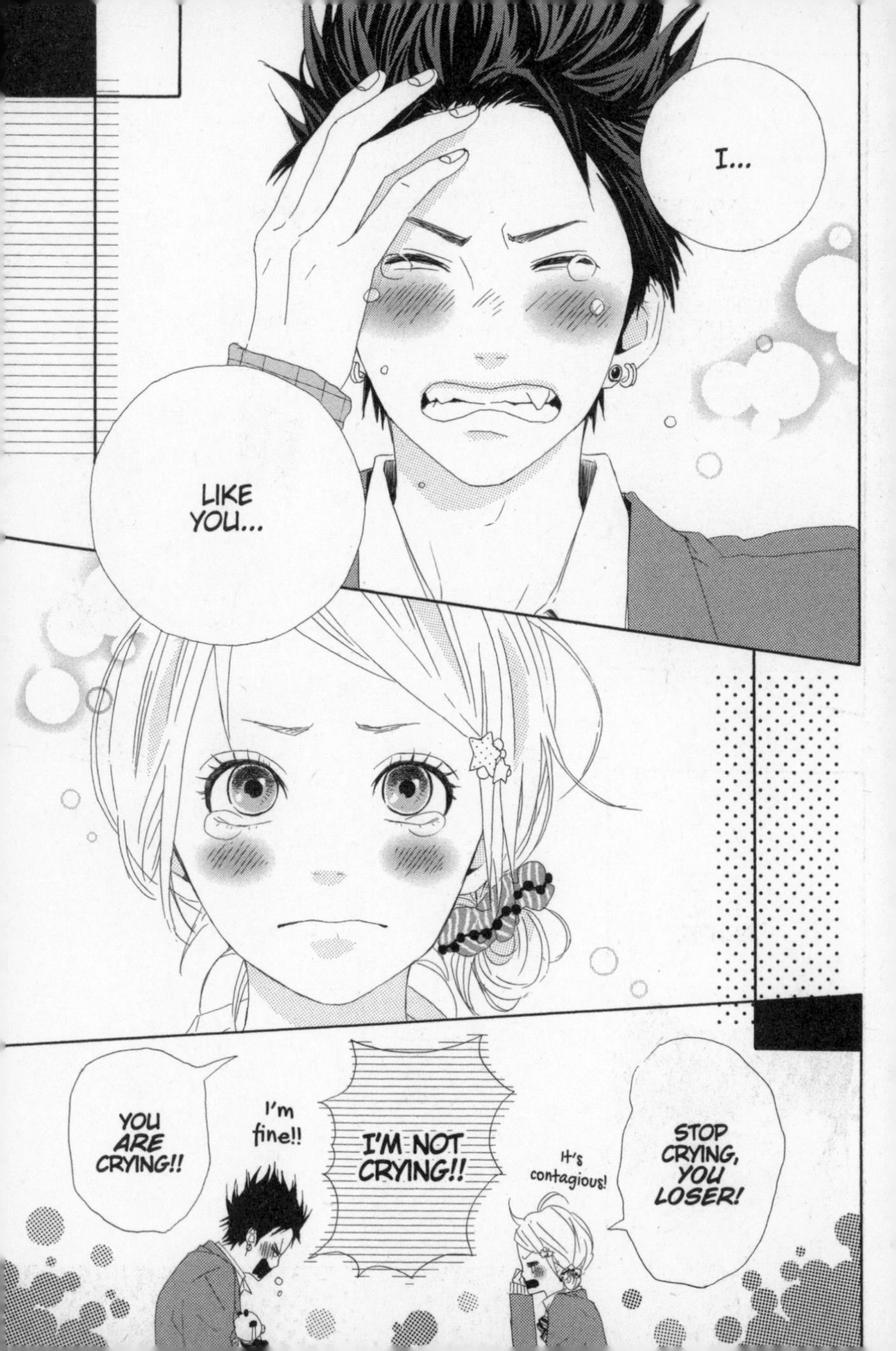
I...
LIKE YOU...
STOP CRYING, YOU LOSER!
It's contagious!
I'M NOT CRYING!!
I'm fine!!
YOU ARE CRYING!!

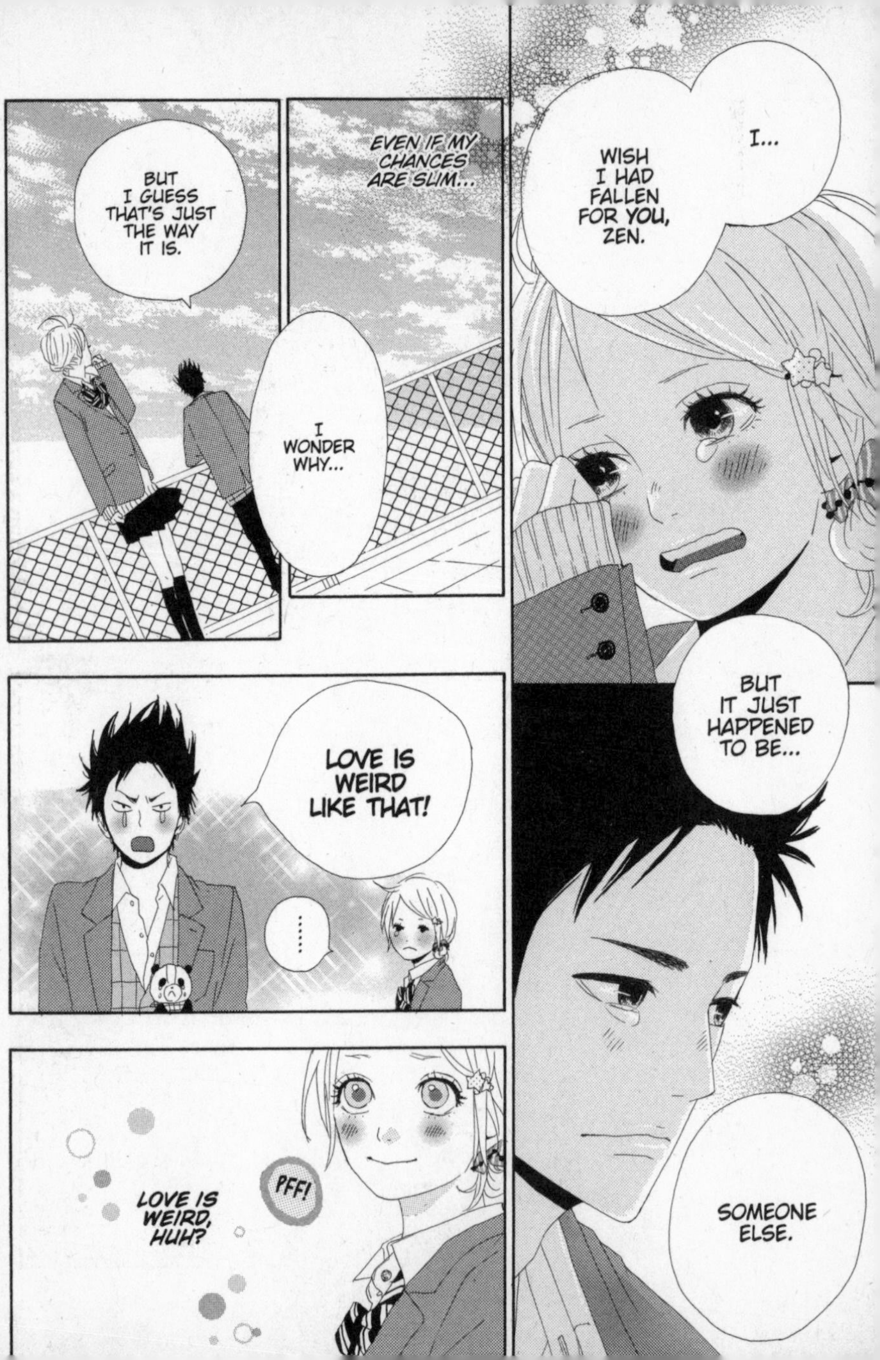
I...
WISH I HAD FALLEN FOR YOU, ZEN.
BUT IT JUST HAPPENED TO BE...
SOMEONE ELSE.
EVEN IF MY CHANCES ARE SLIM...
I WONDER WHY...
BUT I GUESS THAT'S JUST THE WAY IT IS.
LOVE IS WEIRD LIKE THAT!
......
PFF!
LOVE IS WEIRD, HUH?

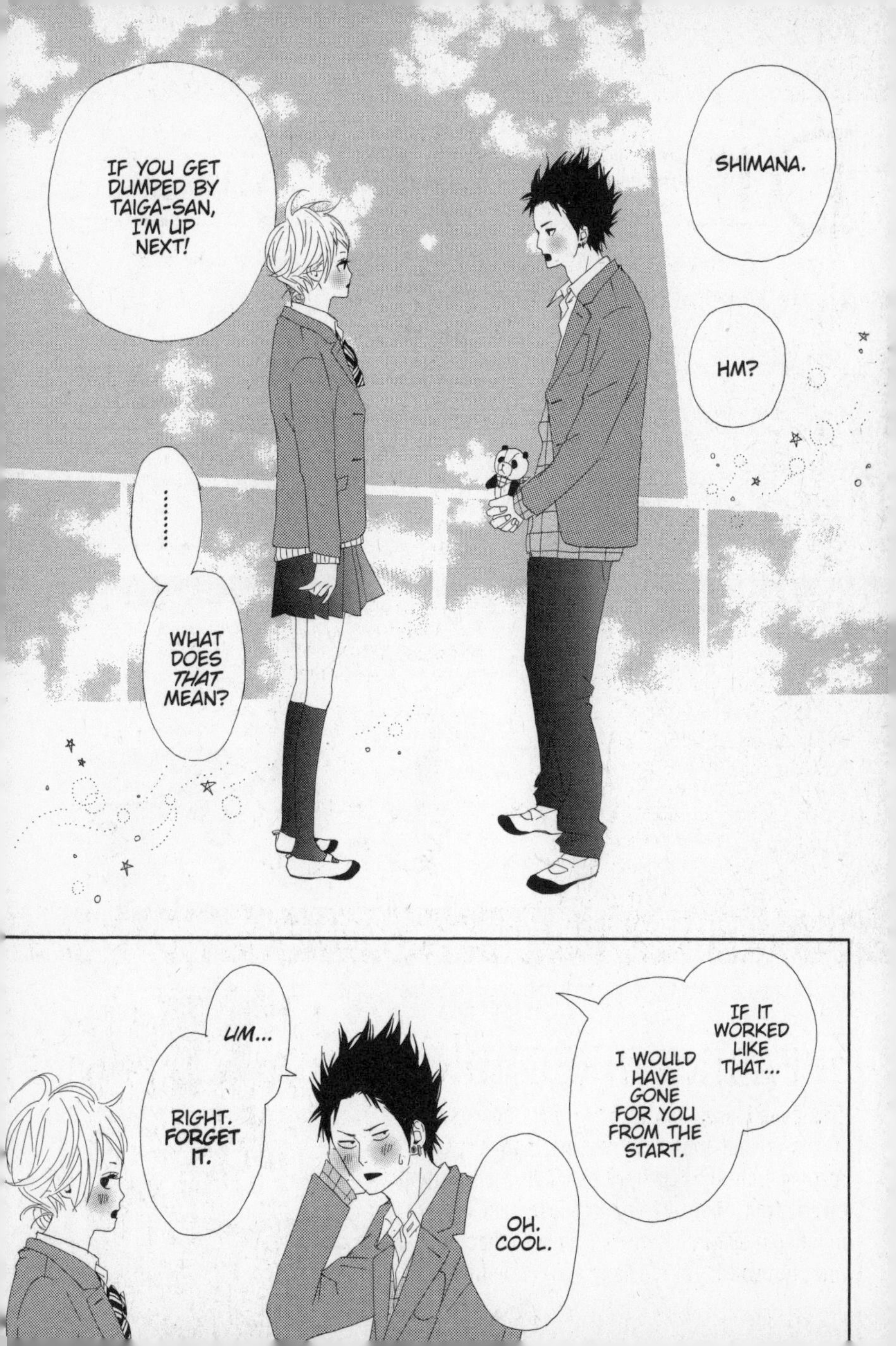
SHIMANA.
HM?
IF YOU GET DUMPED BY TAIGA-SAN, I'M UP NEXT!
......
WHAT DOES THAT MEAN?
IF IT WORKED LIKE THAT...
I WOULD HAVE GONE FOR YOU FROM THE START.
OH. COOL.
UM...
RIGHT. FORGET IT.

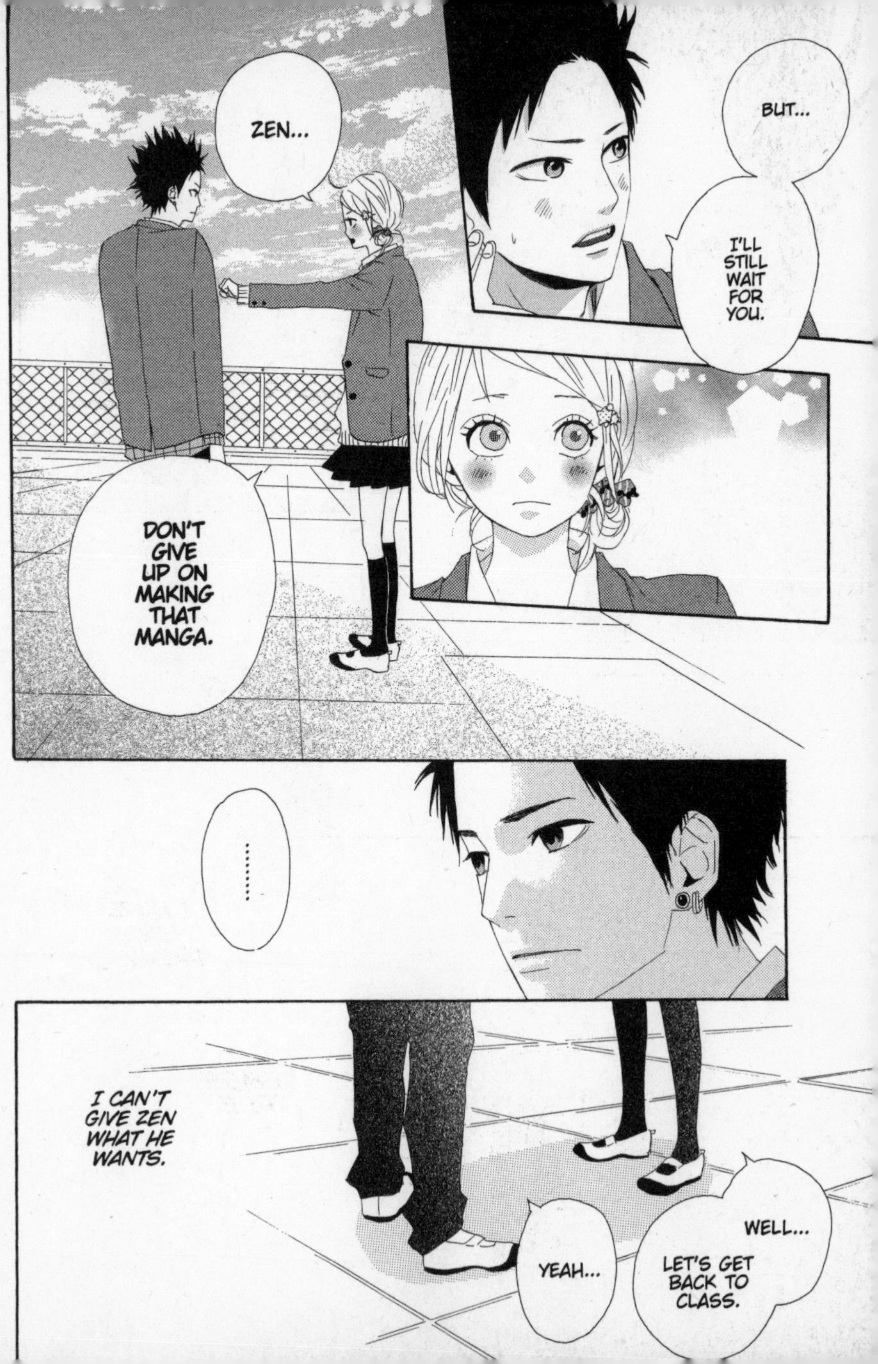
BUT...
I'LL STILL WAIT FOR YOU.
ZEN...
DON'T GIVE UP ON MAKING THAT MANGA.
......
WELL...
LET'S GET BACK TO CLASS.
YEAH...
I CAN'T GIVE ZEN WHAT HE WANTS.

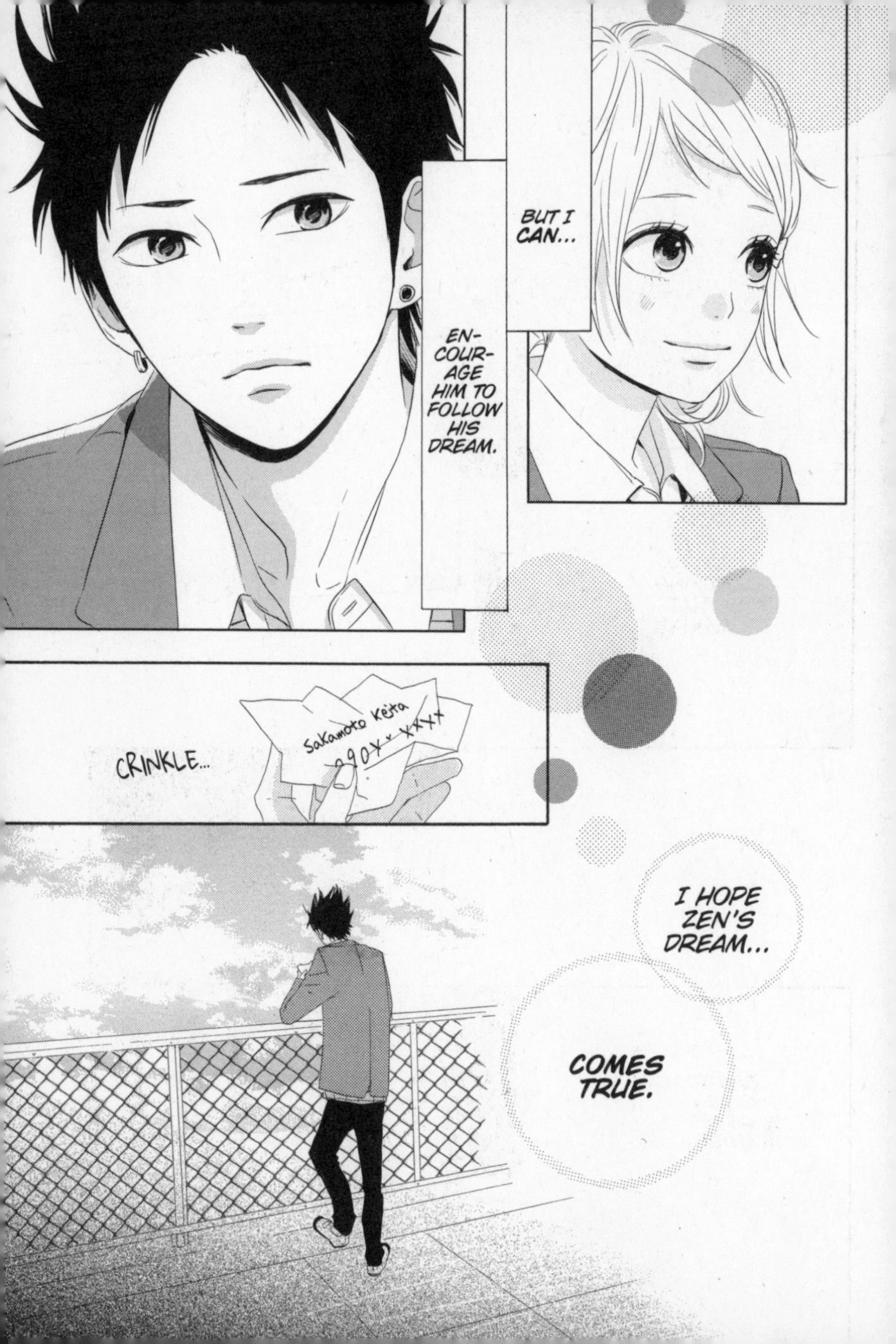
BUT I CAN...
EN-COUR-AGE HIM TO FOLLOW HIS DREAM.
Sakamoto Keita
090X-XXXX
CRINKLE...
I HOPE ZEN'S DREAM...
COMES TRUE.

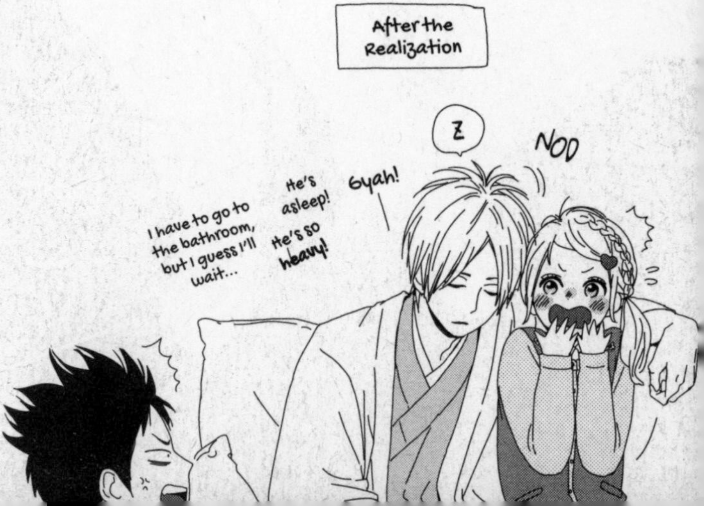
After the Realization
Z
NOD
Gyah!
He's asleep!
He's so heavy!
I have to go to the bathroom, but I guess I'll wait...

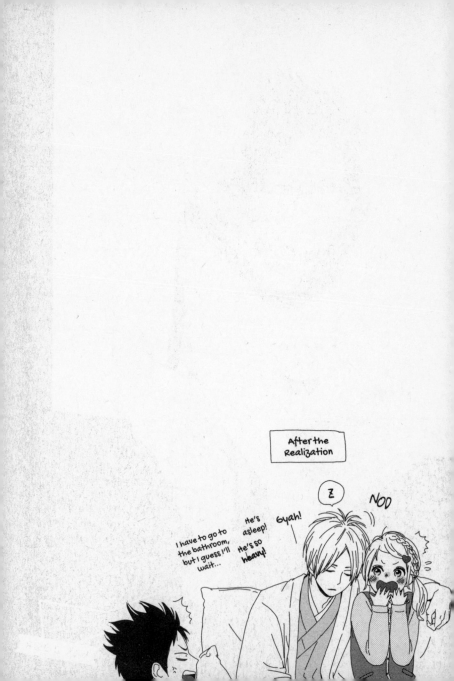

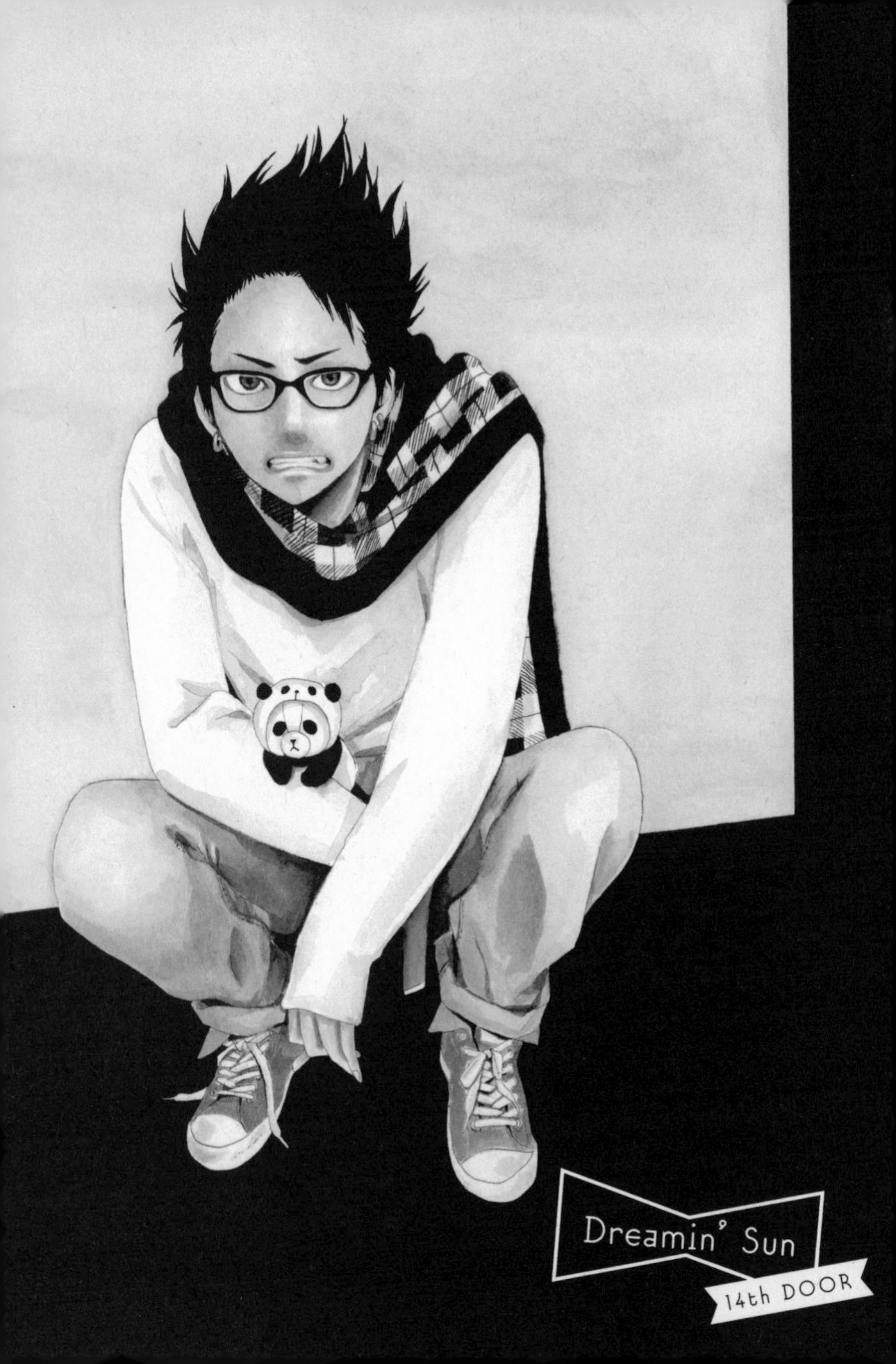
Dreamin' Sun
14th DOOR

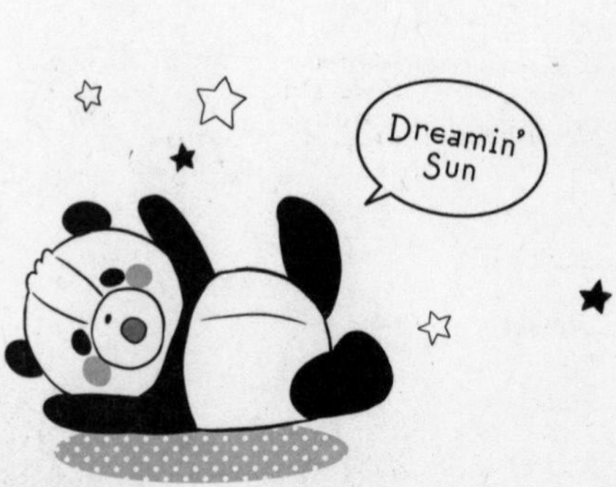
Dreamin' Sun

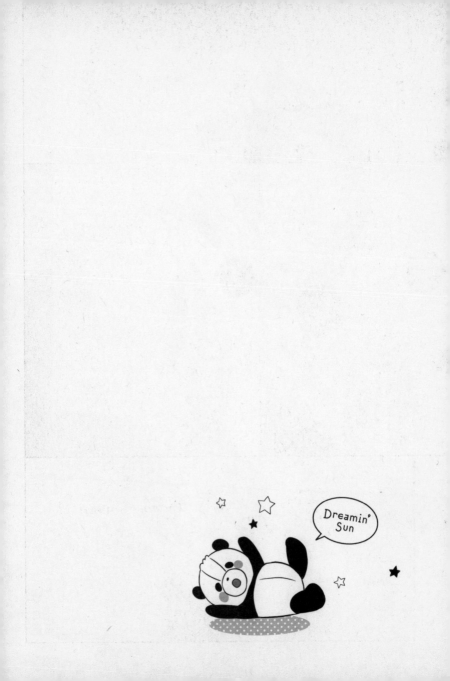

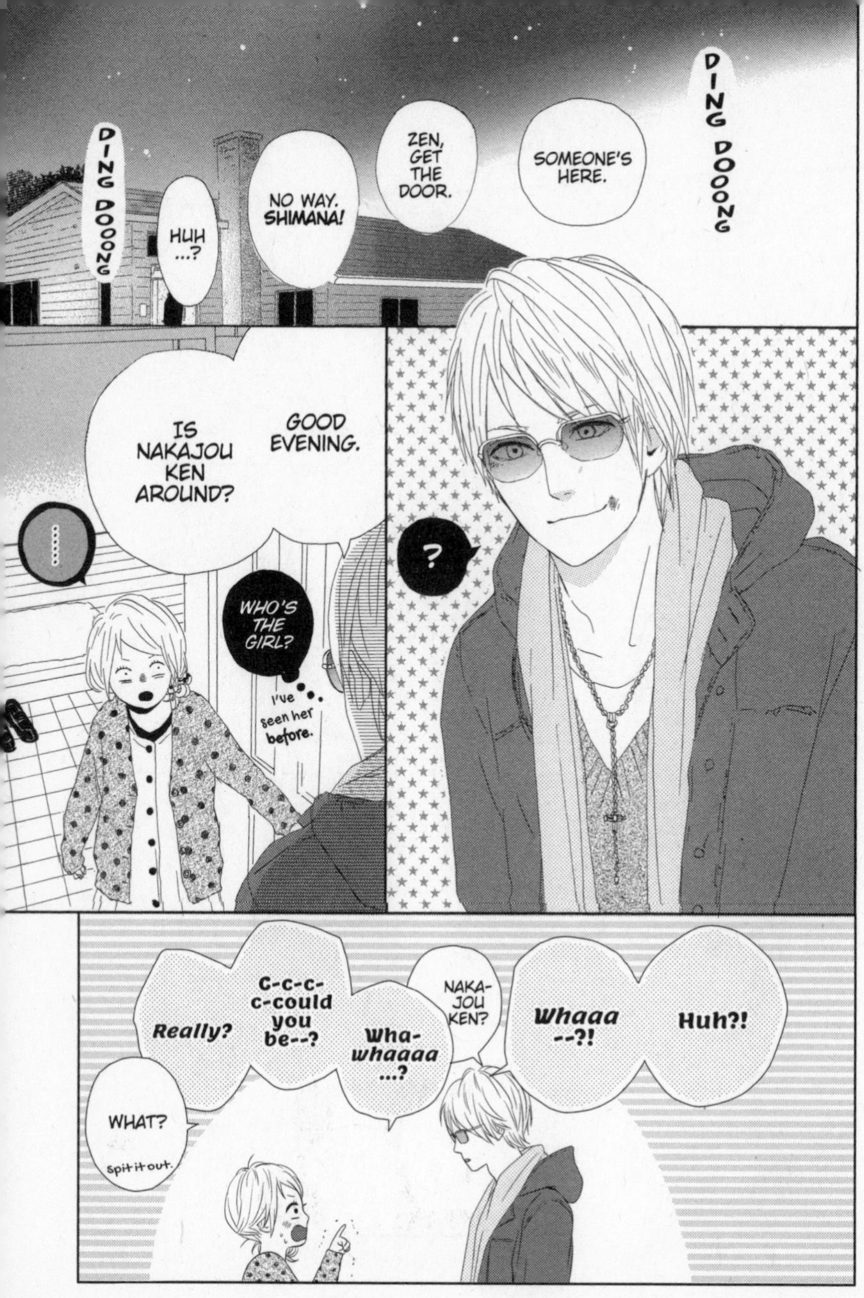
DING DOOONG
SOMEONE'S HERE.
ZEN, GET THE DOOR.
NO WAY. SHIMANA!
HUH ...?
DING DOOONG
?
GOOD EVENING.
IS NAKAJOU KEN AROUND?
WHO'S THE GIRL?
I've seen her before.
......
Huh?!
Whaaa --?!
NAKAJOU KEN?
Wha-whaaaa ...?
C-c-c-c-could you be--?
Really?
WHAT?
spit it out.

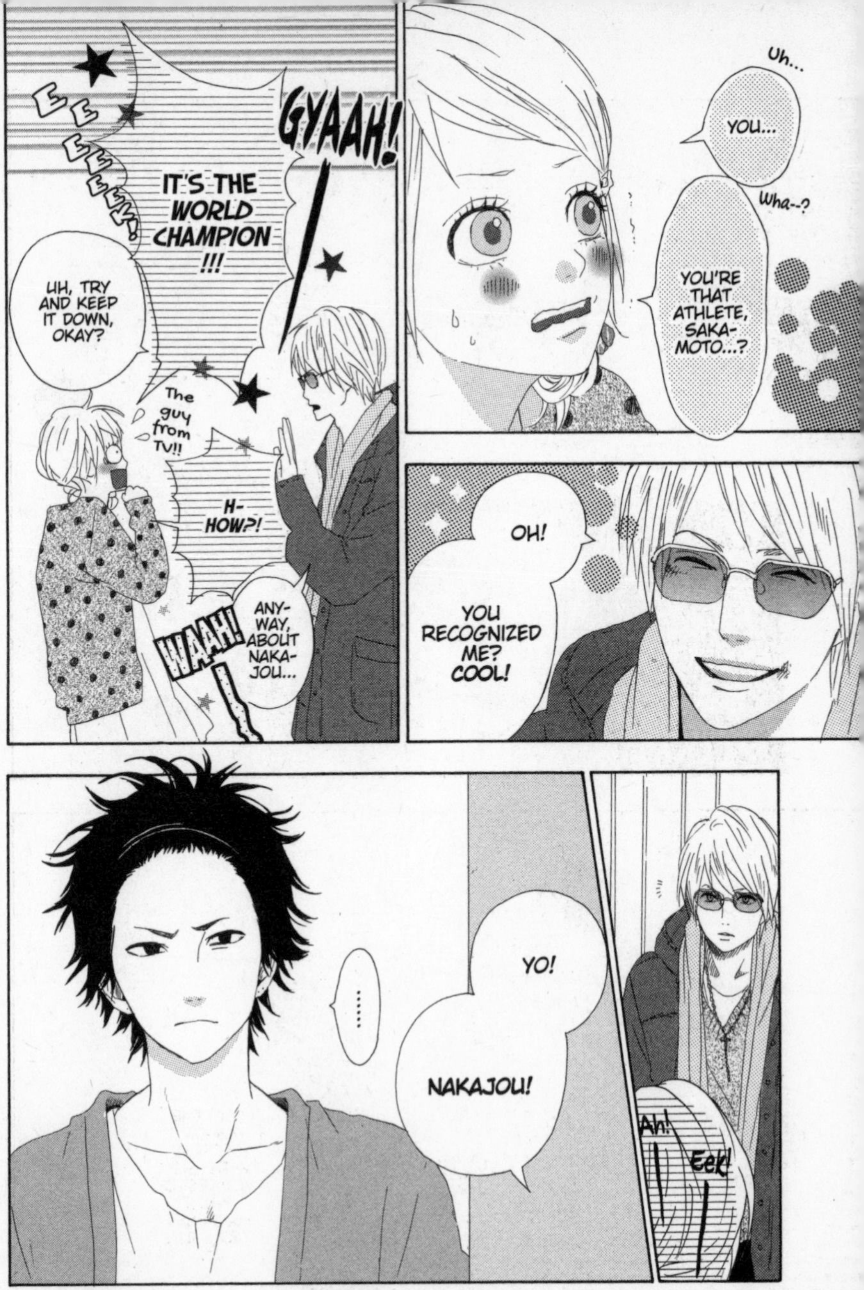
Uh...
YOU...
Wha--?
YOU'RE THAT ATHLETE, SAKAMOTO...?
OH!
YOU RECOGNIZED ME? COOL!
GYAAH!
IT'S THE WORLD CHAMPION!!!
EEEEEK!
UH, TRY AND KEEP IT DOWN, OKAY?
The guy from TV!!
H-HOW?!
ANYWAY, ABOUT NAKAJOU...
WAAH!
Ah!
Eek!
YO!
NAKAJOU!
......

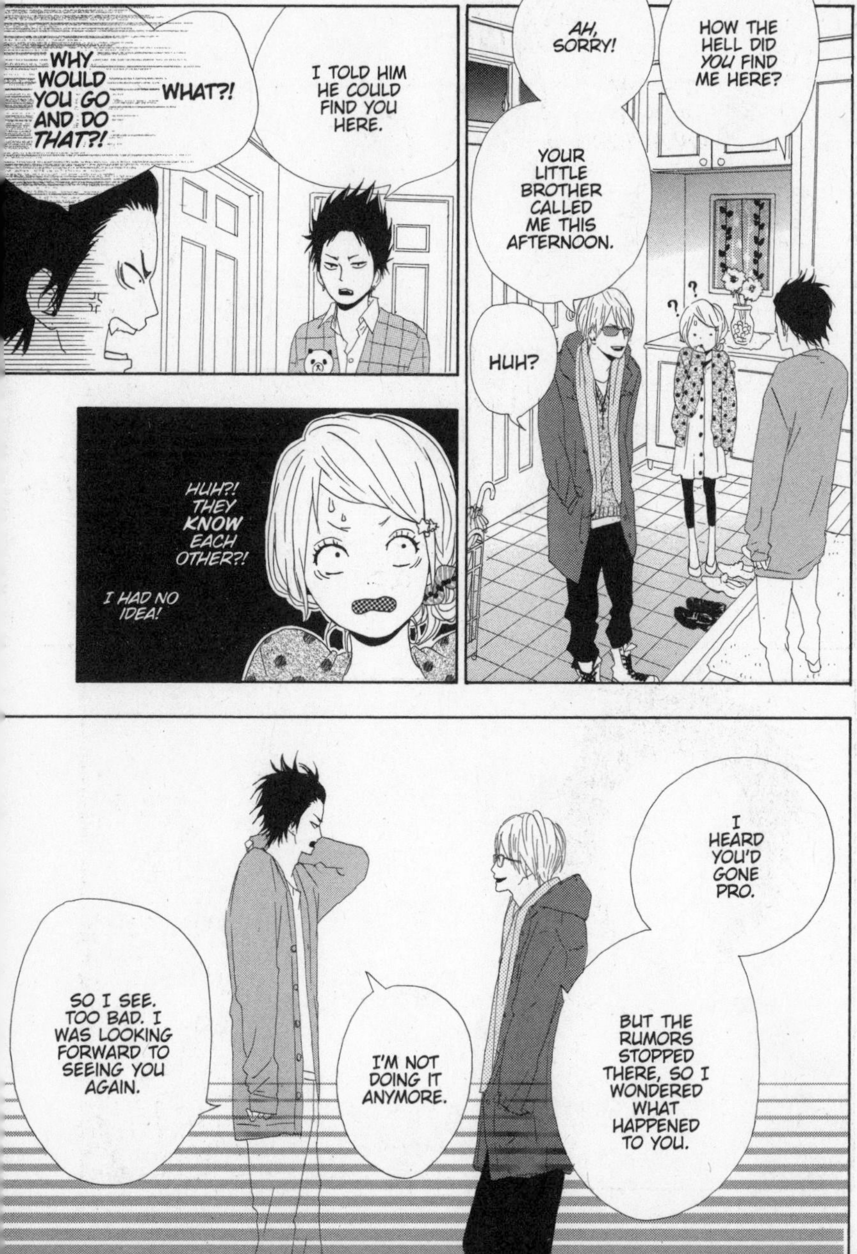
HOW THE HELL DID YOU FIND ME HERE?
AH, SORRY!
YOUR LITTLE BROTHER CALLED ME THIS AFTERNOON.
HUH?
I TOLD HIM HE COULD FIND YOU HERE.
WHAT?!
WHY WOULD YOU GO AND DO THAT?!
HUH?! THEY KNOW EACH OTHER?!
I HAD NO IDEA!
I HEARD YOU'D GONE PRO.
BUT THE RUMORS STOPPED THERE, SO I WONDERED WHAT HAPPENED TO YOU.
I'M NOT DOING IT ANYMORE.
SO I SEE. TOO BAD. I WAS LOOKING FORWARD TO SEEING YOU AGAIN.

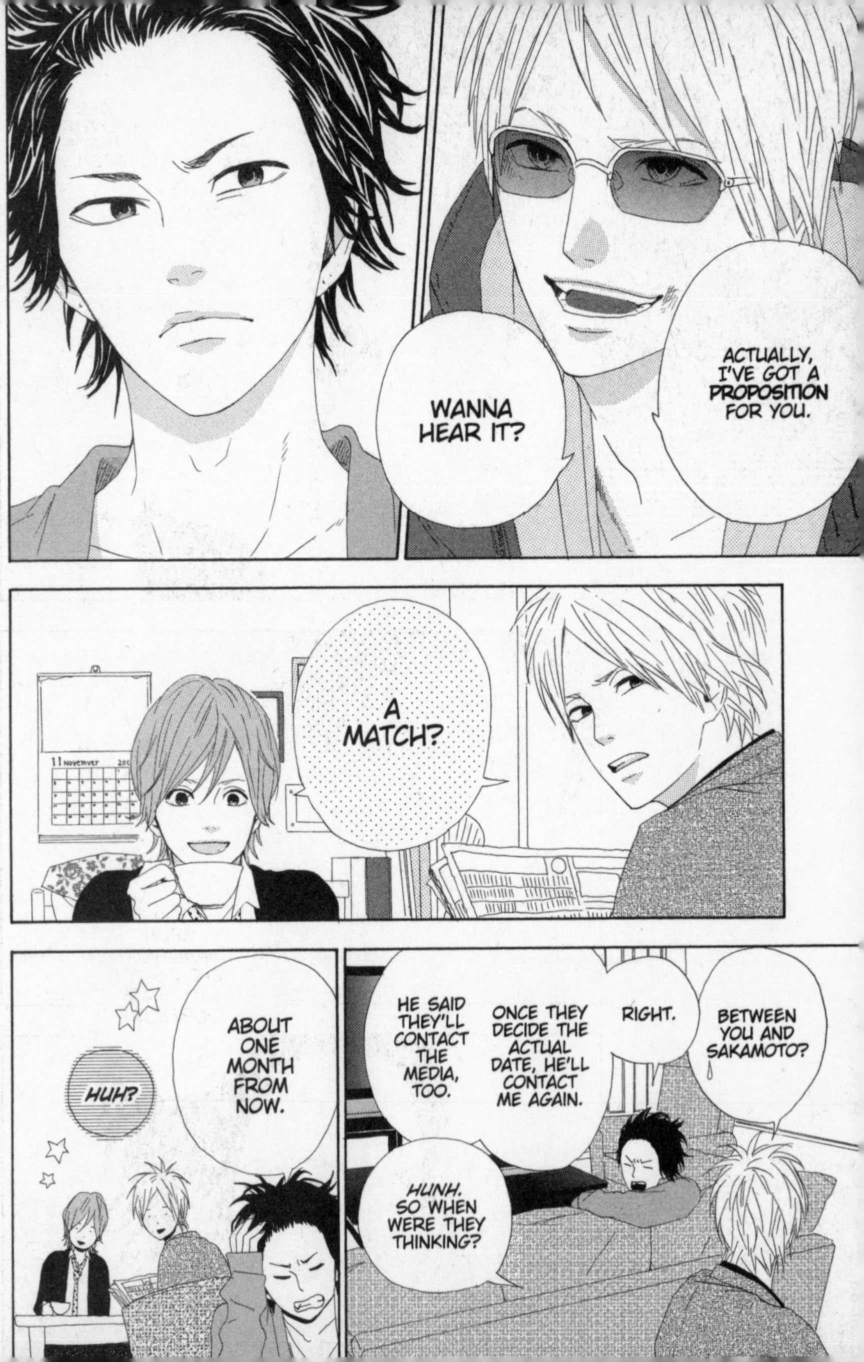
ACTUALLY, I'VE GOT A PROPOSITION FOR YOU.
WANNA HEAR IT?
A MATCH?
BETWEEN YOU AND SAKAMOTO?
RIGHT.
ONCE THEY DECIDE THE ACTUAL DATE, HE'LL CONTACT ME AGAIN.
HE SAID THEY'LL CONTACT THE MEDIA, TOO.
HUNH. SO WHEN WERE THEY THINKING?
ABOUT ONE MONTH FROM NOW.
HUH?

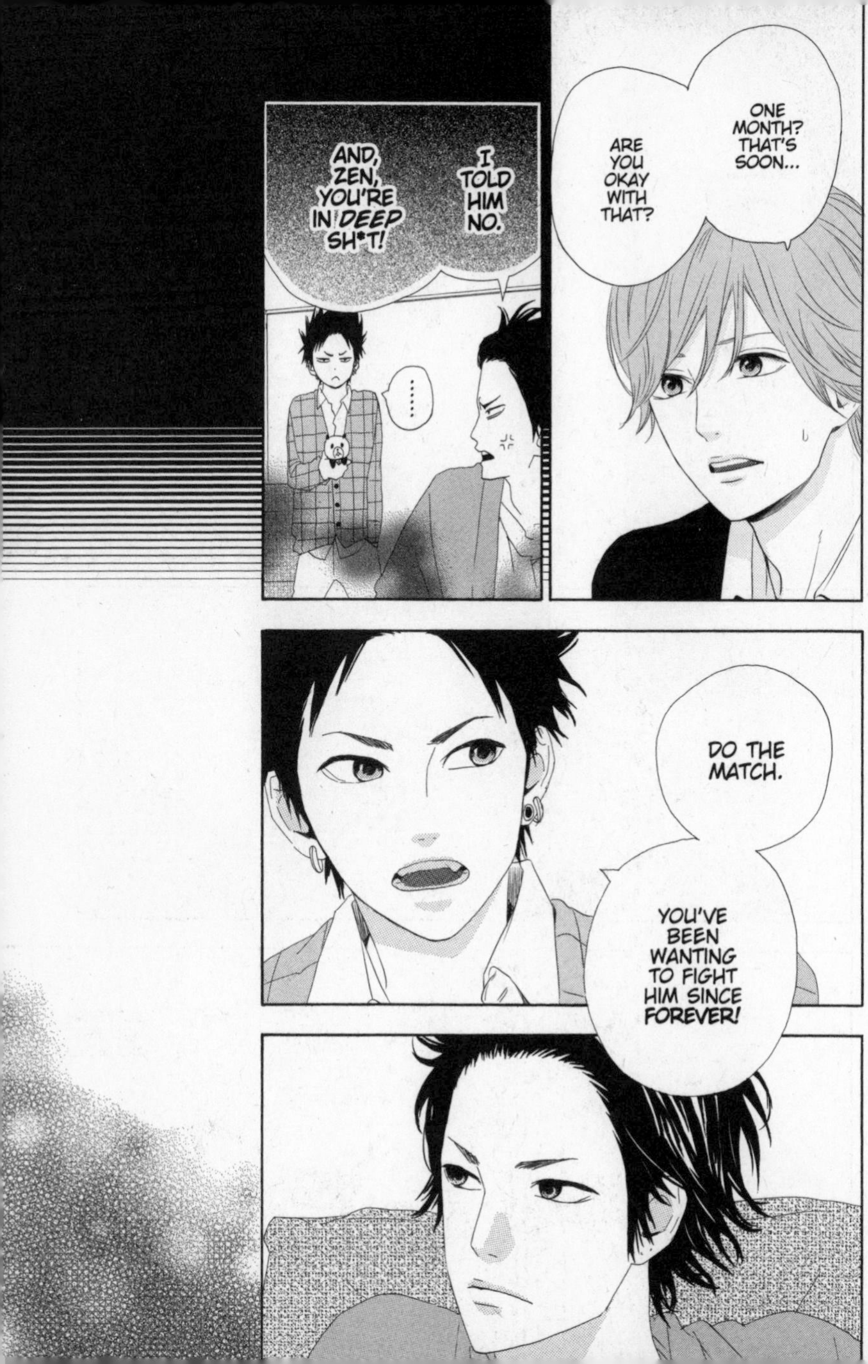

ONE MONTH? THAT'S SOON...
ARE YOU OKAY WITH THAT?
I TOLD HIM NO.
AND, ZEN, YOU'RE IN DEEP SH*T!
......
DO THE MATCH.
YOU'VE BEEN WANTING TO FIGHT HIM SINCE FOREVER!

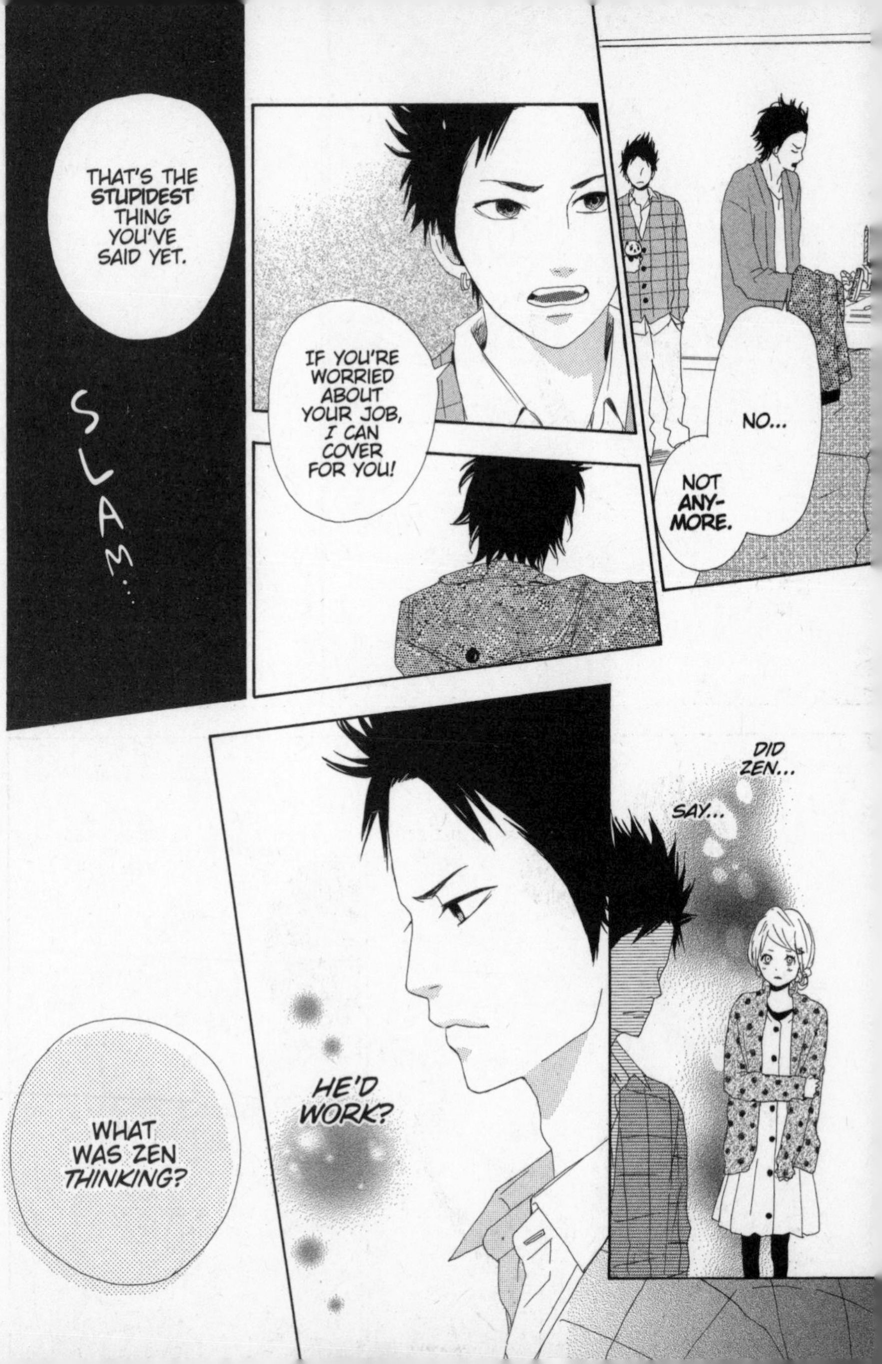
NO...
NOT ANYMORE.
IF YOU'RE WORRIED ABOUT YOUR JOB, I CAN COVER FOR YOU!
THAT'S THE STUPIDEST THING YOU'VE SAID YET.
SLAM...
DID ZEN...
SAY...
HE'D WORK?
WHAT WAS ZEN THINKING?

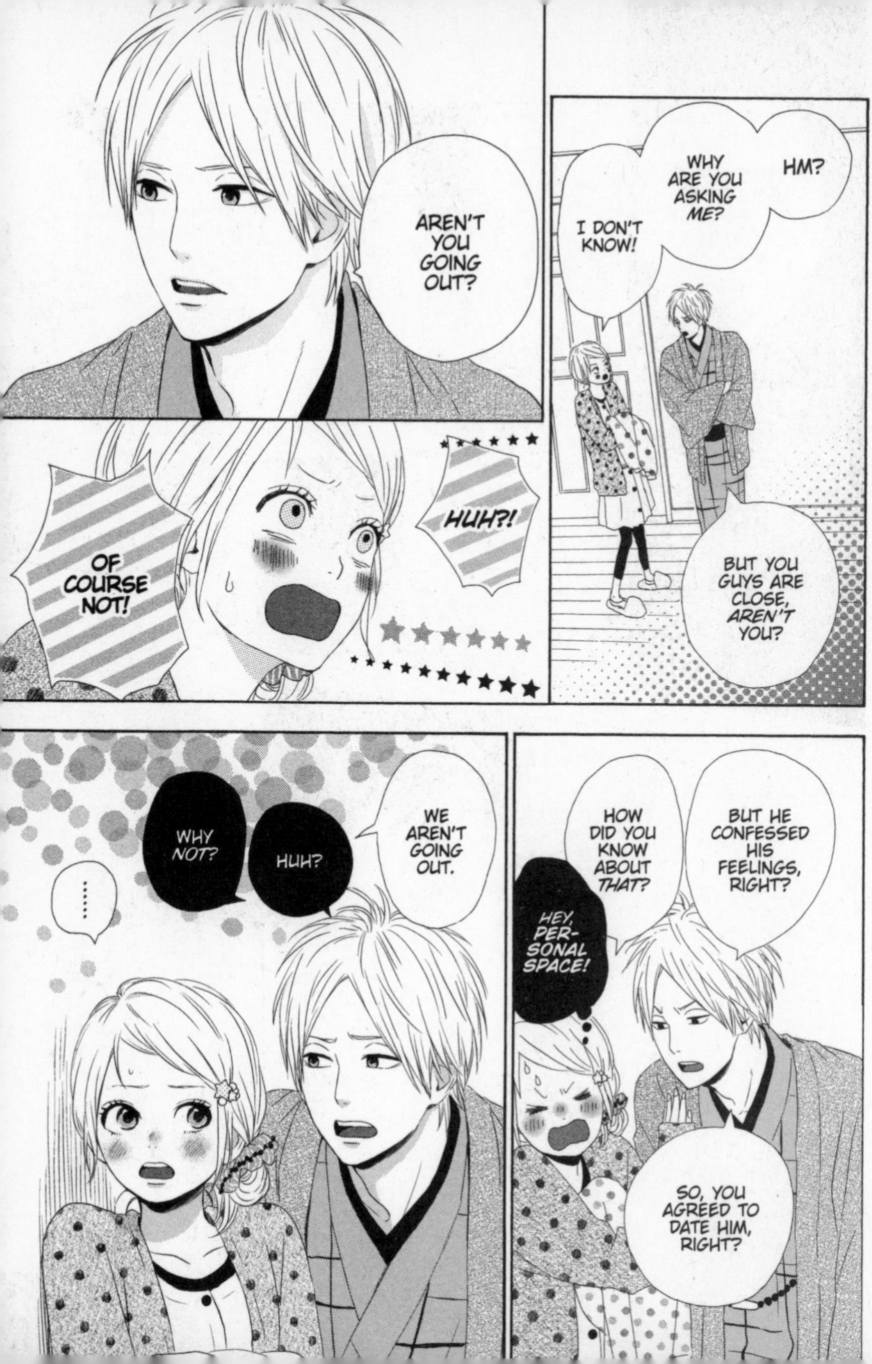
HM?
WHY ARE YOU ASKING *ME*?
I DON'T KNOW!
BUT YOU GUYS ARE CLOSE, *AREN'T* YOU?
AREN'T YOU GOING OUT?
HUH?!
OF COURSE NOT!
BUT HE CONFESSED HIS FEELINGS, RIGHT?
HOW DID YOU KNOW ABOUT *THAT*?
HEY, PER-SONAL SPACE!
SO, YOU AGREED TO DATE HIM, RIGHT?
WE AREN'T GOING OUT.
HUH?
WHY *NOT*?
......

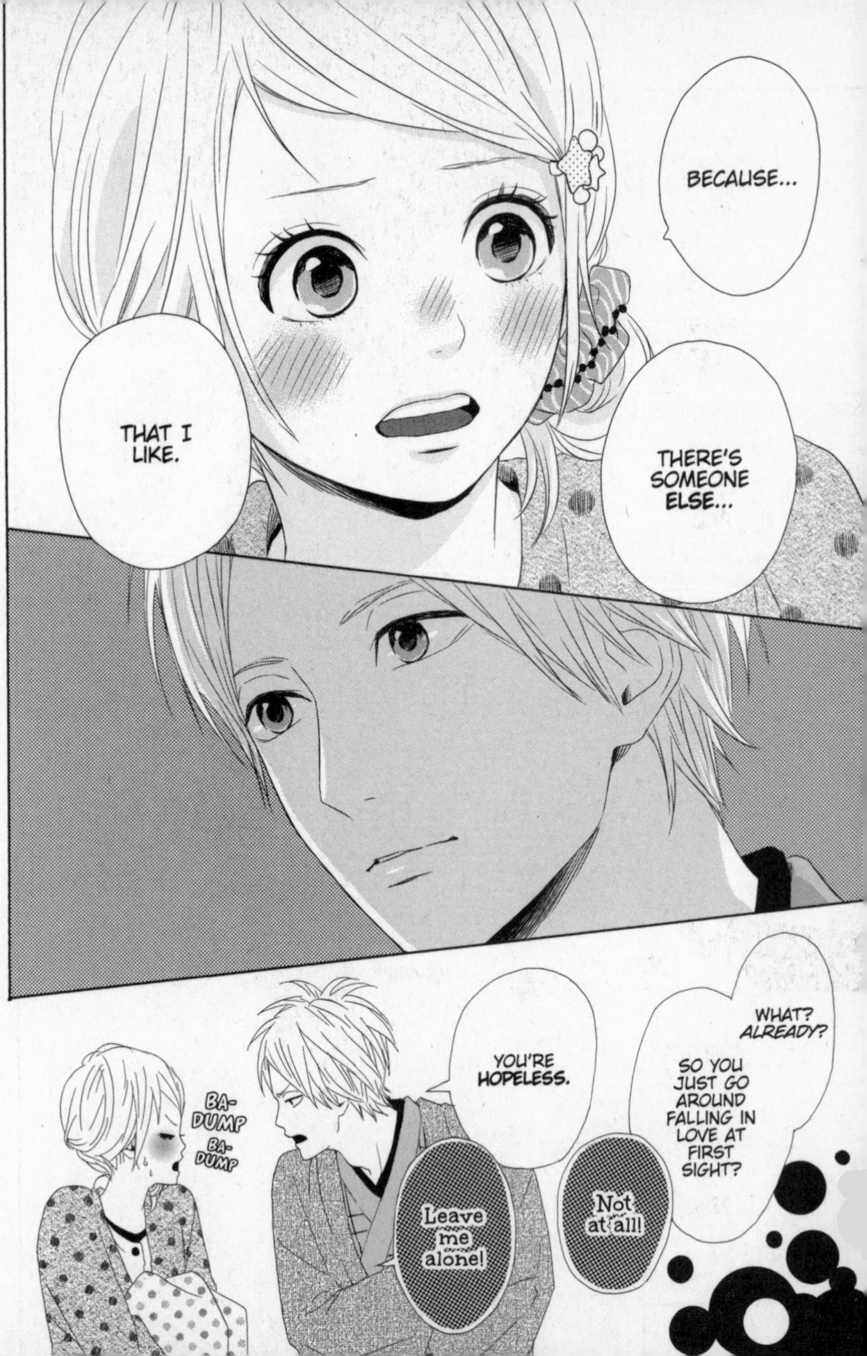
BECAUSE...
THERE'S SOMEONE ELSE...
THAT I LIKE.
WHAT? ALREADY?
SO YOU JUST GO AROUND FALLING IN LOVE AT FIRST SIGHT?
Not at all!
YOU'RE HOPELESS.
Leave me alone!
BA-DUMP BA-DUMP

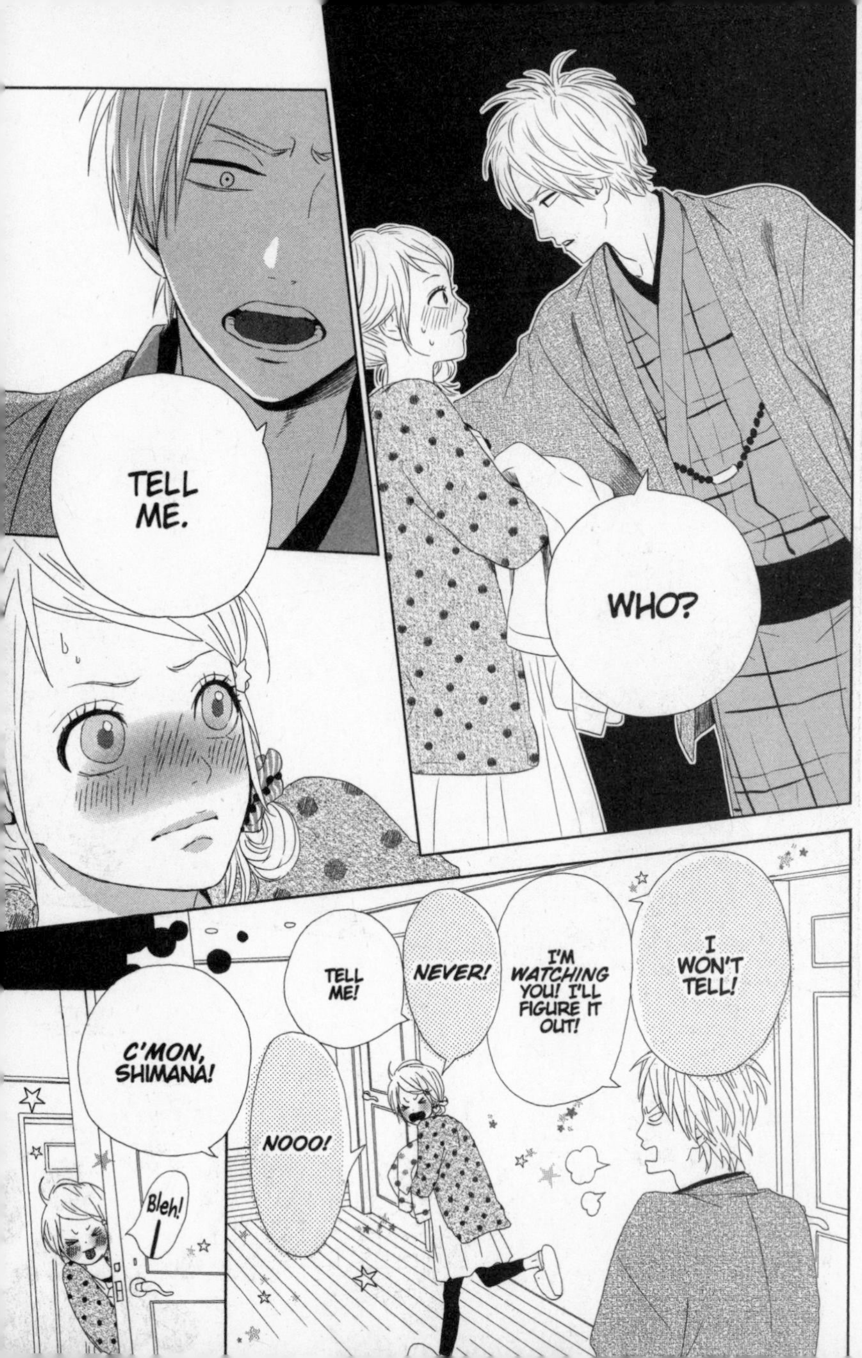
WHO?
TELL ME.
I WON'T TELL!
I'M WATCHING YOU! I'LL FIGURE IT OUT!
NEVER!
TELL ME!
C'MON, SHIMANA!
NOOO!
Bleh!

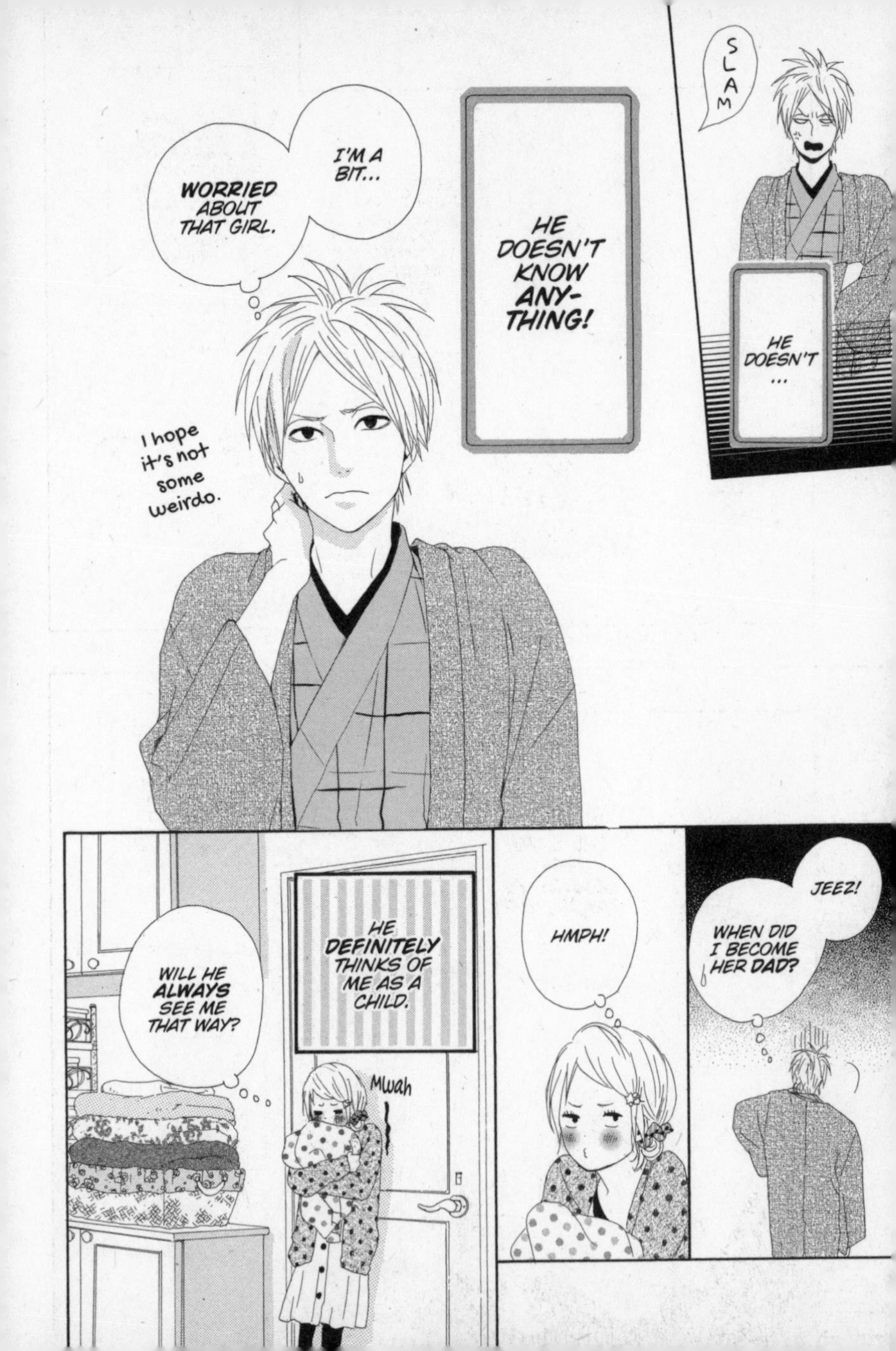
SLAM
HE DOESN'T ...
HE DOESN'T KNOW ANY-THING!
I'M A BIT... WORRIED ABOUT THAT GIRL.
I hope it's not some weirdo.
JEEZ! WHEN DID I BECOME HER DAD?
HMPH!
HE DEFINITELY THINKS OF ME AS A CHILD.
Mwah
WILL HE ALWAYS SEE ME THAT WAY?

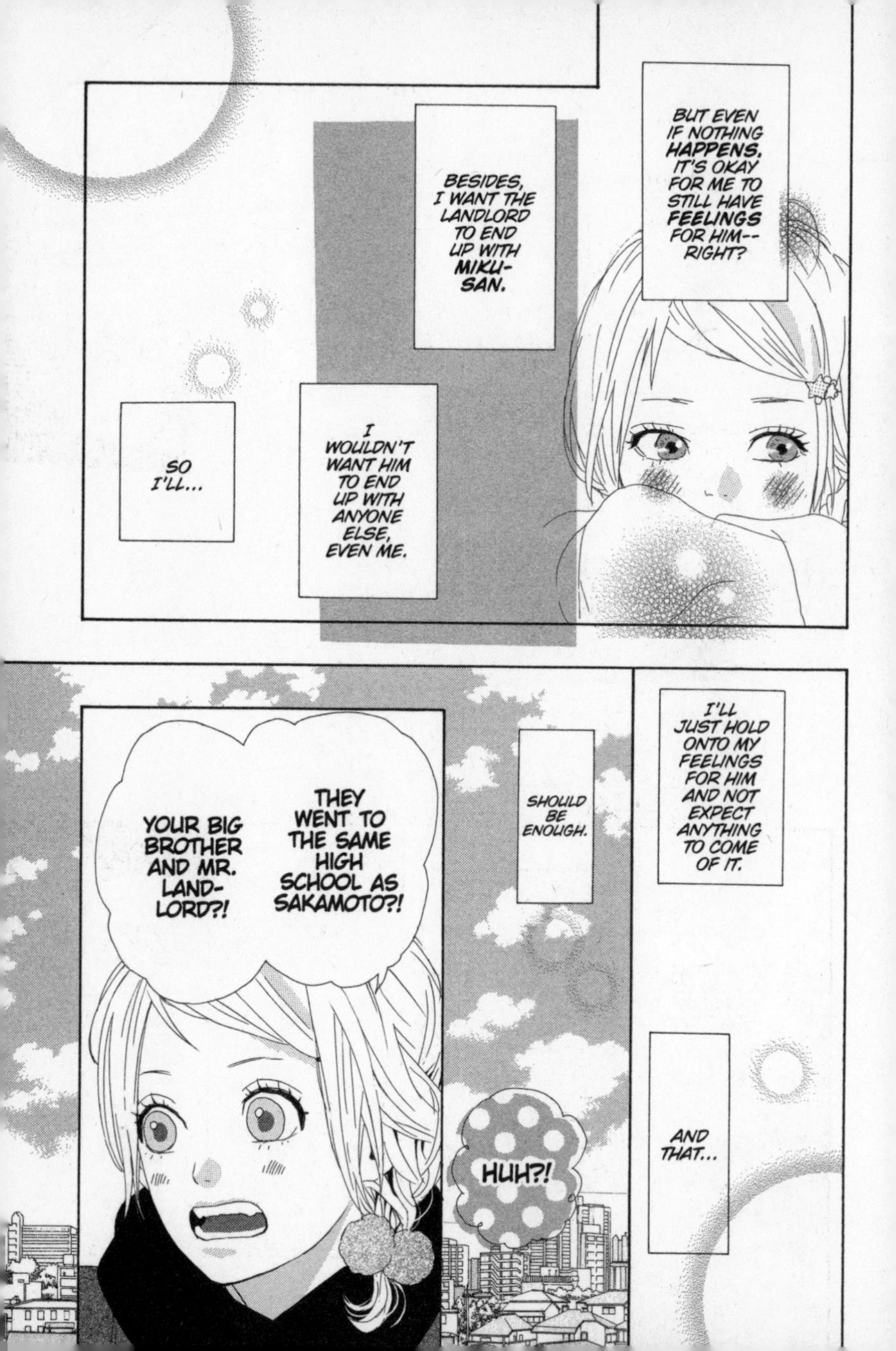
BUT EVEN IF NOTHING HAPPENS, IT'S OKAY FOR ME TO STILL HAVE FEELINGS FOR HIM--RIGHT?
BESIDES, I WANT THE LANDLORD TO END UP WITH MIKU-SAN.
I WOULDN'T WANT HIM TO END UP WITH ANYONE ELSE, EVEN ME.
SO I'LL...
I'LL JUST HOLD ONTO MY FEELINGS FOR HIM AND NOT EXPECT ANYTHING TO COME OF IT.
AND THAT...
SHOULD BE ENOUGH.
THEY WENT TO THE SAME HIGH SCHOOL AS SAKAMOTO?!
YOUR BIG BROTHER AND MR. LANDLORD?!
HUH?!

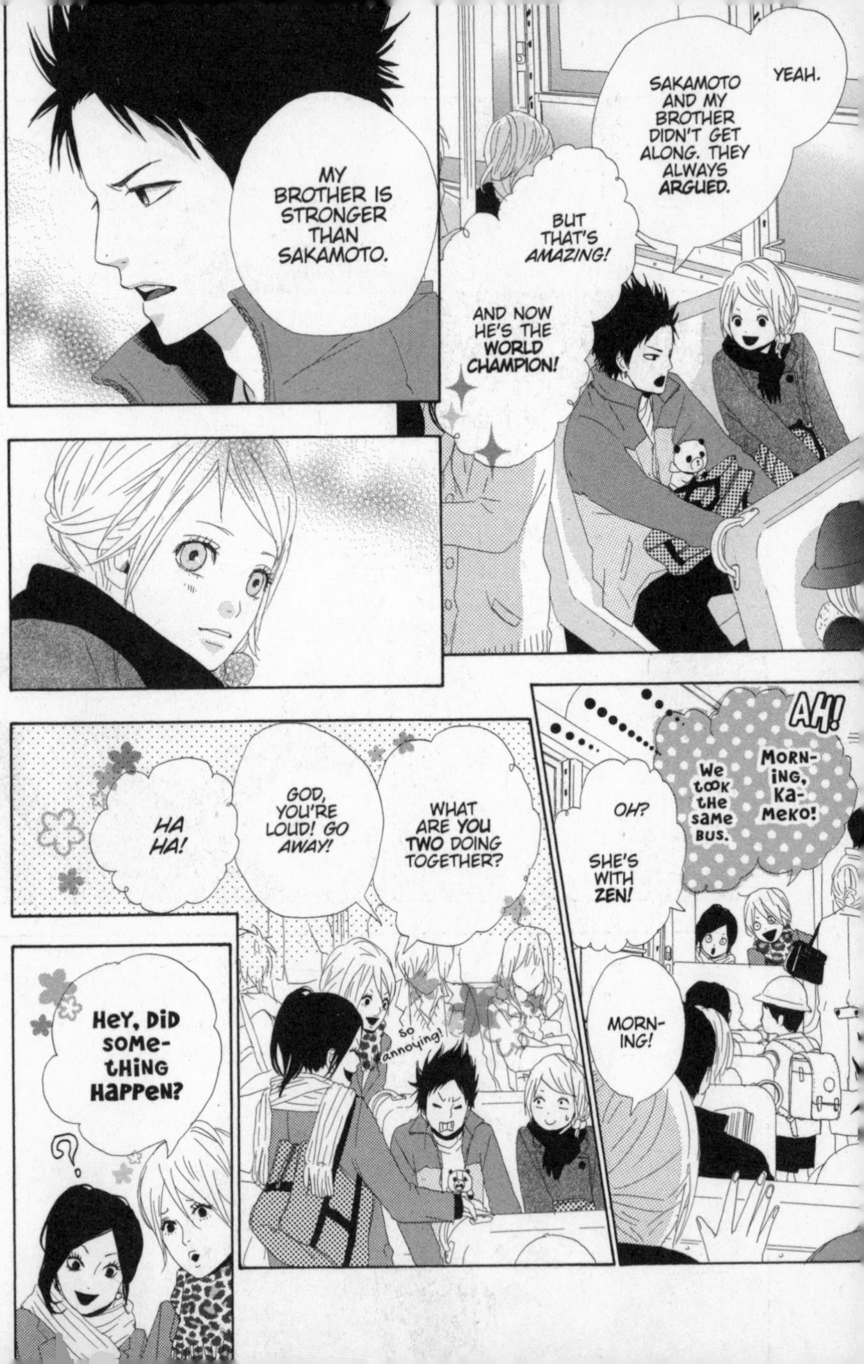

YEAH.
SAKAMOTO AND MY BROTHER DIDN'T GET ALONG. THEY ALWAYS ARGUED.
BUT THAT'S AMAZING!
AND NOW HE'S THE WORLD CHAMPION!
MY BROTHER IS STRONGER THAN SAKAMOTO.
AH!
MORNING, KAMEKO!
We took the same bus.
OH?
SHE'S WITH ZEN!
MORNING!
WHAT ARE YOU TWO DOING TOGETHER?
GOD, YOU'RE LOUD! GO AWAY!
so annoying!
HA HA!
HEY, DID SOMETHING HAPPEN?

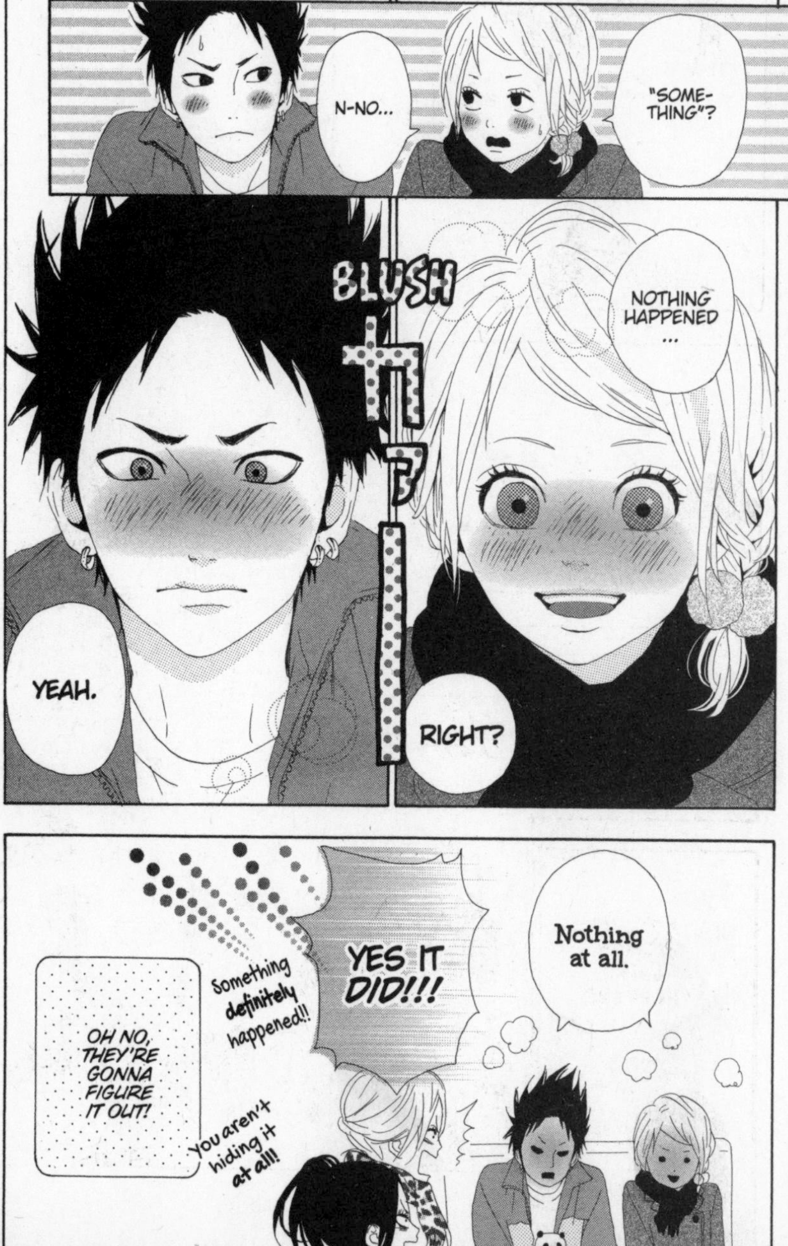

"SOME-THING"?
N-NO...
NOTHING HAPPENED ...
BLUSH
RIGHT?
YEAH.
Nothing at all.
YES IT DID!!!
Something definitely happened!!
OH NO, THEY'RE GONNA FIGURE IT OUT!
You aren't hiding it at all!

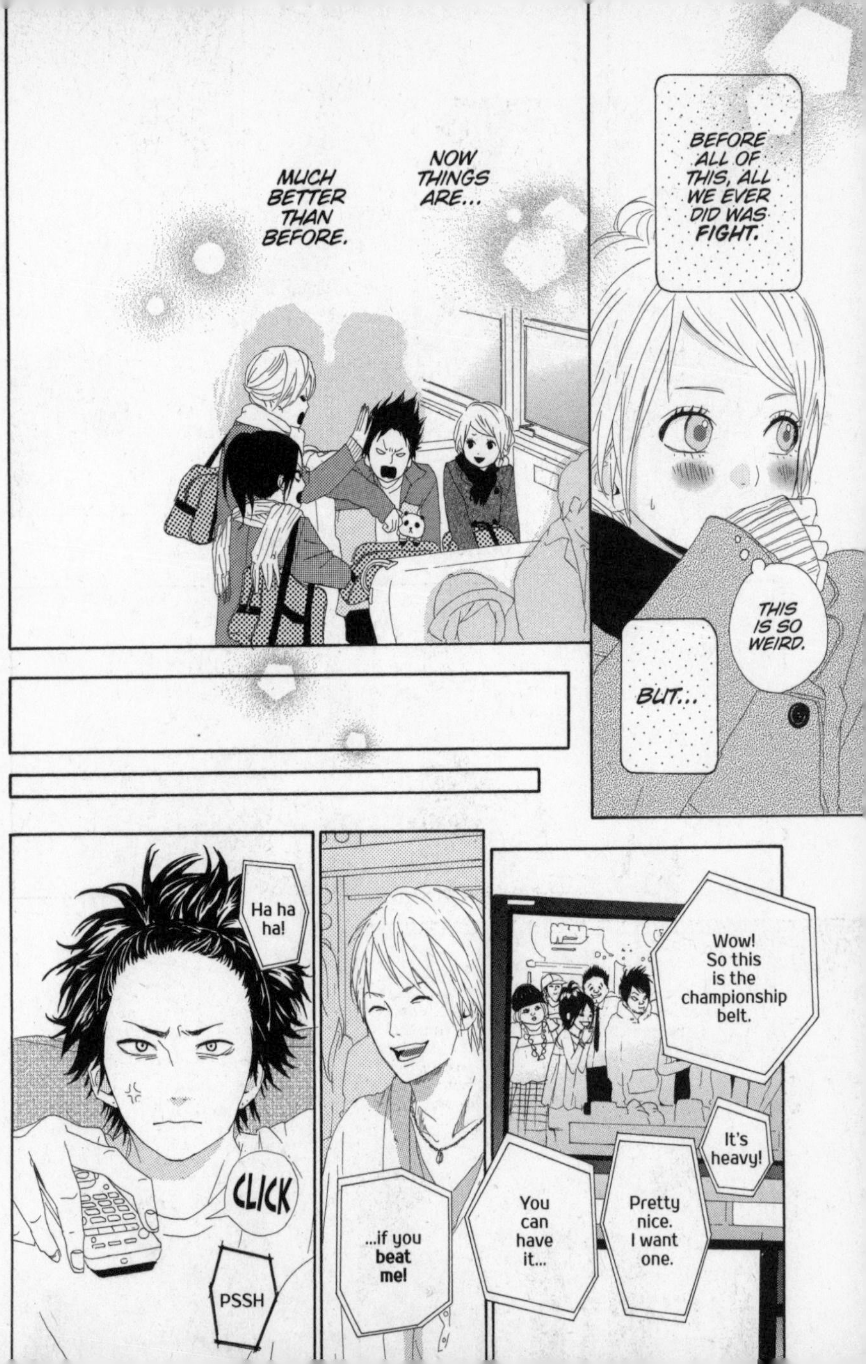
BEFORE ALL OF THIS, ALL WE EVER DID WAS FIGHT.
THIS IS SO WEIRD.
BUT...
NOW THINGS ARE...
MUCH BETTER THAN BEFORE.
Wow! So this is the championship belt.
It's heavy!
Pretty nice. I want one.
You can have it...
...if you beat me!
Ha ha ha!
CLICK
PSSH

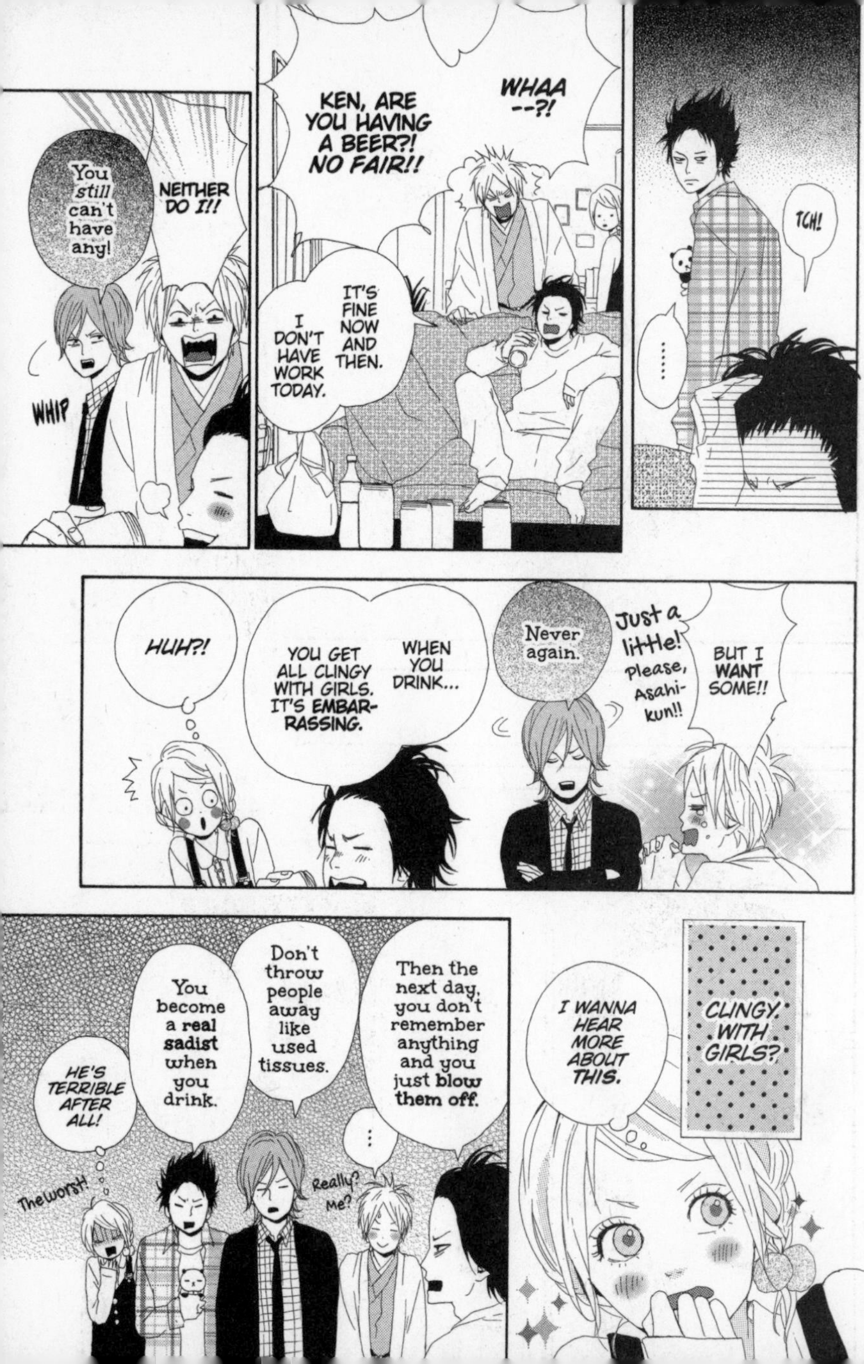
TCH!
......
WHAA --?!
KEN, ARE YOU HAVING A BEER?! NO FAIR!!
IT'S FINE NOW AND THEN.
I DON'T HAVE WORK TODAY.
NEITHER DO I!!
You still can't have any!
WHIP
BUT I WANT SOME!!
Just a little! Please, Asahi-kun!!
Never again.
WHEN YOU DRINK...
YOU GET ALL CLINGY WITH GIRLS. IT'S EMBARRASSING.
HUH?!
CLINGY WITH GIRLS?
I WANNA HEAR MORE ABOUT THIS.
Then the next day, you don't remember anything and you just blow them off.
...
Really? Me?
Don't throw people away like used tissues.
You become a real sadist when you drink.
HE'S TERRIBLE AFTER ALL!
The worst!

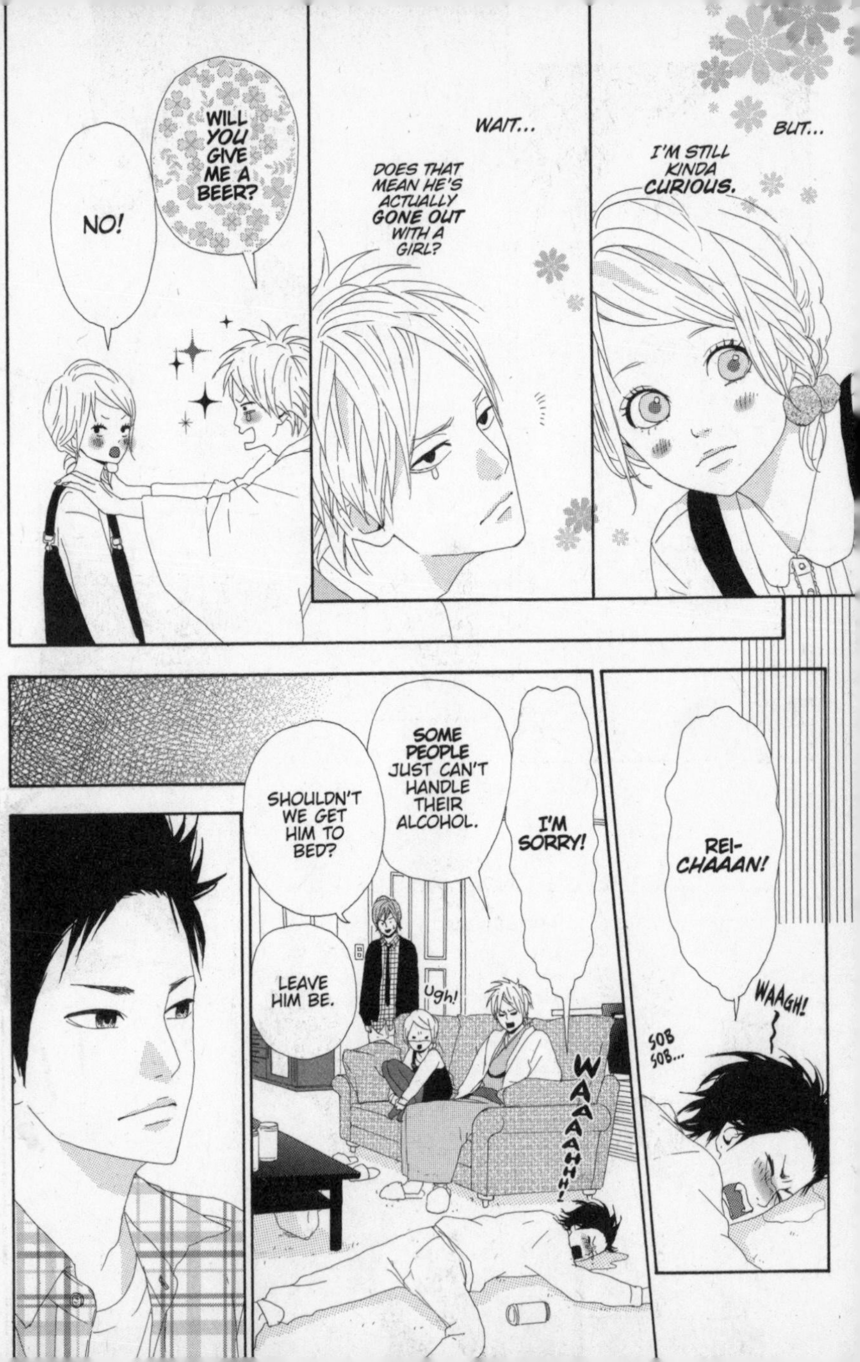
BUT...
I'M STILL KINDA CURIOUS.
WAIT...
DOES THAT MEAN HE'S ACTUALLY GONE OUT WITH A GIRL?
WILL YOU GIVE ME A BEER?
NO!
REI-CHAAAN!
WAAGH!
SOB SOB...
I'M SORRY!
SOME PEOPLE JUST CAN'T HANDLE THEIR ALCOHOL.
SHOULDN'T WE GET HIM TO BED?
WAAAAHH!
Ugh!
LEAVE HIM BE.

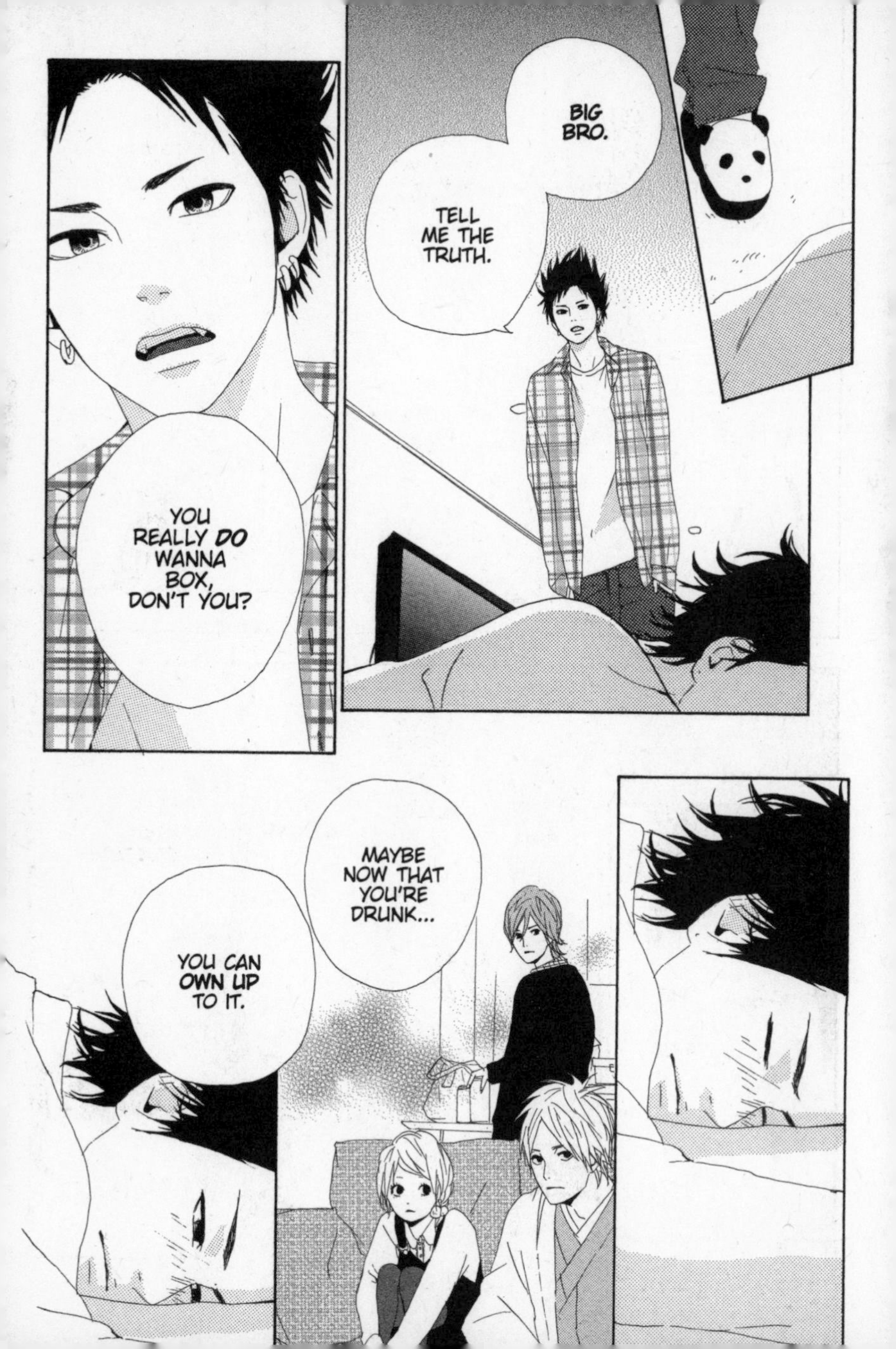
BIG BRO.
TELL ME THE TRUTH.
YOU REALLY *DO* WANNA BOX, DON'T YOU?
MAYBE NOW THAT YOU'RE DRUNK...
YOU CAN OWN UP TO IT.

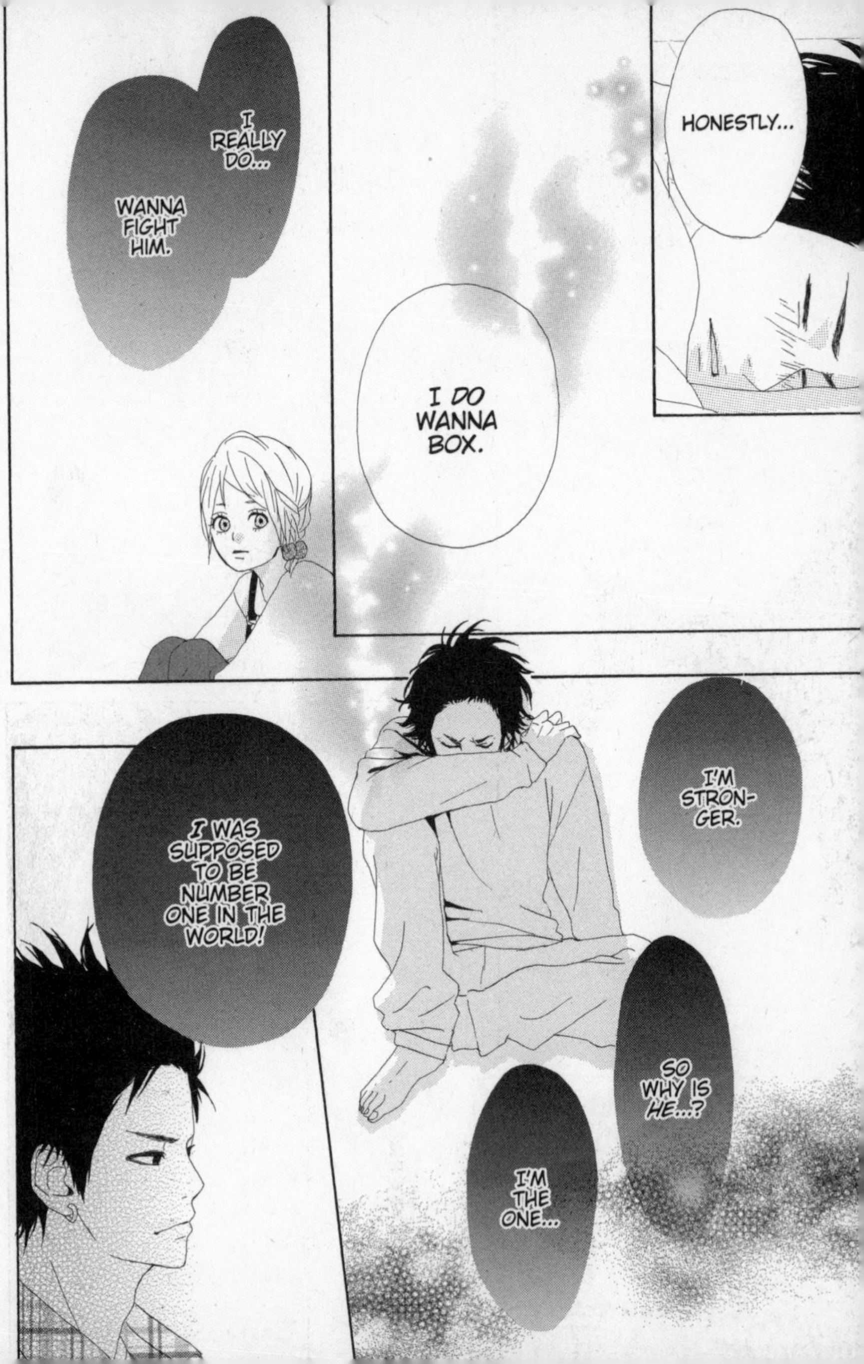
HONESTLY...
I DO WANNA BOX.
I REALLY DO...
WANNA FIGHT HIM.
I'M STRONGER.
SO WHY IS HE...?
I'M THE ONE...
I WAS SUPPOSED TO BE NUMBER ONE IN THE WORLD!

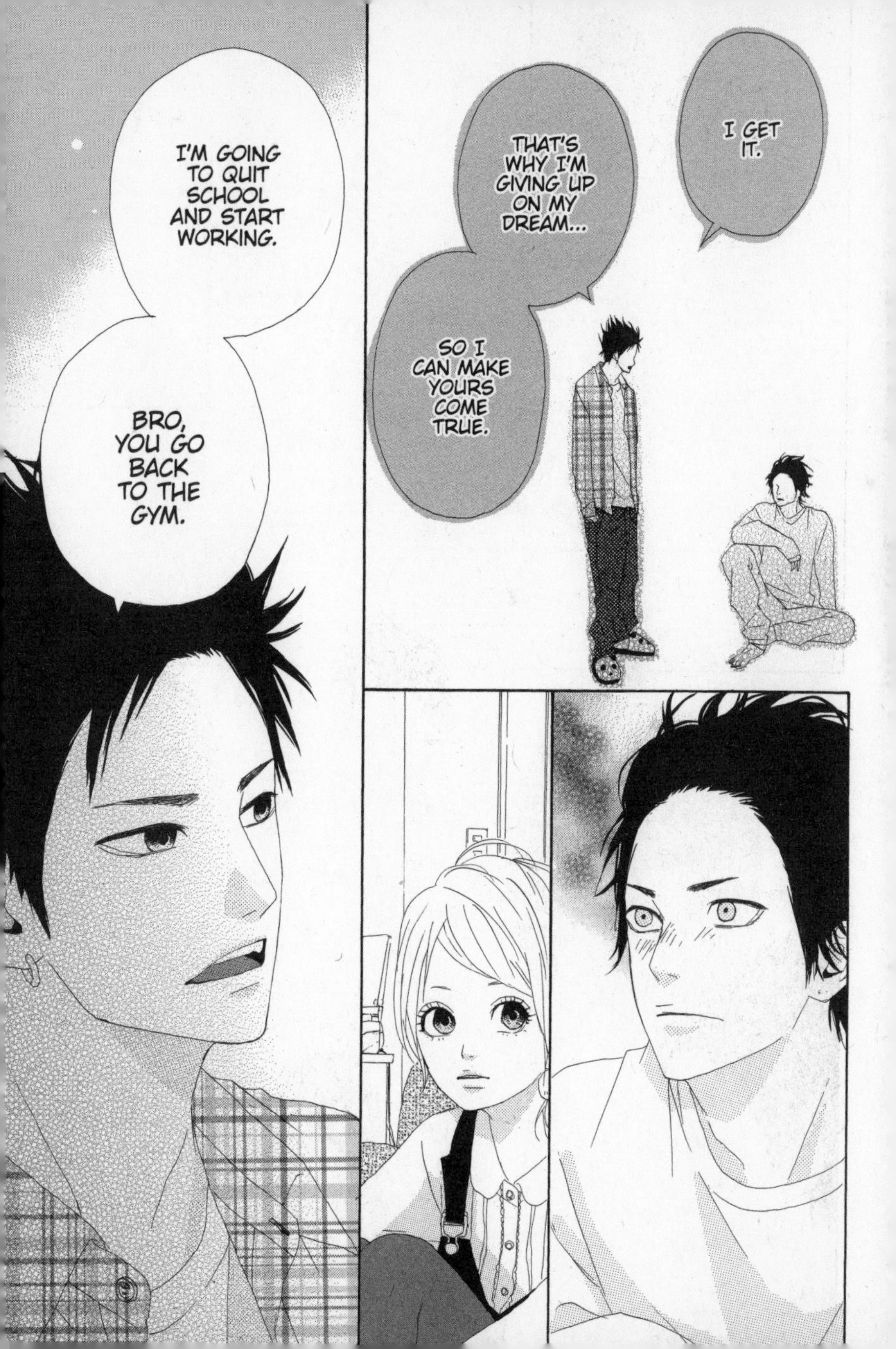
I GET IT.
THAT'S WHY I'M GIVING UP ON MY DREAM...
SO I CAN MAKE YOURS COME TRUE.
I'M GOING TO QUIT SCHOOL AND START WORKING.
BRO, YOU GO BACK TO THE GYM.

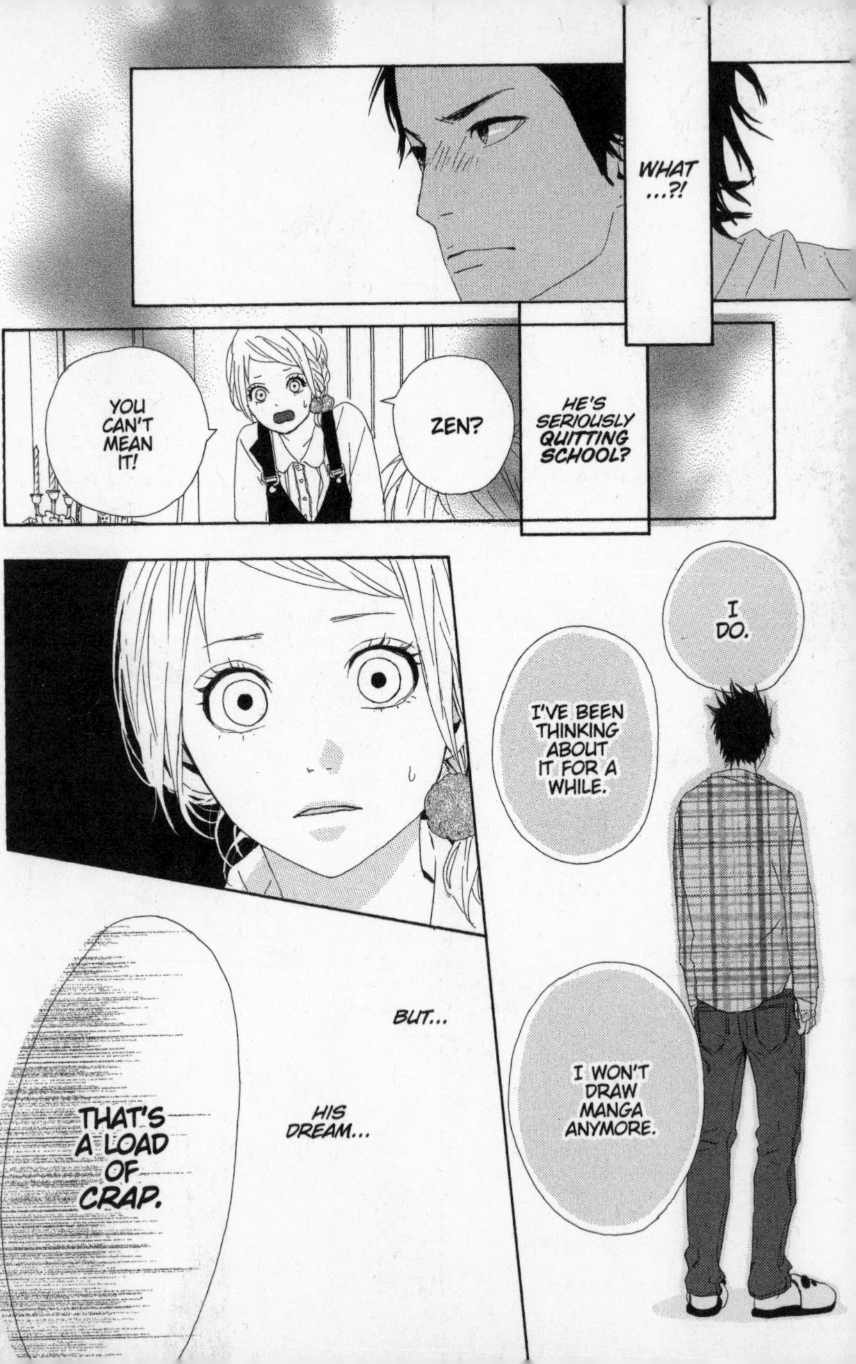
WHAT ...?!
HE'S SERIOUSLY QUITTING SCHOOL?
ZEN?
YOU CAN'T MEAN IT!
I DO.
I'VE BEEN THINKING ABOUT IT FOR A WHILE.
I WON'T DRAW MANGA ANYMORE.
BUT...
HIS DREAM...
THAT'S A LOAD OF CRAP.

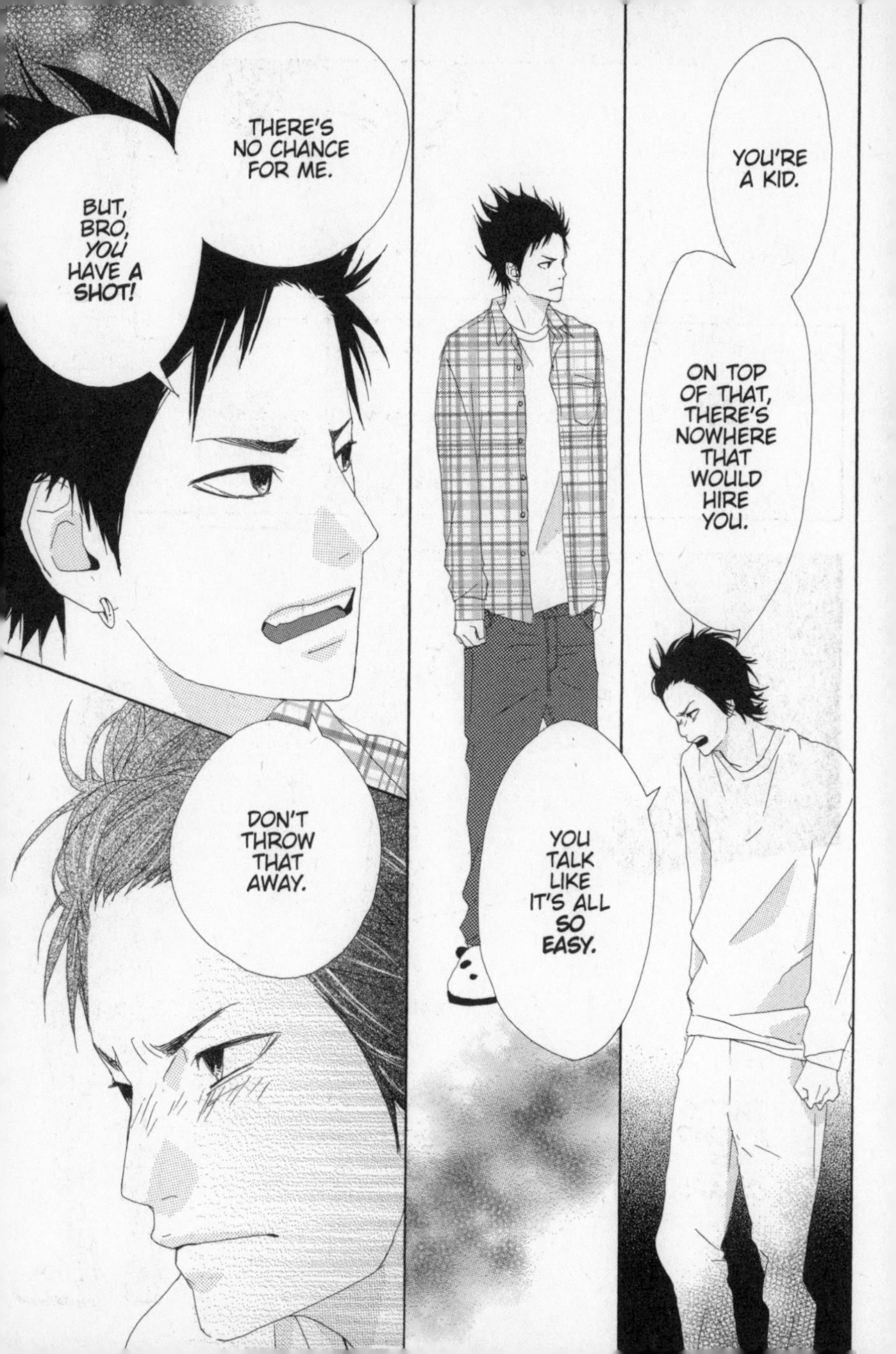
YOU'RE A KID.
ON TOP OF THAT, THERE'S NOWHERE THAT WOULD HIRE YOU.
YOU TALK LIKE IT'S ALL SO EASY.
THERE'S NO CHANCE FOR ME.
BUT, BRO, *YOU* HAVE A SHOT!
DON'T THROW THAT AWAY.

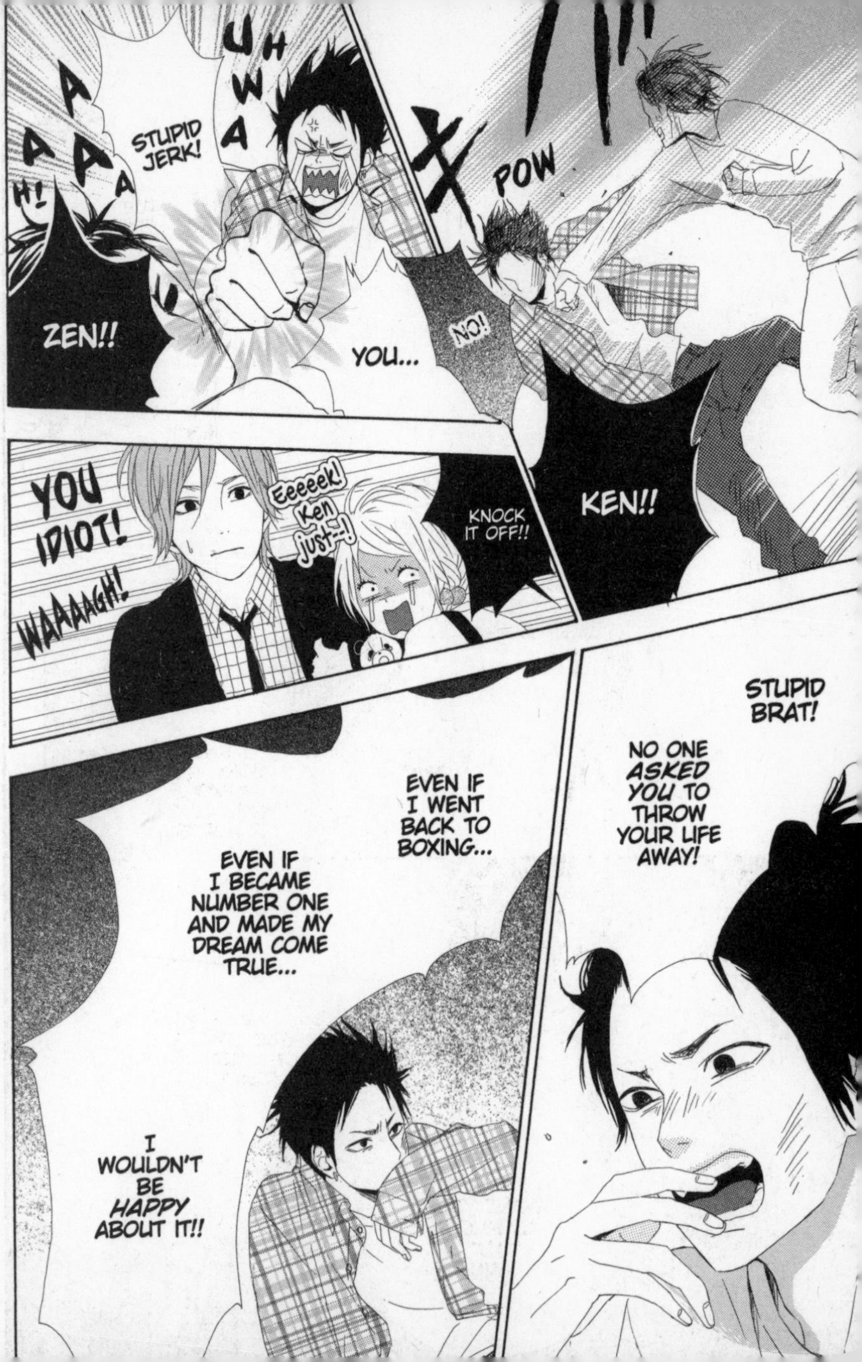

バキ
POW
NO!
KEN!!
UHWA
A
STUPID JERK!
AAAAH!
ZEN!!
YOU...
KNOCK IT OFF!!
Eeeeek! Ken just--!
YOU IDIOT!
WAAAAGH!
STUPID BRAT!
NO ONE *ASKED YOU* TO THROW YOUR LIFE AWAY!
EVEN IF I WENT BACK TO BOXING...
EVEN IF I BECAME NUMBER ONE AND MADE MY DREAM COME TRUE...
I WOULDN'T BE *HAPPY* ABOUT IT!!

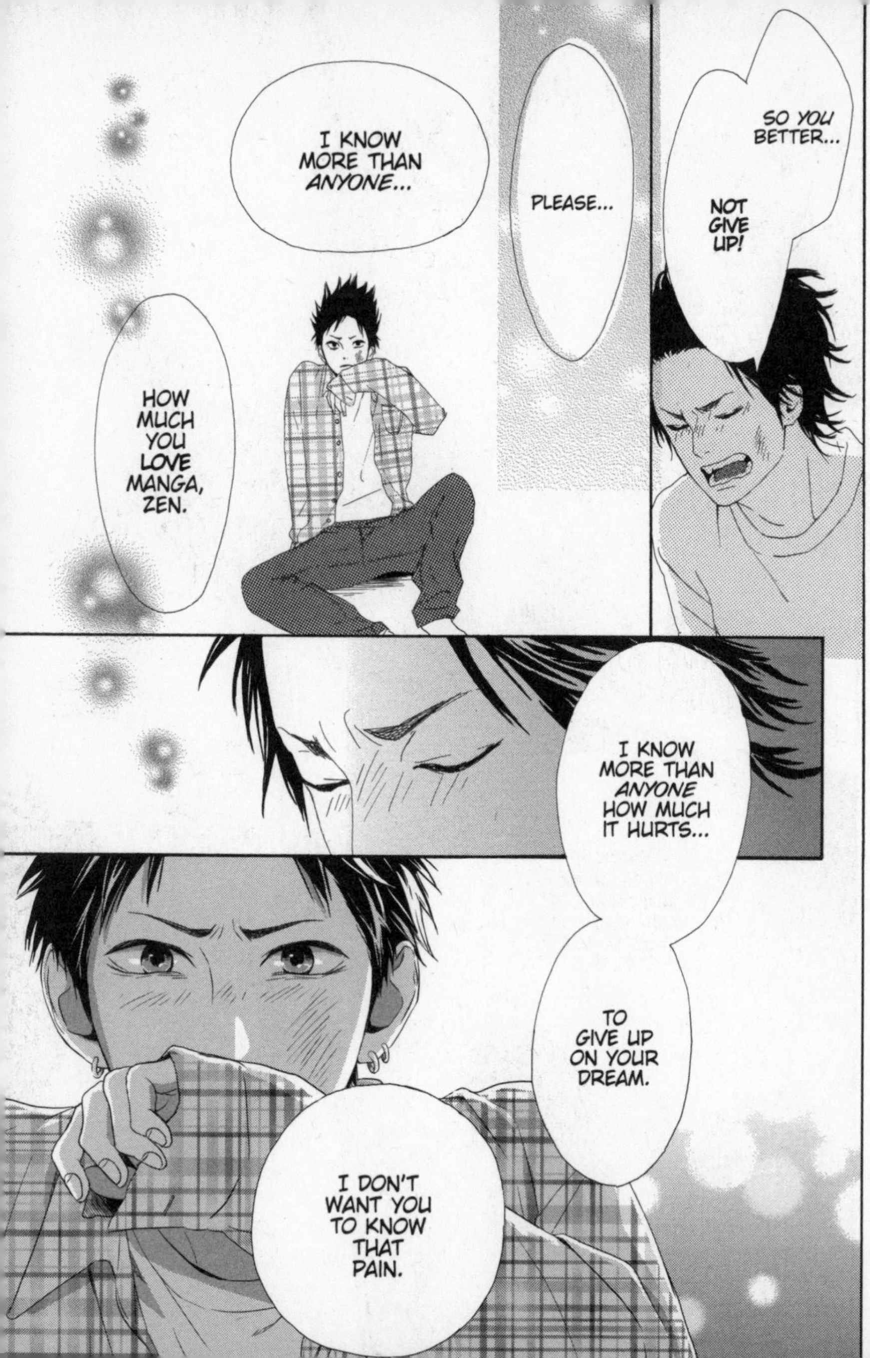
SO YOU BETTER...
NOT GIVE UP!
PLEASE...
I KNOW MORE THAN *ANYONE*...
HOW MUCH YOU LOVE MANGA, ZEN.
I KNOW MORE THAN *ANYONE* HOW MUCH IT HURTS...
TO GIVE UP ON YOUR DREAM.
I DON'T WANT YOU TO KNOW THAT PAIN.

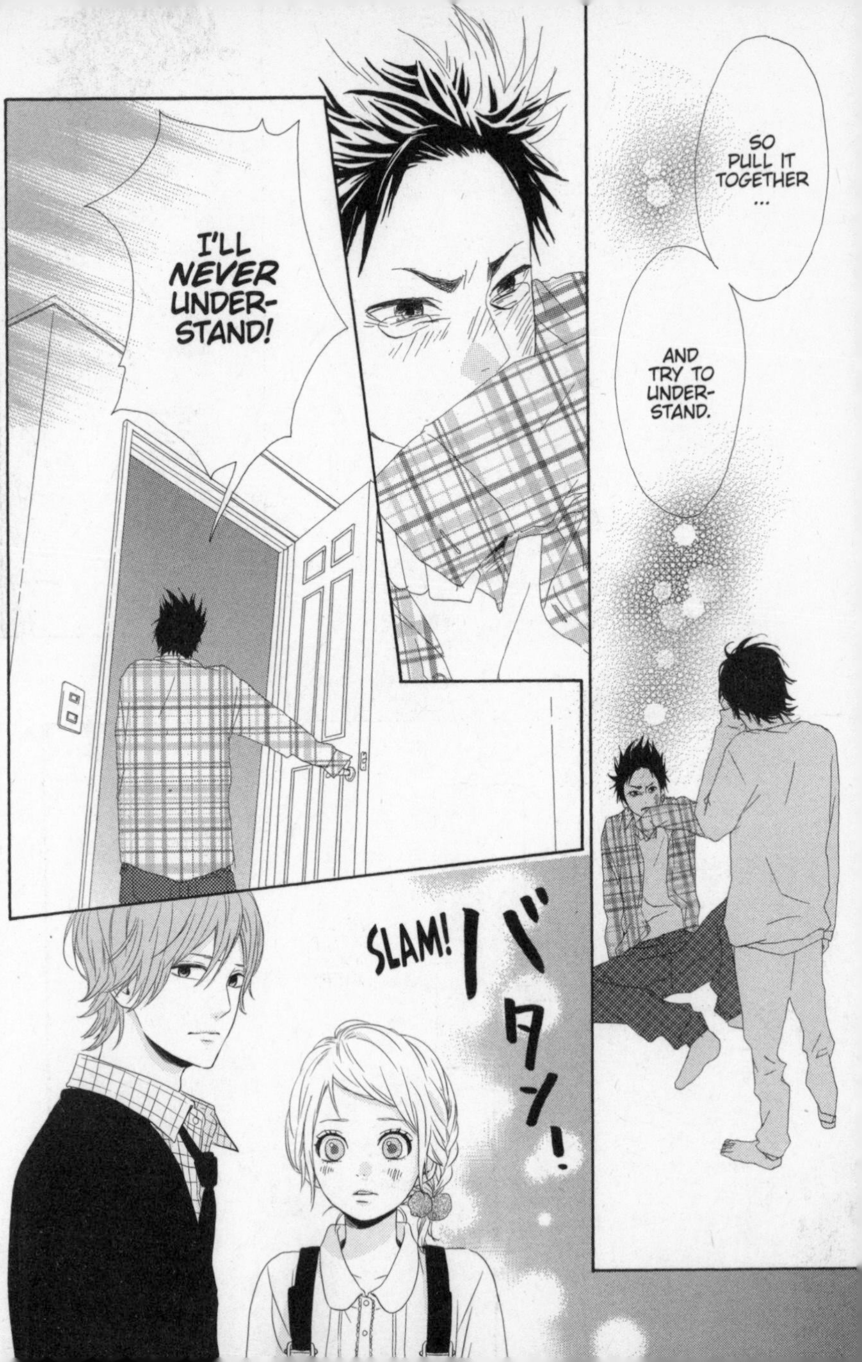
SO PULL IT TOGETHER ...
AND TRY TO UNDER-STAND.
I'LL NEVER UNDER-STAND!
SLAM!
バタン!

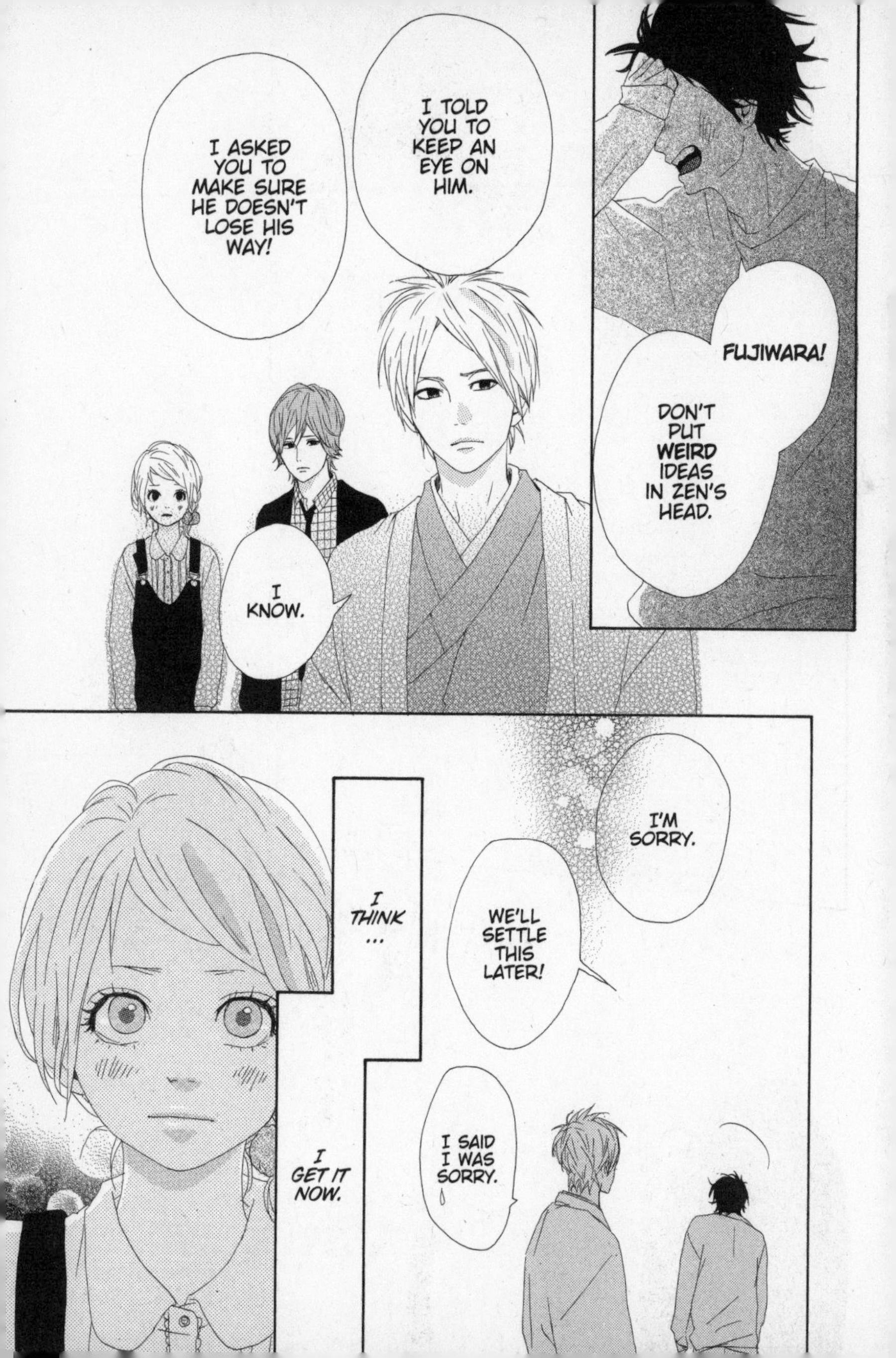
FUJIWARA!
DON'T PUT WEIRD IDEAS IN ZEN'S HEAD.
I TOLD YOU TO KEEP AN EYE ON HIM.
I ASKED YOU TO MAKE SURE HE DOESN'T LOSE HIS WAY!
I KNOW.
I'M SORRY.
WE'LL SETTLE THIS LATER!
I SAID I WAS SORRY.
I THINK ...
I GET IT NOW.

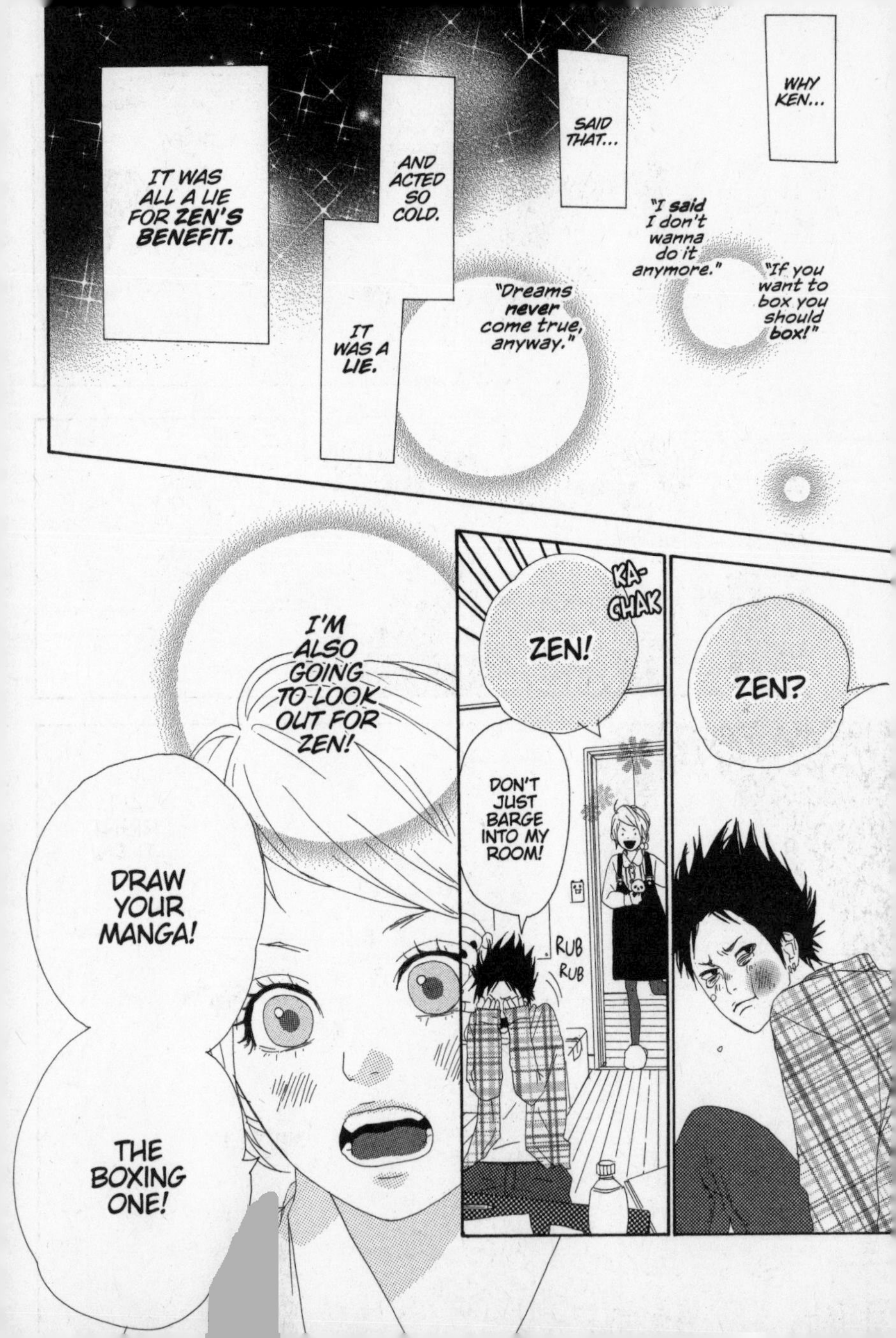
WHY KEN...
"If you want to box you should box!"
"I said I don't wanna do it anymore."
SAID THAT...
"Dreams never come true, anyway."
AND ACTED SO COLD.
IT WAS A LIE.
IT WAS ALL A LIE FOR ZEN'S BENEFIT.
ZEN?
KA-CHAK
ZEN!
DON'T JUST BARGE INTO MY ROOM!
RUB RUB
I'M ALSO GOING TO LOOK OUT FOR ZEN!
DRAW YOUR MANGA!
THE BOXING ONE!

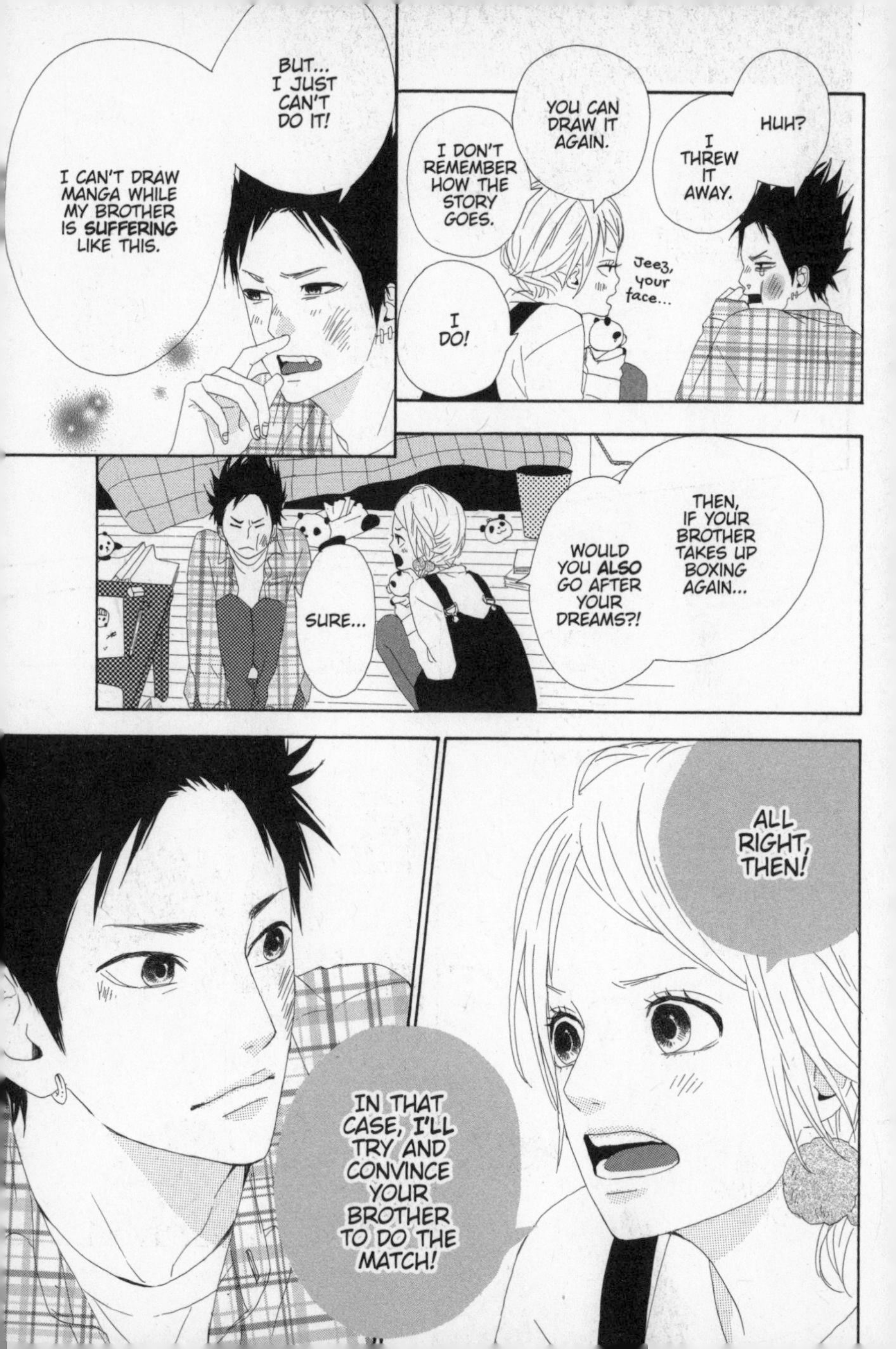
HUH?
I THREW IT AWAY.
YOU CAN DRAW IT AGAIN.
Jeez, your face...
I DON'T REMEMBER HOW THE STORY GOES.
I DO!
BUT... I JUST CAN'T DO IT!
I CAN'T DRAW MANGA WHILE MY BROTHER IS **SUFFERING** LIKE THIS.
THEN, IF YOUR BROTHER TAKES UP BOXING AGAIN...
WOULD YOU **ALSO** GO AFTER YOUR DREAMS?!
SURE...
ALL RIGHT, THEN!
IN THAT CASE, I'LL TRY AND CONVINCE YOUR BROTHER TO DO THE MATCH!

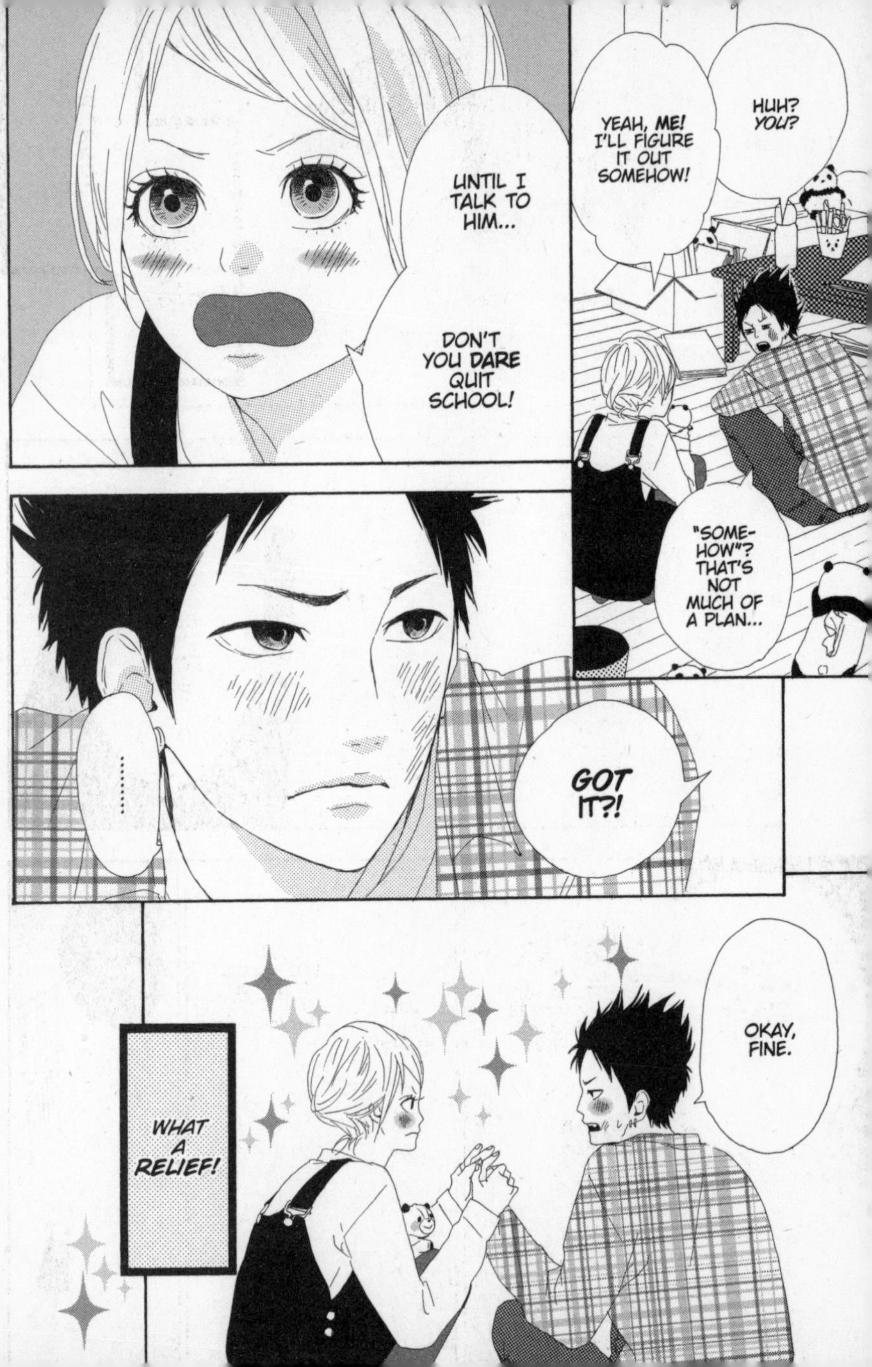
HUH? YOU?
YEAH, ME! I'LL FIGURE IT OUT SOMEHOW!
"SOME-HOW"? THAT'S NOT MUCH OF A PLAN...
UNTIL I TALK TO HIM...
DON'T YOU DARE QUIT SCHOOL!
GOT IT?!
......
OKAY, FINE.
WHAT A RELIEF!

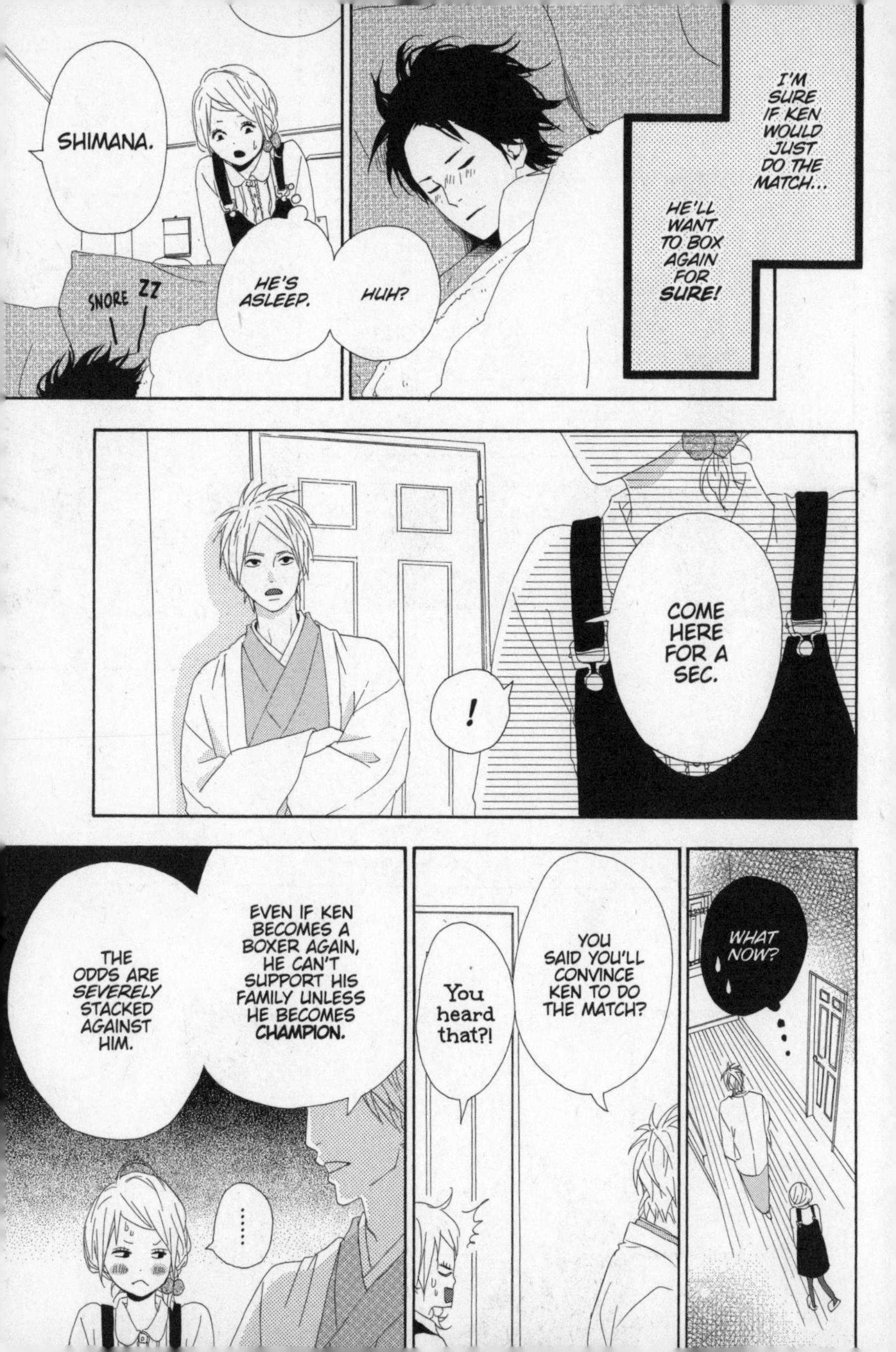
I'M SURE IF KEN WOULD JUST DO THE MATCH...
HE'LL WANT TO BOX AGAIN FOR SURE!
SHIMANA.
SNORE ZZ
HUH?
HE'S ASLEEP.
COME HERE FOR A SEC.
!
WHAT NOW?
...
YOU SAID YOU'LL CONVINCE KEN TO DO THE MATCH?
You heard that?!
EVEN IF KEN BECOMES A BOXER AGAIN, HE CAN'T SUPPORT HIS FAMILY UNLESS HE BECOMES CHAMPION.
THE ODDS ARE SEVERELY STACKED AGAINST HIM.
......

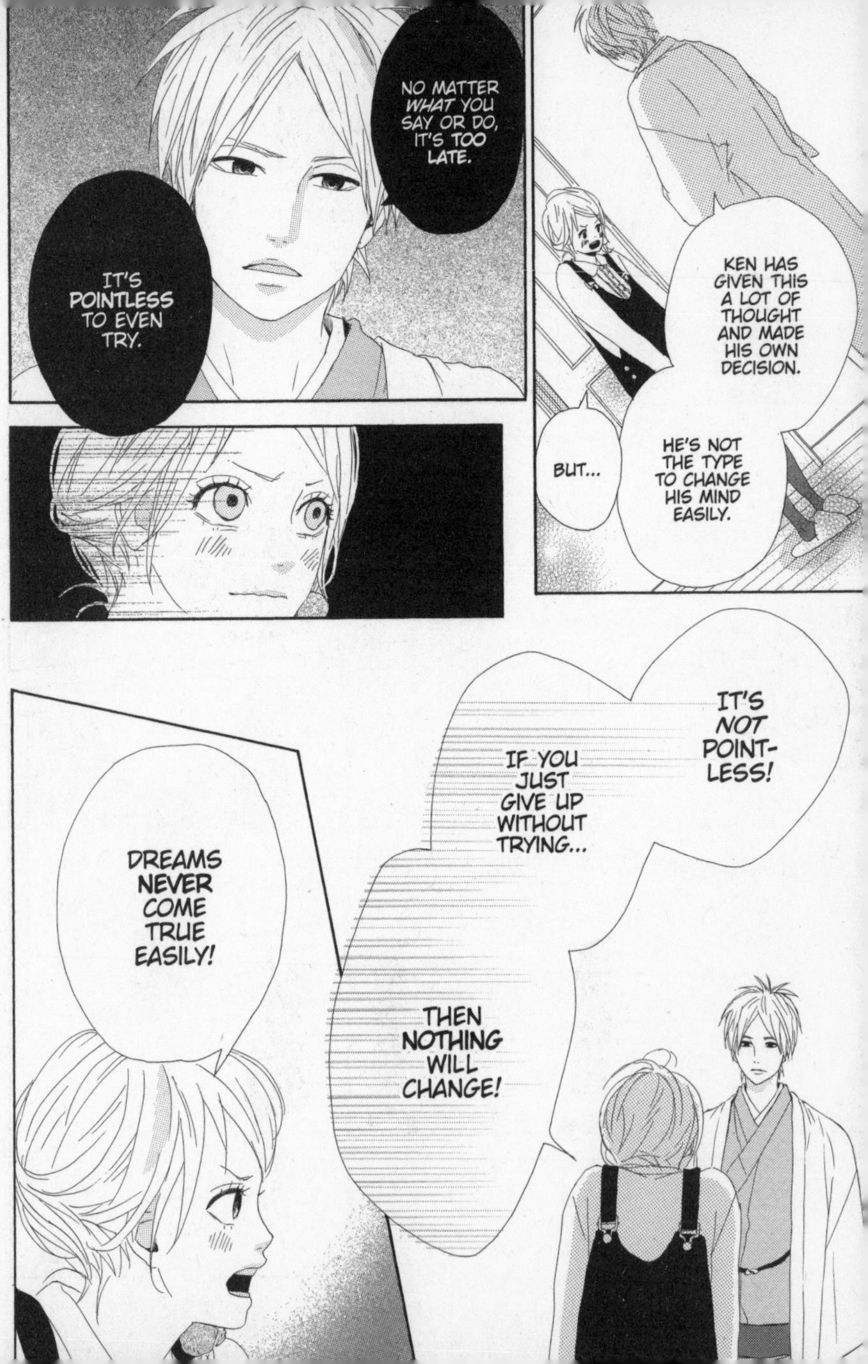
KEN HAS GIVEN THIS A LOT OF THOUGHT AND MADE HIS OWN DECISION.
HE'S NOT THE TYPE TO CHANGE HIS MIND EASILY.
BUT...
NO MATTER *WHAT* YOU SAY OR DO, IT'S TOO LATE.
IT'S POINTLESS TO EVEN TRY.
IT'S *NOT* POINT-LESS!
IF YOU JUST GIVE UP WITHOUT TRYING...
THEN NOTHING WILL CHANGE!
DREAMS NEVER COME TRUE EASILY!

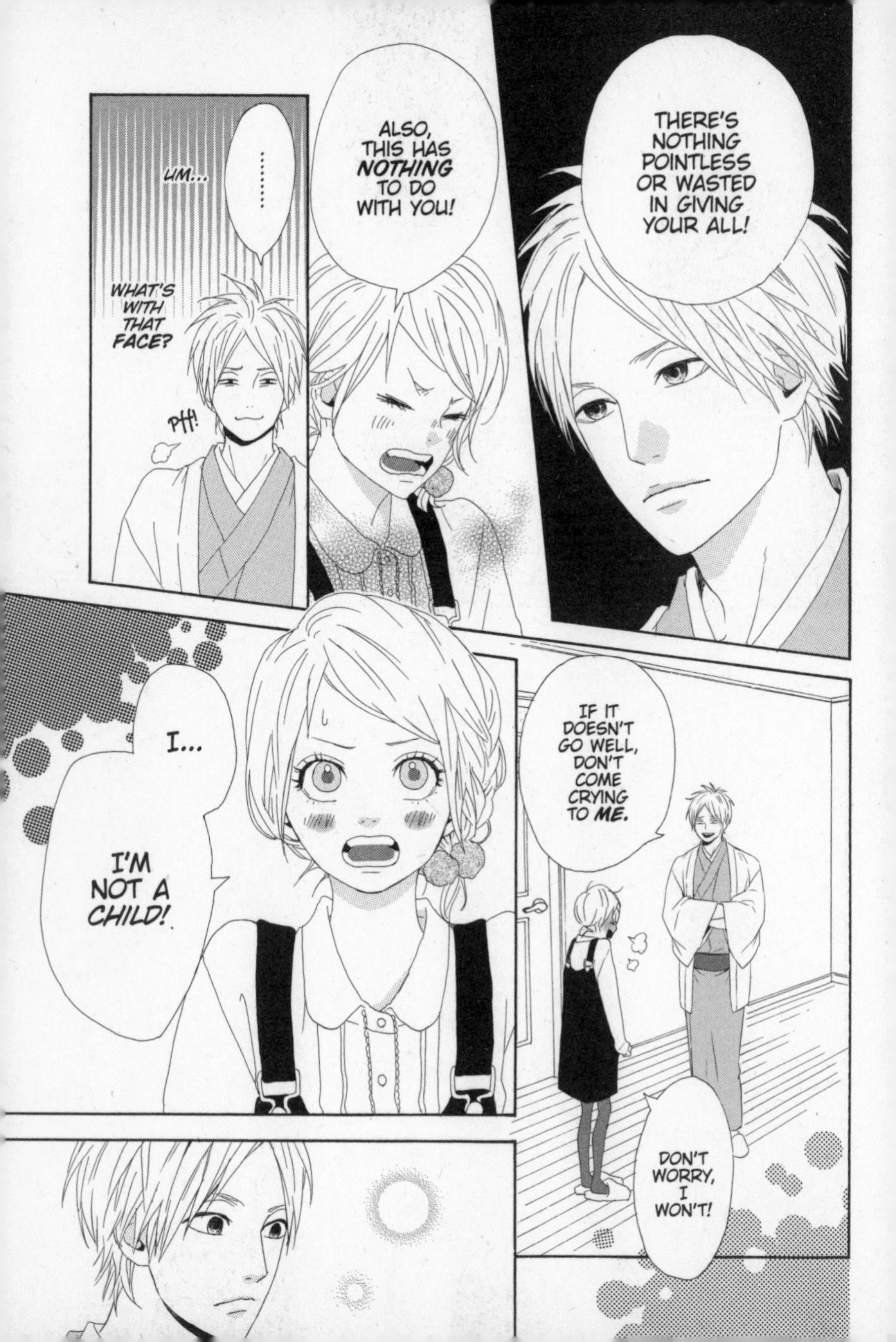
THERE'S NOTHING POINTLESS OR WASTED IN GIVING YOUR ALL!
ALSO, THIS HAS NOTHING TO DO WITH YOU!
......
UM...
WHAT'S WITH THAT FACE?
Pff!
IF IT DOESN'T GO WELL, DON'T COME CRYING TO ME.
DON'T WORRY, I WON'T!
I...
I'M NOT A CHILD!

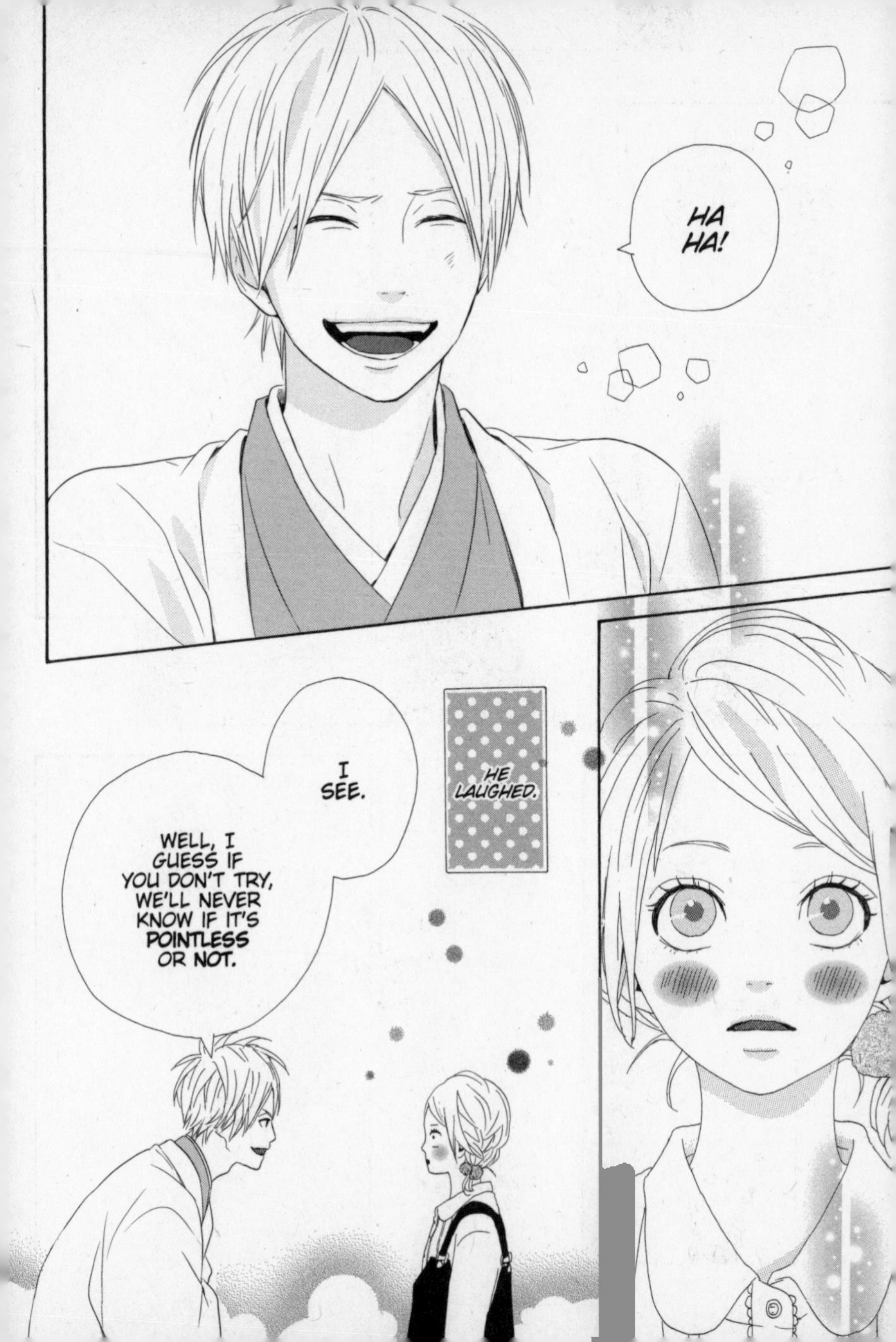
HA HA!
HE LAUGHED.
I SEE.
WELL, I GUESS IF YOU DON'T TRY, WE'LL NEVER KNOW IF IT'S POINTLESS OR NOT.

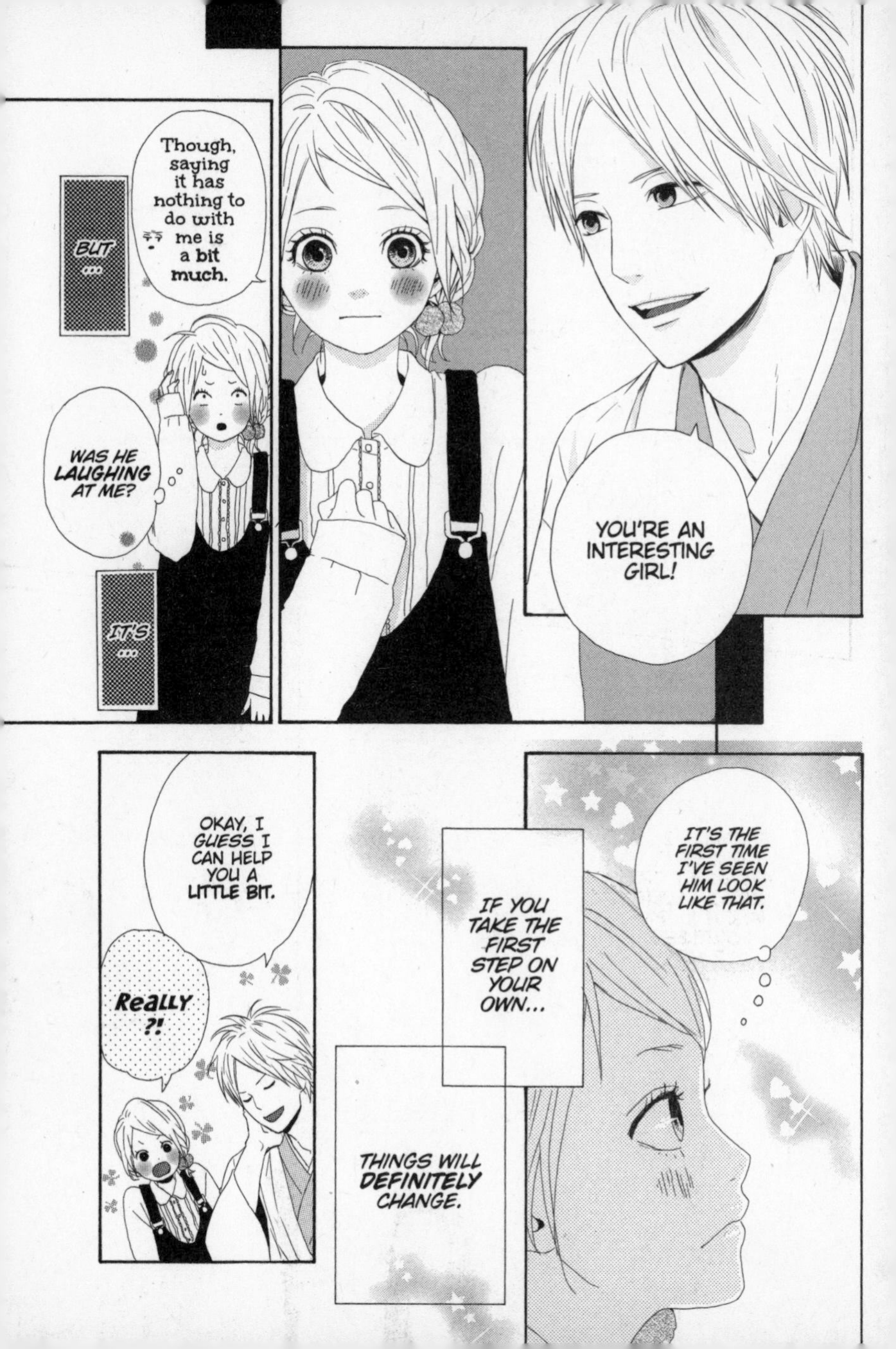
YOU'RE AN INTERESTING GIRL!
Though, saying it has nothing to do with me is a bit much.
BUT...
WAS HE LAUGHING AT ME?
IT'S...
IT'S THE FIRST TIME I'VE SEEN HIM LOOK LIKE THAT.
IF YOU TAKE THE FIRST STEP ON YOUR OWN...
THINGS WILL DEFINITELY CHANGE.
OKAY, I GUESS I CAN HELP YOU A LITTLE BIT.
Really ?!

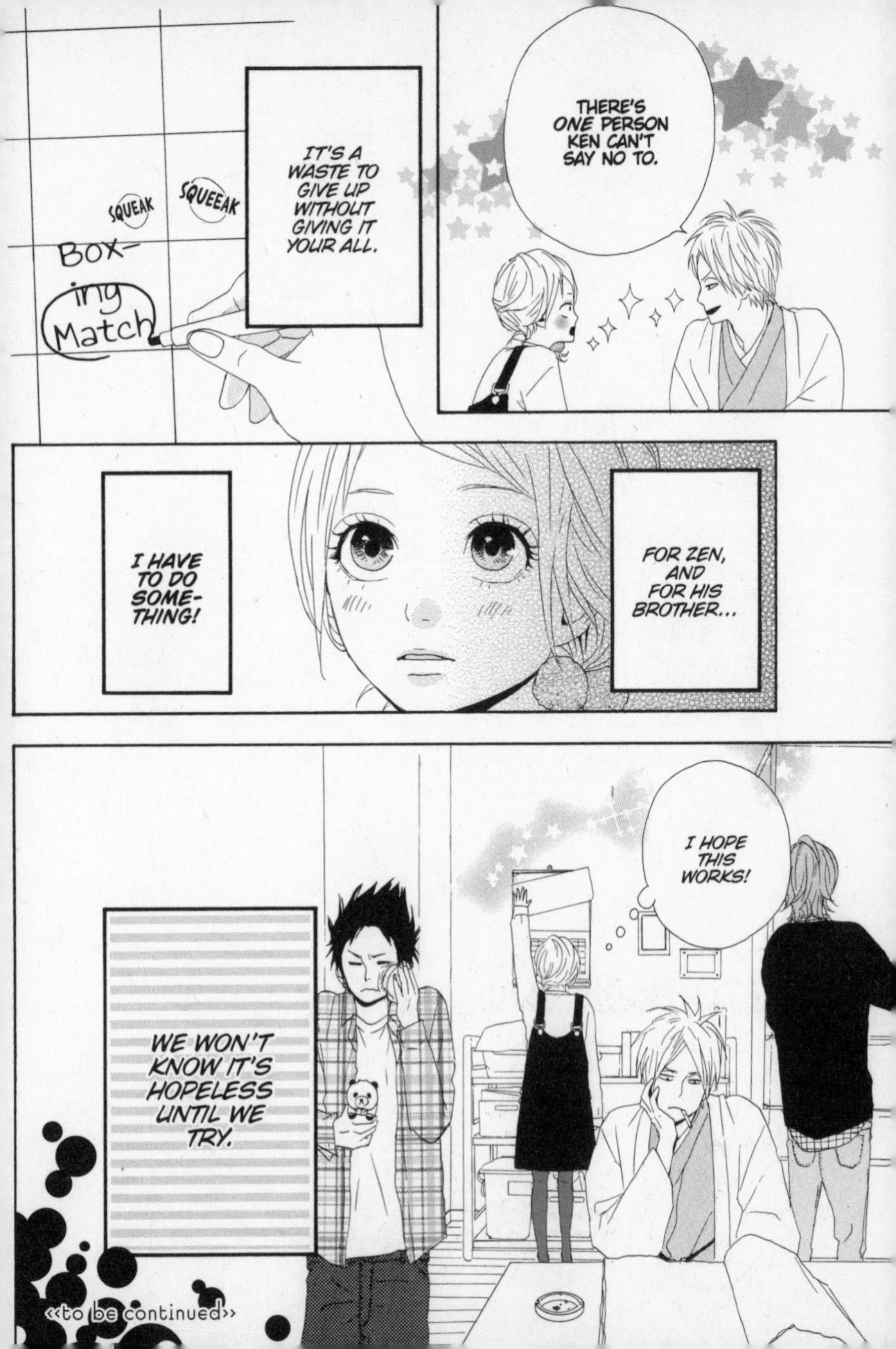
THERE'S ONE PERSON KEN CAN'T SAY NO TO.
IT'S A WASTE TO GIVE UP WITHOUT GIVING IT YOUR ALL.
SQUEEAK
SQUEAK
Box-ing Match
FOR ZEN, AND FOR HIS BROTHER...
I HAVE TO DO SOME-THING!
I HOPE THIS WORKS!
WE WON'T KNOW IT'S HOPELESS UNTIL WE TRY.
«to be continued»

THE FIND POKO GAME

Poko is hidden throughout the manga! Find him!

This time, there are 6 POKOS.

BONUS MANGA

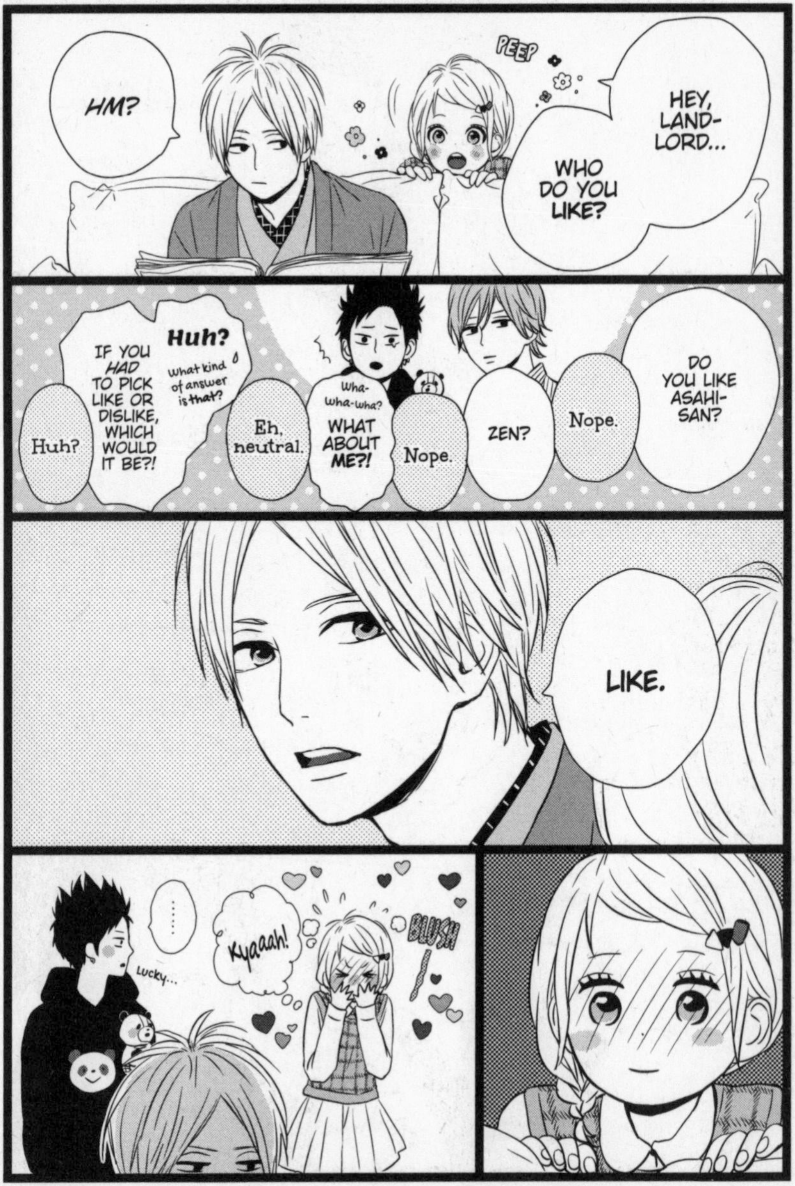
PEEP
HEY, LANDLORD...
WHO DO YOU LIKE?
HM?
DO YOU LIKE ASAHI-SAN?
Nope.
ZEN?
Nope.
Wha-wha-wha?
WHAT ABOUT ME?!
Eh, neutral.
Huh?
What kind of answer is that?
IF YOU HAD TO PICK LIKE OR DISLIKE, WHICH WOULD IT BE?!
Huh?
LIKE.
BLUSH
Kyaaah!
......
Lucky...

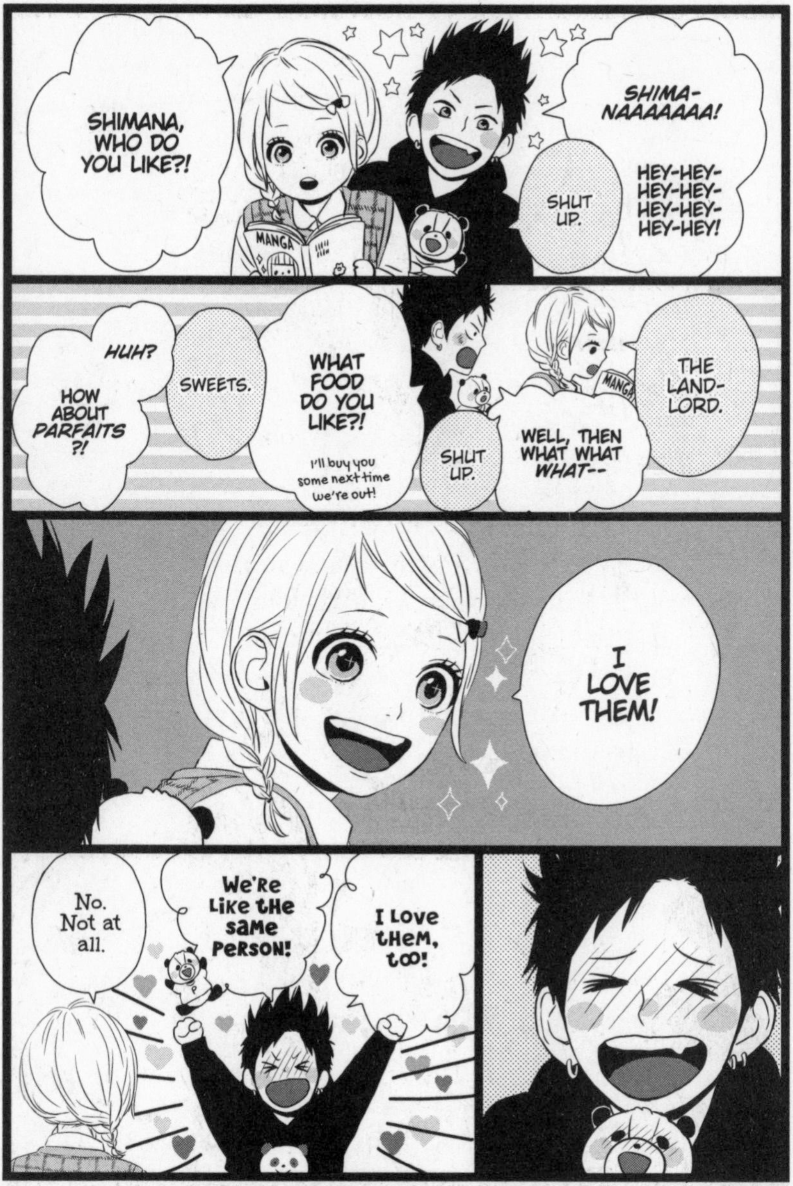
SHIMA-NAAAAAAA!
HEY-HEY-HEY-HEY-HEY-HEY-HEY-HEY!
SHUT UP.
SHIMANA, WHO DO YOU LIKE?!
THE LAND-LORD.
WELL, THEN WHAT WHAT WHAT--
SHUT UP.
WHAT FOOD DO YOU LIKE?!
I'll buy you some next time we're out!
SWEETS.
HUH?
HOW ABOUT PARFAITS?!
I LOVE THEM!
I Love them, too!
We're Like the same person!
No. Not at all.

THE END

The New Release Version of the Hit Romantic Comedy!

With its redrawn artwork, it's even cuter than before!

"With love, giving up means it's over."

Zen has confessed his feelings to Shimana! And even though she doesn't feel the same way, Shimana still wants to encourage Zen to follow his dreams.
Having realized her own feelings for the landlord, she strives to get closer to him... But Fujiwara merely treats Shimana like a child. When Zen's brother Ken shows her the landlord's high school yearbook, what secrets will she find within...?! Find out in the next volume!

Ichigo Takano presents
Dreamin' Sun 4
Coming Soon!

By Ichigo Takano, creator of the Eisner Award-nominated *orange*!

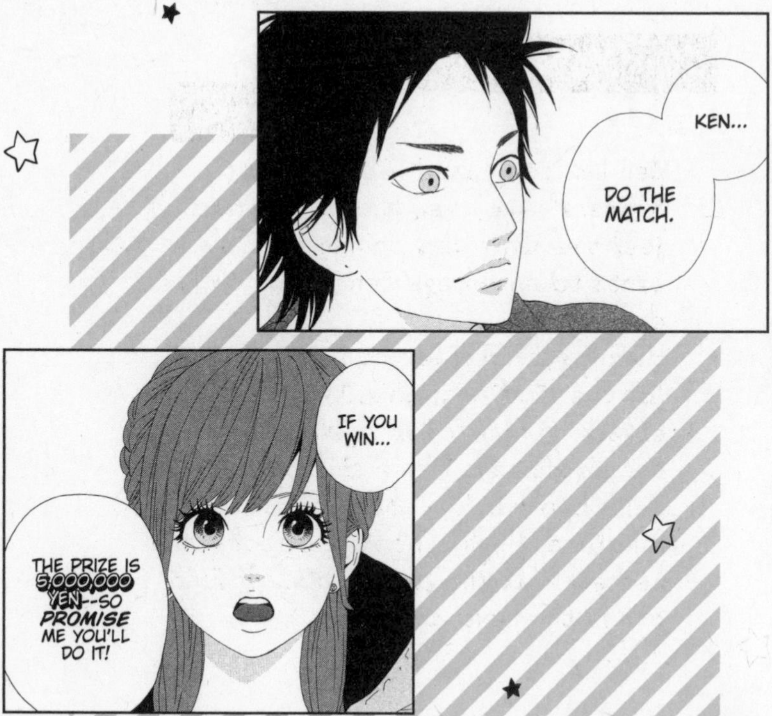
KEN...
DO THE MATCH.
IF YOU WIN...
THE PRIZE IS 5,000,000 YEN--SO PROMISE ME YOU'LL DO IT!

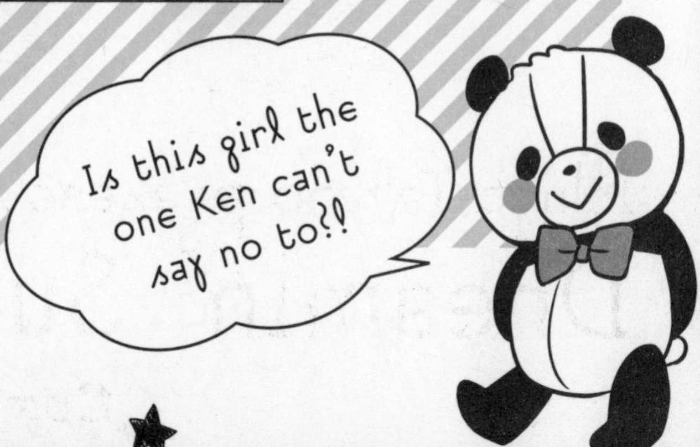
Is this girl the one Ken can't say no to?!

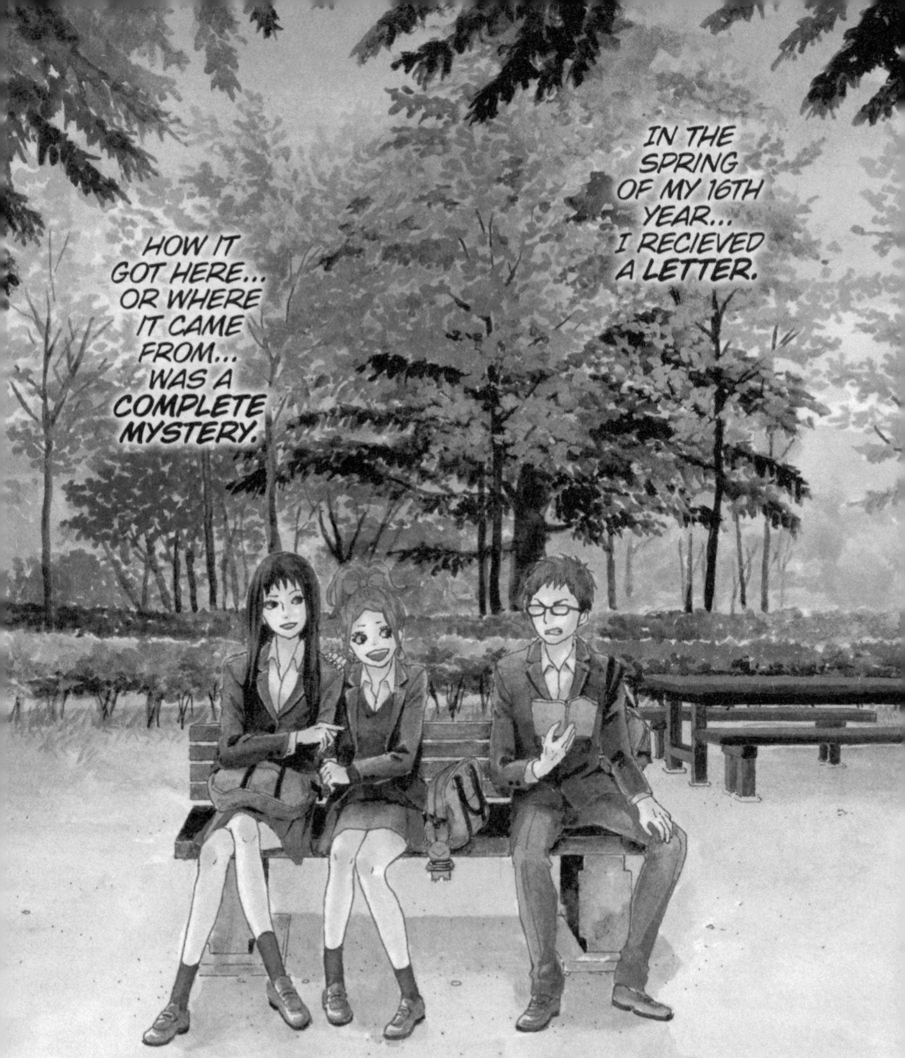
IN THE SPRING OF MY 16TH YEAR... I RECIEVED A LETTER.
HOW IT GOT HERE... OR WHERE IT CAME FROM... WAS A COMPLETE MYSTERY.

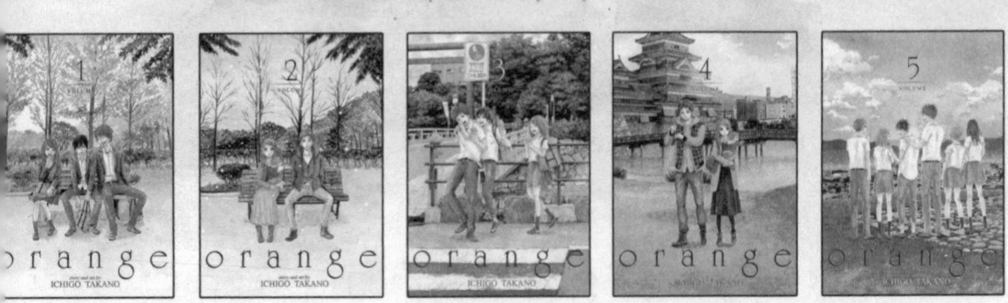
orange
ICHIGO TAKANO